Romanesque Architecture and Sculpture in Wales

Romanesque Architecture and Sculpture in Wales

by
Malcolm Thurlby

Logaston Press

LOGASTON PRESS
Little Logaston Woonton Almeley
Herefordshire HR3 6QH
logastonpress.co.uk

First published by Logaston Press 2006
Copyright © Malcolm Thurlby 2006

All rights reserved. No part of this publication
may be reproduced, stored in a retrieval system,
or transmitted, in any form or by any means,
electronic, mechanical, photocopying, recording
or otherwise, without the prior permission,
in writing, of the publisher

ISBN 1 904396 50 X

Set in Times New Roman by Logaston Press
and printed in Great Britain by
Biddles Ltd., King's Lynn

Front cover illustration: St Davids cathedral: looking east along the nave

Contents

	Acknowledgements	*vii*
	Preface	*ix*
	Introduction	*xiii*
1	Chepstow and Ludlow	1
2	Norman Church Architecture in the March and Glamorgan down to 1120	49
3	Cathedral, Castle and Monastery post 1120	73
4	Church Architecture and Sculpture for Norman Patrons	157
5	The Patronage of Gruffudd ap Cynan, Prince of Gwynedd	189
6	Church Architecture, Shrines and Fonts for Welsh Patrons	239
7	St Davids Cathedral	281
8	Epilogue	339
	Glossary	345
	Bibliography	351
	References	365
	Index	377

Acknowledgements

It is a pleasure to acknowledge the help of many friends with the research on this project. From the beginning, Eric Fernie, teacher, mentor and friend, has answered countless questions about the European contextualization of the Welsh works. Also, with characteristic generosity, he read the penultimate draft of the text and raised numerous questions ranging from factual detail to broader aspects of interpretation of the material. Ron Baxter, Research Director of the *Corpus of Romanesque Sculpture in Britain and Ireland*, kindly answered questions pertaining to a number of sites in Cheshire. Hans Böker generously shared his expertise on parallel material in Germany. Peter Coffman provided important information on restoration reports and references in nineteenth-century architectural periodicals, and scanned the illustrations from my slides. The Very Reverend Wyn Evans, Dean of St Davids cathedral, always provided a warm welcome to his church, along with an unbounded enthusiasm for research on the fabric. Richard Gem has been especially helpful in interpreting Chepstow, Penmon and Ewenny priory churches. Richard Halsey helped me to refine ideas on Ewenny. Stuart Harrison generously contributed his vast knowledge on all aspects of Cistercian work, especially in connection with Strata Florida abbey. He provided images of architectural fragments at St Dogmaels abbey, and informative debate in connection with the barrel vaults at Monkton. Duncan Givans kindly supplied me with a copy of his excellent Ph.D. thesis 'Romanesque Portals with tympana in the British Isles, sculpture iconography and display', and answered questions about comparative material for Welsh tympana and lintels. John Goodall and John Kenyon provided sage advice on all aspects of secular architecture, and the latter has been of unfailing help with bibliographical and archival matters, and with interpretation of Chepstow and Newcastle castles. Rosie Humphries permitted full access to the keep of Usk castle and was an informed discussant on the fabric. Jeremy Knight provided invaluable assistance with the interpretation of Usk castle. Aimee Pritchard, who is currently researching Romanesque in North Wales for a Ph.D. degree at the University of Bangor, freely shared her profound knowledge of the material, provided excellent company for fieldwork in Anglesey, and answered innumerable question on specific details of Romanesque in north Wales. Ann Rainsbury, curator of Chepstow Museum, was an excellent guide to the material in her care that pertained to Chepstow priory. Mark Redknap of the National Museum of Wales, generously gave me access to his forthcoming publication (with J.M. Lewis), entitled, *A Corpus of Early Medieval Inscribed Stones and Stone Sculpture in Wales, vol. 1, Breconshire, Glamorgan, Monmouthshire, Radnorshire, and geographically contiguous areas of Herefordshire and Shropshire*. Matthew Reeve read the text and raised important questions. David Robinson contributed significantly to the interpretation of Usk priory. Roger Stalley's good humour and provocative thoughts have been a constant inspiration, even though we have agreed to disagree on certain matters concerning St Davids cathedral. Sophie Stewart kindly supplied a copy of her report on the restoration of the wall painting in the presbytery of Ewenny priory from which her reconstruction of the Romanesque decoration is reproduced here (Plate 11). Rick Turner provided a copy of his text on the great tower of Chepstow castle, prior to its publication in the *Antiquaries Journal*, and was an informed and helpful guide to files at Cadw. He also read the sections of my text on Chepstow and Ludlow castles and offered important comments. Cadw also provided help concerning the plans for various buildings, and these are reproduced with their permission. Needless to say, I take responsibility for any errors.

At Logaston Press Andy Johnson's editorial and organizational expertise has been invaluable. My wife, Carol, accompanied me for most of the fieldwork and provided excellent navigation to even the most remote sites. At home during the writing stage she supplied all the necessary sustenance for the grey cells.

Financial support for the fieldwork was provided by Specific Research Grants from York University, Ontario, and a Research Grant from the Social Sciences and Humanities Research Council of Canada.

Preface

In the preface to David Walker's book entitled *The Norman Conquerors*, published in 1977 as a volume in the *New History of Wales*, the editors of the series observed that during the previous quarter century much research had been completed on the history of the country.[1] They explained that this was mainly available in academic journals and therefore not accessible to the general public, and consequently that the aim of the series was to bring the research into the public domain. Since that time, historical research has flourished, with particularly significant studies in ecclesiastical history and the lives of saints. There have been important contributions to the study of Norman castles. Yet for the most part the castles have been seen in secular isolation with little attempt to consider them in relation to the ecclesiastical architecture and sculpture that was produced at the same time and often for the same patrons. Three historical surveys, A.D. Carr's *Medieval Wales*, Keri Maund's *The Welsh Kings*, and Roger Turvey's *The Welsh Princes: the native rulers of Wales, 1063–1283*, provide concise accounts of the period but with little reference to visual documentation, as opposed to written documentation.[2] Indeed, it is sad that Maund's otherwise excellent study is accompanied by illustrations of buildings and works of art that are so poorly integrated with the text. The publication in 2003 of Peter Lord's, *The Visual Culture of Wales: Medieval Vision*, in a large format with excellent colour plates and at an affordable price, contributes to our understanding of the period. Lord illustrates and discusses many fonts, the richly carved arch in the church at Aberffraw (Anglesey) and the shrine at Pennant Melangell (Montgomery), few of which had previously escaped from the confines of academic journals. However, the almost reluctant inclusion of a minimal amount of architecture detracts from the overall value of the volume, and his dating of many works, not least some of the Anglesey fonts, is open to reconsideration, as we shall see later in this book.

The approach adopted here is to start with the objects — the churches, castles, fonts, shrines and so on, and then try to explain them in their historical context. To the historian accustomed to dealing with written documentation, this may seem like putting the cart before the horse. However, it is not that far removed from Nerys Ann Jones and Morfydd Owen's reading of mid-twelfth-century poems to St Cadfan and St Tysilio in relation to the secular politics of the time and place.[3] We are dealing with a time in which the written documentation that pertains to works of art is woefully thin, and, where it exists, it is only rarely specific enough to allow a particular work to be connected with a specific patron. It therefore makes sense to glean all we can from the visual evidence, to observe their associations with works of art elsewhere, not just in Wales, or even in Norman England, but throughout Europe. These gleanings may then be integrated with what we know of the likely patrons with the view to understanding the motives behind the creation of the works and their possible meaning in the society of the day. Our task is not unlike that of Sherlock Holmes or Miss Marple trying to solve the crime with only a few clues at their disposal. The clues have been closely observed and photographed in detail to facilitate comparative analysis with related works of art. This approach allows us to understand general trends in the period, to identify regional traits, and even to locate the training of specific craftsmen. At a time when there is no documentation whatsoever on the artists and masons, this will prove especially valuable in considering how masons were recruited. This will be well illustrated with the Norman cathedral at Llandaff, with patrons like Gruffudd ap Cynan, prince of Gwynedd (d.1137), in works like Aberffraw and Penmon priory, and in the late twelfth-century cathedral at St Davids.

In undertaking to compile an introductory survey of the Romanesque architecture and sculpture in Wales, I had to ask myself when is the work 'complete'? On the one hand, the answer is likely to be 'never'. On the other hand, there came a point at which I felt that I had probably visited and photographed more Romanesque sites in Wales than anyone else, had formulated some views about the works in their historical context, and had the information with which to write this book. I am only too aware of the amount of research that remains to be done. While the measurements of some buildings are presented in the text there are many more to measure. Geological analysis of stone used for fonts would go a long way to determining their place of origin and contribute a great deal to our understanding of centres of production. A comprehensive list of fonts would contribute to our knowledge of the creation of the parochial system in the twelfth century. This will be done under the auspices of the *Corpus of Romanesque Sculpture in Britain and Ireland* under the expert guidance of Ron Baxter, the director of that project. The Corpus is being published on the Internet (http://crsbi.ac.uk). The list could go on. I hope at this stage that the specialist and non-specialist alike will feel sufficiently inspired by the contents of this book to get out and explore the rich visual heritage of Romanesque Wales. There is no substitute for seeing the monuments first hand. I hope you will expand on my terms of reference and refine or correct the views expressed here. And, for those who teach history as an academic subject, whether in school or university, please make every effort to include this visual evidence of Welsh history in your classes.

In one respect my work on this book may be taken back to the early 1970s when I first visited Llanthony priory on a bitterly cold and misty winter's day. Not deterred by the inclement conditions I continued to make occasional sorties from Canada to visit Welsh medieval buildings. In the 1980s, when I was working on the reconstruction of lost vaults in English Romanesque architecture, one church in particular, Ewenny priory, became of great interest because unlike buildings in England, it preserved its Romanesque presbytery vault. This research led to a separate article on the Romanesque fabric of Ewenny priory church.[4] Then, in writing *The Herefordshire School of Romanesque Sculpture*, certain Welsh analogues were evident.[5] In retrospect, I am inclined to think that I did not give the Welsh sources due emphasis but at least my interest in things Welsh was stimulated. In the first place, it was concerned with the continuing Celtic artistic tradition but, as research progressed, it soon evolved into trying to understand that aspect alongside Norman forms. Thus most of the research for this book has been undertaken over the last five years with visits to as many buildings as possible. The last was completed in a month-long trip in September 2004. The seemingly constant rainfall brought to mind Henry II's campaign to enter Wales to confront the Welsh under the leadership of Owain Gwynedd. It was defeated not by the Welsh army but by the weather; Henry's army was driven back by the 'summer' storms as it tried to make its way across the mountains.[6] I subsequently learned that back at home in Ontario, September 2004 was particularly sunny and warm. The news was not welcome but at least I'm pleased to report that, unlike Henry, this intrepid adventurer was not driven back by the rain. On a more positive note, much of the fieldwork brings back happy memories of magnificent scenery and spectacular settings for many buildings. In all seasons a visit to Llanthony priory is a sublime experience. No less the drive, whether over the mountains from Hay-on-Wye or up the valley from the A465 to the south. If the latter, be sure to take the slight detour to the east to the church at Cwmyoy. The journeys to Pennant Melangell and Patrishow are especially fine, whilst Aberdaron, Capel Lligwy, Llangwyfan, Mynt, and Pistyll all have wonderful coastal locations. At Manorbier it is not hard to realize why in the twelfth century Gerald of Wales praised it as 'the most pleasant place by far' in Wales.[7]

When I began to visit English medieval churches some forty years ago, the majority of them were open and I suspect that that was also true of the Welsh churches. Unfortunately that is not the case today; the seemingly constant threat of theft and vandalism means that doors are locked. This is understandable and in most cases mandated by insurance companies. In such cases it would be very helpful to find a list of key-holders with addresses and telephone numbers. In time let's hope that the situation comes full circle for a writer of a letter to *The Builder* in 1848 entitled 'Access to Churches', complained of the frustration that he so often had 'to utter the invariable cry — "Where are the church keys?"'.[8]

Tessa Garton's review of my book *The Herefordshire School of Romanesque Sculpture* stated that it 'contains much that is useful and thought provoking, and has much to offer both to the scholar and to the general public'.[9] It is hoped that *Romanesque Architecture and Sculpture in Wales* can also stimulate research into the monuments and encourage the general public to visit, enjoy and understand this rich heritage.

Introduction

With the possible exception of the great tower of Chepstow castle, the Romanesque architecture of Wales is not well known, and the sculpture even less so. Indeed, until recently, even the late twelfth-century fabric of St Davids cathedral had been considered as little more than a minor, old-fashioned offshoot of more important, progressive architectural developments in England.[j] It is true that Wales has no Romanesque cathedral or abbey church to compare with the monumental scale of a Durham or a Peterborough. Yet it does preserve some remarkable eleventh- and twelfth-century treasures. The nave of Chepstow priory provides evidence of an early high stone vault that is of European significance. The presbytery of Llandaff cathedral has a richly articulated eastern arch that speaks unequivocally of Bishop Urban's connection with Anselm, Archbishop of Canterbury, and the Normanization of the church. Ewenny boasts one of the best-preserved small priory churches in Britain and has the rare distinction of retaining its original presbytery vault and clear traces of the original polychrome. Quite apart from the importance of this in its own right, it is invaluable in aiding our understanding of lost high vaults in Romanesque England. Another small priory church, at Penmon (Anglesey), has an amazingly rich decoration in the south transept that is closely allied to contemporary work in Chester. The nave of Margam abbey church is a fine example of the bold simplicity of the early architecture of the Cistercian order. The nave of Newport St Woolos introduces some interesting examples of variety in its arcaded nave and boasts intriguing carved capitals on the west doorway. The font at the former priory church at Brecon, now the cathedral, is intimately related to the well-known Herefordshire School of sculpture. Smaller but no less interesting are the numerous fonts in Anglesey carved mainly with a rich variety of patterns inherited from a well-established insular tradition. A variety of fonts in Breconshire, Cardiganshire and Radnorshire, reflect an awareness of major work in Europe. Fonts in Glamorganshire and Pembrokeshire are closely allied to those in Devon and Somerset and in some cases were imported into Wales. The elaborate arch at Aberffraw (Anglesey) has connections with Cheshire, Cornwall, Cumbria, Scotland and Ireland, and has fascinating repercussions with regard to the use of a church and possible imperial connections, associated with Gruffudd ap Cynan (d.1137), the celebrated prince of Gwynnedd. Similar princely connections with the church at Meifod (Montgomery) lead to the exploration of grand imperial associations concerning the planning and use of the church. Pennant Melangell (Montgomery) preserves an original twelfth-century shrine, unique in the British Isles, and of pan-European significance. The sculptural decoration of the shrine belongs to a thriving school in the north of Wales in the late twelfth and early thirteenth centuries. In one respect it may also be affiliated to Sarum Cathedral as remodelled by Bishop Roger 1102–39. Roger was one of the most munificent patrons of the day and, not surprisingly, his work was highly influential. He founded a priory at Kidwelly of which all traces are gone, but time and again we will find parallels between Welsh details and Sarum, in the north as well as the south of the country. The Augustinian priory church at Llanthony is a key monument for the beginnings of Gothic in the west of England and Wales. St Davids cathedral is one of the most intriguing churches of the late twelfth century anywhere is Europe. Two disasters — the fall of the crossing tower in 1220 and the earthquake of 1247/8 — have led to the rebuilding of the church commenced by Bishop Peter de Leia in 1182. To determine the sequence of construction, the original design and subsequent modifications has required much sleuthing. And in addition to the grandeur of the great tower of Chepstow castle, the keeps at Ogmore and Tretower preserve features rarely encountered elsewhere, and the hall at Manorbier is a fine example of twelfth-century secular architecture.

This situation suggests that there is much from the Romanesque period to be explored in Wales. Yet until now there has been no attempt to bring the material together in an easily accessible format and to illustrate it well. The book does not pretend to be comprehensive; new material has a habit of cropping up all the time. Be that as it may, I have tried to include the majority of the works from the great cathedrals, abbey churches and castles, to the single-cell church. The emphasis is on architecture and sculpture that can still be seen with the result that earthworks play a very minor role in our discussion. While they are of enormous value in charting the Norman incursion into Wales, they are not a focus for the study of architecture and sculpture of the period.

The geographical and temporal parameters of our study require some explanation in the context of the organization of the book. We start with 1067 and the establishment of the Norman lord William fitzOsbern at Chepstow where he is built a castle and founded the priory. FitzOsbern also built or rebuilt castles at Clifford, Ewyas Harold, Richards Castle, Wigmore and Monmouth, but nothing at those sites remains from his time. Castles were already erected on the border and after the Conquest the pattern was accelerated, as one would expect under Norman control. Hen Domen was erected by Roger of Montgomery, Earl of Shrewsbury (d.1094), but only the earthwork remains and therefore is not considered here.[1] On the other hand, I have included a discussion of the Lacy castle at Ludlow (Salop). This is an important survivor of a major masonry castle in the March, and provides certain insights into the relationship with ecclesiastical architecture in the west midlands. Aspects of its design are also directly relevant to churches and castles in Wales.

The division between the second and the third and fourth chapters is established chronologically around 1120, a date chosen with reference to the start of construction of Llandaff cathedral. The patron, Bishop Urban, was a Norman appointment and was subject to the authority of the Archbishop of Canterbury. Urban's new cathedral was a most emphatic statement of the Normanization of this part of Wales. Ewenny priory may have been begun before this, even as early as 1111, but as the date of construction is not precisely established it seemed better to stick with 1120. Similarly, while Monmouth priory was in use by 1101–1102 the surviving fabric at the west end of the nave is unlikely to predate Bishop Urban's work at Llandaff. The buildings and sculptures discussed in chapter two are all typologically earlier than Llandaff cathedral, while the sculpture at Llyswyrny, Llanrhidian and Llantwit Major (all Glamorgan) reflect, at least in part, earlier sculptural traditions of southern Wales. At the same time, reference to English work is made in an effort to understand the beginnings of aspects of the Romanesque style in Wales. Whatever the aims of the patrons, one could hardly expect local craftsmen to master the new style instantaneously. Contact had to be made with craftsmen working in England and with this in mind early sculpture on Welsh lintels is explored in relation to contemporary work in Herefordshire and further north along the border.

The third chapter examines the major work of the patrons of the Norman administration. Llandaff cathedral, and the monastic churches at Monmouth, Ewenny, Llangennith, Monkton, St Dogmaels, Brecon, Malpas and St Clears are investigated in the context of West Country Romanesque architecture and sculpture. Monmouth and Usk castles are considered alongside the priory churches in both places, and Ogmore castle with the nearby Ewenny priory. Kenfig castle and Margam abbey are presented under the auspices of Robert, Earl of Gloucester and Lord of Glamorgan (*circa* 1121–1147). The castles at Newcastle-Bridgend, Manorbier and Tretower are viewed separately as is the account of Llanthony priory. These monastic and secular works are discussed according to a chronological order.

The fourth chapter covers smaller churches and fonts in the Marches that were built as a result of English Norman Patronage and are presented geographically — Glamorgan, Gwent/Monmouthshire, Breconshire, Pembrokeshire and the single example of Chirk — as well as in what I see as a reasonable chronological fashion.

Chapter five conforms temporally with chapters three and four but is treated as a separate entity because it has been possible to associate a number of the works with one patron, Gruffudd ap Cynan, Prince of Gwynedd (d.1137). The architecture of Bangor cathedral and the sculpture of Penmon priory and Aberffraw (Anglesey) are examined in connection with contemporary work at Chester. These comparisons provide clues on the training of the craftsmen, and at the same time provide insights into the aims of the patron. Examination of this particular aspect of the investigation throws the net even wider, to encompass Ireland and Scotland, Scandinavia, and Europe. In a couple of cases we even explore indications of patrons' wishes to be associated with the grandeur of the Holy Roman Empire. These views are reinforced with the examination of other works in Anglesey, especially the large number of richly decorated fonts.

Chapter six covers the same time period and considers works produced by other Welsh patrons. At Twywn (Merioneth), Meifod and Kerry (Montgomery) there are significant remains of the Romanesque churches built for Welsh patrons on a scale to match similar Norman work and, especially in the case of Meifod, with remarkably prestigious associations. The reconstructed shrine at Pennant Melangell and related fragments in the vicinity incorporate traditional Welsh aspects with features inherited from high-quality Norman work. The patronage of Rhys ap Gruffudd, Prince of Deheubarth (d.1197) from the Cistercian abbey at Strata Florida to the large number of fonts in Cardiganshire, shows him to be as ambitious as similar Norman patrons.

For the end of our survey there is no precise date. I have chosen to include St Davids cathedral as commenced in 1182. This is some years after the Gothic choir of Canterbury Cathedral or the establishment of the early Gothic design of Wells Cathedral, and over a quarter of a century after northern French Gothic elements were introduced in the choir built by Archbishop Roger of Pont l'Évêque at York Minster (1154–81).[2] Yet there are many aspects of the design of St Davids that preserve a strong link with the Romanesque, so much so that Roger Stalley concluded that 'In many respects St Davids was the last great expression of English Romanesque, and perhaps deliberately so'.[3] Thomas Lloyd *et al* in the introduction to the Pembrokeshire volume of *The Buildings of Wales*, asserts that St Davids is 'one of the last great Romanesque churches of Britain, barely aware of the Gothic then well underway elsewhere.[4] In the detailed account of St Davids cathedral in the same volume, Professor Roger Stalley reiterated boldly that 'St Davids was more Romanesque than Gothic'.[5] Stalley continues, 'unfortunately the sequence of construction is difficult to determine with precision, the situation clouded by two disasters that befell the cathedral in the C13'. The crossing tower collapsed in 1220 and an earthquake in 1247/8 destroyed a 'great part' of the church. The rebuilding of the cathedral after these events was in many respects conservative, with the result that the sequence of construction has not been satisfactorily determined. In order to try to remedy this situation our examination of the fabric takes us to the mid-thirteenth-century rebuilding of the cathedral.

On the other hand, the rebuilding of Llandaff Cathedral, probably under the auspices of Bishop Henry of Abergavenny (1193–1218), reads as a largely Gothic work. Elements continue Romanesque practice of the West Country school and discussion will be confined to these.

1

Chepstow
and Ludlow

As the old A48 approaches Chepstow from the north-east, the road descends to the River Wye and then turns to the right over the bridge. At this point we are afforded an excellent view of the two great symbols of Norman authority in the town, the castle and the priory. The castle dominates the Welsh bank of the Wye; the priory occupies land a few hundred yards to the east. Much has changed since Norman times. The priory's west tower dates from the early eighteenth century but the ecclesiastical presence of the Norman administration would have been equally well marked by the former crossing tower of the church. The castle has expanded considerably from the end of the twelfth century onwards but the dominant building is still the great Norman tower.

The pairing of ecclesiastical and secular foundations was standard practice for the Norman ruling élite. To cite just a few examples in England in the late eleventh century,

Fig. 1 Chepstow castle: exterior of the great tower from the north-east

Fig. 2 Chepstow castle: exterior of the great tower from the east-south-east

the cathedrals of Durham, Lincoln and Norwich were each accompanied by adjacent castles. Castles were located close to monastic or collegiate churches at Bramber (Sussex), Castle Acre (Norfolk), and Portchester (Hants.), while at Kilpeck (Herefs.) and Castle Rising (Norfolk) the parish church is nearby the castle.[1] This pairing insured the imposition of Norman authority in both the secular and religious realms.[2] The same pattern is encountered in Wales. As at Chepstow, a number of daughter houses of French Benedictine houses, known as alien priories, were founded before 1100. William fitz Osbern possibly built a castle at Monmouth, and before 1086 Wihenoc of Monmouth founded a priory church in the town as a daughter of St Laurent at Saumur (Maine-et-Loire).[3] At Abergavenny, Hamelin de Ballon, Lord of Abergavenny, constructed a motte-and-bailey castle soon after 1087. Before 1100 he gave to St Vincent of Le Mans (Sarthe) the chapel of his castle and appurtenances of the church of Abergavenny and land for making a principal church in which monks should serve.[4] The motte and part of the outline of the bailey of the castle to the north are still to be seen but only the font remains from the Norman priory. Further west in Pembrokeshire, Monkton was founded about 1098 as a daughter of Sées (Orne), to accompany the castle at Pembroke.[5]

CHEPSTOW CASTLE: THE GREAT TOWER

The great tower of Chepstow castle has been associated with William fitz Osbern, Earl of Hereford (1067–1071), on the basis of a reference in Domesday Book that he built a castle at Chepstow (figs. 1–3).[6] Other references record that he built or rebuilt castles at

Richard's Castle, Clifford, Ewyas Harold, Wigmore (all in Herefordshire) and possibly Monmouth.[7] Recently, the association of Chepstow's great tower with William fitz Osbern has been challenged, and the suggestion made that William the Conqueror may have been the patron following his 1081 visit to Wales.[8] No evidence has been found for the use of masonry from fitz Osbern's time at his other castles, and, therefore, it seems logical to conclude that they were wooden constructions. Why should Chepstow be any different? Against this, there is nothing in terms of the style of the building to preclude a *c.*1070 date for the great tower at Chepstow. So, given a documented connection with fitz Osbern, and no mention of any architectural patronage by William I at Chepstow, my preference would be for the earlier date. This will also be supported by documentation in relation to one of fitz Osbern's associates in Herefordshire, and another in Gloucestershire.

In addition to the debate over the date of the great tower, there is disagreement as to its function. Specifically, was there a hall and chamber on the first floor, or did an audience hall occupy this entire space? John Clifford Perks, author of the Department of the Environment's Official Handbook to Chepstow castle in 1967, believed that there was a wooden partition in the first storey in the eleventh century, which was replaced with a stone double arch in the thirteenth century, the springers of which remain today.[9] This putative wooden partition may have provided the division for hall and chamber. This is the interpretation followed by John Newman in his account of the castle in the Gwent/

Fig. 3 Chepstow castle: exterior of the great tower from the south

Monmouthshire volume of the *Buildings of Wales*.[10] There is no physical evidence for the partition and in the most recent article on the castle, Rick Turner, Cadw Inspector of Ancient Monuments, has reconstructed an open hall without any subdivision.[11]

Description and Function

The tower is an irregular rectangle measuring approximately 120ft by 45ft and was originally of two storeys — the third storey was added in two separate building campaigns in the thirteenth century.[12] The outer wall is articulated with pilaster buttresses, two bays by five (figs. 1–5). There is a battered plinth on the south and east walls (figs. 1–3), and a plain plinth on the north and west wall, all of sandstone ashlar (figs. 4–5). For the most part, the walls are built of roughly squared stones with some reused Roman brick and ashlar dressings — a diverse collection of stones analysed in detail by John Allen and Rick Turner.[13] A string-course of reused Roman brick runs along the west, south and east exterior of the hall. It turns the north-east and north-west angles but is not continued along the north wall. This string-course provides external expression of the internal division between the two floors. The top of the first storey is marked externally on the west wall

Fig. 4 (left) Chepstow castle: raking view of the exterior of the west bays of the north wall of great tower from the north-east

Fig. 5 (right) Chepstow castle: exterior of the west wall of the great tower

Figs. 6 and 7 Chepstow castle: eastern doorway to the great tower (with pilaster buttress alongside), with detail of the arch and tympanun

by a sandstone string-course above which there are two courses of ashlar (fig. 5). Immediately above this there are two circular windows, one in the centre of the wall above the pilaster buttress, the other set centrally in the bay to the left. These windows differ in size and constructional detail. The central one is smaller and is cut from two stones, while the one to the left is composed of several roughly shaped stones (damaged at the bottom). The top string-course and upper two ashlar courses continue on to the south wall (fig. 3).

The east wall contains the elaborate portal in the right bay, while in the left bay there is a narrow, round-headed window that lights the top of the staircase in the thickness of the wall (figs. 2, 6 and 7). The lintel, tympanum and arch of the portal are carved with chip-carved saltire crosses (figs. 6 and 7). The lintel is composed of three joggled stones; the one in the centre tapers from top to bottom so as to be secured against the side blocks. On the tympanum, crushed Roman tile is mixed with the mortar to impart a strong pink colour. The Roman-brick string-course does not encompass the entire arch of the doorway but just the upper segment between ten and two in terms of a clock face.

The north wall is thinner than the other three walls. In the easternmost bay there is a rectangular doorcase to the undercroft. Three round-headed, single-splay windows light the ground floor, one in each of the middle three bays (fig. 4). Above the doorway to the undercroft there remains the only Norman window to the first floor in the north wall — interestingly it is not splayed but cut straight through the wall (fig. 9). There is evidence for original windows in the other bays except bay four (counting from the east). In the westernmost bay, the exterior of the blocked window has its head cut from a single stone and is centred in the bay. However, on the inside the window is not centrally placed within

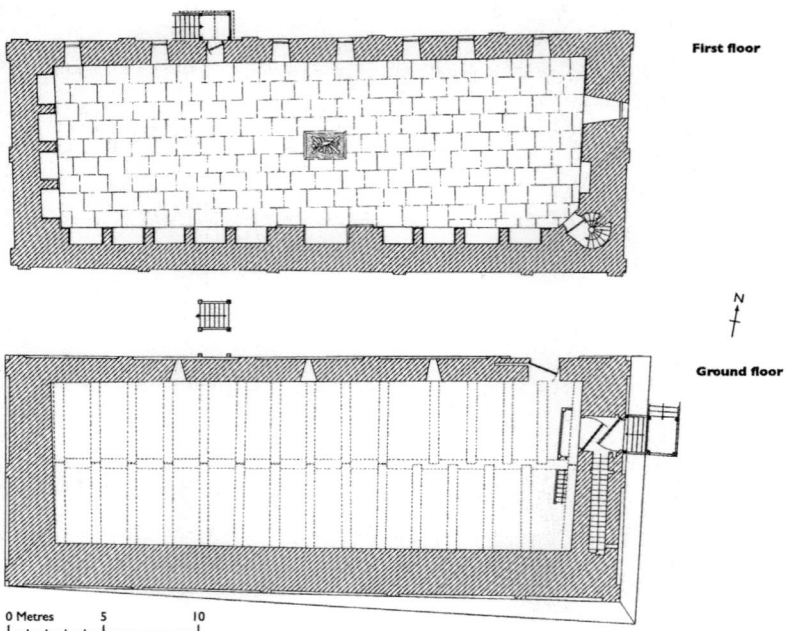

Fig. 8 Plan of the great tower at Chepstow castle

Fig. 9 Detail of the interior of the east window in the north wall of the great tower at Chepstow

the bay; the left jamb is adjacent to the north-west corner (fig. 10). Thus, from the point of view of the interior, placement of the window took no account of the thickness of the west wall, meaning that external rather than internal symmetry was the design preference. There is clear evidence on the exterior for two windows in the third bay from the east; to the left both jambs are extant, whilst to the right just the right jamb can be seen. In the second bay from the east just the left jamb of the right window survives.

The Roman-brick string-course is only used in the western part of the western bay of the north wall and in the north-east pilaster buttress. This suggested to Turner that a lean-to structure abutted here. In the fourth bay of the first floor there is a tall but somewhat narrow doorway that would have been reached by a dog-legged wooden stair (figs. 3, and 10–12). The return of the stair is cut into the

Fig. 10 Interior north-west corner of the great tower showing the closeness of the blocked window on the left to the corner of the building, indicating that external, rather than internal symmetry was more important

Fig. 12 The first-floor doorway in the western bay of the north wall of the great tower, with square sockets below for the floor beams also supported on posts down the centre of the basement

adjacent pilaster — as seen clearly in figure 4 — which indicates that the stair was entered from the west. On the exterior the doorway has an irregularly shaped monolithic lintel.

On the interior of the east portal there is a plain, tripartite lintel and a plain tympanum composed of eleven stones in three rows (fig. 14). There are two orders in the arch which are plain except for one stone in the outer order carved with saltire crosses. It must have been a

Fig. 14 Detail of the interior of the eastern doorway in the great hall

Fig. 11 Interior of the great tower looking west-north-west

Fig. 13 Interior of the north wall of the great tower from the south-west

Fig. 15 Interior of the south and east walls of the great tower

Fig. 16 Detail of the blind arcade on the interior of the north wall of the great tower

'spare' from the other side of the doorway — it would have been covered by the floor of the upper storey, as indicated by the large socket immediately to the right of the arch (fig. 14).

The floor of the basement is bedrock and slopes up significantly from east to west (figs. 11, 13 and 18). There are large, square sockets in the middle of the east and west walls for the ends of beams that would have been carried on posts down the centre of the basement (figs. 11 and 15). In the north and south walls there are square sockets for the joists of the floor of the hall (figs. 10, 11, 13 and 18). These would have been covered with ceiling planks on which it is likely that three was a layer of bedding sand and a flagged floor.

The articulation of the interior of the first-floor hall can be reconstructed with some degree of accuracy. At the west end there are the four blind niches and there is a similar range of four niches at the western end of the south wall (figs. 11 and 15–16). In the second niche from the left on the west wall the plastered tympanum has a white lattice pattern on a red ground, a simplified version of the reticulated masonry on the tympanum of the east portal (plate 1, figs. 6 and 16). It will also be noticed that the impost between the two left niches has a cable moulding below two quirks, in contrast to the plain chamfers of the other imposts. To the left of the four niches at the west end of the south wall, the most obvious feature is the

Fig. 17 Norman arches to eiher side of thirteenth-century south respond of crossing arch

Fig. 18 Detail of the arch to the right (west) of thirteenth-century respond illustrated in fig. 17

13

respond and springing of the thirteenth-century cross arch. However, careful examination of the masonry to the right of this later respond reveals that a Romanesque arch springs towards the respond from the same impost as the fourth niche (figs. 17 and 18). Before considering this further, let us move to the left of the thirteenth-century work to the eastern section of the south wall. Reading left to right from the angled entrance arch in the south-east corner, there is a round-headed niche on chamfered imposts, somewhat larger in size than the niches in the western section of this wall (fig. 18). There follows another niche — opened as a window in the thirteenth century — but there is only an impost on the right. This impost continues for some distance to the right after which the wall is plain for about the same distance. The impost then starts again just to the east of the thirteenth-century respond. It is significant that this impost is set at a lower level than the imposts that carry the arches of the niches further west (fig. 17). The imposts to the east are also longer than those to the west. The difference in the levels indicates that the arch that springs from the impost immediately to the right of the thirteenth-century respond would not have extended to the impost to the left. Indeed, it would seem from the trajectory of the voussoirs that this arch would have been of the same size as those to the right (figs. 17–18). This would leave ample room for a wooden partition in the Norman hall. While we can never be sure that such a partition ever existed, the difference in articulation of the two sections of the southern wall at least implies that there was some division in function between the two spaces. It is therefore significant that the doorway in the north wall is located immediately to the left of the respond of the thirteenth-century cross arch to provide a separate entrance to the western section of the hall (figs. 11 and 13). There is no evidence that the tower was residential, and Turner has suggested that it functioned as a grand audience hall. In this case the more richly articulated western end of the hall would have had a dais for the high table to be occupied by fitz Osbern and his immediate circle. If that were the case, then the putative wooden partition would have taken the form of an arched or trabeated screen, rather than a solid divider pierced only by doors. There is no evidence in the walls for a fireplace so presumably there was an open hearth in the hall.

Turner has questioned whether the east portal functioned as the main entrance to the hall. He pointed out the difficulty of reconstructing an appropriate wooden staircase for access to the portal, and explained the elaboration of the portal as an appropriately grand frame for the lord of Chepstow when appearing ceremonially to his subjects gathered on the ground below. The theory has much to recommend in that it is analogous to Roman practice, as at Diocletian's Palace at Split. At the same time there seems little reason to preclude its use as a portal, for the only alternative would have been to use the doorway in the north wall. The location of this doorway towards the west end of the hall would mean that a visitor would pass by the grand east portal and then walk alongside most of the side of the hall before gaining entry. It has been mentioned above that the dog-legged wooden stair to the north doorway was entered from the west (fig. 4), which would be unusual if it was intended for the visitor approaching from the east. Moreover, the north doorway is so narrow as to preclude the entry of more than one person at a time, something difficult

Fig. 19 Looking aloing the east wall of the great tower to the south-east corner, showing the corner entry at first-floor level

to equate with the idea of a grand entry into a ceremonial hall (figs. 4, 12 and 13). The lack of any sort of ornamentation or articulation of the doorway is also hard to explain for a main entrance, and is in stark contrast to the elaborate, near-contemporary main portals at Scolland's Hall at Richmond (Yorks.) or Colchester castle (Essex). Here it seems significant that Pamela Marshall has referred to the Chepstow north portal as 'a back door or opening to a balcony'.[14] For the visitor to the great tower at Chepstow, to enter the east portal, turn left to climb the stairs and then exit in the south-east angle of the first floor (fig. 19), is not fundamentally different from the arrangement in the great tower at Castle Hedingham (Essex). Visitors to Hedingham would reach the richly ornamented portal by an external stair. They would pass through the doorway and turn immediately left to enter the spiral stair and walk up one storey to exit in the corner of the great hall. At Chepstow the exit from the top of the stair in the south-east corner of the first floor is set on an angle and is about twice the width of the north doorway (figs. 12, 13 and 19). It is therefore far better suited in scale to a grand entry into the hall.

Sources and Affiliations

The closest parallel for the rectangular plan and two-storey arrangement with a first-floor hall above a ground-floor storage area is Scolland's Hall at Richmond.[15] Richmond castle was founded around 1070 by Alan Rufus, nephew of William the Conqueror, and commander of the Breton contingent of the Norman army at the Battle of Hastings. A first-floor hall is also represented in the Bayeux Tapestry in the scene depicting King Harold dining at his manor at Bosham (Sussex). William fitz Osbern may have been responsible for the construction of a large castle, possibly centred on a donjon, in Breteuil, and he would have been familiar with eleventh-century stone towers.[16]

Anglo-Saxon, Norman and Roman affiliations are suggested by various motifs or techniques of building. The building technique with cut-stone facing on a rubble core is of Roman derivation and was in regular use in Normandy well before the Conquest. The pilaster buttresses also reflect Norman practice, as do the arches with cut-stone radiating voussoirs. One important exception to this is in the arch from the staircase in the south-west corner of the first floor. Here, instead of the neat, cut-stone radial voussoirs, there are smaller, non-radial stones — contrast the inside of the east portal and the arch from the staircase, illustrated in figure 19. This is surely an indication of non-Norman workmanship and one that is unknown to me in any major post-Conquest building. As such it is one of the best indications that we are dealing with William fitz Osbern's castle erected before 1071, rather than a building of the 1080s commissioned by William I.

Two other details have pre-Conquest associations. First, the circular window that surmounts the pilaster in the centre of the west wall is cut through a squared flat frame in the manner of the circular openings at the top of the eleventh-century west tower at St Benet's, Cambridge. Secondly, the inclusion of the cable and quirks on the impost between the two left niches in the west wall of the hall recalls a pre-Conquest interest in variety in detail. This can be seen in the piers and responds at Great Paxton (Hunts.), and it finds

Fig. 20 Beaumais (Calvados): the south doorway showing use of chip-carved saltire crosses

its fullest expression in variously shaped and moulded window frames in the stair turret of the west tower at Hough-on-the-Hill (Lincs.). It must be admitted that allied variations are found in the abaci of the arcades in St John's chapel in the Tower of London, built for William I after 1070. However, the aesthetic of these details at Chepstow has more in common with a pre-Conquest tradition than with one in eleventh-century Normandy.

In contrast to any lingering Anglo-Saxon elements, the construction of the lintel, and the chip-carved saltire crosses on the lintel, tympanum and arch of the great portal, reflect the latest practice in Normandy. The three-stone form of the lintel with the tapered central block is paralleled on the north nave portal at Saint-Nicholas at Caen, in which the tympanum is composed of three rows of plain ashlar as on the inner face of the Chepstow portal.[17] The chip-carved saltire crosses are used extensively on arches and capitals in La Trinité or Abbaye-aux-Dames at Caen, the abbey church founded by Duke William and his wife, Matilda, in 1059 or 1060, and consecrated on 18 June 1066.[18] The motif enjoyed considerable popularity in Normandy, as witnessed in the abbey church at Graville-Ste-Honorine (Seine-Maritime),[19] and in the arch of the south portal at Beaumais (Calvados) (fig. 26), and in a secular setting on the tympanum on the Exchequer at Caen.[20] The motif appears in England in the capitals of Durham castle chapel as early as 1072.[21] It is also used on the lintel of the south doorway at Winstone (Glos.) where the tympanum is incised with a reticulated lozenge pattern, like the stones in the Chepstow tympanum but without the chip-carved decoration (figs. 7 and 21). Here, it may be significant that the same reticulated pattern appears on the tympanum of the portal at St Leger-de-Rôtes (Eure), about 30km south-east of Cormeilles.[22] William fitz Osbern had founded a Benedictine monastery at Cormeilles, of which Chepstow priory was a daughter house.[23] In 1086 Winstone was held by Ansfrid de Cormeilles, and the overlordship of the manor descended with the honor of Cormeilles.[24] It seems likely that the incisions on the Winstone tympanum would have been used as guidelines for the geometric painted decoration as on the Romanesque painted plaster from St Mary's abbey, York (fig. 22). This provided a rather neater pattern than the coloured-plaster examples in the niches at the west end of the Chepstow hall (plate 1). There is a version of the motif composed of single stones, as in the Chepstow east portal, on the tympanum of the north doorway at St Leonard's, Hatfield (Herefs.) (fig. 23), where there is also a joggled lintel of three stones, albeit

Fig. 21 St. Bartholomew's Winstone (Glos.): south doorway showing a tympanum incised with a reticulated lozenge pattern

stepped rather than wedged as at Chepstow (figs. 7 and 14). The Domesday Book records that the manor of Hatfield was held by Hugh l'Asne,[25] a member of fitz Osbern's household who held land on the earl's estates in Normandy, and was made one of the tenants-in-chief in Herefordshire by the earl.[26] In light of the formal similarities between the Hatfield and Chepstow portals, this personal connection between William fitz Osbern and Hugh l'Asne may indicate that the Hatfield portal design was based on that at Chepstow. Moreover, it tends to reinforce the case for fitz Osbern as patron of the work at the castle.

The vogue for chip-carved decoration on tympana in England lasted well into the twelfth century. In Kent, examples of chip-carved tympana occur in the main entrances to two churches associated with Canterbury cathedral, at Eynsford and Godmersham.[27] Here the principle of applying the richest decoration to the main entrance of a church is the same as in a secular context in the great tower at Chepstow.

Fig. 22 *St Mary's abbey, York: fragment of painted plaster now held in the Yorkshire Museum*

The hood mould of the Chepstow doorway that continues to either side of the arch as a string-course, does not envelop the entire arch but only the section between 10 and 2 in terms of a clock face (figs. 6 and 7). It is made of Roman brick and probably reflects a Roman source in which a cornice is continued around an arch as in Diocletian's Palace at Split.[28] At Split, an architrave and frieze fill the space between the springing of the arch and the cornice of the entablature, but these elements have been omitted at Chepstow. It is possible that they were

Fig. 23 *St. Leonard's, Hatfield (Herefs.): tympanun above the north doorway showing incised decoration akin to that at Chepstow. Hatfield manor was held by Hugh L'Asne, one of fitz Osbern's tenants-in-chief*

originally executed in paint or coloured plaster, in the manner of the painted articulation of the interior of the first-floor room of the Carolingian gatehouse at Lorsch (plate 2). There is also a good precedent for the combination of masonry and painted articulation in the first storey of the westwerk at Corvey (873–885), where the profile of a carved impost is continued along the wall in paint (plate 3). Local inspiration may have come from the Roman remains at Caerleon or Caerwent. On the former, Gerald of Wales recorded that of the Roman work,

> You can still see many vestiges of its one-time splendour. There are immense palaces, which, with the gilded gables of their roofs, once rivalled the magnificence of ancient Rome. They were set up in the first place by some of the most eminent men of the Roman state, and they were therefore embellished with every architectural conceit. There is a lofty tower, and beside it remarkable hot baths, the remains of temples and an amphitheatre.[29]

It is worth noting that brick courses are often interspersed with ashlar facing in Roman buildings, such as the frigidarium at Nice-Cimiez (Alpes-Maritimes), where we also find a precedent for the joggled lintel construction of the east portal at Chepstow (figs. 2, 7 and 82).

The motif of the '10-2' hoodmould that continues to either side of the arch as a string-course, is paralleled on the west arch of the bishop's chapel at Hereford (1079–95) and the east presbytery arch of Hereford cathedral (1107–15).[30] In the 1120s, under Anglo-Welsh influence, it is used on the west front of Ardfert cathedral (Kerry) (fig. 24), where it

Fig. 24 Ardfert cathedral, Kerry: west front showing a hoodmould that continues as a string-course, as paralleled over the doorway to the great tower at Chepstow

is also interesting to see friezes of reticulated masonry in the walls beneath the blind arches that flank the portal.

There seems to be little reason to doubt that William fitz Osbern was the patron of the great tower at Chepstow. The association between fitz Osbern and Hugh l'Asne, allied with the formal comparison between the Chepstow and Hatfield doorways, support the idea that fitz Osbern built a stone castle at Chepstow. A similar link to the south doorway at Winstone through Ansfrid de Cormeilles reinforces this interpretation. Moreover, as Perks has indicated, it would have been most difficult to erect a wooden structure on the bedrock that provides such a firm foundation for the great tower.[31] William of Poitiers recorded that Duke William 'loved fitz Osbern above the other members of his household since they had been boys together'.[32] In light of this close relationship with the new king, it seems entirely appropriate that fitz Osbern should have commissioned the masonry great tower at Chepstow. It created a powerful symbol of the new Norman authority, one to be matched in the ecclesiastical realm by the new priory founded by fitz Osbern just across town. The Roman analogues cited for aspects of the great tower at Chepstow are pertinent in connection with the locations of a number of Norman castles, including the Tower of London and Colchester. In London, William's great tower was built on the edge of the Roman city, and at Colchester the great tower was erected on or around the site of the podium of the temple of Claudius.[33] Such appropriation of either a Roman site and/or Roman motifs speaks clearly of the imperial aspirations of the Normans.

If the association of the Chepstow great tower with William fitz Osbern is correct, then it raises questions about the dating of a number of other Anglo-Norman castles. It implies that work on the Tower of London and Richmond castle could have commenced soon after 1070. Perhaps construction of Colchester castle was also started at this time, and in the ecclesiastical realm there are related questions regarding the starting dates of a number of buildings, not least with Chepstow priory.

CHEPSTOW PRIORY CHURCH

The Benedictine priory of Chepstow was a cell of William fitz Osbern's foundation of Cormeilles abbey (Eure).[34] None of the documentation specifically names William fitz Osbern as the founder of the daughter house at Chepstow, but William Coxe, author of *An Historical Tour through Monmouthshire* (1801), recorded that the foundation was made by 'one of the proprietors of the castle soon after the Conquest'.[35] This makes William the most likely candidate, unless it is suggested that his son, Roger de Breteuil, founded the priory in commemoration of his father. William fitz Osbern died in Flanders in 1071 and was succeeded by Roger, who conspired with Ralph, Earl of Norfolk and Suffolk and Waltheof of Northumbria, to overthrow King William. In 1075 Roger was captured and imprisoned by the king and his estates were forfeited to the crown.

How soon after the foundation of the priory, work commenced on the stone church is not easily determined because the eastern arm, crossing and transepts of the church are destroyed, with the exception of the lowest courses of the north-west crossing pier (fig. 25).[36] An engraving of 1800 shows the west responds of the north and south crossing

Fig. 25 (above) North-west crossing pier at Chepstow priory
Fig. 26 (right) Interior south nave elevation, and exterior of the priory from the south-east (after Coxe, 1801)

arches extant (fig. 26), while an 1844 drawing illustrates the upper half of a former crossing pier re-erected after the destruction of the eastern bay of the nave in 1841 (fig. 27).[37] Joseph Millerd's map of 1686 shows the crossing tower and eastern arm of the church but without recognizable details, while Charles Heath's 1793 description of the church indicates that the eastern arm had arcades on piers like the nave.[38] Of the original six-bay nave, five bays remain, less the aisles, which were destroyed in 1840–1841 (figs. 28 and 29). For the distinguished nineteenth-century historian Edward A. Freeman this was the culmination of 'accumulations of successive periods of barbarism'.[39] Prior to 1841 there was a north doorway of two orders with zigzag in the arch.[40] There is an elaborate west doorway flanked by single, narrow blind arches, and three windows above (fig. 30). Following the collapse of the crossing tower in 1701, a west tower was built behind the façade wall in the western bay of the nave in 1705–1706, in which fragments of the Romanesque crossing tower were reused.

Fig. 27 A re-erected crossing pier from Chepstow priory (after Wallace 1904)

In the late nineteenth century, the Rev. E.J. Hensley observed that the 'nave is one of the few Norman buildings in England originally designed to be vaulted'.[41] Subsequently, architect and antiquary Charles Lynam suggested that there was originally a high groin vault over the nave, for which he cited comparative evidence for a groin vault in the nave of St Mary the Virgin at Copford (Essex).[42] Sir Alfred Clapham dated the nave *circa* 1120 and McAleer observed that 'the west façade may be later as it has much chevron enrichment'.[43] There can be no doubt that both Hensley and Lynam are correct that the nave was vaulted, although, as we shall see, the vault would have been ribbed rather than groined. Recent research has demonstrated that master masons in the south-west Midlands were at the forefront of high-vault construction in the late eleventh and early twelfth centuries.[44] The vaults and other aspects of Romanesque Chepstow priory must be placed within this context. This involves a close examination of all aspects of its design in relation to the date of the church; was it really commenced before 1071 or was there a delay between the foundation of the monastery and the beginning of construction of the stone church?

Description

The nave has a three-storey elevation that comprises main arcade, triforium and clerestorey (figs. 28 and 29). The main arcade is round-headed with two orders to the unmoulded arches. The inner order is corbelled out from the simple rectangular pier but this arrangement dates only from the 1840–41 remodelling, and there is conflicting evidence as to the

Fig. 29 (left) South nave elevation looking west
Fig. 28 (right) North nave elevation looking west

original appearance of the Romanesque piers. On the one hand, it appears that the original disposition is preserved in the first pier of the south nave arcade (fig. 31) — now the east respond — and on the west side of the west pier of both the north and south arcades. Here the inner order of the arch is articulated from the ground on a projecting section of the pier and springs from a chamfered impost now removed from the east respond of the south arcade. On the other hand, the engraving of the south elevation of the nave published by Coxe shows the piers with shafts (fig. 26). How far the engraving is to be trusted is a moot point. As we shall see, its accuracy is in doubt as a record of any evidence for high vault shafts, and it shows two nook shafts between the first and second orders of the arch without any evidence for corresponding mouldings in the arch. There is, however, firm evidence that the arcade responds were differently treated at the east and west ends. At the west end of both arcades the inner order of the arch is carried on a single half column (fig. 32). At the east end twin shafts carried the inner order while the outer order was carried on nook shafts (fig. 25). The original east respond of the north arcade formed part of an elaborate crossing pier which carried the arches of the crossing and the arch from the north transept to the north nave aisle. In each case the articulation was different. The arch from the north transept to the north nave aisle had two orders: the inner one was carried on paired shafts, while the outer order had a nook shaft towards the aisle but just a squared section towards the transept. The north crossing arch had two orders with nook shafts and paired soffit shafts. In contrast there are triple shafts for the western arch but no nook shafts or any projection for an outer order (figs. 25 and 27). Mrs. Ormerod's drawing of the pier shows the use of both cushion and double-scallop capitals (fig. 25). There are no projections from the nave piers towards the aisles and there is regularly coursed ashlar masonry in the spandrels, but this probably dates from the 1840–41 restoration (figs. 33 and 34). Above,

Fig. 31 (above) Eastern bay of the south nave arcade
Fig. 32 (right) West respond of the north nave arcade

Fig. 33 (left) Exterior of the priory from the north-west
Fig. 34 (right) Exterior of the priory from the south

pilasters articulate the 'outside' of the false gallery and clerestorey. Returning inside, the triforium openings on the north do not match those on the south (figs. 36 and 37). The former are plain single arches in each bay. The latter have paired, two-order unmoulded arches with the inner order supported on half shafts, while the outer order are carried on nook shafts on the outside and paired shafts in the centre. The back of the south triforium is framed with large, round-headed, enclosing arches but these are not used on the north side (figs. 33 and 34). The clerestorey has plain, single-order, round-headed openings without a wall passage. In the south nave elevation the trace of a former pilaster is filled with plaster and this is continued in a stilted-arch form above the clerestorey (fig. 29). On the north side the pilaster is only marked at main arcade level; above the whole wall is plastered except for the ashlar frames of the triforium and clerestorey openings (fig. 28).

The western piers of the arcades are 11 inches longer than the other piers, 90 inches versus 79 inches (fig. 34). This indicates that twin western towers were intended although there is no evidence that they were built. Two storeys of the central section of the west front remain from the Romanesque fabric flanked by two-stepped pilasters that enclose vices (fig. 30). The elaborate round-headed doorway has six orders. The heavily restored inner order is continuous with an angle roll. The other orders have shafts and capitals

Fig. 30 (left) The west front of Chepstow priory
Fig. 35 (right) Looking at the west end from inside the nave

with single flat leaves at the angles and a simple foliage spray on a stalk between. Orders 2 and 6 have furrowed chevron and this is also used on the single blind arches that flank the doorway. Order 4 has an angle roll and a quirked hollow roll on the face, while orders 3 and 5 are chip-carved, the former with a series of diamond shapes, the latter with small triangular wedges. Above the doorway, three windows light a passage in the thickness of the wall that is articulated on the inner plane with segmental arches on columns with scalloped capitals (figs. 35 and 36). At the back of the columns arches are thrown across the passage from corbels immediately below the capitals to land on corbels between the windows. The central window is elaborate, with three orders of different types of chevron in the arch; spaced lozenge chevron on order 1, 90-degree chevron on the second order and continuous lozenge on the outer order (fig. 37). The inner order has plain chamfered jambs, while the second and third orders have shafts and scalloped capitals; those on the right and the inner capital on the left with two scallops on each face, while both faces of the

Fig. 37 (above) The west windows, of which the central one has three types of chevron in the arch
Fig. 36 (right) The passage in the west wall behind the windows, looking south

outer left capital have three scallops. The quirked chamfered abaci extend to form the impost of the plain, single-order windows to the side, although this feature is not repeated on the lateral springers of these arches. A single-billet hood mould is used above all three windows.

Reconstruction, Analysis and Sources
Both Hensley and Lynam were quite correct to reconstruct a high vault over the nave on the evidence of the traces on the south wall (fig. 29). There would have been a pilaster at the front of each pier that carried the transverse arches of the high vault in the manner of the Hereford cathedral presbytery as reconstructed by Scott, albeit with different details.[45] George Ormerod's description of the church in 1838 provides crucial evidence in this connection:

Over the round arches of the nave were and still remain Triforia, and over them a row of Clerestory windows, all clearly Norman, and the roofs over the side aisles and nave as shewn by fragments, had been vaulted with arches of tufa placed between ribs of oolite. The arches were sprung from vaulting shafts, omitted in Hoare's elevation [fig. 34], but ascending from the first string course in front of every pier.[46]

Thus there were shafts towards the nave and one must imagine a stepped respond as in the north nave aisle at St Peter's abbey (now cathedral) Gloucester (fig. 38), although probably with a three- rather than a five-shaft group. Moreover, the description makes it clear that both the aisles and the main span were rib vaulted and not groined as suggested by Lynam.

Fig. 38 St Peter's abbey (now cathedral), Gloucester: the north nave aisle looking west showing a five-shafted stepped respond. Chepstow priory probably originally had a similar three-shafted arrangement

There is no evidence for abutment at gallery level (figs. 33 and 34) but this does not seem to have concerned Anglo-Norman architects. There are barrel vaults over the galleries in St John's chapel in the Tower of London, and half barrels in the presbytery galleries of St Peter's, Gloucester. In each case they provided abutment for a Romanesque high vault. However, there are more cases of former Anglo-Norman high vaults without abutment over the galleries. Examples are in the Benedictine abbey churches of Tewkesbury and Pershore, in the presbytery of Hereford cathedral, and throughout Durham cathedral and Lindisfarne priory.[47] In this connection it should be pointed out that at least some of these West Country vault webs probably used tufa webbing as at Chepstow. Tufa is 'a generic name for porous stones, formed of pulverulent matter consolidated and often stratified' and may be further classified as either calcareous or volcanic tufa.[48] It is the calcareous type that was used in English medieval vaults, 'a porous or vesicular carbonate of lime, generally deposited near the sources and along the courses of calcareous springs'.[49] Its texture ranges in appearance from bread to clustered popcorn, and it is much lighter in weight than either limestone or sandstone, a feature that especially recommends its use in vaulting. Fragments of tufa, which possibly come from the former Romanesque high vault, are (re)used in the jambs of the fourteenth-century clerestory windows in the eastern bays of the nave of Tewkesbury abbey.[50] The large amount of tufa reused in the infill of the arches of the upper storey of the bishop's chapel at Hereford, makes it likely that the vaults there made use of this material. Willis recorded that the chapter house vault at Worcester cathedral is made of tufa.[51] Geographically closer to Chepstow is Caerleon where it has been suggested that the Roman legionary fortress baths were either groin- or barrel-vaulted using tufa.[52] As already mentioned, Gerald of Wales recorded 'remarkable hot baths, and remains of temples and an amphitheatre at Caerleon'.[53] Later in the twelfth century tufa is used for the vault web in the chapter house at Much Wenlock priory (*c*.1160), the chapter house at Keynsham abbey, in the western bays of the south nave aisle at Worcester cathedral, and, after 1185, in the Great Church at Glastonbury abbey.[54] In his contemporary description of the new work in the choir of Canterbury cathedral (1175–84), the monk, Gervase, tells us that the high vault is 'beautifully constructed of stone and light tufa'.[55]

The single shafts on the west responds of the nave arcade that carry the inner order find parallel in the West Country School of Romanesque architecture in the west responds of the presbytery arcades at St John's, Chester, and the east responds of the nave at Shrewsbury abbey.[56] The paired shafts of the east responds of the nave arcades that carry the inner order are paralleled in the west responds of the presbytery arcades at St Peter's, Gloucester. Chepstow is exceptional amongst these churches, however, in having compound piers rather than columns for the arcades. The latter are the norm in the West Country School, although compound piers are used in the presbytery of Hereford cathedral and were formerly in the nave of Worcester cathedral.[57] The Chepstow piers as they appear today, are paralleled in the ground storey of the former bishop's chapel at Hereford built by Robert de Losinga (1079–95), although on a considerably smaller scale than at Chepstow, and with single-order, rather than two-order arches. Their stepped form may also be compared with the nave arcade piers at St Albans abbey (commenced 1077), where it is also important to recall the use of Roman brick and flint.[58] Is it possible that there was Roman inspiration for the design of the Chepstow piers? The Chepstow piers may certainly be read in light of Roman work in the simple stepped piers of the Basilica Julia in Rome, where there were groin-vaulted aisles, the evidence for which looks remarkably like that for the high vaults at Chepstow.[59] Such inspiration may have come from the Roman remains at Caerleon. A close parallel is also found in the nave arcade piers of the former Benedictine nunnery at Elstow (Beds.) which was founded *c*.1075. Analogues with the church of Saint-Germain at Pont Audemer (Eure) may also be significant, Pont Audemer lying just 17km north-east of Cormeilles. The two-bay presbytery there is covered with a heavily restored groin vault but one that must have been planned from the first given the stepped articulation of the vault responds (fig. 39). In the nave, the main arcade has plain arches of two orders on simple rectangular piers with attached shafts to carry the inner

Saint-Germain at Pont Audemar (Eure), which has analogues with Chepstow priory:
Fig. 39 (left) Interior north wall of the presbytery
Fig. 40 (right) North elevation of the nave

orders like the west responds of the Chepstow nave arcades (fig. 48). Similar piers appear in the nave at Bernay abbey (Eure), just 28km south-east of Cormeilles, so in both cases we may be dealing with affiliates of the pier form and sanctuary high vault in the mother house of Chepstow.[60] In light of these parallels it is tempting to offer an early date for the Chepstow piers, but against this idea it is sobering to introduce the plain square piers in the nave at Davington priory (Kent) (fd.1153). Geographically closer to Chepstow, this is reinforced with reference to the nave triforium piers at Leominster priory (fd.1123) introduced after the abandonment of the more elaborate plan to vault the nave.

The single, plain openings of the Chepstow nave north triforium (fig. 28) are paralleled in the transept triforia at Tewkesbury abbey.[61] The south triforium openings at Chepstow (fig. 29) are conceived as a more elaborate version of the transept and nave triforia openings at Tewkesbury.[62] At Tewkesbury they have plain, single-order arches and jambs, and a single central shaft and capital. At Chepstow the arches are also plain but they have two orders, the inner carried on cushion and scalloped capitals atop half shafts, the outer on moulded imposts on shafts without capitals. The absence of the capital on the outer order is unusual in a Norman context although a similar arrangement, but without bases, occurs in the two openings above the western crossing arch at Attleborough (Norfolk). This seems to be more in keeping with an Anglo-Saxon tradition in which capitals are often omitted. Indeed, an excellent pre-Conquest comparison is found in the east and west crossing arches of St Mary-in-Castro, Dover (Kent); a good post-Conquest example is the chancel arch at Clayton (Sussex).[63] In structural terms the inclusion of the large enclosing arch behind the triforium is exactly paralleled in the nave of Bernay abbey (Eure) where the triforium openings are also akin to those on the south side of the nave at Chepstow (figs 29 and 33).[64] The enclosing arch at triforium level then appears in the West Country in the nave of St Peter's, Gloucester, and in early Gothic dress in the western bays of the nave at Worcester cathedral and throughout the late twelfth- and early thirteenth-century work at Wells cathedral.[65] The plain clerestorey without wall passage is most closely related to the presbytery at Durham cathedral where there was also a Romanesque high rib vault. This may read as a cautionary measure so as to avoid weakening the upper wall with a wall passage.

The asymmetrical and complex form of the remaining crossing pier at Chepstow (figs. 25 and 27) is unusual in a West Country Romanesque context in which the piers are generally elongated on an east-west axis without protruding shafts to obstruct the choir stalls. Good examples of this are in the great Benedictine abbey churches of Gloucester, Tewkesbury and Pershore. Be that as it may, St John's, Chester, provides a very close parallel for the north-west crossing pier at Chepstow, with the juxtaposition of three shafts on the face towards the nave, and two shafts towards the transept. St John's, Chester, was possibly designed as early as 1075, when it became a cathedral, although stylistically it appears to have been built well after this time.[66] Triple shafts are also used on the crossing piers at Binham priory (Norfolk) (founded *c.*1090), Norwich cathedral (commenced 1096) and possibly in the crossing of Bury St Edmunds abbey commenced in 1081. In turn, this may be read as an adaptation of the pre-Conquest crossing piers at Great Paxton (Hunts.), a minster church probably built under the patronage of Edward the Confessor.[67] Paired shafts are already used in the crossing at Jumièges abbey church (1040), and they appear subsequently at La Trinité at Caen.

Fig. 41 South capitals on the western tower arch at Chepstow priory

The construction of the present western tower in 1706 incorporated masonry from the Romanesque crossing tower, which had collapsed in 1701 (fig. 35). The first clue as to the reuse comes with the damage to the capitals of the inner order and the eastern nook shaft capitals, which are in fact reused Romanesque bases (fig. 41). The capitals are a volute type with two rows of symmetrical upright leaves below the volutes. They are not precisely paralleled elsewhere, but they belong to the same family as a capital in the crypt at Bayeux, commenced 1044/49,[68] and the south capital of the western crossing arch at Stogursey priory (Somerset), founded between 1100 and 1107.[69] Along with this, it is important to refer to Mrs. Ormerod's drawing of the reconstructed crossing pier complete with cushion and scalloped capitals (fig. 27). These are in sharp contrast to the volute capitals reused in the western crossing arch, and this may indicate that the more elaborate, foliage capitals were used on the eastern crossing arch to emphasise the entrance into the sanctuary. The arch mouldings of the present tower arch are likewise reused and comprise a simple soffit roll and an outer order to the east with a recessed angle roll and an undulating hollow roll to the second order.

The use of scalloped capitals and mouldings in the crossing arches is of crucial concern in regard to the date of construction of the church. The earliest datable post-Conquest scalloped capital is generally considered to be in St John's chapel in the Tower of London, which was commenced sometime between 1070 and 1077. In West Country Romanesque we seemingly have to wait until the crypt of St Peter's abbey, Gloucester, commenced in 1089. However, it is possible that the scalloped capital was already in use in pre-Conquest England. The case rests on the report of a number of fragments from Southwell Minster described and illustrated by James Dimock (fig. 42). Here it is important to quote Dimock at length. With reference to the possibility of mid-eleventh-century work at Southwell, Dimock states:

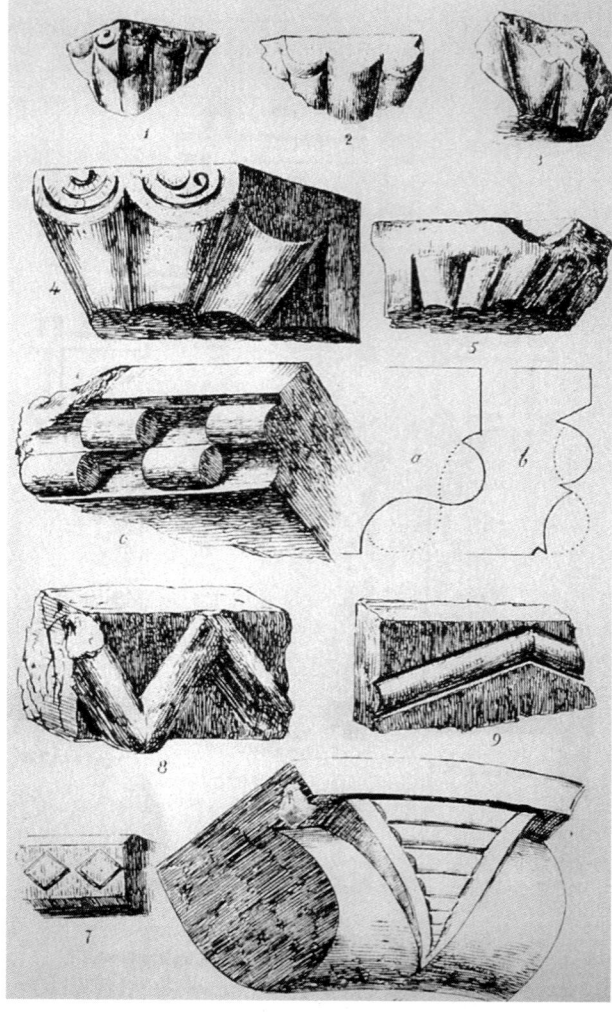

Fig. 42 Southwell minster: fragments (after Dimock)

> And to this date, perhaps, belong a number of fragments of capitals, mouldings etc., which have been found, during recent repairs, *some in the foundation of the*

south wall of the nave, others worked up in the piers of the central tower [emphasis mine]. They tell of a church, rudely indeed, but fully as much ornamented in its way, as the subsequent Norman structure in which they were entombed. Independently of their historical value, they are interesting in an architectural point of view, as comprising forms which are generally considered to be characteristic of even the later Norman. Supposing that the present nave and transepts were erected in the first half of the twelfth century, these fragments must have belonged to a building erected at the latest before the end of the eleventh century. But several of them have every appearance of having been subjected to the action of atmosphere, for ages before the church of which they were a part was destroyed, and themselves were made use of in later building. I cannot help fancying it possible, that some of these fragments may have belonged to a church, not only of the middle of the eleventh century, but of even a far earlier date. I may add, that there can be *no doubt of their being earlier than the Norman work in which they were imbedded: they are not, as has been suggested, mere wasters from the stones preparing for this later work: the capitals have very evident remains of colouring; and however close an identity there may be in some instances in character, the execution of these mouldings is much rougher, and the section perfectly distinct from that of similar mouldings in the present Norman portions of the church* [emphasis mine].[70]

In Germany, a double-scallop capital at Lorsch has been dated as early as the eighth century,[71] otherwise, examples are more common from the mid-eleventh century onwards, as at St Lucius at Werden, 1049–63 (fig. 43). Here the capital tops a four-shafted pier like those in the pre-Conquest nave arcades at Great Paxton, less the rolls or angle fillets between the shafts.[72] So, if a pre-Conquest pier form is associated with near-contemporary German work, is there any reason to exclude the scalloped capital from a similar equation? In this light, is it unreasonable to see scalloped capitals used in the crossing at Chepstow around 1070?

Turning to arch mouldings, it seems that, in general, major churches constructed

Fig. 43 St Lucius, Werdun: presbytery north arcade from the north, showing a double-scallop capital

in the first generation after the Conquest have plain arches, as at Archbishop Lanfranc's cathedral at Canterbury, commenced in 1070, and Bishop Walkelin's Winchester cathedral, commenced in 1079. These stand in sharp contrast to the richly moulded arcades of churches of the second generation after the Conquest, exemplified by Durham cathedral (1093) and Norwich cathedral (1096). A clear demonstration of this typology is seen in the transepts of Ely cathedral, where there is a break in construction between 1093 and 1100. Here unmoulded arches of the first phase of construction are surmounted by moulded arches of the second phase.[73] Typologically sound and chronologically convenient as such a guideline may be there are reasons for doubting such an absolutely clear-cut division. The soffit roll is not common in West Country Romanesque, although there is a close parallel for its use at Chepstow in the transept chapel arches at Worcester cathedral (1084–89) and the chancel arch of the former collegiate church at Quatford (Salop) (1086).[74] Also at Worcester, but on a smaller scale, the soffit roll is used in the blind arcade of the eastern slype. Here Philip Barker observed that the irregular construction of the arches indicates that the voussoirs are reused Anglo-Saxon work.[75] Moreover, the soffit roll is used in the arch to the former south-east porticus of Deerhurst priory (Glos.). This probably dates after the gift of Deerhurst to the abbey of Saint Denis in 1059.[76] At Wittering (Northants.) the elaborate chancel arch is likely to be pre-Conquest or at least before the masons of Ely Cathedral started using the quarries at Barnack in the early 1080s.[77] In Normandy, the soffit roll is used in the second quarter of the eleventh century at Bernay abbey and after 1066 in the crossing at Saint-Etienne at Caen where it is flanked by a further three rolls.[78] The angle roll appears in the transepts at Le Mont St Michel either before or after 1058.[79] At Saint-Nicholas at Caen, a building mentioned in a charter of Duke William of Normandy of 1083 as 'recently constructed',[80] is especially interesting in this context. There are roll-and-hollow mouldings on the lower windows of the apse, one order on the exterior, and two on the interior (fig. 44).[81] Ruprich-Robert placed the start of construction of Saint-Nicholas at 1070.[82]

In England, the chancel arch at Holy Trinity, Bosham (Sussex), has the closest

Fig. 44 St Nicholas, Caen (Calvados): detail of apse capitals and rolls-and-hollow mouldings on the window arches

Fig. 45 Holy Trinity, Bosham (Sussex): northern capitals on the chancel arch

Fig. 41 Chepstow Priory. south capital on the western tower arch

juxtaposition of soffit roll, recessed angle roll and hood to Chepstow (figs. 41 and 45). The Bosham chancel arch is an insertion into a pre-Conquest fabric and is usually dated around 1090.[83] However, its proximity to Chichester may suggest a somewhat earlier date. The seat of the bishopric was moved to Chichester from Selsey in 1075 but architectural historians long held that work on the new cathedral was not started until the time of Bishop Ralph de Luffa in 1091. However, as cathedral archaeologist Tim Tatton-Brown has argued, it is most unlikely that start on the new work would have been delayed some sixteen years and consequently it makes more sense that the Norman fabric was commenced in 1075.[84] The remarkably close parallel between the Chichester mouldings and the doorway in the chapel at Corfe castle suggests that the latter may be the work of William the Conqueror.[85] Elsewhere, the crossing arches at Milborne Port (Somerset) have three moulded orders.[86] It is generally agreed that the church there was commenced around 1080, and was commissioned by Regenbald, who held the manor at Domesday.[87] Regenbald was a clerk to Edward the Confessor and one of the 'survivors' of the Conquest, and therefore the church may have been started somewhat sooner after the Conquest. Between 1050 and 1080, the north doorway of St Botolph's at Hadstock (Essex) has an angle roll, and the soffit roll is used on the chancel arch at St Martin, Wareham (Dorset).[88] Some Anglo-Saxon doorways like the west doorway at Earls Barton (Northants.) have multiple mouldings on the face, while other near-contemporary doorways are plain. Similarly, in Normandy, plain and moulded orders of an arch appear at the same time, and even in the same building, as in the external articulation of the apse of Saint-Nicholas at Caen.

One difference between the Chepstow and Bosham arch mouldings is that the outer order at Chepstow is a wave moulding rather than the simple hollow roll at Bosham. The only parallel I know for this profile at Chepstow is on the arch to the north porch at Tewkesbury abbey (figs. 41 and 46), and this is possibly problematical for an early date for Chepstow. The Tewkesbury porch probably dates from the second decade of the twelfth century and at the earliest was not designed until the abbey was founded after 1087. On the other hand, if the wave moulding is seen as something that evolves directly from a hollow roll then the Tewkesbury parallel is not crucial from a dating point of view.

The voussoirs of the Chepstow arch do not show any signs of having been recut for use in their present position. Therefore, it may be assumed that the arch as seen

Fig. 46 Tewkesbury abbey: wave moulding on the exterior arch of the north porch

Fig. 47 Chepstow priory: west portal with wave moulding on the outer order

reflects its original span. It is too narrow for the eastern or western crossing arches and therefore must have come from the north or south crossing arch. The difference in diameter between axial and transeptal arches in a crossing is relatively common in Romanesque architecture in Britain not least in the West Country as at Gloucester, Tewkesbury, Pershore and Hereford, and possibly reflecting pre-Conquest sources as represented by Dorchester abbey (Oxon.) and Wimborne Minster (Dorset).[89]

The use of mouldings for the crossing arches, but not for the nave main arcades, is relatively unusual. There is a selective use of mouldings at Saint-Etienne at Caen where the crossing arches are richly detailed but the two-order main arcade and gallery arches in the nave only have simple angle roll mouldings to the outer order of the arch. An even better comparison is with Blyth priory (Notts.) where the surviving western crossing arch is richly moulded but the two-order arches of the nave arcades are plain.[90] It is likely that in these cases the crossing area is emphasized as the place of the liturgical choir.

The west doorway of six orders (figs. 29 and 47) belongs to a tradition established in the West Country in the west portal of the bishop's chapel at Hereford, continued at Tewkesbury abbey and Hereford cathedral. Of these only Tewkesbury is extant and has moulded arches like the bishop's chapel.[91] The Hereford cathedral portal was destroyed with the collapse of the west tower in 1786, but engravings indicate that it was richly ornamented although it is not possible to be sure about the details of the design.[92] Both the Hereford and Tewkesbury connections are important for our understanding of the Chepstow. The geometric ornament of the Chepstow doorway is closely allied to Hereford. There we find parallels for the furrowed chevron in the enclosing arches of the presbytery galleries.[93] The inclusion of the roll moulding on the inner and fourth orders alongside orders with chip carving only on the face of the order is akin to the east arch of the presbytery at Hereford (figs. 47 and 48). The second order of this Hereford arch provides the closest analogue for the third order of the Chepstow arch. The saltire crosses on the abaci of the presbytery east arch at Hereford, while renewed, give a good comparison for the fifth order of the Chepstow arch. The Chepstow capitals evolve from a Norman volute type

Fig. 48 Hereford cathedral: detail of the eastern arch in the presbytery

represented by Graville-Sainte-Honorine.[94] Large-scale variants in England are in St John's chapel in the Tower of London and in the nave arcades of Blyth priory.[95] The capitals are unusual in a West Country context, in which there is a preference for scalloped types, but volutes do appear in the nave triforia at Tewkesbury and in the south transept clerestorey at Hereford. It is one of the latter capitals that provides the closest comparison for Chepstow albeit with volutes which are missing at Chepstow. The profile of the abaci is also similar except for an additional quirk on the upright at Chepstow.

The Chepstow west doorway is flanked by single-order blind arches, which continue the chevron of the outer order of the doorway (fig. 46). The motif of blind arches flanking a central doorway is not a common one in Britain, but appears on the west front of St Botolph's priory at Colchester, at Rochester cathedral, Stewkley (Bucks.) and Iffley (Oxon). It also appears on the west front of Meuvaines (Calvados) and St-Georges at Saint-Martin-de-Boscherville (Seine-Maritime).[96] However, it is common in western France as at Corme-Ecluse, Echebrune, Biron, Echillais, Ecurat, Fontaine d'Ozillac (all Charente-Maritime), Gensac-la-Pallue (Charente), and elsewhere.

The triple windows above the west doorway are a Norman inheritance, as at Caen, Saint-Etienne and La Trinité. Unlike these Caen churches, however, there is an arcaded passage inside the west front (figs. 35 and 36), a feature associated with West Country practice. There was a passage at this level in the west wall at Hereford cathedral.[97] The arches across the passage also betray a Hereford link. They are corbelled out from the west wall, which is not an unusual detail, but instead of springing from the capital on the column, they are corbelled out from the bottom of the stone below the capital (fig. 36). This differential level for the springing of arches at right angles to each other is paralleled in the arcade columns of upper storey former bishop's chapel of Hereford cathedral. The segmental arches of the inner arcade of the passage also recall the transverse arches of the 'nave' of the upper storey of the Hereford chapel (fig. 35). The scalloped capitals of the central west window find many parallels in the West Country, as in the nave aisle responds at Gloucester, the nave triforia at Tewkesbury, and at Hereford cathedral, where is also encountered the dagger between the cones of the scallops. The hyphenated chevron of the inner order may initially be regarded as 'late' — for instance the varieties of the type in the Lady Chapel of Glastonbury abbey (1184–86/9).[98] However, the basic hyphenated chevron appears much earlier in the twelfth century in the crossing arches of Hereford cathedral (1108/15–25),[99] and in the north portal of Cormac's Chapel at Cashel (Tipperary) (1127–34). Rudimentary versions of the continuous lozenge of the outer order appear on string-courses in the vestry of Hereford cathedral and on the chancel arch at Bridstow (Herefs.).[100] On the latter, the outer order of chevron is the same three-row, ninety-degree type as on the second order of the Chepstow window. Returning to the continuous lozenge chevron we may compare the 'bridges' at the east end of St Peter's, Gloucester and the apse ribs at Kilpeck (Herefs.). These comparisons suggest that the earliest date for the Chepstow window would be in the second decade of the twelfth century.

Conclusion
There are documented cases of permanent stone buildings being commenced significantly later than the foundation of a particular monastic house. It is possible that this was the case with Chepstow priory church, and that the traditional associations of arch mouldings and scalloped capitals with works of the 1090s are correct. Against this, William fitz Osbern was a very important and influential figure in the new Norman administration, and it is unlikely that he would have tolerated any delay in the start of work on the priory. Even though he died in 1071, construction would have continued under his son and, after 1075, with funds from his old friend William I. Furthermore, when dealing with the dates of buildings according to style and typology, it is sobering to recall the case of the donjon at Loches (Indre-et-Loire). It was often attributed to *c*.1100, even though it was documented as by Fulk Nerra, Count of Anjou, 997–1040. It is now dated by dendrochonological evidence between 1012 and *c*.1035.[101]

The construction of a vault in the nave of Chepstow priory raises an important question about the eastern arm of the church. Throughout Romanesque architecture high vaults were never built in the nave of a church without a high vault in the presbytery. A presbytery vault provided a permanent ciborium over the high altar, as we shall see later in Wales at Ewenny priory. Thus, if construction at Chepstow commenced with the pre-1071 foundation it would have had one of the earliest high vaults in Britain; we may compare Lanfranc's Canterbury cathedral (1070), and Remigius's Lincoln cathedral (*c*.1072/5). In Normandy, Le Mont St Michel has barrel-vaulted transepts, which means that there was a high vault in the presbytery, although whether this was commenced in 1023 or 1058 is a moot point.[102] Notre-Dame-sur l'Eau at Domfront (Orne) has a groin-vaulted sanctuary probably of the mid-eleventh century. Vaults were used throughout the bishop's chapels at Hereford, and Copford and Great Clacton (Essex) and St John's chapel in the Tower of London.[103] In the West Country the great Benedictine abbey churches of Tewkesbury and Pershore abbey were fully vaulted while at Gloucester there were high vaults in the presbytery and nave but the transepts were wood-roofed.[104] In the north of England Durham cathedral and Lindisfarne priory were both given high vaults throughout.[105] In Normandy, the abbey church of Lessay (Manche) was fully vaulted, while both La Trinité and Saint-Etienne at Caen had presbytery vaults in the eleventh century but were initially constructed with wooden roofs in the transepts and nave. These analogues put Chepstow priory church into a high-status category. Along with these it is important to add in a 'West Country' context, Cormac's Chapel at Cashel, a royal chapel built between 1127 and 1134 with a rib-vaulted chancel and a barrel-vault nave.[106]

The use of ribs in the nave at Chepstow also raises questions about the exact form of the presbytery vault in the church. Throughout Romanesque architecture where different types of vaults were used in a single church or monastic complex, rib vaults were used as a mark of greater liturgical or hierarchical importance. Thus, as we shall see at Ewenny priory, a rib vault is used above the high altar in the eastern bay of the presbytery while the other two bays are barrel vaulted (fig. 120). Or a chapter house may be rib vaulted while a dormitory undercroft would have groin vaults, as at Kirkstall abbey (Yorks.).[107] Such reasoning suggests that the Chepstow presbytery vault would have been ribbed and if so it would be amongst the earliest rib vaults in Europe. The rib vaults in Milanese churches, such as San Nazaro Maggiore, probably date immediately after the 1075 fire in the city.[108] Architectural historian Peter Kidson has suggested that Lincoln cathedral had rib vaults in the presbytery of Remigius's church, 1072/5–92.[109] After this the apses of the transept crypts and the south transept chapel at Christchurch priory, Twyneham (Dorset) are rib vaulted, and the south transept chapel at Tewkesbury abbey has a rib vault.[110] It may be that the Chepstow presbytery had a high groin vault and that the use of ribs in the nave and nave aisles represents a typological progression. Analogues for this are found at St Peter's abbey, Gloucester, and Southwell Minster, where groin vaults were used in the presbytery aisles but the nave aisles were rib-vaulted.[111]

LUDLOW CASTLE

As at Chepstow, a general view of the town of Ludlow immediately advertises the former Norman presence. Seen from the west, the castle dominates the foreground, while the later medieval tower of St Lawrence's church marks the site of its Norman predecessor (fig. 49). Construction of the castle is not documented and various candidates have been nominated as the first patron. There is Walter de Lacy (d.1085), whose status in the March after the Conquest was originally second only to William fitz Osbern.[112] Walter's son Roger has also been credited with the commencement of the stone castle.[113] He forfeited his lands in 1096, after which his brother, Hugh (d.1115?), took over and may have commenced or continued construction.[114] A large amount of the Norman fabric remains but often in modified form. The recent publication of the multi-authored volume on Ludlow castle has contributed significantly to our understanding of the fabric of the Norman castle and its chapel.[115] Here I shall concentrate on aspects of the buildings that pertain to work in Wales and their place in West Country Romanesque architecture.

The plan of Ludlow castle is significantly different to Chepstow, for instead of the great tower there is the gate tower, a curtain wall and four other Norman towers. The closest near-contemporary parallel is with Richmond castle (Yorks.) which was probably

Fig. 49 General view of Ludlow from the south-west

Fig. 50 The gate tower of Ludlow Castle from the outer bailey with the shadow of the original entrance arch in the ground floor

Fig. 51 Sherborne castle: exterior of the gate tower with a central arch similar to what once existed at Ludlow castle

founded by Count Alan Rufus around 1070.[116] We will encounter reduced variants of this arrangement in Wales at Manorbier and Newcastle (Bridgend). There is also the round chapel, which is well preserved, with the exception of the chancel.

Looking at the façade of the gate tower, in the centre of the ground floor we see the arc of the former entrance arch now infilled with red sandstone ashlar (fig. 50). Above and to the left, in the first storey there is a Norman window, but above the main entrance the Norman work has been replaced. To visualize the original appearance of the large round-headed entrance arch, the best terms of reference are the gate towers at Sherborne (Dorset) (fig. 51) and Newark (Notts.) castles.[117] For the first storey at Ludlow, Derek Renn has reconstructed two more windows like the one on the left, and has made interesting comparisons with ecclesiastical architecture including the west block at Jumièges abbey (fig. 52), where three windows light the first floor, and Charlemagne's palace chapel at

Fig. 52 Jumièges abbey: west front   *Fig. 53 St Pantaleon, Cologne: west front*

Aachen.[118] To these we might add the west block at St Pantaleon, Cologne (984–991). Here we find the large round-headed entrance arch that leads to a porch with side niches — a three-dimensional version of the dado arcade at Ludlow — and three large windows above in the first storey (figs. 49 and 53). Geographically and temporally closer is the former bishop's chapel at Hereford (1079–95) where there was a paired opening on the first floor above the large entrance arch.

The side walls of the gatehouse are articulated with a dado arcade, a motif usually reserved for prestigious churches (fig. 54). At Ludlow the dado arcade is also used in the chapel. Local late eleventh-century parallels are in the slype at Worcester cathedral and the treasury of St Peter's abbey, Gloucester. For a dado in an entrance porch there is precedent in Germany in the western porch of the early eleventh-century abbey church at Limburg-an-der-Hardt. Parallels in England are all twelfth-century side porches and are ecclesiastical: Bishop's Cleeve (Glos.), Malmesbury abbey, Sherborne abbey, Southwell Minster.

The capitals of the dado arcade are of particular interest for two reasons (fig. 54). First, both cushion and scalloped types are used. Secondly, they are without abaci, a feature later to be found in a number of Welsh buildings. The use of the cushion capital in the gatehouse at Exeter castle, as early as 1068, raises the question of whether this type of capital was used before the Conquest.[119] Architectural historian Richard Gem has argued that it was not, and that the cushion capital was introduced into England with Archbishop Lanfranc's rebuilding of Canterbury cathedral starting in 1070.[120] Most commentators have accepted Gem's case, although Eric Cambridge questioned it in relation to the north doorway of the west range at Jarrow, datable to the 1070s.[121] Cambridge indicated that influence could have spread to Jarrow from Canterbury but that it is surely significant that the Jarrow capitals are unmitred cushions as opposed to the mitred type at Canterbury. The unmitred type that appears in Belgium in the crypt of Notre-Dame at Huy is so close in appearance to Jarrow that it would be remarkable if Jarrow was influenced by Canterbury and yet produced a capital so similar to Huy.[122] The inclusion of the cushion capital and the triangular-headed arch in the west range at Jarrow and, so soon after the Conquest at the other end of the country, in the Exeter castle gatehouse, surely suggests that the motifs were inherited from Anglo-Saxon practice. This is supported with reference to part of a pre-Conquest cross shaft with a cushion capital atop a baluster shaft from St Augustine's, Canterbury.[123] Similar forms are used in crosses in Cumbria, and at Clulow (Cheshire), and Stapleford (Notts.).[124] In this context it is worth mentioning that at Canterbury, one Blithere was described in 1091 as 'the very distinguished master of the craftsmen and director of the beautiful church' of St Augustine's, Canterbury.[125] Blithere also held Seasalter (Kent) of the monks of Canterbury cathedral which suggests that, in addition to his appointment at St Augustine's, he was involved with the building of Lanfranc's cathedral and may even have been master mason there.[126] Blithere is an English name, and Jean Bony has associated this with Anglo-Saxon taste for the carved shafts in the 'dark entry' at Canterbury cathedral.[127] While not mentioning Blithere, Eric Fernie suggested that the stepping back of the storeys of the former north-west tower of Canterbury cathedral is paralleled in the pre-Conquest west tower at Earls Barton, and may reflect the Anglo-Saxon cathedral at Canterbury.[128] Is it possible that the use of cushion capitals in the cathedral, as opposed to the

Fig. 54 Detail of the dado arcade in the ground floor of the gate tower at Ludlow castle

Fig. 42 (left) Southwell minster capital no.4 illustrated by Dimock
Fig. 54 (right) Capitals in the ground floor dado in the gate tower at Ludlow castle showing single and double scallops with similar incised decoration

volute capital so popular in Normandy, also reflects Blithere's Anglo-Saxon sensibilities? Perhaps we should revert to Zarnecki's view of 1951: 'Cushion capitals had already been used in Anglo-Saxon buildings and were derived, no doubt, from Germany, where they were quite common from the beginning of the eleventh century. The sudden popularity of cushion capitals in England after the Conquest indicates that the Normans were not totally unfriendly to local achievements, and that once they adopted a feature from Anglo-Saxon buildings they used it widely'.[129] It is also worth recording that cathedral archaeologist, Philip Barker, long believed that many of the shafts, capitals and abaci in the crypt of Worcester cathedral (1084–89) were reused from an earlier structure.[130] He further suggested that the bases, shafts and capitals of the wall arcades in the Worcester slype are reused Anglo-Saxon.[131] Thus it is interesting that the bulbous bases in the Worcester slype arcades are the closest I know for this feature at Jarrow. Similar forms also appear in the crossing at Milborne Port where they are accompanied by cushion bases.[132]

The case for the Anglo-Saxon cushion capital accompanies the one made above for use of the scalloped capital before the Conquest. Of the capitals from Southwell minster illustrated by Dimock, number 4 is most interesting in relation to those in the Ludlow dado (figs. 42 and 54). It combines single and double scallops, and on the shields of the double scallops there are incised arcs and spirals as at Ludlow. There is no way of knowing whether or not the Southwell capitals had abaci but cushion capitals without abaci are used in the bishop's chapel at Hereford. Given the many associations between this Hereford chapel and the Holy Roman Empire, it is worth pointing out that cushion capitals without abaci occur in Lorraine in the nave of Froville and the crypts of Saint-Vanne at Verdun and Saint-André at Esley.[133] It also seems significant that capitals without abaci, albeit not cushion or scalloped, are used in the crossing and in the pilaster articulation on the south wall of the chancel at Milborne Port. Some of the motifs used at Milborne Port are clearly introduced from Normandy, while others, which have no Norman parallels, almost certainly reflect an Anglo-Saxon tradition. The capitals of the south portal and chancel arch at St Margaret, Knook (Wilts.) are also without abaci.[134] The capitals of the south portal are carved cushions and support a heavy roll moulding in the arch that surrounds a tympanum carved with two affronted beasts entwined in foliage. Sir Alfred Clapham compared this with manuscript illumination of the early eleventh century and suggested that perhaps the tympanum was executed about 1050.[135] Sir Thomas Kendrick concurred with Clapham's parallel but dated the tympanum around 1000, while the Taylors dated the doorway between 1050 and 1100.[136] Sir Nikolaus Pevsner acknowledged the striking similarity between the tympanum and Anglo-Saxon motifs, but he cautioned 'that this is not enough to consider the tympanum Anglo-Saxon'.[137] Whatever the absolute date of the sculpture at Knook, there is no denying that it represents the tradition of pre-Conquest work. I do not know of any examples of Norman capitals without abaci and therefore it seems reasonable to suggest that they derive from Anglo-Saxon models. In this regard, it is worth referring to a little-known article entitled 'Anglo-Norman ornament compared with designs in Anglo-Saxon MSS', in which the author, J. Park Harrison, indicated that architectural details as represented in pre-Conquest manuscripts showed affinities with Anglo-Norman architectural motifs.[138] I have never come across a reference to this work in the literature on Norman architecture. Perhaps it is time to follow it up rather more closely.

In the vestibule of the hall in the gate tower at Ludlow, the arch from the staircase is enclosed in a tall arch that reaches to the top of the wall (fig. 55). The left or west jamb has been cut back at a later date but may be reconstructed with reference to the three original stones still remaining at the bottom of the order, and to the extant jamb on the right (east) of the arch. This motif is known as the giant or colossal order and is an arched adaptation of the trabeated design described in the Roman architectural treatise by Vitruvius.[139] It is paralleled most closely in the transepts at Tewkesbury abbey where the giant arch frames the arch from the transept to the presbytery aisle and creates the arch to the gallery.[140] The same principle is also witnessed in a window on the west side of the entrance

Fig. 55 Detail of east vestibule to the first-floor hall at Ludlow castle

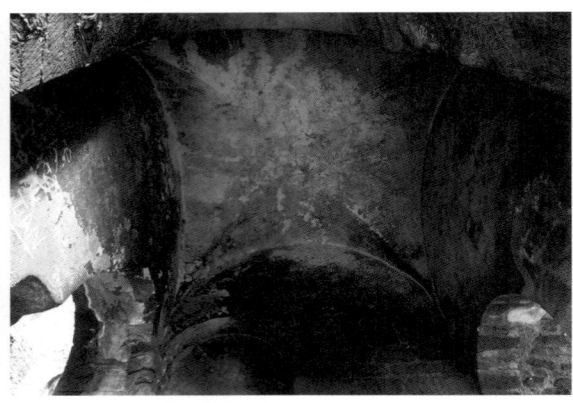

Fig. 56 (left) Detail of the exterior of the south window in the gate tower at Ludlow castle
Fig. 57 (above) Groin vault in the east vestibule to the first-floor hall at Ludlow castle

tower at Ludlow in which the aperture itself is framed in an enclosing arch that springs from capitals set at the springer of the aperture (fig. 56). A similar arrangement is also witnessed in a window in the keep at Corfe castle. This arch-within-an-arch motif is one selected by Brakspear as characteristic of the West Country School of Masons and is first encountered in the transept clerestorey at Worcester cathedral and subsequently in the nave clerestorey at Gloucester.[141] The groin vault in the vestibule is constructed with a segmental trajectory and without any articulation to the ground (fig. 57). This is the manner of the groin vaults in the presbytery aisles and the crypt of St Peter's abbey, Gloucester. The segmental trajectory is also used for the arch to the kitchen in the south-west tower at Ludlow, like the arches in the crypt at Gloucester, the south doorway at Wheathill (Salop), and in the so-called Monks' Bar at the Fleece Hotel, Gloucester.

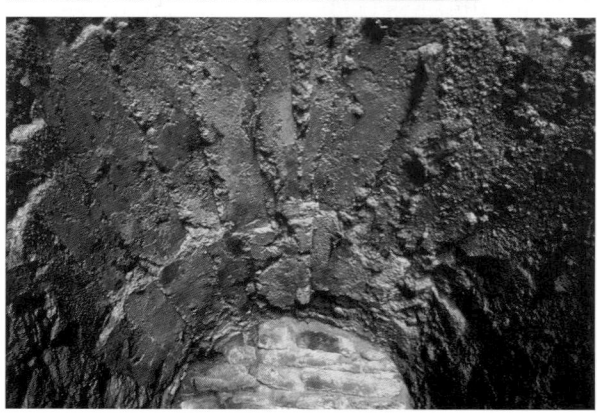

Fig. 58 Detail of barrel vault over stair to the first floor in the gate tower at Ludlow castle

The barrel vault of the staircase preserves an important detail: the marks of the wooden planks of the centering used for the construction of the vault (fig. 58). The finished vault would have been plastered but following the abandonment of the staircase as the main entrance to the first floor, the plaster would have been allowed to deteriorate, and was not replaced.

Above the doorway from the west wall walk to the first floor of the gate tower, the tympanum and lintel are formed from a single stone (fig. 59). In other words, the tympanum has wing-like projections to create the end of a lintel and double as the lowest stones of the voussoirs. This unusual technical trait is found above the doorway from the first-floor chamber to the staircase in the keep at Goodrich castle, and in churches at Dymock and Pauntley (both in Glos.), Brinsop, Kilpeck and Mathon (all in Herefs.), and Kinlet (Salop).[142]

Fig. 59 Detail of tympanum above the exit from the west wall of the gate tower at Ludlow castle at first-floor level

The above parallels indicate that aspects of the design of the gate tower at Ludlow have much in common with ecclesiastical architecture. The parallels do not assist in the matter of dating but a start under the patronage of Walter de Lacy in 1075 has much to recommend it, when Walter's holding became directly of the Crown.[143] Moreover, as Renn has observed, Walter's death in 1085 after a fall from scaffolding whilst supervising work on a church in Hereford, suggests that he took a close interest in masonry buildings.[144]

The chapel of St Mary Magdalene in the bailey of the castle has a round nave that stands to its full height from which projected a chancel with one square bay and an apse. The chancel is marked by the foundations of the north and south walls, and by excavation of a three-sided apse. In plan this is the same as in the radiating chapels at St Peter's abbey, Gloucester.

Fig. 60 Detail of the dado arcade in the round chapel at Ludlow castle

Also on the wall above the east face of the chancel arch there are radiating stones of a former vault. This may have been groined, as in the Gloucester chapels, or a barrel as reconstructed on a large scale in the high vaults of the abbey churches at Tewkesbury and Pershore. Perhaps the latter is more likely in light of the barrel vault in the chancel at Kempley (Glos.), a church probably constructed by the Lacy family.[145]

Other aspects of the Ludlow chapel are of interest in the context of the West Country School of Romanesque architecture. The nave interior is adorned with a dado arcade. On the one hand, this may be seen as a more developed version of that in the tower entrance in that it has scalloped capitals without abaci but with decorated arches, the chevron and moulded patterns of which alternate from bay to bay (figs. 54 and 60).[146] On the other hand, dado arcades are relatively unusual in a West Country context. Examples have been cited in the chapter houses at Worcester cathedral and St Peter's Gloucester, but the only parallels for this motif in the church itself in the first third of the twelfth century are in the presbytery aisles at St John's collegiate church, Chester, the south transept of Hereford cathedral, and the south transept at Penmon priory (Anglesey).[147] The exact profile of the chevron on the outer order of the chapel doorway (fig. 70) is found on the south doorway at St Mary's, Dymock (Glos.), and at St John's, Pauntley (Glos.).[148] Scalloped capitals without abaci are also used in the blind arcade of the apse at Dymock,[149] and other parallels for the Ludlow chapel are found in the Dymock School of Sculpture. The alternation of thick and thin rolls in the right-angled chevron on the inner order of the Ludlow chapel portal is paralleled on the outer order of the chancel arch at Bridstow (Herefs.),[150] and on the south doorway at Middleton-on-the-Hill (Herefs.). Unfortunately, none of these buildings is dated by documentary evidence, but there is good reason for attributing Dymock to the patronage of Miles of Gloucester around 1125–30. A similar date seems appropriate for the Ludlow castle chapel.

Fig. 61 Detail of the west doorway to the round chapel at Ludlow castle

2
Norman Church Architecture in the March and Glamorgan down to 1120

The division between this chapter and the one following is determined with reference to the 1120 start of construction of Llandaff cathedral. The patron at Llandaff was Bishop Urban, a Norman appointment who was subject to the authority of the Archbishop of Canterbury, and his new cathedral boldly proclaimed the Normanization of ecclesiastical authority. The buildings and sculptures discussed here are all typologically earlier than Llandaff cathedral and seem to represent the first attempts of Norman patrons to impose a new ecclesiastical architecture as they moved into Wales. St Andrew at Presteigne (Radnorshire) introduces us to the use of tufa masonry and a proportional system of church planning favoured elsewhere by the Normans. Tufa is also used at St Pierre (Gwent), while herringbone masonry, which is often associated with construction in the late eleventh or early twelfth century, occurs at St Peter at Dixton (Gwent) and St Peter at Cogan (Glamorgan). Similarly, the details of the imposts of the chancel arch at St Cadoc at Llancarfan (Glamorgan) speak of Norman parentage. Norman impact in the field of sculpture is witnessed in the carved lintels at Holy Trinity or St David at Llanddew, St Bilo at Llanfilo (Breconshire), St Tydfil at Llyswyrny (Glamorgan), and St Lywell at Llanlowell (Gwent). At the same time, details of the Llyswyrny lintel relate to the enigmatic stone at Llanrhidian (Glamorgan). The latter has been variously dated but it is here suggested that it, along with some sculpture from Llantwit Major (Glamorgan), dates from the late eleventh or early twelfth century and reflects earlier sculptural traditions of southern Wales. Such an interpretation is analogous to contemporary sculpture in England where indigenous Anglo-Saxon elements continued in use alongside features introduced from Normandy.

PRESTEIGNE (RADNORSHIRE), ST ANDREW

Of the early Norman church of St Andrew at Presteigne, there remains the eastern half of the north aisle wall, in which there are two blocked windows (fig. 62), and it seems likely that the rest of the north aisle wall is also Norman.[1] The northern half of the former chancel arch is immured in the east wall of the north nave aisle, and the southern half of the former west doorway is located to the south of the west respond of the north nave arcade (fig. 63). The window frames and the former chancel arch are built of squared tufa, while the west doorway is primarily limestone ashlar with some tufa blocks in the arch (figs. 63–64). From the later Norman fabric there are the two western columns reused in the fourteenth-century north nave arcade (fig. 65).

Fig. 62 Presteigne, St Andrew: exterior of the nave and north aisle

Fig. 63 Presteigne, St Andrew: north aisle looking east showing the former chancel arch immured in the east wall

The account of the fabric by H.M. and Joan Taylor in *Anglo-Saxon Architecture* presented a complicated early-building history, albeit one they emphasize is most tentative.[2] In the north aisle wall they identified three different building periods. The lowest four to five feet of the eastern half of the north wall is of coursed grey ragstone, the upper section 'of roughly squared brown stone separated by courses of thin stones almost the shape of tiles' (fig. 62).[3] The western half of the north nave wall has a different character of rubble and is set on a slightly different alignment than the eastern half of the wall. The Taylors argued that the upper part of the eastern section is fixed as early Norman by the form of the windows. The lower section of the wall may therefore be pre-Conquest but they added that 'there is no confirmatory evidence such as would be provided by a surviving door, or window or quoining'.[4] They noted that 'the north wall is 3ft 4in thick and therefore receives no support for pre-Conquest date on grounds of thinness'.[5] Moreover, differences in the character of masonry may indicate nothing more than different sources for the stonework, as in the great tower of Chepstow castle, especially on the exterior of the west wall (fig. 5).

Of the two blocked, north windows, the western one retains its round-headed frame inside while only the upper section of the western jamb and the corresponding arch springer remains of the eastern window (fig. 63). On the exterior, the eastern window preserves its jambs and arched head, the latter cut from a single stone (figs. 62 and 64). The western window is larger and has a square head which seems to result from a later reworking; witness the telltale fragment of tufa immediately below the right side of the lintel, which indicates that a window, like the one to the left, has been cut back.

Fig. 64 Presteigne, St Andrew: blocked east window in the north nave aisle illustrating the use of tufa

Fig. 65 Presteigne, St Andrew: north nave arcade

The difference in date between the western and eastern halves of the nave is difficult to determine. However, the use of some tufa voussoirs in the west arch and the rough diagonal tooling on the ashlar of the jamb suggest a date not too advanced in the twelfth century. The use of tufa is generally associated with an early date in the Norman period although, as David Parsons has indicated in his study of Herefordshire churches, it is not a foolproof tool.[6] Be that as it may, it may be significant that the windows at Presteigne are considerably smaller than the tufa-framed windows at Tedstone Delamere and Moccas (both in Herefs.). Tedstone Delamere is difficult to date, but the sculptural details at Moccas suggest that the work there is of the 1120s. Moccas is constructed primarily of neatly squared tufa blocks and the apse windows have two orders rather than the single order of the Presteigne windows. The less accomplished squaring of the tufa at Presteigne has much more in common with the south doorway at Edvin Loach (Herefs.). There the tympanum is composed of three courses of squared tufa, in the manner of the sandstone ashlar on the inner tympanum of the east portal of the great tower at Chepstow.[7] While this does not prove an early date for Presteigne, it suggests that a date before 1100 is most probable.

The nave is long and narrow, 81ft 0in (Taylors give 82ft) by 18ft 4in (Taylors give 19ft 0in), dimensions that suggest the master mason used the proportional system of the side of the square to the diagonal, that is one to the square root of two or 1:1.4142. The length of the nave is generated by multiplying the width of the nave by 3, and adding the diagonal of a square based on the width of the nave: $18.3333 \times 3 + (18.3333 \times 1.4142) = 80.9265$. Quite what this indicates in terms of the training of the mason is difficult to determine. The use of the proportional system of the side of the square to the diagonal seems to be the most regular one used in Norman England.[8] However, the system was used in ancient Rome and throughout medieval Europe, so its occurrence at Presteigne is not indicative of any specific aspect or location of the training of the master mason.

Fig. 66 St Pierre: exterior from the north

The blocked chancel arch indicates that there was a clear architectural division between the nave and sanctuary in the Norman church. Whether the sanctuary was of one or two bays, and either apsidal or square-ended, could only be determined through excavation.

The two western columns of the north nave arcade differ from the columns further east in being round rather than octagonal, are larger in scale and built of larger blocks of ashlar (fig. 65). The western column has a round capital surmounted by an octagonal abacus but the second column has an octagonal capital and abacus that seem rather too small for the column. The eastern columns are fourteenth century but the western two and the capital of the western column appear to date from the twelfth century. Clearly they are not *in situ* but they probably mark the addition of an aisle to the original aisleless church at some point in the twelfth century.

ST PIERRE (GWENT), ST PETER

The aisleless nave and chancel of the church are in one, but a straight vertical joint in the north wall indicates that the original design has been modified (fig. 66). The masonry is different to either side of the straight joint, and the ashlar immediately to the right of the joint has the appearance of quoining at the north-east angle of the Norman nave. This may suggest that the Norman church had a separately articulated and smaller chancel. There is a Norman window immediately to the east of the later north porch (fig. 66). It is widely splayed to the interior where it is framed with ashlar and has tufa voussoirs in the upper section of the arch head (fig. 67). There is a blocked west doorway, which is round-headed on the interior but segmental on the exterior (fig. 67). The latter is constructed with non-radiating voussoirs, which, as we have seen in the great tower at Chepstow castle, is an indication of an early date after the Conquest.

Fig. 67 St Pierre: interior looking west

Dixton (Gwent), St Peter

There is a section of herringbone masonry exposed beneath the plaster on the inner face of the north nave wall. Although there are no other identifiable Norman features in the nave, the space is long and thin, 67ft x 16ft 9in, or proportionally 1 to 4. In this respect it is not far removed from the nave at Presteigne.

Fig. 68 Cogan, St Peter: exterior from the north

Cogan (Glamorgan), St Peter
(Penarth, off Sully Road)

St Peter's, Cogan, is a classic example of a small, Norman, two-cell church with aisleless rectangular chancel and nave (fig. 68). Herringbone masonry is used on the exterior of all three walls of the chancel and on the north wall of the nave. There are no windows in either the east wall of the chancel or the north wall of the nave. The later fenestration in the north and south chancel walls and the south wall of the nave presumably expands former Norman apertures. The later south doorway is located midway down the nave which almost certainly reflects the Norman arrangement as elsewhere in Glamorgan at Colwinston, Llandow and Monknash, and at Winson (Gloucestershire). The plain, rubble, round-headed chancel arch sits on simple imposts. Although it is crudely executed, it reflects the scale of more-accomplished Norman work (fig. 69).

Fig. 69 Cogan, St Peter: chancel arch

Fig. 70 Llancarfan, St Cadoc: detail of the south impost on the chancel arch

LLANCARFAN (GLAMORGAN), ST CADOC

This important former *clas* church was given to St Peter's abbey Gloucester by Robert fitz Hamon (d.1107), as part of the Normanizing process of the newly conquered territory.[9] It was an important centre of learning; Lifris, the author of the *Life of St Cadog*, and the son of Herwald, the late eleventh-century Bishop of Llandaff, was probably based at Llancarfan.[10] Unfortunately, little remains of the Norman fabric of the church. The later chancel arch rests on chamfered imposts carved on both the upright and chamfered faces with chip-carved saltire crosses (fig. 70).[11] There is something similar on the chancel arch at Middleton-on-the-Hill (Herefs.) where two rows of saltire crosses adorn the face of the imposts above the chamfer (fig. 71). The plain jambs of the Middleton arch preserve some of the original painted decoration in the form of white crosses, and it is possible that something similar was also used at Romanesque Llancarfan. However, the plastered and limewashed finish of the Llancarfan responds make it more likely that the painted decoration would have been in red, as on the east respond of the south nave arcade at Blyth priory, commenced in 1088 (plate 4). A small two-light round-headed window with (restored) central shaft reused in the tower, point to the former existence of an early Norman church with chancel, nave and tower.[12]

Fig. 71 Middleton-on-the-Hill (Herefs.), St Mary: north jamb of the chancel arch

EARLY CARVED LINTELS, AND AN ALLIED STONE AT LLANRHIDIAN (GLAMORGAN)

The churches of Holy Trinity or St David at Llanddew, St Bilo at Llanfilo (Breconshire), St Tydfil at Llyswyrny (Glamorgan), and St Lywell at Llanlowell, preserve interesting early Romanesque lintels that have been all but ignored by art historians[13] Another carved stone, which has been variously dated and is now reset on the west bench inside the south porch of St Rhidian and St Illtyd at Llanrhidian (Glamorgan), has also been published as a lintel.[14] It will be argued here that the Llanrhidian stone was originally part of a screen, and associations will be suggested with the lintel at Llyswyrny and other Romanesque sculpture. Just two of the lintels remain *in situ*, those of the (blocked) north doorway at Llanfilo and the south doorway at Llanlowell. The lintels do not form a single group but rather indicate aspects of diversity, both in execution and in stylistic affiliation, that are so informative in the quest to understand the beginnings of Romanesque sculpture in Wales.

Fig. 72 Llanfilo, St Bilo: lintel over the north nave doorway

Fig. 73 Llanfilo, St Bilo: exterior from the north

The old red sandstone lintel of the blocked north doorway at Llanfilo measures 5ft 5in by 1 ft 3in, and is chip-carved with two rows of saltire crosses framed above and below by lozenges, and to the left by lozenges and triangles (fig. 72). The plain ashlar jambs of the doorway contrast with the almost tile-like rubble of the north wall (fig. 73). The stones immediately beneath the lintel are larger than the others in the jambs, and the top right block extends significantly along the wall in a manner that recalls massive Anglo-Saxon impost blocks, as in the chancel arches at St Laurence, Bradford-on-Avon (Wilts.) and All Saints, Wittering (Northants.). The fragmentary lintel built into the east wall of the south porch at Llanfilo is ornamented with a central row of raised lozenges the points of which are met, above and below, with raised triangles (fig. 74). In each of the intervening recessed lozenges there is a straight central stem flanked by single pellets.

Fig. 74 Llanfilo, St Bilo: lintel reset in the south porch

Fig. 75 Llanddew, St David: lintel fragment in south porch

Fragments of two chip-carved lintels are kept in the south porch at Llanddew (figs. 75 and 76). On one, the left half of the stone there is a row of saltire crosses both above and below a central row of lozenges. To the right of this there is cross with flared arms, the ends of which have paired triangular incisions, and there are roughly formed circular or polygonal panels in the interstices. Immediately to the right, a later vertical channel damages the face of the stone, and further to the right there are two vertical rows of saltire crosses. On the second lintel, there is a central row of lozenges on the surface of the stone with recessed triangles in the interstices. Below, and originally above (now damaged), there are two rows of triangles arranged point-to-point, and between them there are diagonally recessed triangles carved back-to-back against the vertical axis.

The Llyswyrny lintel is reused on the exterior of the south nave wall towards the south-east corner (fig. 77). Across the lower section of the stone there is a single row

Fig. 76 Llanddew, St David: lintel fragment in south porch

Fig. 77 Llyswynny, St Tydfil: lintel fragment reset in the exterior of the south wall

of saltire crosses. Above, to the left, there is a tree with three pairs of stylized, loosely spiralled leaves to either side of a central vertical stem. Immediately to the right there are two further leaves set at a forty-five degree angle and attached to a stem that curves in a semicircle beneath the tree. To the top right there is a horizontal tree above a row of incised chevron and a wavy line.

The Llanddew and Llanfilo lintels are related to four examples just over the border in Herefordshire, three of which are *in situ* and are part of an architectural context with more datable features than the Welsh examples. Examination of these works as a group will provide an appropriate context for the Welsh sculptures as both a regional and a European phenomenon.

Unlike the Llanddew and Llanfilo lintels, those in the north and south nave doorways of St Andrew, Bredwardine, the south nave doorway of St John the Baptist, Letton, and the south doorway of St Mary Magdalene, Willersley (all in Herefordshire) have attracted considerable attention of art historians.[15] There is general agreement that they are examples of early Norman carving, *circa* 1100–1120, and that they pre-date the Dymock School of sculpture, *circa* 1120–1130, and the flowering of the Herefordshire School of sculpture, *circa* 1130–1150.[16] However, a number of matters remain unresolved. It has been suggested that the Bredwardine and Letton lintels were inserted in earlier doorways.[17] Is this supported by the internal archaeological evidence and by comparative analysis with near-contemporary doorways elsewhere? While there can be little doubt that the lintels come from the same workshop, to what degree are they an isolated phenomenon? Or, do they form part of a more widespread trend in Romanesque sculpture?

The lintels of both doorways at Bredwardine are of red sandstone and this stone is also used for the capitals of the south doorway and the jambs of the north doorway (figs. 78–80). The arch and tympanum of both doorways, and the jambs of the south doorway, are of calcerious tufa. The design and proportions of the Bredwardine doorways are quite different from each other. The south doorway has a full semi-circular tympanum set above the carved lintel and is framed by a heavy roll moulding carried on carved cushion capitals atop shafts and moulded bases. The north doorway lacks the shafts, capitals and moulding in the arch, while the tympanum and arch are segmental rather than semi-circular. The richer

Fig. 78 Bredwardine (Herefs.), St Andrew: north portal

articulation of the south doorway suggests its greater importance and concomitantly that it was the main entrance into the church. The difference in the lintel-tympanum relationship is less obvious. It must be admitted that, at first sight, one is tempted to concur with the view that the lintel of the north doorway is an insertion because without it the plain arch and tympanum may be reconstructed to a full semi-circle. Be that as it may, there is good reason to believe that what we see is the original

Fig. 79 Bredwardine (Herefs.), St Andrew: south portal

arrangement. In early Norman times segmental arches are used in the bishop's chapel at Hereford built by Robert de Losinga, bishop of Hereford, 1079–1095.[18] The south doorway of the nave at Mathon (Herefs.) has the plain tympanum and lintel carved from a single stone and the arch of the tympanum is segmental.[19] On the bottom of the Mathon lintel a single cable is carved, and a variant of this minimalist approach to sculptural enrichment is encounted in the south doorway at Kinlet (Salop). Here the tympanum and lintel are carved from a single stone, as at Mathon, and the bottom of the lintel has a row of chip-carved saltire crosses topped with a shallow band of recessed sawtooth. The same arrangement, less the carved decoration, occurs in the doorway into the gate tower from the west wall-walk at Ludlow castle (fig. 59) and the tympanum of the great hall at Goodrich castle (Herefs.).[20] There are similar proportions carved on one stone with incised imitation voussoirs above the door to the stair of the former central axial tower at Dymock and, without the incised voussoirs, on the south chancel doorway at Castle Frome (Herefs.).[21] Segmental tympana appear carved with the Agnus Dei on the north doorway at Preston-by-Dymock (Glos.), Castlemoreton (Worcs.) and Upleadon (Glos.).[22] A later example of

Fig. 80 Bredwardine (Herefs.), St Andrew: detail of the underside of the lintel of the south portal

Fig. 81 Letton (Herefs.), St John the Baptist: detail of the lintel of the south portal

a plain segmental tympanum without lintel is in the south doorway at Astley (Worcs.). Much further afield, there is a close formal comparison for the large lintel and segmental tympanum at Bredwardine on the central portal of the west façade of the cathedral at S. Agata dei Goti in Campania.[23] This is not to suggest any direct connection between the two works but rather that both are likely to reflect a practice established in Roman times.

The theory that the lintels are inserted into pre-existing doorways is not supported by any archaeological evidence and would be hard to understand as a mode of operation. In each case did the carved lintel replace an earlier, presumably plain, lintel? Or was there no lintel at all and concomitantly a taller door? The difference in stone types in the Bredwardine and Letton doorways is explained by the desire to have carved lintels and, in the case of the Bredwardine south doorway, carved capitals (figs. 79 and 81). These were executed in old red sandstone because tufa is ill-suited for carving, as witnessed on the hood of the Letton south doorway. Moreover, the juxtaposition of a large lintel with a single-order round-headed arch derives from Roman sources, as in the frigidarium of the baths at Nice-Cimiez (Alpes-Maritimes) (fig. 82). This is repeated in uncarved form in the south doorway at Barrow, and the north and south doorways at Silvington (both in Salop). The early eleventh-

Fig. 82 Nice-Cimiez (Alpes-Maritimes): the firgidarium of the Roman baths

63

century carved lintels of the west portals at Saint-Génis-des-Fontaines (1019–20) (fig. 83) and Saint-André-de-Sorrede in the Roussillon carry single-order arches. On the north portal at Meuvaines (Calvados), a lintel carved with the Last Supper is set beneath a plain multi-block tympanum and single-order arch.[24]

The use of a carved lintel with either a plain or carved tympanum is not uncommon in English Romanesque.[25] The south doorway at Winstone (Glos.) has three rows of chip-carved saltire crosses on the lintel, a tympanum with finely incised reticulated lozenges, and a heavy roll moulding in the arch like the south doorway at Bredwardine (figs. 27 and 92). There is something similar at Holy Cross, Morton Morrel (Warwickshire) where the tympanum, lintel and a fragment of the enclosing arch are reset on a sill of a north nave window.[26] The tympanum is plain while the right half of the lintel has three rows of saltire crosses, while to the left is a horizontal placed Latin cross with a tapering shaft and a ring-head. The lintel of the south doorway at Hampton Bishop (Herefs.) is carved with two rows of saltire crosses beneath four rows of scale pattern.[27] Above, there is a plain tympanum, composed of twelve separate stones, surrounded by a single-order arch with chevron and a hood mould with single billet. Also, as at Bredwardine and Letton, the lintel is carved in a different stone than the tympanum and arch. There are also three fragments of chip-carved stones possibly from lintels preserved at St Mary, Bowdon (Cheshire).[28] Yellow sandstone is used for the lintel while old red sandstone is used for the tympanum and arch.

Fig. 83 Saint-Génis-des-Fontaines (Pyrénées-Orientales): west portal

The plain tympana were almost certainly rendered and painted. While no painted tympana above doorways have survived in Britain, the tympanum area in the niches of the interior west wall of the great hall at Chepstow castle are painted with reticulated lozenges (fig. 16). Red dots are painted above the carved part of the tympanum at Leckhampstead (Bucks.).[29] In France, good examples of painted tympana are found inside the nave west doorways at Saint-Savin-sur-Gartempe (Vienne) and at Ougy in Burgundy. These are figurative and it is possible that figurative subjects were used in our tympana. The juxtaposition of a carved figurated tympanum and a chip-carved lintel is not uncommon. The south tympanum at Great Washbourn (Glos.) is carved on an irregular shaped stone with a single row of stars for the 'lintel' and an equal armed cross on the plain tympanum with alternating chip-carved roundels and paired star pattern in the 'arch'.[30] At Stratton (Glos.), the tympanum of the south doorway has a triple row of star on the lintel and a Tree of Life on the tympanum with an animal and serpent on either side.[31] At Kencott (Oxon) the south doorway has a single-star lintel and Sagittarius firing an arrow into the jaws of a dragon.[32] At Newton Purcell (Oxon) the south, formerly the north, tympanum has a triple-star lintel with a large bird and serpent curled up behind it amidst foliage.[33] The south doorway at Croxdale (Co. Durham) has single-star ornament on the lintel, with a 'Tree of Life' on the tympanum with a head at the apex said to represent our Lord crucified on the Tree of Life.[34] At Findern and Tissington (Derbs.) there is allied work with a cross in the tympanum and double star on lintel.[35] At Pennington (Lancs.) there is a single-star lintel with demi-figure of an archangel on the tympanum over a doorway of Beckside farm.[36] In the north doorway at Moreton Valence (Glos.), St Michael fights the dragon on the tympanum above a lintel with chip-carved scales and chevron, while on the tympanum of the south doorway at Leckhampstead (Bucks.) two affronted dragons battle over a tiny human figure, above a lintel with chip-carved saltire crosses.[37]

Recently, it has been suggested that chip-carved lintels with saltire crosses represent the firmament and that six-petalled stylized flowers represent stars.[38] Such interpretation is possible but given the chip-carved saltire crosses on the lintel, tympanum and arch of the doorway to the great tower of Chepstow castle, and on the doorway to the Exchequer at Caen, one should guard against reading too much 'meaning' into these motifs.

The chevron on the doorway at Letton is potentially significant in regard to date. Chevron is traditionally associated with the second campaign of construction at Durham cathedral after 1115.[39] More recently, however, earlier examples have been suggested — the east crossing arch and apse arch at Cerisy-la-Forêt (Calvados) and the east processional doorway at Malvern priory.[40] Cerisy is not documented but probably dates around 1080–1085 while Malvern was founded in 1085. The immediate inspiration therefore seems to be Norman, but Anglo-Saxon associations must not be overlooked. One may compare the simple incised chevrons on the north lintel at Bredwardine with this feature on the arch in the scene of Egil defending his home on the seventh-century ivory Frank's casket (London, British Museum).[41] This ivory panel also has decorated shafts although the more direct connection would be with post-Conquest examples in the dormitory at Canterbury cathedral and the famous incised piers at Durham cathedral.

The figures on the north lintel at Bredwardine have been variously interpreted (fig. 78), as the Gods of Egypt, Bes and Thoth, and also two Indian divinities, Ganesh the elephant God, and Hanumen the monkey god.[42] Marshall suggested that the figure on the left is a basilisk and on the right is the figure of our Lord.[43] He read Christ's right hand in blessing and the left as if holding a book 'but it is too weathered to see the exact details. Behind the head is what appears to be a halo'. Keyser referred to them as two grotesque figures.[44] For Zarnecki this may represent the Temptation of Christ.[45] While the iconography may be difficult to decipher, there can be little doubt that the sculptor of the Bredwardine north lintel also worked at Hereford cathedral. There, two seated figures, probably God the Father and God the Son, carved on a capital from the presbytery east arch, have a similar pose to the right figure at Bredwardine with knees apart and feet close together.[46] The carving on the cushion capitals of the Bredwardine south doorway (fig. 78) is comparable to the 'small tympanum' from Hereford cathedral, and the left capital of the south doorway at Moccas (Herefs.).[47]

At Letton there are two heads on the upper right side, the one on the right is bearded, and each is surrounded by rays like an aureole. Marshall suggested that they might represent Father and Son, and this seems entirely possible given this pairing at Hereford.[48] Below, there is a scorpion and a frog, 'possibly spirits of evil'.[49]

The doorways at Bredwardine are unusual in that they are not opposite each other; the north doorway is set further to the west than its southern counterpart. This is also the case at Dymock (Glos.). At Llanfilo, it works the other way round, the north doorway is set further east than the south doorway. At Letton there is a south and west door, the latter is uncarved and therefore the less important. A west doorway in a small church is unusual but finds parallel in Herefordshire, complete with the south doorway, at Castle Frome. We have also seen west and north doorways at St Pierre (fig. 67). The precise significance of these differences is difficult to determine but they are surely reflective of differences in liturgical practice.

Returning to the Welsh lintels, the saltire crosses on the north lintel at Llanfilo, one fragment at Llanddew, and at Llyswyrny, parallel those on the upper right segment of the Bredwardine south lintel (figs. 72, 75, 77 and 78). The faceted triangular pattern on the second Llanddew lintel is the same as that on the hood mould of the Letton south doorway. The lozenges along the centre of both Llanddew lintels, and at the top and bottom of the Llanfilo north lintel, are simplified variants of this motif, as indicated by the slightly botched transitional patterns at the left end of the Llanfilo north lintel.

The execution of the Llanlowell lintel (fig. 84) is quite different from Llanddew, Llanfilo and Llyswyrny. The lintel tapers from right to left, and instead of chip-carved decoration, the designs are finely incised on to the surface of the stone. At the top there are two rows of imbrication, below which there are four horizontal lines that run from an encircled, six-petal flower on the right to two vertical lines that extend about one inch above and below the horizontals. There is a single row of rectangles at the bottom of the lintel above a slight chamfer on the bottom of the stone. Different as the technique may be, the motifs on the Llanlowell lintel are associated with those on the Herefordshire lintels. Encircled six-petal flowers appear at Letton, and on the underside of the lintel of the south doorway at Bredwardine (figs. 80 and 84). The scale pattern is a larger version of this

Fig. 84 Llanlowell, St Lywell: detail of the lintel to the south portal

Fig. 85 Willersley (Herefs.), St Mary Magdalene: detail of the lintel to the south portal

motif on the lintel of the south doorway at Hampton Bishop, and the incised lines along the centre of the Llanlowell lintel may be read as an extended version of the graduated squares on the Willersley lintel (figs. 84 and 85). Finally, the band of squares at the bottom of the lintel suggests a starting point for a repeating pattern. It is possible that the Llanlowell incisions represent the beginnings of a design intended to be chip-carved. Alternatively, the incisions may just be guidelines for the painter, as seen on the Romanesque plaster from St Mary's abbey, York (figs. 22 and 84).

The chip-carved saltire crosses on the Llyswyrny lintel are a strong indication of an early Romanesque date, with parallels on the east doorway of the great tower at Chepstow castle (1067–71), to the lintel of the south doorway at Bredwardine and associated Herefordshire lintels of around 1120. Moreover, the form of the stylized tree on the left of the Llyswyrny lintel recalls the painted decoration on the capital of the east respond of the south nave arcade of Blyth priory church, commenced in 1088 (fig. 77 and plate 4). The juxtaposition of a band of chip-carved crosses at the bottom of the lintel with foliage forms at Llyswyrny is allied to the Beaumais (Calvados) lintel (fig. 20), although the arrangement of the Welsh example is less structured than the Norman one. The triple band of ornamentation at Beaumais, however, does relate to the lintels at Llanddew and of the north doorway at Llanfilo.

The Llanrhidian stone is not easily interpreted.[50] According to a notice in the porch it was found in 1856 and was moved to the porch in 1910. It is 6ft 7in long, 2ft 5in maximum height, and 1ft 1in in depth (figs. 86 and 87). In an article published in 1888, J. Romilly Allen recorded that the stone was found 'a few years ago, almost buried out of sight, beneath the accumulated soil just in front of the western doorway of the tower'. It is generally believed to be pre-Norman in date. The Royal Commission suggested that 'the stone probably served as a lintel over a doorway or some other architectural function', and cited parallels in Ireland in support of this interpretation'.[51] In his account in the Glamorgan volume of *The Buildings of Wales*, John Newman followed this interpretation and gave a date of the ninth or tenth century for the stone.[52] In his corpus of *The Early Christian Monuments of Wales*, Nash-Williams noted parenthetically '?part of a monolithic sarcophagus or hog-back'.[53] The notice in the porch suggests that it may be part of a Viking tombstone.

The front of the stone is carved in low relief and with incised patterns. In the centre are two highly stylized human figures whose rectangular bodies are without arms and have inverted-pear-shaped heads with simply rendered eyes, noses and mouths but no

Fig. 86 Llanrhidian, St Rhidian and St Illtyd: frieze in the south porch

Fig. 87 Llanrhidian, St Rhidian and St Illtyd: view from above showing the depression behind the projecting animal head

ears or hair. The body of the right-hand figure is decorated with opposed diagonal frets; the edges of the garment extend down to form inward-curving spiral 'feet'. The left-hand figure has prominent squared shoulders below which there are blank areas with lower curved terminations that are probably stylized breasts. Below this the figure is clothed in a garment decorated with an asymmetrical double-line design.

Between the heads of the figures are two decorative, low-relief panels. To the right is a square filled with a pattern like the garment of the right-hand figure, with incised rings outside the corners. To the left, the design is not easy to read but there seems to be an eight-pronged linear star pattern.

To either side of the central pair of figures are stylized animals. To the right, eyes protrude at the top of the head and the long snout terminates in spirals, the upper one touching the shoulder of the right-hand figure. The body of the animal has a pronounced backbone, in the tradition of the treasures from the seventh-century Sutton Hoo ship burial, which terminates in a knotted leg.[54] This creature almost completely encloses a much smaller, dog-like animal that sniffs behind the snout of the larger beast. The left-hand creature faces away from the central group and, like the right-hand creature has a pronounced backbone, but has a tiny, ill-defined head with a long snout that turns down at the end snout. The back leg seems to return in a spiral beneath the body to terminate in a pointed trilobe tail set below the snout.

In the report on the Swansea Summer Meeting of the Cambrian society in 1920, it was stated that the right-hand side of the stone 'is shaped to represent the head and throat of an animal. There is no ear or nostril or eye, but the snout; the nose is there, and also a decided mouth, much larger than in the engraving, and the lower lip and jaw, and the throat is perfectly carved. Inside the mouth are two pointed teeth, one in the upper, one in the lower jaw'.[55] Careful examination of the stone confirms this reading and thereby precludes the use of the stone as a lintel over a doorway. The projecting animal head may be allied to those above the west doorways of Deerhurst (Glos.) priory church, although at Deerhurst the heads are not attached to a carved panel (figs. 86 and 88). For an animal head projecting at the end of a carved panel there are the examples on the western angles of the nave at Kilpeck (Herefs.).[56] There the panels are much shorter and are just carved with foliage rather than the figures at Llanrhidian. Nevertheless, it leads to the suggestion that the Llanrhidian stone may have been part of a frieze. In this connection, it is worth noting that a section of the pre-Conquest frieze reset in the south aisle at Breedon-on-the-Hill (Leics.) has two human heads projecting at one end at right angles to the sculpture on the frieze.[57] Also, at the south-east angle of the late twelfth-century chancel at Barfreston (Kent) there is a quadruped carved on the same stone behind a projecting head corbel. An undecorated variant of this is encountered at the western angles of the nave at Tedstone Delamere (Herefs.) and in Irish Romanesque churches. The location is similar to that at Kilpeck except that instead of a projecting animal head there is simply a projecting section of stone curved on the underside, while the body of the stone stretches back in the wall. Good examples are seen at St Saviour and Trinity at Glendalough (Wicklow).

Fig. 88 Deerhurst (Glos.), St Mary: west front

At the lower left end the Llanrhidian stone terminates in an arc that seems too neat to suggest that it is the result of damage. The arc has a wider radius than the one beneath the projecting head at the opposite end of the stone. It would appear to be consistent with the ornamented head of a window, as in the late eleventh-century blocked nave windows at St Mary Magdalen at Twyning (Glos.), or the narrow arches of an arcade as on the shrine of St Melangell at Pennant Melangell (Montgomeryshire) (fig. 415).

One aspect of the stone is most difficult to explain; the roughly circular depression at the back of the stone immediately behind the projecting animal head (fig. 87). It is 12½in wide and 6in deep, and may be secondary. On the other hand, it may be seen as an integral part of the initial carving of the stone to serve as socket for a wooden post. The almost complete loss of carved woodwork from the early medieval and Romanesque British Isles makes it impossible to prove such a theory. One possible parallel is with the Oratory of Gallerus (Kerry), where above the lintel inside the west doorway there project two stones each pierced with a substantial circular hole. It is usually suggested that they functioned in connection with doors but it is possible that they served as sockets for supporting wooden posts connected with something above the doorway. However, pushing the analogue with the Pennant Melangell shrine a little further, it is worth considering that the Llanrhidian stone may have been a piece of church furniture, possibly part of a screen. The twelfth-century wooden screen on the upper level of the two-storey sanctuary at Compton (Surrey) may reflect lost examples on the transept galleries at Winchester cathedral and Saint-Etienne at Caen. In the latter two cases wooden screens would satisfactorily complete 'unfinished' stone architectural elements, and at Winchester there is even evidence for such fusion of wood and stone in a wooden shaft and cushion capital in the terminal wall of the south transept.

In the south nave aisle at Sutton (Northants) there is seated lion whose tail is swept up on to its back, at which point there is a projection in the stone that is hollowed out in the manner of the Llanrhidian stone (figs. 87 and 89). The Sutton lion is obviously related to those that support columns in Italian Romanesque portals, as at Modena cathedral, and pulpits, as at Cava dei Tirreni abbey near Salerno.[58] It seems likely that the Sutton lion would have performed the same function. The lion is not *in situ* and it is possible that it was part of a screen.

To cite Romanesque associations in the quest to reconstruct the original context, and even the date, of the Llanrhidian stone may seem far-fetched, especially given the decidedly early medieval appearance of the two figures in the centre of the composition and the animal interlace to the left and right. Allen compared the figures with those in the ninth- or tenth-century *Book of Deer* (Cambridge University Library, MS. Ii.6.32, fol. 1b).[59] They are very much in the insular tradition established in the seventh century, as in figures like the Matthew symbol in the *Book of Durrow* (Dublin, Trinity College, MS A.45) or the *Echternach Gospels* (Paris, Bibliotheque Nationale, MS lat. 9389).[60] Here pattern making was infinitely more important than any attempt at naturalistic representation of the human figure. There is also an interesting analogue for the Llanrhidian figures with two of the evangelist symbols on the 'Soiscel Molaise' (the satchel of St Molaise), from Devenish Island in Lower Lough Erne (Fermanagh), now in the National Museum of Ireland.[61] The striated ribbons that articulate the garments of the Matthew and

Fig. 89 Sutton (Northants), St Michael: lion

Luke symbols are akin to the channeled ribbons of the Llanrhidian figures. Moreover, the ribbons to the side of Luke on the satchel terminate at the bottom in inward turning spirals in much the same way as on the right-hand figure on the Llanrhidian stone. Straightforward as such a figurative heritage may seem, it does not necessarily preclude Norman affiliation. The frontally posed human figures with large, completely shaven egg-shaped heads without ears set on small, stylized rectangular bodies may be seen as an insular adaptation of Norman figures like those on the fourth voussoir from the left on the outer order of the reset doorway at Montgaroult (Orne).[62]

While it is true that the figures seem archaic by Romanesque standards, it is worth noting that parallels for the composition at Llanrhidian are found in early twelfth-century work. The gabled lintel at St Bees (Cumbria) has a centrally placed St Michael killing the dragon flanked by panels of interlace.[63] On the north lintel at Bredwardine there are two stylized figures in the centre of the lintel and set beneath and arcade and flanked by two chip-carved roundels and decorated columns (fig. 81). The entire composition at Bredwardine is far more ordered, one may say more Romanesque, than at Llanrhidian, and yet one is struck by the un-architectonic, or un-Romanesque, appearance of the arcade. Indeed, the plant-like growth of the arches from the 'capitals' recalls the eighth-century panels at Breedon-on-the-Hill.[64] Thus the occurrence of parallels with much earlier work would not in itself preclude a Romanesque date for the Llanrhidian stone. With this in mind, it is important that on the Llyswyrny lintel we find a close similarity of the spiral terminations of the creature on the right and the 'feet' of the right 'human' on the Llanrhidian stone (figs. 77 and 86).

LLANTWIT MAJOR (GLAMORGAN)

At Llantwit Major the nave of the church is twelfth century, as indicated by the simple, round-headed south doorway, but the crossing dates only from the years around 1200. It may replace a simpler Romanesque chancel or mark the first extension of a rectangular, single-cell church. In either case, it seems likely that some pre-Norman work was incorporated into the twelfth-century church. Two tapering shafts preserved at the west end of the nave are richly decorated with three panels of 8- and 12-strand plaitwork above a lower frieze of opposing double triangles (figs. 90 and 91).[65] They have grooves at the back and may have been part of a screen arrangement within the church; perhaps they provided the division between 'nave' and 'chancel' in the un-subdivided architectural nave? Two analogues in

Fig. 90 Llantwit Major, St Illtyd: shaft

Spain and one in Norway help the reading of the screen setting for the Llantwit shafts. First, at the Mozarabic church of San Miguel de Escalada (913), near Leon, the screens in the south aisle have been reset away from the responds but on the responds are the cuttings for the screens to be tailed in (fig. 92). In the mid-ninth-century Asturian church of Santa Cristina de Lena, south of Oviedo, the screen is set between two marble columns.[66] In Norway in the screen of the stave church at Hopperstad IV, the frame on the entrance to the chancel is slotted into grooves in the columnar responds.[67] The technique has been described with reference to portals at Hopperstad II and IV and Urnes II where the 'jambs consist of huge columns, with grooves on the side facing the wall planks'.[68] The stave church parallels suggest that the Llantwit Major shafts may reflect a wooden architectural tradition.[69]

The Llantwit Major shafts are difficult to date. Nash-Williams suggested tenth/eleventh century, an opinion adopted by subsequent writers.[70] This may well be correct but given the continuity of plaitwork and richly decorated monolithic shafts in the Herefordshire School of Romanesque sculpture, a date in the twelfth century should not be overlooked. In either case, the shafts demonstrate the respect for the indigenous Welsh sculptural tradition under the Norman administration.

A grotesque animal head at Llantwit Major may have been used like the projecting heads at Kilpeck and, further in relation to the Herefordshire School, it has been paralleled with the heads of the beast on the Chaddesley Corbett (Worcs.) font.[71] If we think of the Llanrhidian stone with its projecting lion's head as part of a screen, then it is possible that the Llantwit Major head had a similar function.

Fig. 91 Llantwit Major, St Illtyd: detail of shaft showing the groove at the back

Fig. 92 Escalada (Castille/Leon), S. Miguel: detail of the screen currently placed in the south aisle

3

Cathedral, Castle and Monastery post 1120

Llandaff cathedral represents the physical appearance of Norman ways in south Wales and was a Romanesque structure on a grand scale, by the standard of the building in the region. Elsewhere the Norman presence was often marked, as it had been in England, by the construction of a castle and monastic foundation in close proximity. There was a monastic church and castle at Monmouth, Ewenny priory and nearby Ogmore castle, Usk priory church and castle and the pairing of Kenfig castle and Margam abbey. The monastic churches at Llangennith, Monkton, St Dogmaels, Brecon, Malpas and St Clears are investigated in the context of West Country Romanesque architecture and sculpture. The castles at Newcastle-Bridgend, Manorbier and Tretower are viewed separately as is the account of Llanthony priory. These monastic and secular works are discussed according to a chronological order.

LLANDAFF CATHEDRAL

The cathedral church of Saints Peter and Paul, Dyfrig, Teilo and Euddogwy, is set on the west side of the River Taff below the escarpment at the top of which is Cathedral Green and the village of Llandaff.[1] The location goes back to the sixth century when St Dyfrig, Bishop of Ergyng (d.612) established a community near the ford through which the Roman road crossed the river. Today, the church is primarily Gothic although it was nearly lost in an eighteenth-century remodelling.[2] Subsequently, starting in 1841, the full force of ecclesiological correctness stripped away the 'pagan' classicism of the previous century and the church was restored to its proper Christian, that is to say its Gothic, form. The work of restoration started under T.H. Wyatt, but from 1843 the major figure was John Pritchard, a local architect who preached the architectural gospel according to Augustus Welby Pugin and his Anglican counterparts at the Cambridge Camden Society. Pritchard continued in the service of Llandaff cathedral until the completion of the new south-west tower and spire, 1867–1869, and his work provides a very instructive barometer for the changing attitudes towards restoration during the period.[3] Fortunately for our purposes, there are important remains of the Romanesque church that include the east arch and some windows in the south wall of the presbytery, and the north and south nave doorways (fig. 109).

Construction of the Romanesque cathedral church of Llandaff was commenced in 1120 or 1121 by Bishop Urban, who had been appointed by the Norman administration in 1107, and was subject to the authority of the archbishop of Canterbury. In keeping with this, the architecture of the new cathedral was a radical departure from the old church. The

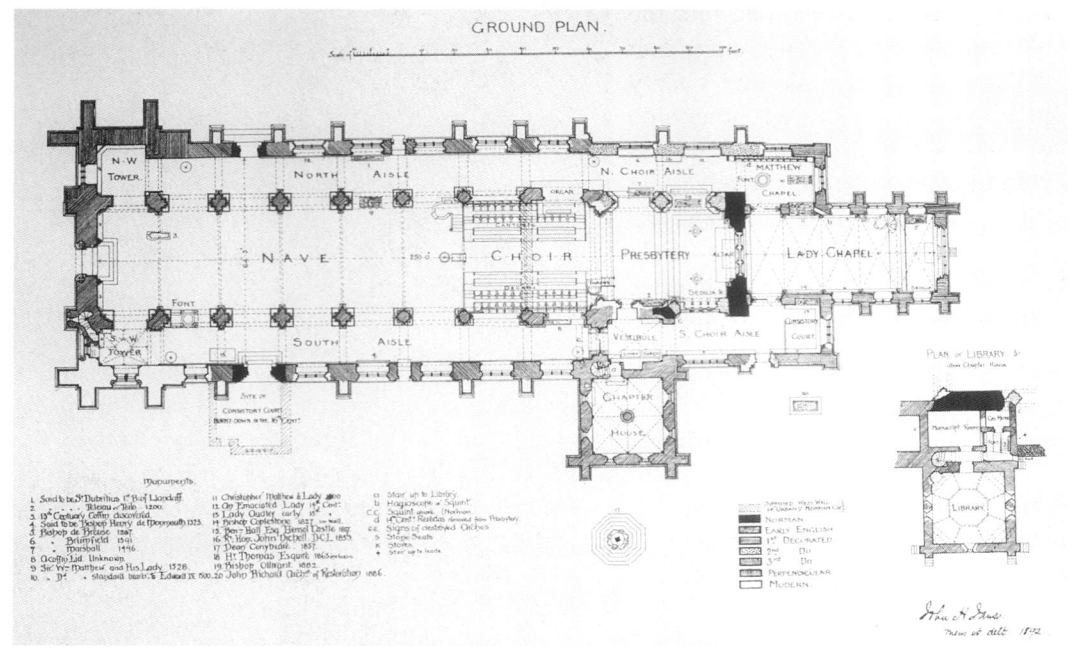

Fig. 93 Plan of Llandaff cathedral from The Builder

Fig. 94 Llandaff cathedral: interior of the presbytery looking south-east

Book of Llandaff recorded that the old church was 'twenty-eight feet in length, fifteen wide and twenty high, with two aisles on either side of but a small size and height, and with an apsidal porticus twelve feet long'.[4] While Urban's church was not conceived on the huge scale of some of the Norman cathedrals in England, when seen against the earlier architectural tradition in Wales, it must have seemed like a giant of a building.

Of the Norman church the monumental east arch and the south windows of the presbytery are richly decorated and speak of a very ambitious building programme (fig. 94). The round-headed east arch has four orders. The inner order is carried on paired shafts with richly foliated capitals and has twin rolls in the soffit of the arch (fig. 95 and plate 5). The foliage palmettes of the capitals grow from heart-shaped surrounds that are either beaded or striated and are clasped with binding ties (plate 5 and fig.96). Order two is plain and has just an impost at the springing of the arch, which continues the beaded cable ornament of the abaci of the capitals of the other orders. Order three has chevron jambs and chevron in the arch, a stylized foliage capital on the left (palte 5), and an angle head on the right capital from which a ribbed stem issues from the mouth and sprouts fluted leaves that grow to either side of the head. The fourth order has another variety of chevron in the arch roll, and capitals carved

Fig. 95 Close up of the southern capitals and the four orders on the west side of the presbytery arch

Fig. 96 Detail of the north soffit capitals on the east side of the presbytery arch

Fig. 97 (left) Detail of the south sofit capitals on the east side of the presbytery arch
Fig. 98 (right) Detail of the west capital in the south window in the presbytery

with trefoil, fluted leaves that spread from a button-like protrusion. The arch is framed with a row of large beaded medallions with sunken patterns. Medallions are also preserved on the exterior of the second and third south presbytery windows where they are framed with a billet hood mould originally on grotesque label stops of which one remains (figs. 98 and 99). The inner order of these windows is continuous and has a narrow chamfer while the second order has a roll moulding carried on foliage capitals without abaci. The same arrangement is seen on the inside of the second south presbytery window, which has a broad outer order of a countersunk chequer pattern (fig. 100). This contrasts with the window to the east in which the equivalent order has two rows of sunken roundels (fig. 94).

Fig. 99 (left) South window in the presbytery
Fig. 100 (right) Detail of the west capital in the second south window in the presbytery

Fig. 101 Gloucester, St Peter's abbey (now cathedral): detail of the north nave triforium and clerestorey divided by a beaded cable string course, like the string-course/abaci on the presbytery arch at Llandaff cathedral

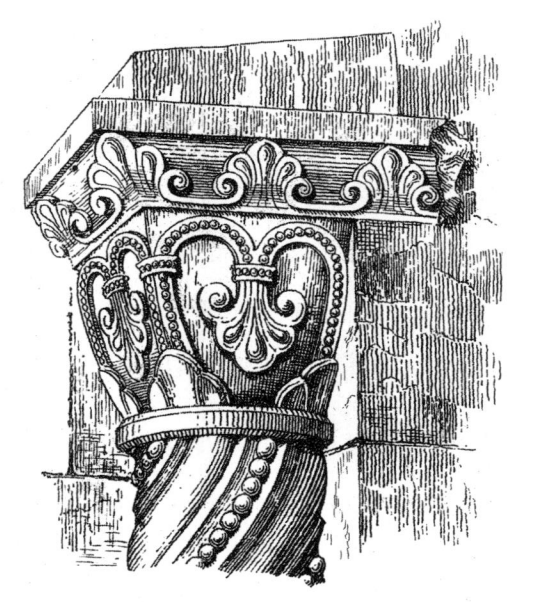

Fig. 102 Wootton (Glos.), St Mary Magdalene: capital (after Brandon) showing a heart-shaped frame and stylised leaves like those at Llandaff

Many aspects of the work indicate that Urban wished to create a top-quality building, and to facilitate this he recruited masons who had been trained and/or worked at two of the major buildings not far away in England — Hereford cathedral and St Peter's abbey, Gloucester. Quite apart from any of the sculptural decoration, the ashlar on the east wall of the presbytery is of the highest quality. The multi-ordered east presbytery arch is paralleled at Hereford cathedral and St John's, Chester,[5] and it probably led into an apsidal or short square-ended chapel. The Hereford arch provides a parallel for the paired shafts of the inner order at Llandaff, but unlike Llandaff it does not have twin soffit rolls. For this we can turn to the nave arcades at St Peter's abbey, Gloucester, and it is in the Gloucester nave that we find a beaded cable string course between the triforium and clerestorey like the string-course/abaci on the Llandaff arch (figs. 94–97, 101 and plate 6). In the Gloucester clerestorey we also see the fragmentary jambs of the former Romanesque minor arches carved with chevron as on order three of the Llandaff arch. The dragon's head label stop on the exterior of the third presbytery window at Llandaff is paralleled in a fragment at St Peter's, Gloucester,[6] as well as at St Oswald's priory, Gloucester and inside the west doorway at Deerhurst priory.[7]

For the foliage capitals at Llandaff the closest parallels are not with St Peter's, Gloucester but in the chapel of St Mary Magdalene at Wootton, on the outskirts of the city. There we find striated and beaded stems with binding ties that create a heart-shaped frame for multi-lobed leaves, and even stylized fluted leaves at the angle of the capital from which stems grow as in the window capitals at Llandaff (figs. 96, 98, 99 and 102). Even closer to the soffit capitals at Llandaff, is the foliage design on the neck of the font at Newnham-on-Severn (Glos.) (figs. 12 and 97). Moreover, the capitals of the arcade on the Newnham bowl are without abaci, as on the window capitals at Llandaff (figs. 98 and 100).[8] The Newnham font is by the workshop that produced the font at Hereford cathedral.[9] Also at Hereford, reused in the remodelling of the south transept clerestorey passage, are two medallions of the same type as at Llandaff.[10] Similar medallions are also used on a window of the keep at Longtown castle (Herefs.) and at Sarum cathedral.[11] The latter connection is an interesting one in that the work at Sarum was commissioned by Roger, bishop of Salisbury 1102–1139, one of the most munificent patrons of the day.[12] Whatever the exact date of Roger's work, we may be certain that a significant part of it must have been completed by 1127–1134, when at least one sculptor from Sarum worked on Cormac's Chapel at Cashel (Tipperary).[13] Roger also founded a castle and priory at Kidwelly (Carmarthenshire) of which all traces have now gone. He was established as lord of Kidwelly in 1106 and he probably wasted no time in getting on with the construction of the castle,[14] and subsequently, in 1114, founding a priory at Kidwelly as a dependency of Sherborne abbey.[15] The west face of the east crossing arch at Sherborne is decorated with medallions of the same family as those at Llandaff,[16] and one is left to wonder whether there might have been similar work at Kidwelly. As it is there is just a record of a Norman capital from the castle that is now lost.[17]

Returning to the Hereford orbit, details of the heads on the capitals of the chancel arch at Tarrington (Herefs.) suggest that they belong to the same family as the head on the middle right capital of the Llandaff east arch.[18] Many details at Tarrington relate closely to the Romanesque work at Hereford cathedral. This is important because the inside of the arch head of the east window in the north chancel wall at Tarrington has sunken roundels like those on the first presbytery window at Llandaff. I do not know of another example of this motif, and it therefore serves to reinforce the connection between the Llandaff and Hereford masons. It is also worth noting that in the wall paintings in the chancel at Kempley (Glos.), the arches above the apostles on the north and south walls are decorated with small roundels. Moreover at Kempley, the soffit of the chancel arch and the splays of the north and south chancel windows are painted with a red-and-white-chequerboard pattern, a painted version of the hood of the second window in the Llandaff presbytery.

For the roll mouldings of the windows we have to go slightly further afield to the arch to the south transept chapel at Worcester cathedral, or the east processional doorway at Malvern priory. The latter also has capitals without abaci, albeit plain rather than sculpted, and this feature we have mentioned in connection with the dado arcade at Ludlow castle's gate tower and chapel and in the bishop's chapel at Hereford. Given the possibility of a connection between Llandaff and the work of Bishop Roger of Salisbury, it is worth mentioning that capitals without abaci also appear atop the mid-wall shafts of the crossing tower at St John's, Devizes (Wilts.), a building that has much in common with Sarum cathedral. It is probably through a connection with Bishop Roger's work that the motif also appears in Ireland as in the upper external nave blind colonnade at Cormac's Chapel at Cashel, and in the nave blind colonnades at Kilmalkedar (Kerry). We will encounter the motif again in Wales.

Unfortunately, nothing remains of the Romanesque structure of Llandaff cathedral above the level of the presbytery arch and the south presbytery windows. However, a two-storey elevation seems most probable seeing that it is most unlikely that when the cathedral was rebuilt in the early Gothic period there would have been a reduction in the number of storeys in the building.

Of the Romanesque nave of Llandaff cathedral, the bases of an arch connecting the nave with the presbytery were found during restoration.[19] In 1850 these bases were not known to Edward A. Freeman, who reconstructed the present presbytery as the Romanesque aisleless nave, and conjectured a chancel to the east of this, and a tower-porch to the south where the early Gothic vaulted bay is now located (fig. 93).[20] In his 1873 *Handbook to the Cathedrals of Wales*, Richard King adopted Freeman's reconstruction in principle but took account of the Romanesque bases beneath the present chancel arch and added a one-bay galilee.[21] While such a small scale for a cathedral is not impossible — compare, for example, St Rule's at St Andrews (Fife) — we have already seen something more monumental in Wales at Chepstow priory. Then, there is the construction of the Benedictine priory church at Ewenny (Glamorgan) between 1111/1116 and 1126 on much grander lines. This suggests that something on a more ambitious scale might be appropriate for the cathedral, as would rivalry with the cathedral at St Davids, commenced in 1115. The complete rebuilding of St Davids from 1182, however, deprives us of any physical remains of its Romanesque predecessor. Be that as it may, in the 1140s a poem compared the church at Tywyn (Merioneth) with both Bangor and St Davids cathedrals.[22] Tywyn has a nave flanked by north and south aisles, and it is likely that Bangor was the same.[23] Such circumstances imply that Llandaff cathedral would have had an aisled nave.

Architectural historian, E.W. Lovegrove suggested that the change in design between bays 4 and 5 in the present early Gothic at Llandaff nave may be the result of a break in construction brought about by the demolition of the Romanesque nave that stood to the east of this point.[24] The theory is appealing and may be supported with reference to the proportional system employed at Ewenny priory where the nave is twice as long as the square-ended presbytery. Applying this to Llandaff, a nave twice as long as the presbytery starting from the presbytery west arch would place the Romanesque west front in line with the fourth pair of piers of the Gothic nave arcade. Against this theory it should be pointed out that this would make the nave only about half the length of the nearest English cathedral at Hereford. Therefore, a longer nave may have been planned but not completed. This arrangement would leave the Romanesque cathedral without a crossing tower and transepts, unlike the contemporary cathedral at Bangor, and the priory churches at Chepstow and Ewenny. However, James tells us that 'the bases of the jamb of a Norman doorway were found during the restoration of 1857 where ... one now opens from the presbytery into the vestibule of the Chapter House ... This would have been the door leading from the porch into the nave of the Urban Church' (fig. 93).²⁵ James's interpretation is not easy to understand and less so his idea that the vaulted bay at the west end of the presbytery aisle 'might have been a tower attached to the Norman church'.²⁶ The presence of the richly decorated Norman window here precludes a tower in this bay, or for that matter a porch of any great height. In the absence of any evidence for a crossing surmounted by a tower at Llandaff, it seems most likely that the Norman doorway led to a low passage to a Norman tower on the site of the present chapter house. This plan may be associated with the former Romanesque eastern towers of Hereford cathedral, although a better parallel would be with the transeptally placed towers of Exeter cathedral, and the twin towers at Cormac's Chapel, Cashel.²⁷ Lovegrove also drew attention to two chapter seals of the late twelfth century that depict 'a cruciform church with an aisleless nave, a central tower, and two lesser towers east of the choir flanking the apse'.²⁸ He believed that the seals gave an accurate depiction of the Romanesque church but, given the artistic conventions of architectural representation in the twelfth century, this is a bold assumption.

Following the death of Bishop Urban in 1134, there is no evidence of work on the cathedral until the time of Bishop William Saltmarsh (1186–91), which was almost certainly in response to the

Fig. 103 and 104 Llandaff cathedral: south (above) and north (below) portals to the nave

commencement of the rebuilding of St Davids cathedral in 1182. Saltmarsh was previously chamberlain of St Augustine's, Bristol,[29] and the form of the decoration of the gatehouse there is so close to the nave north and south doorways at Llandaff that it is tempting to suggest that the same craftsmen worked in both places under Saltmarsh's patronage. The round-headed doorways in question at Llandaff are in the third bay from the west of both the north and south nave aisles. The south doorway has four orders, the inner one continuous and carved with spaced chevron (fig. 103). The other three orders are carried on multi-scalloped capitals atop detached shafts. Orders two and four have single chevrons to either side of a thin angle roll, while order three is enveloped by lattice chevron. The hood is ornamented with greek key. The north doorway has three orders alternating continuous and non-continuous (fig. 104). Order one repeats the chevron of orders two and four of the south doorway, while order three has the same lattice chevron as the third order of the south doorway. The second order of the north doorway is carried on multi-scalloped capitals with sunk faces atop detached shafts and is carved with triple chevrons at right angles to a thin angle roll. The dog-tooth hood mould rests on dragon's head label stops like those in the nave of Malmesbury abbey (Wilts.), and there is the head of a bishop at the apex of the arch.[30]

The alternating continuous and non-continuous orders of the north doorway are paralleled on the main north arch of St Augustine's gatehouse, Bristol, while the multi-scalloped capitals of the south doorway go with the southern arch of the

Figs. 105 and 106 Bristol, St Augustine (now cathedral): detail of the north arch (above) and south arch (below) to the gatehouse

gatehouse (figs. 103–106). More specifically, the inner order of the north doorway and the outer order of the south doorway at Llandaff are slightly simplified variants of the outer order of the north arch and the inner order of the south arch of the Bristol gatehouse. The lattice chevron on the third order of the south doorway and the outer order of the north doorway at Llandaff repeats the second order of the south arch at Bristol, minus the foliage in the outer triangles.[31] The precision of these parallels makes the attribution of the Llandaff doorways to Bishop William Saltmarsh most appealing. But what of the circumstances associated with the erection of the doorways? Did Saltmarsh envision a radical remodelling of the cathedral or did he simply wish to extend or complete the Romanesque church? The latter theory is more likely in view of the major style change between the doorways and the early Gothic work of the nave and west front probably commenced by Saltmarsh's successor, Henry of Abergavenny (1193–1218).

Before leaving Llandaff cathedral a word must be said about the dedication of the church, in light of the Normanization of the administration under Bishop Urban. Obedience to Canterbury has already been mentioned and in turn there is direct reference to Rome by way of the dedications to saints Peter and Paul. It is well known that, starting with St Albans in 1077, many of the great English abbey and cathedral churches were rebuilt on a scale that matched the great Constantinian basilican churches of early Christian Rome.[32] At the same time, and also starting at St Albans, it was a local saint that was promoted, and this continued with St Swithin at Winchester, St Edmund at Bury St Edmunds, St Ethelreda at Ely, St Erkenwald at Old St Paul's in London, and St Cuthbert at Durham. At Durham cathedral (1093–1133) not only were precise measurements of the building taken from Old St Peter's, but the spiral decoration on the columns in the presbytery and transepts, and the ribs of the high vaults were iconographically inspired by the baldacchino there.[33] We thus find a clear visual expression of the association of the local saint, Cuthbert, with a top, premier-league saint, Peter. Such promotion of the local saint made excellent political sense, not least to show the new Norman rulers as the legitimate heirs of England, as claimed by William I. At Llandaff cathedral we witness an allied approach. While the scale of Urban's cathedral was not that of Durham or Old St Peter's, the sculptural decoration was every bit as lavish as anything built in England up to that time. With its original painted decoration the church must have had a shrine-like quality to house its relics. The writing of the *Book of Llandaff* was another aspect of this promotion of the local saints.[34] St Teilo, the second bishop of Llandaff, was buried at the cathedral, and in 1120 the relics of St Dubricius (Dyfrig), the former 'archbishop of Caerleon', were 'imported' from Bardsey with the approval of Gruffudd ap Cynan, Prince of Gwynedd, and the newly appointed Bishop David of Bangor. The dedication of Llandaff cathedral associated the resting place of their local saints with St Peter and St Paul.

Monmouth Priory and Castle (Gwent)

In the Domesday survey Monmouth castle is recorded in Herefordshire under the land of the king, in the charge of William son of Baderon.[35] The priory church of St Mary at Monmouth was founded by William fitz Baderon between 1074 and 1086 as a dependency of St Florent, Saumur, and was dedicated by Hervé, Bishop of Bangor, in 1101–2.[36] However, as church historian F.G. Cowley has indicated, there is no precise evidence in extant charters as to when the priory became conventual, and this may not have happened until the latter part of the twelfth century.[37] Robert de Bethune, Bishop of Hereford (1131–48), confirmed the earlier donations at the request of Baderon of Monmouth.[38] The secular and monastic foundations conform to the pattern established in the region at Chepstow by William fitz Osbern immediately after the Conquest. Subsequently, Monmouth castle chapel was given by William fitz Baderon II (c.1108–70/6) to St Florent at Saumur.[39] William fitz Baderon II seems to be the most likely candidate for builder of the present castle.

The priory church has undergone extensive remodelling but with the remains of the Romanesque fabric and a late seventeenth-century drawing, it is possible to reconstruct the rudiments of the original church. To the Romanesque west front a tower and spire were added in the fourteenth century and the latter was replaced with the present one by Nathaniel Wilkinson of Worcester shortly before 1743.[40] After the Dissolution the presbytery and transepts were disused and fell into ruin but the nave was taken over as the parish church. Between 1736 and 1737 the church was rebuilt by Francis Smith of Worcester, and in turn the core of Smith's church was replaced between 1881 and 1883 with the present structure complete with a new east end to the design of George Edmund Street.

Of the Romanesque fabric, there remains the demi-columnar west respond of the nave south arcade and the west front, less most of its central section which was lost when the arch of the fourteenth-century tower was built (fig. 107). Between them there is enough information to reconstruct the Romanesque nave elevation. The demi-columnar respond makes it most likely that the nave arcade was carried on columnar piers, as in the presbytery of St Peter's

Figs. 107 Monmouth priory: the demi-columnar west respond of the nave south arcade

Figs. 108 (left) and 109 (right) Monmouth priory showing the remains of the Romanesque west façade protruding to either side of the later tower, showing (right) the string courses detailed in figures 110 and 111

abbey, Gloucester, or the nave of Shrewsbury abbey. Like these examples, the arches at Monmouth probably would have been round-headed with two plain orders, as we shall also see in the naves at Ewenny priory (fig. 126) and St Woolos at Newport (fig. 216). The north and south extremities of the Romanesque west front protrude beyond the side walls of the later tower (figs. 108–109). With the exception of the use of rubble in the lower section of the north wall, the front is built of good quality ashlar, mainly old red sandstone, except for the top ten courses where tufa predominates. Most importantly, the walls are articulated with string-courses, which are instructive as external indicators of internal divisions in the church, and, in terms of their detail, as pointers to associations for the master mason. The lowest of the string-courses is only on the west face of the northern section of the façade

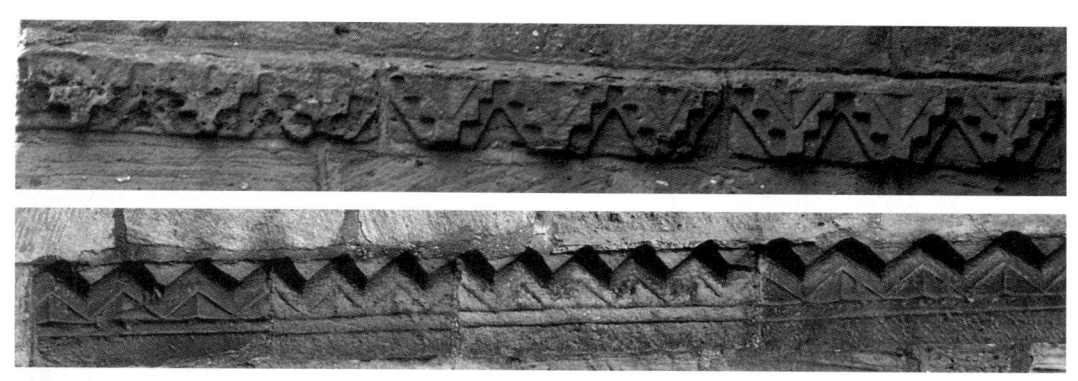

Figs. 110 (above) and 111 (below)
Details of the string courses on the Romanesque façade

and is carved with zigzag on which there is a raised stepped pattern in the upper triangles (fig. 110). The height of this seems to correspond with the top of the nave arcade respond. Moving up, the next string-course continues round to the east side of the façade and is carved with simple chevron. It is matched on the south side of the façade but the section at the southern extremity of the west wall and along the south wall has been replaced with new plain stonework (fig. 111). This level would have marked the division between the main arcade and the first storey. The next string-course has a quirked hollow chamfer and delineates the division between the first and second storeys. The overall impression of the proportions of the divisions as a whole is best appreciated in the view from the north-east (fig. 108).

Confirmation of this reading of a three-storey elevation is found in blocked openings from the newel staircase in the south-west angle of the façade, so carefully analyzed by Sian Rees.[41] The blocked opening at the second storey indicates that there was a wall passage in the clerestorey. It was therefore different from the nave clerestorey at Chepstow and instead conformed to the Norman arrangement at Saint-Etienne at Caen, St Albans abbey and, in West Country Romanesque architecture, in the presbytery and transepts of Worcester cathedral.[42] The inclusion of the clerestorey passage indicates that the nave would have been covered with a wooden roof rather than a vault. How the first storey would have been articulated is difficult to determine. There would have been room for a squat gallery with round-headed arches of the same diameter as the main arcade. However, it is quite possible that such a round-headed arch may have been used at the back of the wall while the front was articulated with smaller arches as at Chepstow or the nave of St Peter's, Gloucester. While questions will always remain about the details of the elevation, it is important to emphasize the ambitious nature of a three-storey elevation at Monmouth priory. As we have seen, even Romanesque Llandaff cathedral probably had a two-storey elevation, so a three-storey design associates Monmouth with the great abbey churches and cathedrals in England.

In her study of the openings from the newel stair, Sian Rees observed that the 'lowest is north facing' and may have originally led to a Norman passageway within the thickness of the west wall.⁴³ This is quite probable given an equivalent passage in the west wall at Chepstow priory and formerly at Hereford cathedral.

A 1684 drawing of Monmouth priory church by Thomas Dinely shows the ruins of the Romanesque fabric to the east of the nave (fig. 112). The details are sketchy and, for Rees, 'virtually impossible to interpret with any certainty'.⁴⁴ Of course, she is right but we must try to extract what we can from the sketch. To start with what is clear, in the foreground there is a columnar pier from which a round-headed arch springs to the west. Above this arch, at about one o'clock, there is a round-headed, window-like opening, and there seems to be a similar aperture at eleven o'clock, although this is less distinct. In the background to the right there is an arcade of two round-headed

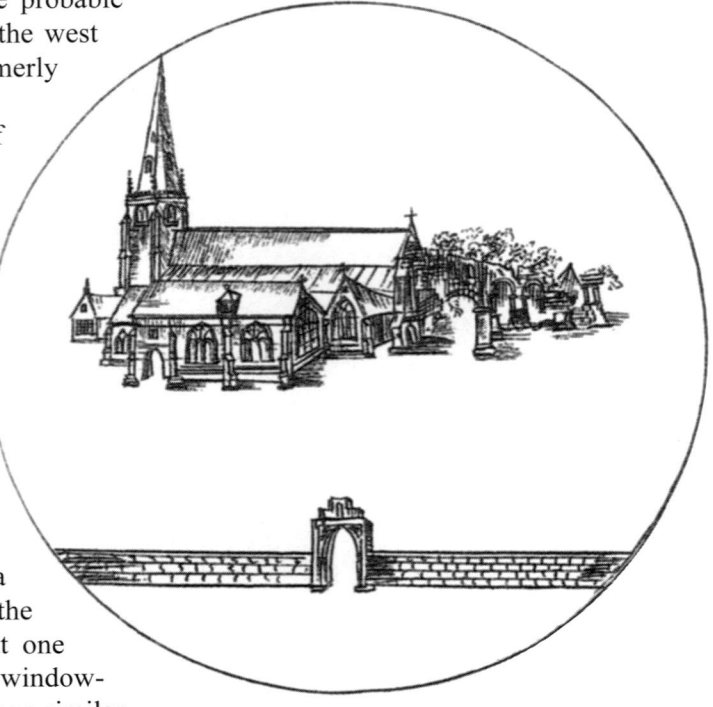

Fig. 112 Thomas Dinely's drawing of Monmouth priory, 1684

arches that share a pier in the middle. The pier seems to have nook shafts, or set-backs, at the angles of the upper half and a square plinth that occupies about half the height of the pier, as in the presbytery arcades at Ledbury (Herefs.).⁴⁵ The appearance of this pier is perhaps best explained by imagining the former existence of choir stalls against the plain lower half of the pier, above which the articulated upper half would be seen. Yet there is a problem of how to interpret this section of the fabric in relation to the columnar pier and arch in the foreground because between the two there is another architectural element. Although partly hidden behind the columnar pier, it seems to have a distinct base and a pier-like bulk. But it is not as tall as either the columnar or the compound piers. Possibly it was an altar, but that would be difficult to equate with the choir stalls. One possibility raised by Rees is that the arcade does not belong to the choir but to the east side of the transept in which the arches would have opened into chapels, as at Ewenny priory.⁴⁶ However, that might be taking perspectival license a little too far. And on the matter of perspective, how are we to read the arch in the foreground? For Rees it is possibly a crossing arch, and this is certainly the reading adopted by the nineteenth-century artist who produced an engraving from Dinely's drawing (figs. 112 and 113). However, it is possible to read the perspective of the drawing to indicate that the arch in the foreground and those of the arcade are of the same height. The arch is lower than the roof of the south nave aisle and, in relation to the height of the west tower, would appear to be of a scale associated with the extant west respond of the south nave arcade. It would be unusual to have a columnar pier as a support at the crossing and therefore it is better to see this bay as one of the regular arcade, and that the two openings above belong to a triforium. If this reading is correct then there is no evidence for a crossing and transept in the church.

A capital unearthed from the west tower is carved with foliage on beaded stems of the same type as the Kilpeck (Herefs.) tympanum and one of the Hereford cathedral crossing capitals.[47] There is also a triple-scalloped capital with collars on the cones reused as the base of a stoup that is allied to the apse capitals at Kilpeck, the nave triforium capitals at St Peter's abbey, Gloucester, and on the main portal to the great tower at Goodrich castle (Herefs.). The chevron string-course on the south section of the west front is of the same type as on the cornice of the Fownhope (Herefs.) tower. A simpler version of this chevron pattern appears on the north section of the Monmouth façade and on the east and south walls of the great tower at Goodrich castle. The stepped motif on the lowest string-course of the north section of the tower is closely paralleled on the scallop faces of a nave arcade capital at Hereford cathedral.[48] These parallels provide the best indicators for the date of the work at Monmouth. Kilpeck was probably built either just before or just after it was given to St Peter's, Gloucester, in 1134. Hereford cathedral was commenced between 1107 and 1115 and was consecrated between 1142 and 1148.[49] St Peter's abbey, Gloucester, was commenced in 1089 and, although there is no documented date for the completion of the Norman nave, it is agreed that the fire damage on the nave arcade piers results from the fire of 1122. This would suggest 1120–1145 for the completion on the work at Monmouth, under the patronage of William fitz Baderon II.

The Romanesque tympanum preserved in the Monmouth Museum is without provenance, other than that it was built into the Williams Bros. shop in Monmouth.[50] It depicts a pair of figures like the fighting knights on the Eardisley (Herefs.) font. Unlike Eardisley, however, the Monmouth knights carry no weapons but each one has rubbery arms, one of which punches the opponent, while the other is intertwined in foliage and

Fig. 113 Nineteenth-century print after Thomas Dinely's drawing of Monmouth priory

grabs at a stem. In this respect the closest parallel is with the knights on Kilpeck corbel no. 10. This is the familiar theme of knights grappling with the forces of evil as elsewhere in the Herefordshire School as on the left jamb of the south doorway at Kilpeck and at Alveley. Although the arc of the tympanum is unusual, the truncation of the top is like the Kilpeck tympanum — a technical detail to further ally the Monmouth work to the Herefordshire School. It is unlikely that such a subject would have come from the local priory church but it may have occupied the castle chapel.

Monmouth Castle

The great tower of Monmouth castle is a smaller version of the great tower at Chepstow, with a two-storey elevation that includes the hall on the first storey. Three bays of the east wall and part of the adjacent section of the south wall are extant, although with some later remodelling (fig. 114). The walls are built of rubble, with ashlar reserved for window and door frames, the quoins of the pilaster buttress at the south-east angle of the tower, and for the projecting angle of the stair turret in the south-east corner of the hall (figs. 114 and 116). In the east wall three round-headed windows light the undercroft; above and to the left a similar window lights the staircase (fig, 114). The clasping pilaster buttress at the south-east angle has one window to the staircase and a shorter one higher on the east wall just below a quirked, hollow-chamfered string course (fig. 115). This string continues a short distance on to the east wall and also on the south wall as far as the one remaining Norman window of the first floor. A later roof crease cuts the lower part of the window, and at ground level a doorway leads to the undercroft. The facing of the doorway appears to be fourteenth century but it may just be a refacing of an earlier doorway. Returning to the east face of the clasping buttress, there is another window near the top of the wall, and higher on the wall to the right there are two corbels carved with human heads.[51]

On the interior (fig. 116), at ground level the three windows in the east wall splay out to segmental-headed niches. The one on the right retains a significant amount of what may be original lime-wash on the arch face. Above these openings there remain four large corbels that would have carried the beams of the hall floor. In the south-east corner is the angled doorway to a newel staircase that

Fig. 114 Monmouth castle: exterior from the south-east

gives access to the first floor through a round-headed doorway with a continuous chamfer, and then up to the top of the tower. In the south wall, there is a niche like those in the east wall but instead of a window it is opened up to a doorway. Above is the large window also with a segmental head.

Fig. 115 Monmouth castle: detail of south-east stair turret

Fig. 116 Monmouth castle: interior looking south-east

The two head corbels are not common in secular architecture, although they are used on the interior of Scolland's Hall at Richmond castle and on the exterior of the stair to the great hall at Castle Rising (Norfolk). Unfortunately, the heads are badly weathered and do not speak clearly of related work elsewhere. In the absence of easily identifiable motifs to help date the great tower, we must look closely at the available features for any clues. The quirked hollow chamfer of the string-course is the same as on the uppermost string-course on the northern section of the west front of Monmouth priory. Moreover, the windows that light the staircase have a chamfered frame as on the lights to the staircase at the south-west angle of the priory. Such chamfers are generally most popular in the later twelfth century but they appear earlier in similar windows in Herefordshire churches, probably around 1130 in the nave at Castle Frome, and around 1134 at Kilpeck. Even more significantly, the motif appears on the window to the staircase in the north-east angle of the great tower at Goodrich castle, a building that has supplied some detailed comparisons for Monmouth priory. At Goodrich we also find the segmental arch used in the main portal. The comparisons between Goodrich and Monmouth priory and castle make even more sense when it is noted that in 1144 William fitz Baderon II granted the church of St Giles of Goodrich castle to the priory of St Mary at Monmouth.[52] Unfortunately, nothing remains of this church, but the documentation serves to firmly associate the link between Goodrich and Monmouth with William fitz Baderon II.

It would therefore appear that William fitz Baderon II was responsible for building both the castle and priory church in Monmouth between about 1120 and 1145.

EWENNY PRIORY (GLAMORGAN)

William de Londres was entrusted with the care of the castle of Ogmore and the land appurtenent to it some time after the late eleventh-century Norman invasion of Glamorgan by Robert fitz Hamon, founder of Tewkesbury abbey.[53] William de Londres built a church at Ewenny, which was probably given to the abbey of St Peter at Gloucester during the time of Bishop Urban of Llandaff (1107–34), who was present at the dedication.[54] Nineteenth-century historians, Arthur West Haddan and William Stubbs recorded that William founded the church in 1111.[55] In *Monasticon Anglicanum* William Dugdale reported a statement of Tudor antiquary, John Leland, that the priory had been founded by Sir John Londres, lord of Ogmore castle, and added 'probably in the early part of the twelfth century'.[56] In *The History and Antiquities of Glamorganshire and its Families* Thomas Nicholas named William de Londres as the founder and added that Maurice de Londres made Ewenny a cell of St Peter's, Gloucester.[57] *The Chronicle of the Princes* recorded that in 1116 William de Londres, for fear of attack from Gruffudd ap Rhys, 'left his [Ogmore] castle and all his cattle and all his precious wealth'.[58] Quite what that disruption had on the foundation of Ewenny is difficult to determine. On the one hand, it is possible that the 1111 foundation date recorded by Haddan and Stubbs is correct, and is quite in keeping with 'the early part

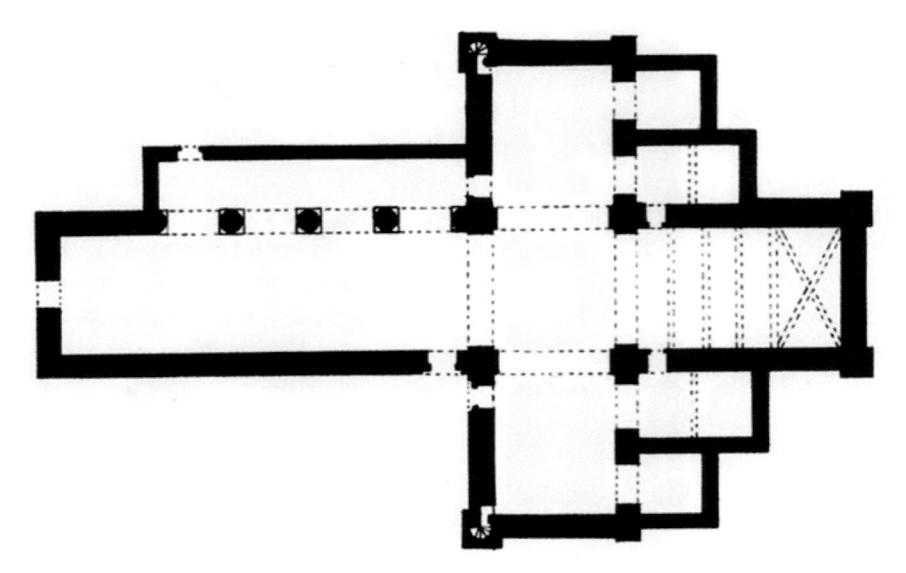

Fig. 117 Ewenny priory: reconstructed plan of the Romanesque church

of the twelfth century', recorded by Dugdale. On the other hand, perhaps the foundation took place with William's return to Ogmore, after the threat of attack had passed. William was dead by 1126 and therefore the church should be dated 1111/1116 to 1126. In a confirmation charter granted by King Stephen in 1138 the churches of Ewenny and St Brides are listed as belonging to Gloucester abbey.[59] Then in 1141 'Maurice de Londres, son of William de Londres, gave to the church of St Peter at Gloucester, the church of St Michael at Ewenny, the church of St Bridget (St Bride's Major) with the chapel of Ogmore ... and all their possessions ... in order that a convent of monks might be formed'.[60] C.A. Ralegh Radford, author of the Department of the Environment guidebook to Ewenny priory, suggested that 'the gift of 1141 represents a provision for the foundation of the priory, the deed doubtless confirming to the parent abbey the properties previously granted by the founder and his family'.[61]

Does the present fabric of Ewenny church date from the time of William de Londres or is it the product of rebuilding in connection with the 1141 gift? In a short article on the church, Miss E. Picton Turberville stated that it was built by William de Londres and his son, Maurice de Londres, and was completed before 1141.[62] Radford suggested that the church was the product of three separate building campaigns, and this interpretation was followed by Lawrence Butler in the *Glamorgan County History*, and Hague in his 1984 account of the priory.[63] This fragmented chronology was deemed untenable by the present author in 1988 who saw the church as the product of a single build between 1116 and 1126.[64] This dating was accepted by Irish architectural historian, Tadhg O'Keefe, but was challenged by John Newman in his account of Ewenny priory in the Glamorganshire volume of *The Buildings of Wales*.[65] Newman pointed out that a three-bay eastern arm could only be associated with a monastic community and that, as Maurice de Londres is described as the founder the church, the church should be dated *circa* 1141. In the context of the foundation of monastic houses in Wales, this discrepancy between the initial establishment of the house and creation of the full conventual organization was not unusual. We have already seen that this was likely the case at Monmouth, and the situation seems to have been similar at Abergavenny.[66] Reassessment of the fabric sheds further light on the matter.

The church has a cruciform plan with a three-bay, aisleless presbytery that terminates in a flat east wall (figs. 117 and 118). There is a low crossing tower and aisleless transepts of two bays, fully preserved on the south but in ruin on the north following a collapse in 1803. Each transept had two square-ended eastern chapels en echelon and it is significant that the chapel walls are thinner than the taller transept walls, a feature especially noticeable in the ruined north wall of the north transept and the adjacent wall of the north transept chapel. The nave has a four-bay aisle to the north and originally extended one bay further west; remains of the north wall make this clear, and its appearance was recorded in the late eighteenth century.[67] In the east bay of the nave there is a processional doorway immediately next to a doorway into the south transept. The north aisle communicates with the north transept through a doorway and beneath the western crossing arch there is a later medieval screen.

Fig. 118 Ewenny priory: exterior from the north-north-east

The east wall of the presbytery is distinct from the rest of the fabric of the church in that it is faced with ashlar whereas the rest of the church is of rubble masonry with ashlar dressing for quoins and arches (fig. 140). This may have iconographic significance to mark the importance of the eastern bay of the presbytery as the place of the high altar. There are three stepped, round-headed windows in the east wall and one window in the eastern bay of the north and south walls to maximize the illumination of the high altar in the eastern bay. The presbytery is vaulted with a quadripartite rib vault over the eastern bay and a barrel vault over the other bays with alternating transverse arches and transverse ribs (fig. 119). The latter have the same profile of two rolls separated by an angle fillet as on the ribs of the vault in the eastern bay. The eastern ogives and the transverse arches of the barrel are carried on scalloped capitals atop shafts that sit on bases on the chevron string-course that runs around the presbytery and the level of the window sill.

On the south wall of the sanctuary there is a rebuilt, round-headed piscina which, if it reflects the original, is an early example of this feature. In the west bay of the north wall immediately to the east of the door to the north transept chapel there is a large, round-headed aumbry (fig. 120). Here the uninterrupted coursing of the ashlar with the east jamb of the doorway demonstrates that the aumbry is coeval with the Norman fabric.

The jambs and arches of the east windows and the north-east rib of the quadripartite rib vault preserve important remains of original painting which is almost certainly contemporary with the building of the church. This painted scheme was then modified around 1200 and we have to thank Sophie Stewart for clearly differentiating the two programmes of decoration in her exemplary restoration of the painting.[68] The best

Figs. 119 and 120 Ewenny priory: the presbytery from the crossing (left) and looking west (right), the latter showing the door to the north transept chapel to the right of the screen and adjacent round-headed aumbry

preserved of the original work is seen on the right side of the left window and shows imitation masonry joints picked out in thick red lines (plate 7). The same treatment is seen clearly on the north-east rib (plate 8). In neither case do the imitation joints coincide with the real masonry joints. Between the north and central window at the level of the springing of the north window, there is a frieze of painted red lozenges as if to indicate a capital or large impost (plate 9). In contrast to this between the central and south window, the analogous space is ornamented with a fictive segmental blind arch (plate 10). It sits on moulded capitals; the one on the right is better preserved. There are also traces of red paint on the chevron ornament on the south respond of the east crossing arch. Sophie Stewart's reconstruction of the original appearance of the painted articulation of the east wall is illustrated in plate 11.

The chevron string-course extends from the side walls of the presbytery to the responds of the eastern crossing arch and the adjacent east responds of the north and south crossing arches (figs. 118–119 and 121). Here, and on the matching west responds of the north and south crossing arches, and both responds of the west crossing arches, paired half shafts rest on moulded bases atop these strings and carry scalloped capitals and the inner

Fig. 121 Ewenny priory: south transept looking south-east

Fig. 122 (above) The north transept chapel from the north-east showing evidence for barrel vaulting
Fig. 123 (right) Detail of south label stop on the arch to the north transept chapel

order of the plain two-order crossing arches. The capitals continue to either side in a frieze-like fashion to carry the second order of the arch. The two-order, round-headed arches to the eastern chapels of the south transept both spring from chevroned imposts (fig. 121). The inner arch is slightly larger than the outer one and has square single billet on the hood mould rather than the quirked chamfer above the outer arch. The inner chapel communicated with the presbytery through a doorway in the western bay, exactly as the north transept inner chapel. All the chapels were barrel vaulted, the evidence for which is best preserved in the north transept inner chapel (fig. 122). Here we see the vault spring from above the string-course on the side wall and the thin stones of the webbing, that range from 12 to 14 inches in length, keyed into the wall above the entrance arch. Halfway along the string-course on the south wall there is a corbel that carried a transverse arch of the vault to articulate the chapel in two bays. In keeping with the different ornamentation on the hood moulds in the south transept chapel arches, the hood to the inner chapel has alternating square billet and squat cones (fig. 123). The hood terminates on a dragon's head stop of the same family as Llandaff cathedral.

Returning to the south transept, there are three large round-headed windows in the south wall set one over two, and a doorway to a spiral stair in the south-west corner (figs. 121 and 124). The staircase leads to the triforium in the west wall from which a stair leads up to the crossing tower (fig. 124). The staircase is expressed on the exterior of the transept as a large clasping, ashlar-faced buttress that is corbelled out near the top to form a low turret. The clasping buttress at the south-east angle of the transept is significantly smaller than at the south-west angle. Francis Grose's engraving of 1775 shows a similar differentiation in the scale of the angle buttresses in the north transept, which suggests that there may have been a staircase in the north-west angle.[69] However, there is no such differentiation in John Carter's drawing of the exterior of the church from the north-west.[70] Immediately next to the south-west crossing pier there is a round-headed doorway to the cloister. On the exterior, the doorway is articulated in two orders, the inner one plain with hollow-chamfered imposts at the springing of the arch, the outer with a quirked angle roll moulding in the arch on scalloped capitals and coursed shafts (fig. 125). The hood mould has a quirked chamfer. Immediately to the left of this doorway is one that leads into the nave. It is also of two orders, and the inner order, and the coursed shafts and scalloped capitals of the outer order, are the same as the doorway to the south transept. However, in the arch the second order is decorated with chevron at right angles to the wall, and the hood mould is carved with a cable pattern.

In the nave, the north arcade has plain, two-order, round-headed arches carried on squat columnar piers with scalloped capitals (fig. 126). Round-headed clerestorey windows are set above the piers, a design that allows the lower splay of the window to fall below the level of the top of the arcade. Although not Romanesque, the position of the screen beneath the western crossing arch immediately behind the nave altar probably reflects the liturgical division of the twelfth century. At the east end of the north nave aisle there is the simple Romanesque doorway to the north transept (fig. 125).

Fig. 124 West wall of the south transept

Fig. 125 South transept and nave processional doorways

Fig. 126 (above) Ewenny priory nave looking east
Fig. 127 (right) The east bay of the north nave aisle

The original west front was one bay further to the west and its form is recorded in a drawing of *circa* 1795, and one by John Carter *circa* 1800.[71] The west doorway has been re-erected in a private garden (fig. 128). Its form is the same as the east processional doorway to the nave except that the hood mould has a quirked hollow chamfer. Originally, above the doorway were three plain, round-headed windows, of which the central one is shown wider and taller in the *circa* 1795 drawing but not so by Carter.

The plan of the church is not precisely paralleled elsewhere but it has much in common with Romanesque priory churches in Wales and England. The simple cruciform plan with aisleless presbytery and transepts is used for priory churches in England after the Conquest like Bramber (Sussex), founded before 1073, and Lastingham (Yorks), 1078–85; Stogursey (Somerset), founded 1100–1107, Pamber (Hants) and Leonard Stanley (Glos.).[72] Aisleless cruciform plans are also associated with Anglo-Saxon minster churches, as at St Mary-in-Castro at Dover (Kent), or at Great Paxton (Hunts.) where nave aisles are incorporated.[73] Similar planning is also found in Normandy at Notre-Dame-sur-l'Eau at Domfront (Orne). A single nave aisle is often associated with Augustinians as at Brinkburn (Northumberland), but was also used in Wales by the Tironensians at St Dogmaels (Pembrokeshire).

The three-bay rather than a two-bay presbytery, as at Leonard Stanley, is rather ambitious, as is the inclusion of the vault with the differentiation between the rib-vaulted eastern bay and the barrel-vaulted western bays (figs. 119–120). Why should there be this difference in vault type in such

Fig. 128 Former west portal at Ewenny priory

a relatively small space? The answer is threefold. In the first place, the four-part rib vault allows for the use of side windows in the eastern bay to augment the illumination provided by the triple eastern windows for the high altar. The use of side windows in the other bays is precluded by the use of barrel vaults in the side chapels. Secondly, while it would have been possible to build rib vaults in the western bays of the presbytery, the barrel is easier and cheaper to construct than the rib vault. Thirdly, and most importantly, the rib vault provides a permanent ciborium over the high altar. This adapts a well-established tradition that goes back to Early Christian Rome, as in Old St Peter's. Subsequently, it is reflected in the early eleventh-century ciborium in Milan, Sant Ambrogio (fig. 129), and in the twelfth century in the ciborium of the nave north altar at San Juan de Duero at Soria (Castille).[74] In Liguria, the apse at Ventemiglia cathedral is rib vaulted while the other main spans are barrel-vaulted, and the same arrangement is common in Romanesque Provence, as at Saint-Paul-Trois-Chateaux, Saint-Restitut and elsewhere.[75] In the Romanesque rib-vaulted apses in Provence, the ribs course consistently with the ashlar web of the vault and, therefore, the ribs have neither specific structural nor constructional value, instead serving an iconographic purpose, to mark the high altar. The Ewenny presbytery vault was almost certainly modelled on the one in the presbytery of the mother-house of St Peter's, Gloucester, in which there is good evidence to suggest that there was a four-part rib vault in the three-sided apse and a barrel vault over the straight bays.[76] It is also possible that the apse of the barrel-vaulted presbytery at the nearby St Mary at Tewkesbury was also rib vaulted; the south transept chapel there has a rib-vaulted apse and a short barrel-vaulted forebay. The same juxtaposition of rib-vaulted apsidal altar space and barrel-vaulted 'choir' is found in the transept crypts at Christchurch (Twyneham) priory.[77] At Saint Martin at Saint-Georges-de-Boscherville (Seine-Martime) ribs are used in the apse while the two-bay choir is groin-vaulted.[78]

The closest formal comparisons for the placement of the shafts of the rib vault on a string-course at windowsill level at Ewenny, are in the rib-vaulted chancels of Heddon-on-the-Wall and Warkworth (Northumberland).[79] Both churches reflect the designs in the three-storey elevations at Durham cathedral and the closely dependent Lindisfarne priory. In the presbytery and east elevation of the transepts at Durham and in the nave of Lindisfarne, the shafts of the high vault rest on the sill of the gallery. Heddon and Warkworth therefore read as scaled-down versions of these schemes. The Durham/Lindisfarne pattern was also used in the nave of St Peter's, Gloucester, and the latter is the most likely source for the Ewenny design.[80] The Gloucester high-vault responds were removed when the present vault was built before 1242 but a possible reflection

Fig. 129 Milan, S. Ambrogio: ciborium showing a rib vault over a high altar

Fig. 130 Much Wenlock: south wall of the chapter house

of their form is in the chapter house of Much Wenlock priory (figs. 101 and 130). Here, as in the east bay of the Ewenny presbytery, the vault ribs are carried on columns that sit on a chevron string-course above a plain lower wall (figs. 118 and 130). Moreover, the ribs profile is the same in both places — twin rolls separated by an angle fillet — and in each case the diagonal ribs are carried on diagonally set capitals, a detail not common in Anglo-Norman Romanesque vaulting.[81] Seeing that this rib profile is also used in the north nave aisle of Gloucester cathedral, it seems reasonable to suggest that the responds of the nave high vault there would have been the source for the diagonally set capitals at Ewenny.

One aspect of the articulation of the Ewenny presbytery vault is unusual — the alternation of major and minor transversals. It is true that this may have been paralleled in the original Romanesque high vault in the presbytery of Durham cathedral, but there it was used in connection with a rib vault, and the alternation is between major and minor piers in the main arcades. The best parallel is in wooden vault or wagon-roof construction, as in the late medieval nave of Cullompton (Devon) with major and minor arched braces, the former carried on short hammer beams, the latter just starting at the springing of the roof (fig. 131). In turn this is frequently paralleled in common rafter construction in which the principal rafters are carried on wall posts but the minor rafters are not. There is evidence in the nave of Tewkesbury that in the eastern bays the Romanesque high vault was built of tufa but that the remainder of the nave had a wooden barrel vault.[82] The transept chapels at Ewenny were also barrel vaulted, which gave an architectural significance to these as subsidiary altar spaces.

Turning to the original painted decoration, close parallels for the red fictive joints are found in Archbishop Thomas of Bayeux's work at York Minster, and on the east respond of the south nave arcade and in the nave clerestorey at Blyth priory (plates 4, 7 and 8).[83] Geographically closer to Ewenny similar work can be seen in the passage to the upper

Fig. 131 Cullompton (Devon), St Andrews: the nave roof, a possible parallel for the Ewenny presbytery vault

chapel of the south transept at Tewkesbury abbey, and Tristram recorded analogous paint at St Peter's, Gloucester. For the capital frieze of lozenges between the central and north window, analogues are in the tympana of the niches of the great tower at Chepstow, and on the jambs of the chancel arch at Middleton-on-the-Hill (Herefs.) (figs. 16, 71 and plate 9). More complex renditions of the same theme are found in the chancel at Kempley — on a frieze on the east wall below the window sill and at either end of the barrel vault — and on the some of the piers in the south nave triforium at Leominster priory. The segmental arch painted on the wall between the central and south window of the east wall at Ewenny finds parallels in the bishop's chapel at Hereford cathedral and the undercroft at Monmouth castle, and also in the arches above the westernmost two apostles on the north wall of the Kempley chancel.

The arches to the transept chapels each have different ornamental detail. Such variety is often associated with later, very prestigious Romanesque work as at St Cross at Winchester for Henry of Blois, abbot of Glastonbury (1126–71) and bishop of Winchester (1129–71). In this he follows Bishop Roger of Salisbury (1102–39) and his work at Sarum cathedral from which eighteen different types of chevron are preserved, and the dado arcade of Ludlow castle chapel. The same principle is evidenced in the adjacent doorways in the west wall of the south transept and the south wall of the nave.

Communication between the north nave aisle and the north transepts through a doorway, rather than an open arch, is paralleled at Bishop's Cleeve (Glos.) and Ripple (Worcs.), both of which belonged to the bishop of Worcester.[84] It is therefore possible that this arrangement reflects the original design of Romanesque Worcester cathedral.

The piscina in south wall of east bay of the presbytery is largely rebuilt but there is no reason to doubt its basic authenticity. The architectural integration of the piscina is a feature of early Cistercian churches in England as at Rievaulx, Fountains and Kirkstall, but Ewenny predates these examples. Aumbries, like the one in the north wall of the presbytery at Ewenny, are found at Kempley and Dymock in the north wall of the presbytery, and in the south wall at Rudford (all Glos.).

The triforium in the west wall of the south transept is a feature normally associated with larger churches as at the great Benedictine abbey churches of Tewkesbury and Pershore and St Werburgh's (cathedral), Chester. The motif appears on a smaller scale at the collegiate church at Gnosall (Staffs.) where, as at Ewenny, it leads from a spiral stair in the south-west angle of the south transept to the crossing tower.

The north nave arcade on columns should be compared with the presbytery of St Peter's, Gloucester, the nave of Shrewsbury abbey, and the nave of Malvern priory. In smaller churches, the nave of St Nicholas at Gloucester provides an excellent example, and in Wales similar arcades appear in the nave of St Woolos at Newport (fig. 216). The wide range of scalloped capitals used at Ewenny was also inspired by St Peter's abbey, Gloucester, where they were used in the crypt, and in the nave aisles and triforia.

In conclusion, Ewenny is the best-preserved example of a Norman priory church in south Wales. The fabric was clearly the product of a single building campaign undertaken by William de Londres for the establishment of a group of Benedictine monks, a foundation confirmed in 1141 by Maurice de Londres. All aspects of its design relate closely to near-contemporary work across the border in England, not least to the mother church of St Peter's, Gloucester. The parallels cited for numerous details of the fabric are far more in keping with a date around 1120 and the patronage of William de Londres, than one associated with Maurice de Londres in 1141. The presbytery vault is a unique survival and provides important clues as to the appearance of the lost presbytery vaults at Gloucester and Tewkesbury. This vault along with the rich painted decoration and variety in ornamental detail make it clear that William de Londres was keen to emulate the richness of the larger Benedictine abbey churches in England.

Ogmore Castle (Glamorgan)

The pairing of priory church and castle encountered at Chepstow and Monmouth was matched at Cardiff where just the shell of the polygonal keep survives,[85] while Ewenny was paired with Ogmore where the castle was established by William de Londres. Located on the east bank of the River Ewenny one and a half miles from the sea there are substantial remains of the Norman keep and a contemporary rectangular building to the east known as the cellar.[86] The rectangular keep, measuring 35ft by 20ft, was originally of two storeys with the main hall on the first floor and stood within and to the west in an oval ringwork 170ft by 100ft. The keep has been attributed to William's son, Maurice de Londres, soon after his father's death in 1126, although Randall considered the keep to be late twelfth century.[87] Its west wall remains to its full height surmounted by a later storey above a bold string-course on the exterior. It is of local limestone rubble construction with a pronounced batter and squared Sutton stone quoins at the south-west angle. There is a later stair turret at the north-west corner. There are no buttresses. To the south of the centre of the wall, two windows light the first storey, the southern one of which is complete, while the northern one only has its original head. Inside, the division between the two original storeys is clearly marked by the row of square holes for the joists of the floor of the first storey, as at Chepstow (fig. 132). Against the east wall of the keep there is a large block of masonry which is probably the lower section of the staircase to the former main entrance on the first floor (fig. 132). Immediately to the left of this there are the jambs of the doorway to the basement. Inside the first storey, on the west wall immediately to the right of the right window, there remain three courses of the respond of a former partition

Fig. 132 Ogmore castle: the keep from the south-east

(fig. 132). The top course of the three is set back which indicates that a wooden lintel or arch of the partition sat at this point. In the northern room there is a grand fireplace with the ashlar springers of a segmental arch set on plain cushion capitals without abaci most closely paralleled in the aisle respond of the former bishop's chapel at Hereford (1079–95). Newman notes that this must be one of the earliest chimneypieces to survive in Britain.[88]

On the evidence of the fabric there seems to be no compelling reason to attribute Ogmore castle to Maurice rather than William de Londres. It is reasonable to suggest that work started when William returned to Ogmore after the 1116 attack by Gruffudd ap Rhys.

LLANGENNITH, ST CENNYDD (GLAMORGAN)

Between 1106 and 1115 the church of St Cennydd at Llangennith was granted to St Taurin at Evreux by Henry of Warwick, Lord of Gower.[89] At the east end of the north wall of the nave is a massive, plain tower, which is entered only from the nave through a low, narrow unmoulded pointed arch (fig. 133). In the east wall of the tower there is a blocked, plain, single-order, round-headed arch on plain jambs and chamfered imposts. The stonework of the exterior east wall shows no sign of former attached masonry so it was presumably cleaned up in restoration. The arch may have led to an apsidal chapel or simply to an altar niche. For the latter and the transeptal placement of the tower there is a parallel at Dunblane cathedral and it may possibly reflect Llandaff cathedral. The placement of the tower also relates to a number of parish churches in south-west England, which seem to have been inspired by the transeptally placed towers at Exeter cathedral.[90] Of these, Yarnscombe (Devon) provides a good parallel for the unmoulded, pointed entrance arch, while Stoke-sub-Hamden (Somerset) supplies a simple projection to the east of the eastern arch.

Transeptally placed towers also appear in Kent and Sussex and are popular in Romanesque Normandy. St Edmund at West Kingsdown (Kent) adopts the two-cell plan and south tower which has a large, single-order arch immured in the east wall as at Llangennith.[91] It may have opened into an apse as in the north tower at Godmersham (Kent) and formerly at St Lawrence at Bapchild (Kent) and St Simon and St Jude at East Dean (Sussex).[92] Architectural historian Stephen Heywood has demonstrated that the type is related to the north-east and south-east chapels of Anselm's choir at Canterbury cathedral as represented on the twelfth-century Waterworks

Fig. 133 Llangennith, St Cennydd: exterior from the north-east

Drawing in the *Eadwine Psalter* (Cambridge).[93] In Normandy there is the north-east tower at Tordouet (Calvados) which has a semi-domed apse and groin-vaulted forebay. Saint-Loup-Hors (Calvados) and Lion-sur-Mer (Calvados) each have a rib-vaulted south tower in a similar position to West Kingsdown. The inclusion of a tower suggests a specific use for the space as a chapel as at Canterbury cathedral or at Stoke-sub-Hamden (Somerset) where there is an altar niche in the east wall of the north-east tower. Alternatively it may have served as a baptistery, as later in the twelfth century at All Saints, Orpington (Kent), where the north tower is rib vaulted.[94] Ruprich-Robert suggested that the south-west tower of Saint-André d'Hébertot (Calvados) may have functioned as a baptistery.[95]

MONKTON (PEMBROKESHIRE)

Arnulph de Montgomery established the Benedictine alien priory of Pembroke — alias Monkton — as a daughter house of Sées, shortly after 1098.[96] All that remains of the Norman church is the aisleless nave, in the north wall of which there are two rubble-built, round-headed Norman windows (fig. 134). The south

Fig. 134 Monkton priory: the nave from the north

Fig. 135 (left) Monkton priory: south porch and Fig 136 (right) south portal

porch is entered through a plain, round-headed arch carried on trumpet-scallop capitals without necking and coursed nook shafts with moulded bases (fig. 135). The south doorway has four continuous roll mouldings without bases and with deep hollows between the rolls (fig. 136). It is framed with a hollow-chamfered quirked hood on restored heads.

The nave has a pointed barrel vault which seems to be contemporary with the fourteenth-century chancel arch rather than with the Norman fabric; see the two massive stepped buttresses added to the north wall of the nave (fig. 134). There is also a pointed barrel vault in the south transept, and one wonders whether this is a reflection of Cistercian practice possibly established at Whitland in the twelfth century. The absence of any detail on the north nave windows makes them impossible to date but the trumpet-scallop capitals of the south porch and especially the roll mouldings and hollows on the south doorway bring to mind work at St Davids cathedral after 1182.

St Dogmaels Abbey (Pembrokeshire)

St Dogmaels was founded by Robert fitz Martin between 1113 and 1115 for a prior and twelve monks of the order of Tiron on the site of the clas church of St Dogmael at Llandudoch, just south of Cardigan.[97] In 1120 Abbot William of Tiron consented to the founder's request that it became an abbey, and in that year Abbot Fulchard was installed by Bishop Bernard of St David's.[98] 'In 1138 Gruffudd ap Cynan's sons, Owain Gwynedd and Cadwaladr, in company with princes Anaraud and Cadell, brought a fleet of fifteen Norse ships (probably from Ireland) to campaign against the Normans in Ceredigion which resulted in the sack of the town and abbey of St Dogmaels.'[c99]

The church is in ruins but the crypt beneath the former eastern two bays of the aisleless presbytery is preserved to the springing of the vault. Also preserved are the lower

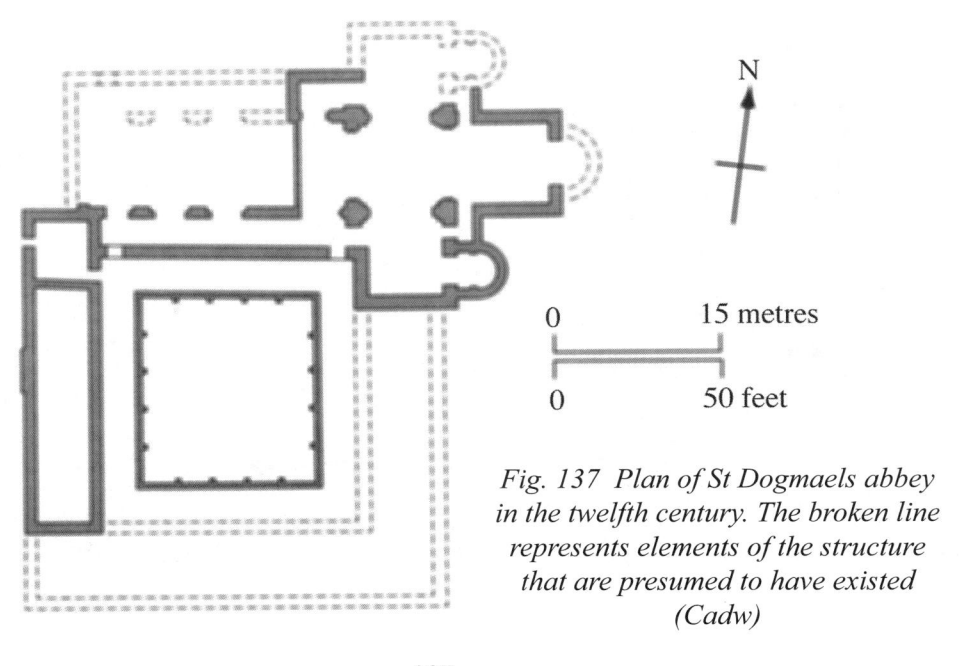

Fig. 137 Plan of St Dogmaels abbey in the twelfth century. The broken line represents elements of the structure that are presumed to have existed (Cadw)

courses of the crossing piers and the eastern wall of the south transept with its semi-circular chapel plus the rectangular piers of the former south nave arcade later immured in the north wall of the cloister (fig. 137).

The chronology of the church has been most fully discussed by Radford in the Department of the Environment guidebook, who detected two major campaigns of building in the twelfth-century church.[100] Of the first church there are the lowest courses of the crossing piers, the aisleless south transept with its apsidal eastern chapel, and the rectangular piers of the south arcade of the nave immured in the later south wall when the aisle was reduced in the thirteenth century. The crypt beneath the two eastern bays of the square-ended presbytery represents a rebuilding of the eastern arm of the church possibly precipitated by damage to the church in the Welsh war of 1191.[101]

One aspect of the planning of the crossing and transepts is unusual and requires comment with regard to the liturgical functioning of the church. Between the south-east crossing pier and the entrance to the south transept chapel there was a narrow opening that provided access to a short passage to the south side of the presbytery. It was probably matched in the north transept in the twelfth century. These entrances provided access to the presbytery past the choir stalls which would have occupied the space beneath the crossing, and would have functioned in a similar way to the doorways from the transept inner chapels to the presbytery at Ewenny priory.

The crossing piers of the Romanesque church have been related to those at Malmesbury abbey.[102] The parallel is based on the use of two half shafts to support the inner order of the east and west crossing arches (fig. 138). However, this feature is rather too common in the twelfth century to suggest a direct relationship. It is standard, for example, in the West Country School in the great Benedictine abbey churches of Gloucester, Tewkesbury and Pershore. The outer order of the responds of the east and west crossing arches, and both orders of the north and south arch responds, are quirked chamfers that are finished in arrow-like terminations. This is an unusual detail but one that is found on the chancel arch at Marcross (Glamorgan) (fig. 252), and, with volute tops, on the chancel arch at St Clears after 1147 (fig. 180).[103] Otherwise, the closest parallel I know is in the third order of the north respond of the chancel arch at Cormac's Chapel at Cashel (Tipperary) (1127–1134). This is important because two of the loose

Fig. 138 St Dogmaels abbey: south-west crossing pier from the north showing the use of two half shafts to support the inner order of the crossing arch, as at Malmesbury abbey

architectural fragments at St Dogmaels (nos. 47 and 48), are from the tops of these chamfers.[104] On no. 47 there is a small human figure, while on no. 48 there is a head carved in the pointed termination. Heads are used both at the top of the chamfered order level with the capitals and on alternate stones in the jambs and arch on the chamfered order of Cormac's Chapel chancel arch (fig. 139). There are also three capitals from the crossing (nos. 44–46), described by Radford as 'reeded',[105] although they are in fact scalloped with 'reeds' between the cones. This is not

Fig. 139 Cashel (Tipperary), Cormac's Chapel: the north capitals of the chancel arch, showing the use of heads, as evidenced at St Dogmaels abbey

especially informative with regard the dating of the work for such capitals are found at Ewenny around 1120 and also on the south doorway of Llandaff cathedral around 1185. The profile of the bases of the half shafts is more instructive for dating the fabric. They are best preserved on the south-west crossing pier and take the form of two stepped and somewhat flattened rolls (fig. 138). This is not a common type, and the earliest examples cited by Stuart Rigold in his detailed study of Romanesque bases are in the slype and south transept at Stoneleigh abbey (Warks.) after 1155.[106] On the east base it is accompanied by a spur that looks like an inflated laurel leaf. Spurs are used in West Country Romanesque architecture from the early twelfth century as at Exeter cathedral, commenced 1112/14, and Hereford cathedral, commenced 1107–1114, but these early examples take on a beaked form rather than the flattened leaf appearance of

Fig. 140 St Dogmaels abbey: south-east buttress to the presbytery

Fig. 141 St Dogmaels abbey: the crypt looking east

Figs. 142 and 143 St Dogmaels abbey: the south-west (left) and east (right) responds in the crypt

St Dogmaels.[107] The St Dogmaels type suggests a date in the second half of the twelfth century. In contrast to this the responds of the arch to the south transept chapel and those to the apsidal end of the chapel are absolutely plain. This probably indicates economy rather than an earlier date for the work.

The ruins of the rebuilt presbytery are set on ground that slopes down to the east with the result that the square sub-plinths of the buttresses are tallest on the east wall. The best preserved is at the south-east angle where the sloping, two-course plinth is topped by a roll moulding (fig. 140). The form is similar to that used in the Lady Chapel of Glastonbury abbey, 1184–1186/89.[108] In the two eastern bays there is a crypt, square in plan and divided into four bays each formerly covered with a four-part rib vault (fig. 141). The corner responds have single, filleted shafts with trumpet-scallop capitals in the eastern angles, and foliage capitals with upright leaves that terminate in volutes (figs. 141 and 142). Triple shafts with trumpet-scallop capitals are used on the responds on the north and south walls (fig. 141), and a variant of this design is used in the middle of the east wall (fig. 143). Here the central shaft has a nib rather than a fillet, and there are narrower lateral shafts and a hollow between the shafts. All

CATHEDRAL, CASTLE AND MONASTERY POST 1120

the abaci are round and the bases are all water-holding.

The details of the crypt accord happily with a date after the war of 1191. Triple shafts with trumpet-scallop capitals conform to Harold Brakspear's late twelfth-century 'West Country School of Masons'.[109] Trumpet-scallop capitals with rounded abaci are used in the presbytery of Llanthony priory after 1171. Fillets are fairly unusual at this time but they make an appearance in the 1170s in the south nave arcade and the doorways at St Mary's, Shrewsbury. This is interesting because the closest parallel for the unusual foliage capital with volutes at St Dogmaels is with the capitals of the south-east crossing pier of Old St Chad's, Shrewsbury (figs. 142 and 144). This may suggest that the mason who designed the St Dogmaels crypt had earlier worked in Shrewsbury.

Fig. 144 Shrewsbury, St Chad: south-east crossing capitals which show carving similar to that at St Dogmaels

BRECON PRIORY (NOW CATHEDRAL)

Brecon priory was founded about 1110 by Bernard de Neufmarché, Lord of Brecon, who built a castle at Brecon and gave the church of St John the Evangelist without the walls to Roger, a monk of Battle abbey.[110] Nothing remains of the Norman fabric of either the castle or the church but the font is related to the Herefordshire School of sculpture.[111] The chalice-shaped bowl sits on a cylindrical stem decorated with fine intersecting arches and a projecting base decorated with a badly worn foliage trail (fig. 145). The top of the bowl has a frieze of symmetrical beaded interlace. The remainder of the bowl was originally occupied with six beaded medallions that issue from the gaping mouths and ears of masks, the mouths deriving from classical theatrical masks.

Fig. 145 Brecon priory (now cathedral): font Now just four of the medallions remain.

Fig. 146 Brecon priory (now cathedral): font

To the right of the damaged section, the first medallion is filled with a dragon carved in profile with head upside down in the lower right of the medallion (fig. 146). Just below the neck there projects a short leg that claws at the elongated lower lip. A wing that curls around the short leg ends up in the mouth of the dragon. The long, beaded tail grows into the bottom section of the medallion to terminate in an arrow-like just below the beast's head. The second medallion is home to a long-necked bird that stands virtually erect with large wings flared down and broadly spread tail feathers (fig. 146). The creature turns its head as if in readiness to preen its back feathers. The third medallion is inhabited by a biped with a long neck, back-turned head, and a long snout (fig. 145). The worn front leg is raised to scratch the side of the adjacent mask. The body extends across the medallion and has a large striated belly, its long tail curling in front of the body and flipping up into the mouth of the creature. The fourth medallion has symmetrical foliage that grows from a central stem that stands on a two-step base (fig. 145). The upper leaves with hollowed lobes spread in palm like fashion while below, smaller leaves grow up from near the bottom of the stem.

The proportions of the chalice-shaped bowl, the stem and base of the Brecon font relate closely to the Herefordshire School font at Stottesden (Salop) on which there is also an interlace frieze and beaded inhabited medallions joined by masks.[112] In the Herefordshire School medallions inhabited by a variety of creatures and joined by grotesque masks appear on the second order of the south doorway at Kilpeck, and on the fourth pillar of the chancel arch at Shobdon.[113] The dragon in the first medallion at Brecon is a cousin of the one on the fourth voussoir from the right on the inner order of the south doorway at Kilpeck. The pose of the beast in the third medallion with back-turned head, raised front leg and tail swept over the hind quarters is a composite of a number of quadrupeds on the fourth pillar of the chancel arch at Shobdon. Interestingly the bird is of a different species to the one most prevalent in the Herefordshire School, in which birds are invariably shown in profile with either crescent-shaped or straight wings. The essentially frontal pose, long neck and flared wings are ultimately derived from Roman imperial eagles like the bronze one in the Coptic Museum in Cairo. The inspiration may have come via Byzantine silks, such as the bird silk preserved in the treasury of Sens cathedral, M 1193, in which the bird inhabits a medallion, as at Brecon.[114]

The quality of the sculpture on the Brecon font falls somewhat below the standard of the best work of the Herefordshire School. It is flatter and lacks precision, factors that ally it more closely with the other fonts that derive from the Herefordshire School at Morville and Linley (Salop), on which there are symmetrically arranged lobes of foliage in medallions similar to those at Brecon.[115] These are also related to a foliated medallion on the font at Rock (Worcestershire).[116]

On the rim of the Brecon font there is a damaged inscription which MacAlister suggested 'seems to be intended for an abbreviation or paraphrase of the account of the baptism of Our Lord, as it is contained in the Gospel of St Mark, I, 9-11, with some suggestions from the parallel text in St Matthew, iii, 13'.[117]

Malpas, St Mary (Gwent)

The present church was built by John Pritchard 1849–50, as an elaborate 'copy' of the twelfth-century chapel of the Cluniac cell of Montacute which had been founded before 1122 by Winibald of Caerleon.[118] William Coxe, in *An Historical Tour In Monmouthshire* (1801), gives the following description of the church before the rebuilding:

> It is a small building of unhewn stone, of an oblong shape like a barn, with a belfry having two apertures for bells. The arched door which is on the western side, the stone frames of the three principal windows, as well as the arch which separates the chancel from the church, are all rounded, and decorated with friezes of hatched moulding, denticles, and receding columns, peculiar to the Saxon and Norman architecture. The arch of the southern window, which seems to have been a doorway, is more elegantly ornamented, and embossed with roses, not unlike the Etruscan style. All the columns, which are mostly of a rude form, have dissimilar capitals and shafts, a striking feature in Saxon structures. Some modern gothic windows have been introduced into the stone frames of the original apertures.

Fig. 147 Malpas, St Mary: exterior from the north-west before 'restoration' (after Westwood)

Coxe also includes an engraving by Sir R.C. Hoare, bart., of the church from the south-west before the restoration.[119] The details in the engraving are not precise but at least some points may be checked against the present church and also compared with drawings made immediately before Pritchard's rebuilding of the church (figs. 147–150).[120] The west central doorway had three orders; there was a string-course above at the level of the base of the gable, and a round-headed, enriched window in the west gable (fig. 147). There is no evidence for the pilaster angle buttresses of the present fabric, and the belfry has been 'Normanized' in the rebuild. The inner order of the west doorway was plain and continuous. Orders two and three both had chevron in the arch and were carried on scalloped capitals with chevroned abaci (fig. 148). The outer left shaft appears to have been decorated although it is unclear whether a chevron or spiral design was used (figs. 147 and 148). Rather than recreating the original west doorway, Pritchard made a copy of the north nave doorway of Llandaff cathedral, even down to the dog-tooth hood mould, but minus the head of the bishop at the apex of the arch. Pritchard seems to have been less inventive with the west window in which the evidence suggests that he based his work on the original. In particular, the left capital copies the original as illustrated by Westwood in his 1879 article on Malpas church (figs. 149 and

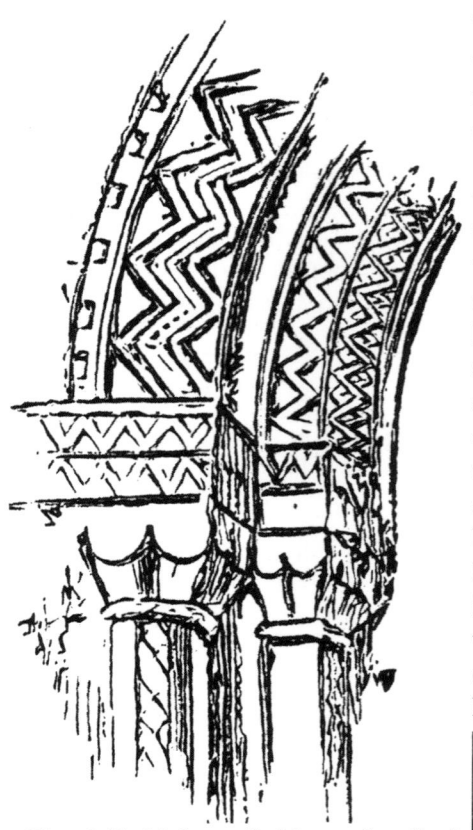

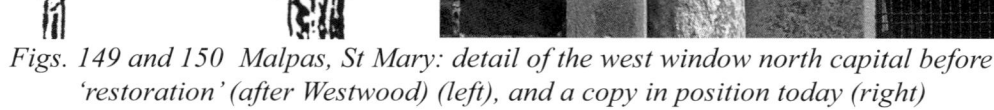

Fig. 148 Malpas, St Mary: detail of the west portal before 'restoration' (after Westwood)

Figs. 149 and 150 Malpas, St Mary: detail of the west window north capital before 'restoration' (after Westwood) (left), and a copy in position today (right)

150).[121] Westwood observed that it was 'very similar in design' to the capitals of the presbytery east arch at Llandaff cathedral (figs. 96, 147 and 150).[122] The right capital belongs with the outer left capital of the same Llandaff arch and also with one of the presbytery south window capitals (plate 5, figs. 100 and 151).

In the south wall there is a round-headed doorway about halfway down the nave, and a string-course above at the level of the sill of round-headed windows. Coxe described roses carved on the south portal but none appear in the present church. Fortunately, Westwood included an illustration of the single-order doorway complete with 'roses' and chevron in the arch, a scalloped capital to the right, and a foliage capital on the left (fig. 152). The 'roses', that look more like daisies, are closely related to those on the abaci of the responds towards the west end of the north nave aisle at St Peter's, Gloucester.[123] Details of Pritchard's side windows of the nave suggest that they may reflect the originals (fig. 153). These have plain scalloped capitals without abaci as in the bishop's chapel at Hereford, and quadrant rolls in the jambs as in the presbytery aisles at St Peter's, Gloucester, and the crossing piers at Milborne Port (Somerset). These motifs are relatively unusual and are unlikely to have been invented by Pritchard.

The chancel arch at Malpas has been heavily restored and the head of the arch appears to be entirely by Pritchard. However, the capitals seem to be original, albeit sharpened up in the restoration. On the south respond the outer order to both the east and west is carried on scalloped capitals each with patterned friezes at the top (fig. 154). On the east side there is incised chevron above chip-carved lozenges, while

Fig. 151 The south capital on the west window

Fig. 152 The south portal before 'restoration' (after Westwood)

on the west horizontal bars are topped with incised chevron. On the west capital there is an angle volute at the top of two fleshy stems that frame a stylized fern leaf. The central capital has a frieze of roundels in which six-petalled flowers flank a central beaded roundel. On the north respond in the centre there is a volute capital with a bird carved on the main face, and this is flanked to the east by a volute capital, and, to the west, with a scalloped capital (fig. 155). The six-petalled leaves in roundels are paralleled on the Bredwardine

Fig. 153 South window in the nave which may reflect the original

Fig. 154 The original, albeit sharpened, south capitals under the new chancel arch

Fig. 155 North capitals on the chancel arch

lintels and we have met the beaded roundel at Llandaff (figs. 78–80 and 154). The volute capitals belong to a tradition established in Normandy in the second half of the eleventh century, although the volute on the west nook shaft of the south respond at Malpas finds its closest family associations in the chancel arches at St Donats (Glamorgan) and St Clears (Carmarthenshire) (figs. 154, 180, 181 and 253). I do not know of exact comparisons for the variations on the scalloped capitals but given the diversity in the details of this motif the lack of a precise parallel should not be surprising. As a whole the range of motifs suggests that there was no delay in starting the work with the foundation of the priory before 1122.

Goldcliffe (Gwent)

The Benedictine priory of Goldcliff was founded in 1113 by Robert de Chandos, lord of Caerleon, for a prior and twelve monks, subject to Bec in Normandy.[124] No trace of the church or monastic buildings remains today but there are two fragments of fret (meander) ornament reused on the exterior south wall of the nave of the parish church of St Mary Magdalen (fig. 156). The high quality of the carving suggests that it is more likely to come from the priory than from an earlier parish church. The motif is not a common one and seems to have been used first in Bishop Roger's cathedral at Sarum, subsequently appearing in the nave of Malmesbury abbey, and on the west portal of St Nicholas, Kenilworth, moved from the Augustinian priory church there.

Fig. 156 Goldcliff, St Mary Magdalene: fragment of meander ornament on the exterior of the south nave wall

Tintern Abbey (Gwent)

In 1131, just three years after the establishment of the first Cistercian house in England at Waverley (Surrey), Walter fitz Richard (d.1138), lord of Chepstow, founded Tintern as a daughter house of l'Aumône (Loir-et-Cher).

Of the early stone church nothing remains above ground and archaeological evidence for its form is far less secure than has been supposed, as David Robinson, an authority on Cistercian architecture in Wales, has clearly indicated.[125] Plans with a short, square-ended, aisleless sanctuary, an undefined crossing area with one- or two-bay transepts to north and south and square chapels to the east, plus an aisleless nave, have been proposed. However, as Robinson observed, 'the plan is by no means as well defined as we might think'.[126]

THE PATRONAGE OF ROBERT, EARL OF GLOUCESTER, LORD OF GLAMORGAN c.1114–1147, & HIS SON WILLIAM, 1147–1183

Robert, Earl of Gloucester, the illegitimate son of Henry I and a major supporter of Matilda from mid 1138 during the period of Anarchy, is a renowned patron of architecture. In Wales, he built the polygonal keep at Cardiff, the castle at Kenfig and founded a Cistercian abbey at Margam shortly before his death. Robert was succeeded by his son, William, who continued with his father's building work at Margam. In 1166 he founded Keynsham abbey and this connection may explain the use of progressive French-inspired motifs on the west front at Margam.

Kenfig Castle (Glamorgan)

At Kenfig the remains of what must have been a magnificent Norman castle have been excavated.[127] The excavation exposed the north-east clasping buttress with its battered plinth faced in fine ashlar, and a scalloped nook-shaft capital of a scale better suited to a window rather than a portal.[128] The castle was established by Robert, earl of Gloucester, Lord of Glamorgan, *circa* 1121–1147.[129] Between 1140 and 1147 Robert granted to Ewenny priory, 'a burgage in the west street ... outside the gate of the vill of Kenefec',[130] but whether or not Robert, or his successor, Earl William (1147–1183), was responsible for the masonry fabric of the great tower of the castle is a moot point. Robert is associated with the construction of a huge keep (estimated at 90ft by 75ft) at Bristol, for which stone was imported from Normandy, and which was described in the thirteenth century as the flower of English keeps.[131] In light of this it seems unlikely that Robert would have been satisfied with anything other than a stone tower at Kenfig.

About 1137 Robert founded the Benedictine priory church of St James at Bristol as a daughter house of Tewkesbury, and shortly before his death in 1147 Robert founded the Cistercian abbey of Margam.[132]

Margam Abbey (Glamorgan)

The first abbot, William of Clairvaux, and a colony of monks arrived from France in November 1147.[133] We have already encountered the Cistercians at Tintern but that community established no daughter houses in Wales. In 1140 Cistercians from Clairvaux were established at Little Trefgarn, near Haverfordwest, under the patronage of Bishop Bernard of St Davids, and in 1147 the former Savignac house at Neath, which had been established in 1130, became Cistercian. Neath was rebuilt in the thirteenth century leaving only a few clues as to the form of the twelfth-century church in the south transept and south nave aisle.[134] The site at Little Trefgarn did not prove suitable, and about 1151 the establishment was moved to Whitland, which was to play an important role in the spread of Cistercian monasticism in Wales, establishing daughter colonies at Strata Florida (1164), Strata Marcella (1170) and Cwmhir (1176). In 1165 Whitland and Strata Florida attracted munificent patronage from Rhys ap Gruffudd, Prince of Deheubarth (d.1197). In light of this important position, it is a pity that Whitland is not better preserved, but it has been excavated to reveal the plan of the twelfth-century church, which is left exposed.[135] This is important because Whitland preserves its twelfth-century, so-called Bernardine plan. There was a short, rectangular presbytery, narrow, two-bay transepts, each with two square eastern chapels separated by solid walls, and an eight-bay nave with cruciform piers. On the one hand, this may be related to Fontenay (Côte-d'Or) (1139–1147) complete with

Fig. 157 Margam abbey: looking east along the nave

Fig. 158 Margam abbey: western bays in the north nave elevation

the unsegregated crossing but possibly not the pointed arches to the arcades. On the other hand, it may indicate the form of the lost twelfth-century eastern arm and transepts at Margam abbey.

It is to the nave of Margam that we must turn to best experience early Cistercian architecture in Wales (figs. 157–159). The eastern arm, transepts and two eastern bays of the nave were rebuilt in the thirteenth century, to leave six bays of the original nave and the west front.[136] It is this twelfth-century nave that was taken over as the parish church after the dissolution. The church underwent 'restoration' in the early nineteenth century, when the present aisles and the gawky façade turrets were built (fig. 160). At this time, the twelfth-century work was either retooled or replaced, but in spite of the nineteenth-century appearance of the surface of the stonework of the west front, much of the detailing is essentially authentic.

The nave arcades have two-order, round-headed main arches that spring from quirked chamfered imposts on compound piers with corresponding squared stepped orders (figs. 157 and 158). In keeping with Cistercian practice, the design is simple and the quality of the ashlar masonry is excellent. However, the ashlar is used economically and is continued for only five or six courses in the spandrels of the arcades, above which there is rubble. The exception is in the jambs of the former clerestorey windows, the lower sections of which are visible above the main arcades where the plaster has been removed in the western bays of the north elevation (fig. 158). The clerestorey windows have been truncated and blocked, but reference to the west front allows us to estimate the original height of the clerestorey and to suggest that the windows would have been round-headed. The nave aisles are now covered with lath-and-plaster groin vaults of circa 1805–1810 and it is possible that this reflects the twelfth-century arrangement (fig. 159).[137] Standard Cistercian practice is to have vaulted nave aisles, as at Fontenay, where transverse barrel vaults cover the aisles, a design adopted in the nave aisles at Fountains abbey (Yorkshire) around 1148. After 1152 rib vaults were used in the nave aisles of Fountains' daughter house at Kirkstall (Yorkshire), while around the same time groin vaults appear in the nave at Pontigny (Yonne). Be that as it may, the lack of any articulation on the aisle side of the main arcade piers, save the continuation of the imposts as a string-course, may indicate that the aisles would have been covered with wood, either a ceiling or open timber. A close parallel for Margam is in

Fig. 159 Margam abbey: south nave arcade from the south-west

Fig. 160 Margam abbey: the west front

the abbey church of Clermont (Mayenne), a Cistercian house founded in 1152 (fig. 161). The nave at Clermont shares with Margam the simple stepped piers — albeit without a step on the aisle side — with arches springing from chamfered imposts, a two-storey elevation without any vertical articulation, and wood roofs over the nave and aisles. In contrast to Clermont and the Burgundian roots of the Cistercians as exemplified at Fontenay, the main arcade at Margam is round-headed rather than pointed. Thus, the regional Romanesque tradition prevailed with the round-headed main arcades possibly looking back to the nave of Chepstow priory (figs. 28 and 29), or in even simpler form with square piers in the nave at Caerleon (Gwent) (fig. 222).

Fig. 161 Clermont abbey (Mayenne): a close parallel for Margam abbey

The simple, two-step plan of the piers is also paralleled in the lower section of the crossing responds at Ewenny priory.

The west front of the nave is heavily restored and yet in many respects reflects the original arrangement (fig. 160). The round-headed doorway has three orders with detached shafts and two sets of annulets, steep bases, richly carved capitals and different mouldings in each order of the arch (figs. 162 and 163). The annulets are not recorded in a 1777 drawing of the west front published by Grose, nor in Carter's drawing of 1803, but they both show annulets on the shafts of the windows above.[138] On the left splay, the capitals have evolved from the standard scalloped type. On the inner capital the scallop faces are deeply drilled and are partly masked with the stylized foliage that grows from the edges of each scallop. The middle capital has slightly recessed scallops and a row of fine holes drilled between each of the cones. The outer capital has undergone something of a metamorphosis in which the cones have become like stylized ribbon ferns, the tops of which merely imply a row of scallops at the top of the capital. It will also be noticed that the necking of each capital is different, and quite elaborate in the case of the outer capital. The outer

Fig. 162 Margam abbey: north capitals on the west portal

Fig. 163 Margam abbey: south capitals on the west portal

Fig. 164 Margam abbey: west windows

Fig. 165 Margam abbey: detail of the northernmost west window

capital of the right splay of the doorway presents another variation on the theme of the scalloped capital. Here the scalloped form is easily recognized but sprouting up from the cable necking there are four laurel-like leaves. The foliage theme then takes over completely on the two other capitals with stylized acanthus leaves. In the arch, the inner order has an angle roll, the middle order a cabled version of this motif, while the outer order has a stepped triple roll. At the bottom of each order of the arch there are variously detailed springing stones.

Above the doorway are three equally sized, round-headed windows each with three orders (fig. 164). The inner order is plain and continuous, while the middle and outer orders both have detached shafts each with three annulets, carved capitals and moulded arches. The capitals again play with variations on the scalloped theme although without the same degree of experimentation as in the doorway. The arch mouldings, on the other hand, are typologically more advanced than in the doorway with their thinner roll moulding set against a broad hollow, and the outer roll enlivened with a gorge (fig. 165).

Fig. 166 Fontenay abbey (Côte d'Or): west front

    The contrast between the richness of this arch decoration on the façade and the austerity of the nave arcades could hardly be greater, and one may be forgiven for thinking that this amazing encrustation of ornament on the façade is alien to the notion of Cistercian simplicity. Comparison with Fontenay (Côte d'Or) (1139–1147) is instructive here. The west front of Margam shares with this Burgundian counterpart the single round-headed doorway, simple pilaster buttresses between the nave and aisle façades, and a reduced version of the fenestration — rather than two tiers of windows at Fontenay, Margam uses a triplet as in the upper tier at Fontenay (figs. 160 and 166). Even the three corbels set just below the windows are common to both façades and are a sure indication that, like Fontenay, Margam had a narthex-like porch. While the Margam doorway is much richer than at Fontenay, the latter is in turn more elaborate than the nave arcades of the church, in that various mouldings are used in the arch. Moreover, in the arches of the chapter house façade at Fontenay every order boasts a different profile and there are even ornamented springing blocks as on the Margam west portal (figs. 162, 163 and 167). This delight in variety in detailing may be paralleled in a Cistercian context in England in the west portal at Fountains abbey. It is also in keeping with the regional aspects of variety that we have seen in Llandaff cathedral and Ewenny priory.

    The details of the capitals and mouldings of the west doorway and windows serve as guides to the date of the façade of the church. The inventive variations of the theme of the scalloped capital, and their use alongside stylized acanthus foliage types, suggests a bracket of 1160 to 1180 for the work. The foliage set against the deeply hollowed scallop faces on the inner left capital of the west doorway finds association with capitals in the west bays of the nave at Worcester cathedral, executed after 1175.[139] Also in this work at Worcester we find the juxtaposition of scalloped and acanthus foliage capitals, but there is one important difference between the two works. At Worcester the scalloped capitals take on a trumpet form whereas at Margam there is only the very slightest hint of this in the inner left capital of the west doorway. All the other scalloped capitals belong to the traditional form that we have seen at Ewenny and as late as the second half of the 1180s in the north and south nave doorways at Llandaff cathedral. The trumpet scallop is the most popular capital type at St Davids cathedral after 1182 and where foliage capitals are introduced it is the stiff-leaf convention, rather than acanthus, that is preferred. Therefore, on the evidence of the capitals the west front of Margam is unlikely to date after the 1180s. A similar conclusion is afforded by the mouldings.

Fig. 167 Fontenay abbey (Côte d'Or): chapter house entrance

The gorged roll was popular in the early Gothic of northern France, and good examples are seen in the windows of the ambulatory chapels of Noyon cathedral in the 1150s.[140] The motif was introduced into England in the presbytery of York Minster as rebuilt by Archbishop Roger of Pont l'Evêque (1154–81) after which it was disseminated throughout the north of England, to St Andrews cathedral-priory (commenced 1160–62) and Kelso abbey in Scotland, and to Trondheim cathedral in Norway.[141] At the same time it appears in the nave arcade of the Temple Church, London, which was finished in 1161, and in the late 1160s in the West Country at Keynsham abbey.[142] The motif never attained the popularity in the west that it did in the north, and its use at Keynsham emphasizes the French connections of the patron, Roger, Bishop of Worcester. Whether or not there is a direct connection between Keynsham and Margam, there can be little doubt that the use of the gorged roll at Margam should be explained by the desire to be up-to-date in design terms. The single roll moulding set in the broad hollow on the windows and the triple-roll

Figs. 168 and 169 St Brides-super-Ely: re-used arch from Margam abbey showing west and east capitals respectively

moulding on the outer order of the doorway are both used at Keynsham. This suggests that a date in the 1170s is more probable that one in the 1160s for the façade. Refinement of this date is at hand in the arch to the south porch at St Brides-super-Ely (Glamorgan) which had been reused from Margam abbey in an almshouse at Margam and was taken to St Brides by Mrs Charlotte Traherne, the rector's wife, sister of C.R.M. Talbot of Margam (figs. 168 and 169).[143] The arch is heavily restored, but the details appear to be authentic. It has two orders, the inner with lozenge chevron in the arch carried on scalloped capitals without abaci and coursed shafts. The outer order has a simple chamfer in the arch with a moulded stop and is carried on foliated trumpet-scallop capitals atop detached shafts. The hood mould is adorned with shuttlecock ornament. The scalloped capitals without abaci conform happily with this well-established type in south Wales, whereas the foliated trumpet-scallops are up to date in terms of Worcester and St Davids cathedrals. The shuttlecock motif appears on hood moulds on the south doorway of St Mary's, Shrewsbury, the right arch of the chapter house façade at Haughmond abbey (Salop), the north nave doorway at St Davids, on a fragment at from the north transept portal at Strata Florida abbey, in the presbytery at Christ Church cathedral, Dublin, and on the east arch of the south arcade of the presbytery at Stogursey priory.[144] St Mary's, Shrewsbury is not documented but probably dates from around 1175–80, and Christ Church, Dublin was commenced in 1186.[145] Although the original location of the St Brides' arch is not known, it seems likely that it would have come from an aisle façade. If this is the case then coupled with all the other evidence, it suggests a date bracket for the façade of 1175–85.

NEWCASTLE, BRIDGEND

A castle at Bridgend was probably established by Robert fitz Hamon by 1106. In his account of Bridgend castle in the Glamorgan volume of *The Buildings of Wales*, Newman observed that the present fabric is datable stylistically to the later twelfth century and 'may even have been built during the short period when it was held by Henry II, 1183–89'.[146] The Royal Commission offers a broader platform to Earl William of Gloucester (1147–83) and note that it is 'based on the current ascription of the gateway to the period 1150–80'.[147]

There is a curtain wall straight along the cliff-top that elsewhere forms an approximately round enclosure that probably follows the line of the late eleventh-century ringwork (fig. 170). To the south there is a mural tower and formerly one to the west, so the plan is a reduced version of Ludlow and is also related to Sherborne (Dorset), built by Bishop Roger of Salisbury (fig. 171).[148] There is an eight-feet-wide portal beside the south tower. This is richly

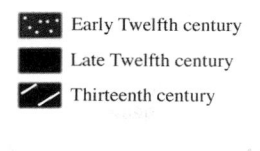

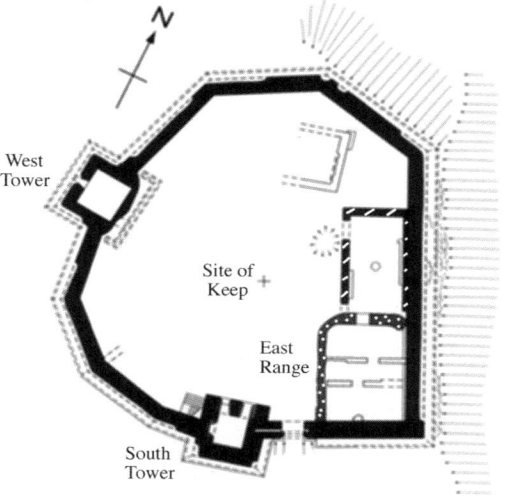

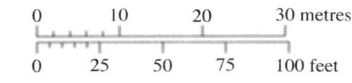

Fig. 170 Plan of Newcastle, Bridgend (Cadw)

Fig. 171 Newcastle, Bridgend: exterior from the south

articulated with a continuous inner order with segmental head and beaded straps, and an outer order with a roll moulding in the arch on volute capitals without abaci on coursed nook shafts (fig. 172). The plain tympanum is of coursed ashlar.

The beaded clasp ornament has been compared with the south doorway at Avington (Berks.), Chirton (Wilts.), the south doorway at Quenington (Glos.), South Cerney (Glos.) and the chancel arch at Stoneleigh (Warks.).[149] None of these is documented but many aspects of the sculptural decoration at Avington have been related to the work of Bishop Roger of Salisbury (d.1139).[150] Hugh de Lacy gave the church of Quenington to St Peter's, Gloucester.[151] South Cerney may have been built by Miles of Gloucester (d.1143). The Chirton doorway is pointed and typologically is the latest of the group in that certain heads in the arch have a naturalistic quality that suggests a date in the last third of the twelfth century. This accords happily with the suggestion that work on the church may be associated with the gift of the church to Lanthony Secunda in 1167.[152] Given this range of dates, it is clear that the beaded-strap motif is of little help in narrowing the date of the portal.

Fig. 172 Newcastle, Bridgend: south portal

The ashlar is finely jointed which may initially suggest a late twelfth-century date but this is a well-known feature of the work of Bishop Roger documented by William of Malmesbury. The segmental head recessed beneath the round-headed enclosing arch is found at Domfront (Orne), the Exchequer at Caen (Calvados), Corfe castle (Dorset), at Egremont castle (Cumbria) which has most recently been dated to the 1120s, in the main doorway inside the forebuilding at Orford (Suffolk) (1165–73), and in the outer forebuilding doorway at Newcastle-upon-Tyne (1168–78).[153] In the late twelfth century, segmental barrel vaults became popular over gatepassages, as in Henry II's inner bailey gatehouses at Dover. In the ecclesiastical realm a round-headed arch enclosing a segmental arch was originally included in the gatehouse of Bury St Edmunds abbey and, following that, in the south doorway at Wissington (Suffolk). Other examples include the north transept west portal at Dorchester abbey (Oxon), in the south portal of Sherborne abbey (Dorset), in the former pulpitum of Ely cathedral, and the south doorway at High Ongar (Essex) and

Plate 1 Chepstow castle: detail of bay 2 of the blind arcade in the interior north wall of the great hall. The tympanum at the back of the arch shows lozenges painted in white against a pinkish-red background. It is a very precious survival of early Romanesque painted decoration and may indicate the sort of coloured pattern that was applied to plain tympana in the Romanesque period

Plate 2 Lorsch abbey gatehouse, Darmstadt, Hesse, Germany: the first floor looking north. This shows the painted articulation of the wall in imitation of coloured marble revetment and a colonnade with Ionic columns. This sort of mimetic painting reflects Roman practice and presages fictive architectural articulation in the Romanesque period

Plate 3 Corvey abbey, Detmold, Westphalia, Germany, westwork: *detail of impost on the interior west wall at first-floor level. This illustrates the fusion of carved and painted articulation in a ninth-century Carolingian building. This tradition continued into the Romanesque period*

Plate 4 Blyth priory (Notts.): east respond in the south nave arcade. This is one of the best-preserved examples of early Romanesque painted masonry in England. The plastered stonework of the shaft is decorated with broad, red, fictive mortar joints. The capital is likewise plastered and painted with leaf designs that derive from classical acanthus foliage

Plate 5 Llandaff cathedral: detail of the north capitals on the eastern arch of the presbytery. These stylized foliage capitals, the chevron ornament and cable moulding on the abaci reflect contemporary work in St Peter's abbey, Gloucester, and Hereford cathedral

Plate 6 Llandaff cathedral: detail of the south capitals on the eastern arch of the presbytery. The angle mask with foliage issuing from the mouth is a popular motif in Romanesque sculpture

Plate 7 Ewenny priory: detail between the northern and central window in the east wall of the presbytery. The original Romanesque painted decoration is shown in the broad, red, fictive mortar joints in the arch and the painted lozenge frieze at the springing of the arch

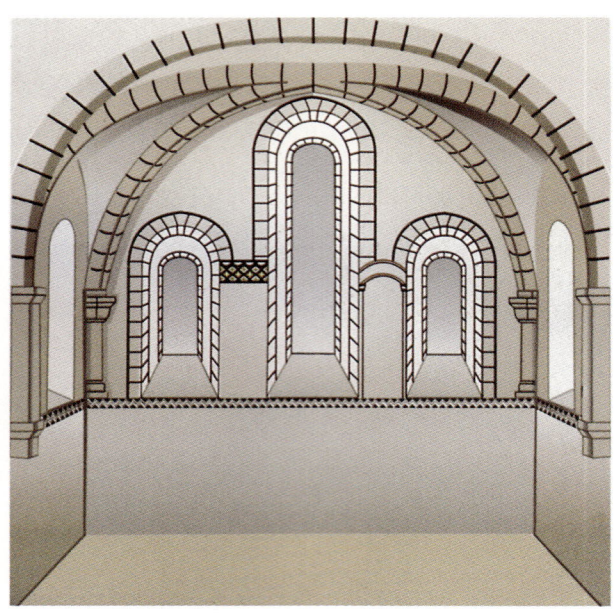

Plate 11 Ewenny priory: reconstruction of the 12th-century Romanesque painted scheme on the east wall of the presbytery (after Sophie Stewart).

Plate 8 Ewenny priory: detail of the vault rib in the eastern bay of the presbytery. This shows the limewash coating of the rib and the imitative mortar joints painted in red. Notice that the imitative joints do not coincide with the real mortar joints!

Plate 9 Ewenny priory: detail of the painted frieze between the northern and central window in the east wall of the presbytery. The lozenge design may be compared with the painted tympanum in the Great Tower at Chepstow castle (Plate 1)

Plate 10 Ewenny priory: detail of the painted arch between the southern and central window in the east wall of the presbytery. This is the sort of painted architectural articulation that derives from the tradition represented in the Lorsch abbey gatehouse (Plate 2)

Plate 12 Tretower castle from the south. In the projecting section of wall, just to the right of centre, is the chimney breast of the kitchen. Blocked Romanesque windows are seen in the wall to the left. The circular tower dates from the thirteenth century

Plate 13 Llanthony priory from the north-west in February snow

Plate 14 Newport, St Woolos: south capital from the north on the west doorway to the nave. The juxtaposition of the fish with the Trinity suggests association with baptism. The two round objects beneath the bird's wings are ampoules of Holy oil used in the sacrament of baptism

Plate 15 Newport, St Mary: the font from the south. Traces of limewash and red paint indicate that fonts like this would have been fully painted

Plate 16 St Davids cathedral: the east wall of the presbytery between the central and northern windows, with a lavish display of varied chevron ornament

CATHEDRAL, CASTLE AND MONASTERY POST 1120

Kirkburn (Yorks.), Shrewsbury St Mary west doorway and Lilleshall priory east processional, refectory and slype doorways.[154] Of these the Bury St Edmunds tower dates from the time of Abbot Anselm (1120–48) and there seems no reason to date High Ongar, Kirkburn or Wissington later than the middle of the twelfth century.

The capitals are not well preserved — on the right there are angle volutes and what appear to be short fat stems in the middle of each side (fig. 173). On the left capital the left volute is relatively intact and there are remains of the other two volutes (fig. 174). There appear to be arced, ribbon-like stems linking the volutes and plain straps, one horizontal around the middle of the capital and a looped one below. We have observed the absence of abaci elsewhere in Wales at Llandaff, Marcross and Ogmore castle. The detailing of the Newcastle capitals, however, is quite different from any of these examples, and also from the scalloped capital from Kenfig castle. The most instructive comparison is with the volute capitals on the chancel arch at St Clears which also provides a parallel for the heavy roll moulding in the arch at Newcastle (figs. 173, 174 and 179). Such details must be set against the more progressive foliage capitals and the more delicate and varied arch mouldings on the west doorway at Margam abbey, of the 1170s or 1180s (figs. 162–164). This contrast tends to weigh against attribution of Newcastle to Henry II. At Newcastle-upon-Tyne (Northumberland) between 1168 and 1178, and at Dover castle (Kent) in the 1180s, the work executed for Henry II was up to date in terms of the latest developments in ecclesiastical architecture. Parallels between Newcastle-upon-Tyne and the galilee chapel at Durham cathedral, and Dover and Canterbury cathedral, indicate that the king wanted nothing less than the latest and greatest in his architectural detailing.[155] In 1183 the Bridgend portal hardly fits these criteria. Moreover, following the death of William, earl of Gloucester, Henry II's work on the castles at Kenfig, Cardiff, Chepstow and Newport, is recorded in the Pipe Rolls.[156] If

Fig. 173 The east capital, south portal

Fig. 174 The west capital, south portal

129

the king was responsible for work at Newcastle then it is strange that the Pipe Rolls did not record it. Thus we are left with attribution to William, earl of Gloucester, and probably in the 1150s or 1160s.

Manorbier Castle (Pembrokeshire)

Manorbier castle was the home of William de Barri, father of Gerald de Barri alias Giraldus Cambrensis or Gerald of Wales, and is first mentioned in 1146.[157] Gerald tells us that 'in all the broad lands of Wales Manorbier is the most pleasant place by far'.[158] The

> fortified mansion ... stands visible from afar because of its turrets and crenellations on the top of a hill which is quite near the sea and which on the western side reaches as far as the harbour. To the north and north-west, just beneath the walls, there is an excellent fish-pond, well constructed and remarkable for its deep waters. On the same side there is a most attractive orchard, shut in between the fish-pond and a grove of trees, with a great crag of rock and hazel-nut trees which grow to a great height. At the east end of the fortified promontory, between the castle, if I may call it that, and the church, a stream of water which never fails winds its way along a valley, which is strewn with sands by the strong sea winds.[159]

Of the twelfth-century castle there remains the old tower and the hall, the former at the east end and the latter with the south-western section of the thirteenth-century curtain wall. The old tower is rubble built and is without distinguishing detail. The two-storey hall is also constructed of rubble and is without either plinth or buttresses (figs. 175 and 176).

Fig. 175 Manorbier castle: exterior of the hall from the west

CATHEDRAL, CASTLE AND MONASTERY POST 1120

Fig. 176 Manorbier castle: exterior of the hall from the east

The hall is topped with merlons that face a wall walk, all seemingly part of the original design.[160] The basement has three parallel barrel-vaulted chambers that occupy the southern two-thirds of the building, and a square, wood-ceiled room at the northern end, above the private apartment. The hall occupied the first floor above the barrel vaults, and is entered through a plain, round-headed doorway on the east side atop a later flight of stairs (fig. 176). Inside the hall to the right of the doorway is a huge fireplace and at the south end there is the head of a window above a later doorway (fig. 177). At the north end of the hall is the private apartment which was formerly separated from the hall with a wall (fig. 178). Above the basement the apartment has two floors, and in the north wall the square holes for the joists are

Fig. 177 Manorbier castle: the fireplace and the window head above a later doorway

131

quite evident. There is one window in the west wall to light each floor (fig. 178). The lower one is little more than a rectangular slit on the exterior but it splays out to a larger rectangular frame inside. The upper window is wider and on the exterior the lintel carries a tympanum of three courses of stonework framed in a semi-circular arch. The round-headed shape is kept throughout the deep splay of the window. In the middle of the north wall of the upper floor of the apartment is a fireplace and to the left of this a round-headed doorway that leads to a staircase on the left to the wall walk and, on the right, to the latrine.

The hall block of Manorbier castle is a very precious survivor of twelfth-century domestic architecture. In terms of the plan of the castle as a whole we may assume that the present curtain wall replaced a wooden precursor. The integration of the hall block with the curtain recalls Chepstow and is allied to Tretower castle. The old tower recalls Ludlow. For the hall block itself, the division of hall and solar may be paralleled with Christchurch (Dorset) and Boothby Pagnell (Lincs.).[161] The use of vaults beneath the hall is also paralleled at Boothby Pagnell, although with two bays of rib vaulting rather than three barrelled units. Boothby Pagnell is normally dated around 1200, and the waterleaf capitals in the rib-vaulted basement at Burton Agnes (Yorks.) indicate a date between 1160 and 1190. While the vaults at Manorbier are the typologically earlier barrel, the mere inclusion of vaults in the basement suggests a date towards the end of the twelfth century.[162]

The absence of architectural detailing precludes close dating of the work but certain aspects call for comment. The construction of the window to the second storey of the apartment with its coursed tympanum recalls the inner face of the east portal in the great tower at Chepstow. The use of a tympanum in a window seems to be exclusive

Fig. 178 Manorbier castle: the internal north-west corner of the hall, showing the deeply splayed west windows on each floor, the fireplace on the upper floor and the round-headed dooorway to its left

to secular architecture in the twelfth century. Examples are at Brough castle (Cumbria) and Portchester (Hants.) over double apertures under an enclosing arch, and with pointed arches in the hall at Oakham (Rutland). It is found in the late tenth century great tower at Langeais (Indre-et-Loire) and is common in Roman city gates and walls.[163] The wall walk with merlons on the outer plane of the wall is particularly fine example — it is interesting that the wall walk is also a feature of the Lady Chapel at Glastonbury abbey (1184–86/89), and one wonders about the iconographic significance of the exchange of this motif.

St Clears (Carmarthenshire)

St Clears was a Cluniac house, founded between 1147 and 1184 as a dependency of St Martin-des-Champs, for a prior and two monks.[164] It was both monastic and parochial. The chancel arch at St Clears is one of the most ambitious in Norman Wales (fig. 179), having three full orders that are articulated in such a way as to suggest even greater multiplicity of ordering. The inner order has a plain arch on chamfered imposts on chamfered jambs carved with a flat ribbon that terminates with a volute at the top, as in the crossing piers at St Dogmaels and the chancel arch at Marcross (Glamorgan) (fig, 252). Orders two and three have heavy roll mouldings in the arch which sit on carved capitals and coursed nook shafts. The moulding in order two is a semi-circular soffit roll and is larger than the more-complete cylinder of order three. This subtle differentiation is also expressed in the jamb shafts. The capitals are paired north and south (figs. 180 and 181). On order two there are volute capitals that terminate spiral rolls which on the south capital are set to either side of long thin stalks topped with simple stylized flowers, while on the north there are central cables. Beneath the angle volute on the south there are two lower legs and feet while to the north there is a depressed lozenge. The outer capitals have four small scallops on each face that top vertical cables separated by angle fillets. The face of the outer order is unadorned and stretches to the sides of the arch to read more like a separate continuous order. The arch is capped with a chamfered hood.

Deformation of the arch is evident yet the depressed trajectory is not simply the result of settlement. Rather it is a form of arch that found favour in the West Country in the late eleventh and early twelfth centuries.

Fig. 179 St Clears priory: the chancel arch

Figs. 180 and 181 St Clears priory: north capitals (top) and south capitals (lower) on the chancel arch

They occur in the crypt of St Peter's, Gloucester, between 1089 and 1100 where they are well suited to the limited height available. Such height limitation was not a factor in the bishop's chapel at Hereford (1079–95), nor was it in the near-contemporary north and south crossing arches of Milborne Port (Somerset). Milborne Port also supplies a good parallel for the heavy roll mouldings. These comparisons suggest that mouldings in the St Clears chancel arch are most conservative. The volute capitals also bring to mind eleventh-century parallels and it is only the cable decoration on the cones of the scalloped capitals that betrays a date in the third quarter of the twelfth century.

CATHEDRAL, CASTLE AND MONASTERY POST 1120

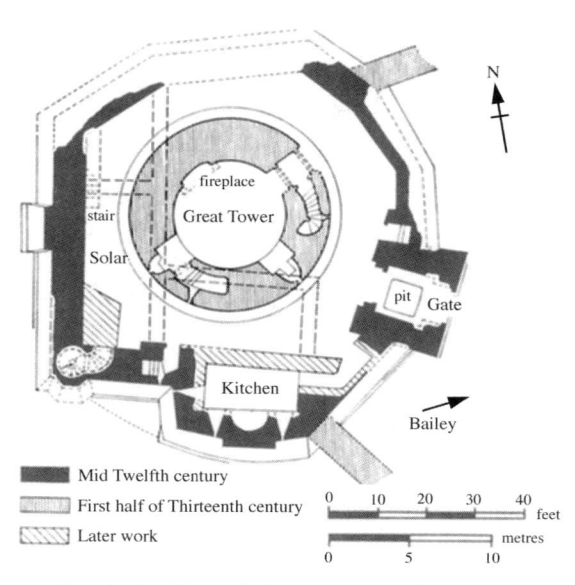

Fig. 182 Plan of Tretower castle (Cadw)

Fig. 183 Tretower castle: detail of the junction of the hall and kitchen

TRETOWER CASTLE (BRECONSHIRE)[165]
A motte-and-bailey castle of around 1100 was built by Picard who received part of the Ystrad Yw district from Bernard de Neufmarché as a reward for having participated in Bernard's occupation of the Usk valley. In the twelfth century a stone curtain was erected and inside (outside the mound) a shell keep was built in the form of an irregular polygon (fig. 182). There was a rectangular east gate tower of which the foundations remain, a first-floor hall with a kitchen on the ground floor off the south side, and a solar, or private living room, at right angles to the hall with a basement against the west wall. The inside walls of the kitchen, hall and solar were destroyed, probably in 1233, and subsequently the great round tower was erected by Roger Picard II,[166] but enough remains of the shell to provide a picture of the remarkably ambitious twelfth-century building. This has been dated to around the middle of the twelfth century, although, as we shall see, there is evidence for putting it closer to 1180.

Reading the exterior of the superstructure from right to left, there is a plain section of wall relieved only by a string-course at about two-thirds of its height (plate 12). Turning the angle there is the south wall of the kitchen in which there projects the chimney with a window to each side in the ground floor. Above the string-course the chimney tapers. The wall returns at right angles on the left to meet the western section of the south wall. The junction is not entirely comfortable especially between the adjacent windows of the first floor (fig. 183). On the left the round-headed

135

window has three orders that are plain and continuous for the first and third orders, and plain in the arch for order two on jambs with narrow coursed shafts and cushion capitals. Immediately to the right of this is the triangular head of a blocked opening set above the continuation of the string-course. To the left of the three-order window in the south wall, there is a smaller window with a continuous, plain outer order and an inner order with chamfered jambs that carry a plain tympanum (fig. 184). The south-west angle collapsed in 1947 but castle historian G.T. Clark described a half-octagonal tower there and his plan shows a spiral staircase.[167] In the west wall there is the projection for the chimney that tapers above the string-course as in the kitchen range (fig. 185). To the right, at first-floor level, there is a blocked window with a plain continuous single order (fig. 185). At the lower right-hand corner of this section of wall, immediately behind the damaged top of the battered plinth, there are the radiating voussoirs of a former arch, and there is similar evidence for an arch at this level towards the northern end of this wall. This indicates that the battered plinth is an addition to the fabric.

Moving inside, in the kitchen the semi-circular fireplace survives except for the hood (fig. 186). At the back of the fireplace there are small square openings that increased the draught for the fire. To the right of the kitchen there is a blocked, round-headed arch which led into the staircase up to the south end of the solar (fig. 187). Above this there is another defaced and blocked arch which is interpreted as a window by Radford and Robinson, the authors of the Cadw guidebook, and as a

Fig. 184 Tretower castle: exterior of window in the south wall of the hall

Fig.185 Tretower castle: exterior from the west showing the tapering outline of a chimney and a blocked window to its right

Figs. 186, 187 and 188 Tretower castle: the kitchen (left), interior looking south (upper right), and blocked doorway to hall (lower right)

doorway by Clark.[168] For the former reading, the level seems to concur with the three-order frame on the exterior at this point (fig. 187). However, the scale of the opening agrees with the blocked doorway below and therefore it may have opened to a stair that led up in the thickness of the wall, the top opening of which is still visible in the truncated end of the wall (fig. 187). The lower courses of the jambs of this doorway survive, albeit in a very weathered condition. There is furrowed chevron ornament to either side of an angle roll (figs. 188 and 189). Adjacent to the right jamb of this doorway is the damaged base and first stone of the jamb of the former doorway between the hall and the solar (fig. 189). To the right of this, in the remaining section

Fig. 189 Tretower castle: detail of the west jamb of the blocked doorway to the hall

Fig. 190 Detail of the south window of the hall showing chevron in the head

of the south wall of the solar, we see evidence for three more damaged arched openings. First, there is the doorway that opened from the staircase from the basement of the hall to the first floor of the solar (fig. 187). Above this there is the left jamb and arch springer of the inner plane of a window. It has two orders, the outer plain and continuous, the inner with traces of spiral ornament on a thin angle shaft, and with chevron in the head (fig. 190). Further to the right, and at a slightly higher level, there is the right jamb of another two ordered opening with a continuous outer order and an inner order on a paired shaft (fig. 187). Nothing remains of the arch which sprang from a higher level than the arch to the left. In the core of the wall, between these two openings, we see the voussoirs of the back of the tympanum window. The reconstruction here is not easy to envisage, but the difference in the level of the two windows indicates that an internal wooden staircase abutted at this point. At the end of this wall, immediately above these windows, there is a blocked wall passage.

Turning to the west wall of the solar we find further evidence for the floor levels. Towards the south and north ends of the basement there are blocked openings which, from their large scale, would appear to be doorways (fig. 191). However, reference to the immured voussoirs visible on the exterior suggests that they were deeply splayed windows, like those in the basement at Monmouth castle (figs. 116 and 185). Above this, the blocked fireplace marks the level of the floor of the solar, and this raises an important detail with regard to the doorway from the hall to the solar (figs.

187 and 191). On the one hand it accords happily with the arch from the stair from the basement of the hall. On the other hand, the threshold of the doorway from the hall is at a higher level and, therefore, it must have led onto a wooden platform from which stairs descended to the west. Above and to the left of the fireplace there is a window of two plain orders which, like the fireplace below, has a segmental head. The position of this window agrees with the frame of the blocked window on the exterior (fig. 185). At the bottom right of the inside of the window there are two projecting stones which may be associated with a gallery at this level reached by the putative wooden stair at the south end of the room. At the north end of the solar there is the arch and outer jamb of a wall passage that led from the solar to the north (fig. 192).

The window with the plain tympanum is a more accomplished version of this motif at Manorbier castle. The alternation between continuous and non-continuous orders on the window frame fits happily in a West Country Romanesque context, and the detail of the narrow angle shaft with cushion capital is happily paralleled in the windows at Dymock (Glos.) (figs. 183 and 193). The paired shaft on the solar south window is used for the outer order of the

Fig. 191 The solar undercroft

Fig. 192 West elevation of the solar showing the blocked wall passage

Fig. 193 Dymock (Glos.), St Mary (left): detail of window to the west of the porch on the south nave showing a narrow angle shaft with a cushion capital, as at Tretower castle

Fig. 194 Tretower castle (above): detail of string course on the south wall

chancel arch at Beckford (Worcs.). The chevron on the jamb of the doorway between the hall and the solar is of the right-angled type found in the nave clerestorey at St Peter's, Gloucester (figs. 101 and 189).

While such embellishment is not remarkable in ecclesiastical architecture, in the secular realm the inclusion of chevron and spiral shafts is ambitious and places it with lavish castles in England including Norwich, Rising (Norfolk), Hedingham (Essex), Sherborne and Goodrich.

The twelfth-century work is generally attributed to about 1150 and to Picard's son, Roger Picard. While there is nothing in the detailing of the castle examined so far to contradict this, the profile of the external string-course with the deep hollow moulding on the underside would be truly remarkable at such a time (fig. 194). On the one hand, the profile may be contrasted with the shallow hollow chamfer used on the strings at Malmesbury abbey in the third quarter of the twelfth century. On the other hand, close parallels are with Wells cathedral, started about 1175, and Glastonbury Lady Chapel and Great Church commenced 1184 and 1185 respectively.

Usk Priory and Castle (Gwent)

The Anglo-Norman priory of St Mary at Usk was firmly yoked to the military and commercial heart of the medieval borough established on the site of Roman *Burrium* by Richard fitz Gilbert de Clare (1130–76), probably in the third quarter of the twelfth century.[169] The precinct housing the priory church and its claustral complex lay within the postulated lines of the borough defences, and on the south-eastern fringe of the market place which was itself focussed on Twyn Square.[170] A little more than 300 yards to the north-west, 'a flight shot' away, the powerful stone castle of the twelfth and thirteenth centuries continues to overlook today's pretty little Monmouthshire town (fig. 195).[171]

At its foundation, the priory at Usk shared a pattern of monastic settlement which had already become widely familiar across the southern March. With very few exceptions,

Fig. 195 Usk: view of town and priory from the castle

the Black Monk priories which had been established during the years 1070 to about 1150 nestled under the shadow of a Norman stronghold, and they were often situated on the commercial fringe of an embryonic new town. There was undoubtedly a colonial flavour to this settlement, with castle, planted borough, and alien priory serving as triple hallmarks of the new authority. Indeed, as historian R.R. Davies reminds us, in their very location the Benedictine priories 'declared that they were the spiritual arm of a military conquest'.[172] Usk, however, stands apart from the group on at least two very significant counts. First, the priory was a notably late foundation, particularly in the context of those neighbouring houses established in the immediate wake of the Conquest at Chepstow, Monmouth, Abergavenny and elsewhere. Secondly, and of even greater interest, St Mary's was the only priory of Benedictine nuns to be established anywhere in Wales.[173]

Soon after the dissolution of the house in August 1536, the nave of the priory was acquired by the townspeople and it has since continued to serve a parochial function. But the east end of the former nunnery, perhaps the most intriguing architectural section of the building, was lost following the suppression. The monastic buildings, too, were largely destroyed, though the gatehouse survives, and parts of a south range appear to have been incorporated in The Priory, which now stands as an essentially Victorian house.

In common with the great majority of nunneries in England and Wales, there is a distinct scarcity of documentary sources from which to start a conventual history of Usk priory. Virtually all that survives in record has been assembled by David Williams, historian of monasticism in Wales.[174] There are, none the less, certain aspects of its foundation and patronage which are worthy of further study, particularly in the general context of women religious, and of patronage, two areas of growing interest within monastic studies.

Usk's original foundation charter has been lost, although a confirmation of grants issued to the nuns in 1330 seems to reflect the priory's initial endowment.[175] It can now be accepted with some confidence that the founder was Richard fitz Gilbert de Clare, earl of Pembroke, known as Richard Strongbow.[176] Local historian, Geoffrey Mein, has suggested Strongbow's original charter must belong to the period between 1154 and 1170.[177] In a more recent note, historian David Crouch chose a date of 1170–76.[178]

Of the Romanesque fabric of the church, there remains the crossing with its impressive tower and projecting circular stair turret, fragments of the transepts, and the entire south wall of the nave (fig. 196). Fortunately, there is sufficient to provide enough information for an assessment of the complete twelfth-century church.

The plan of the church comprised a small, cruciform structure, probably

Fig. 196 Usk priory: the exterior from the north-east

with an aisleless, square-ended presbytery. The north and south transepts were also of squared plan, and were apparently without eastern chapels. Internally, the aisleless nave was approximately 63 feet long by 24 feet wide, and there appear to have been clasping buttresses on the north-west and south-west corners. The southern angle of the south-west pilaster survives, fading into a battered plinth at the base of the wall.[179] The plan also accommodated a strongly projecting circular stair turret at the north-west angle of the crossing (fig. 196). Nothing survives of the contemporary door or window details, and none of the bay divisions can be placed with any degree of certainty.

In attempting to reconstruct the full ground plan, the most contentious aspect is clearly the form of the nuns' church east of the crossing. Stephen Williams was to consider the possibilities in the 1880s, and, as Mein pointed out, his earliest thoughts were for apsidal east walls to the presbytery and to both the transepts.[180] Williams was to revise his opinion on this, and in his later paper the plan drawn by his very competent assistant, Telfer Smith, showed a short, square-ended presbytery projecting some 28 feet from the crossing.[181] Mein recorded the memory of an excavation, which set out to test the Williams theory in 1964.[182] He was content to accept current topographic evidence to suggest that the excavators' trench was located about 8 feet outside the east wall as projected by

Williams.[183] Archaeologist C.N. Maylan went a stage further, suggesting that a 'substantial ... robbed wall' found during excavation outside the east boundary of the church in 1987 may represent the termination of the medieval presbytery.[184] Were Maylan correct, this would mean the entire presbytery measured some 73 feet (22.3m) in overall length, a size equivalent to that of the nave. These suggestions must be discussed in the context of all the other evidence we can recover on the form of the building.

The crossing has two-order, round-headed arches carried on scalloped capitals and coursed half shafts (fig. 197). The bases are hidden by the later raised floor. The crossing arches themselves are plain, except for the inner order of the eastern arch. This is enriched with channelled chevron decoration on its west side, and a large segmental soffit roll which is flanked by angle fillets and thin side rolls (fig. 198). Clearly, the ornament was intended to signify the importance of this arch as the entrance to the sanctuary. In conjunction with this, the abaci of the western crossing arch are decorated with chip-carved saltire crosses. Ornament was therefore used to highlight the visual progression eastwards from the nave, through the crossing, and into the presbytery.

The liturgical importance of the eastern arm of the church was further emphasized architecturally with a stone barrel vault (fig. 199). Fragments of this remain over the

Fig. 197 Usk priory: the crossing looking east

Fig. 198 Usk priory: the north-east capitals on the crossing

Figs. 199 and 200 Usk priory: the exterior from the east (left) showing the outline of the barrel vaulting of the eastern arm, shown in greater detail above

eastern crossing arch in the form of radiating voussoirs of the vault webbing (fig. 200). The voussoirs have a different trajectory and a much rougher finish than the smooth ashlar of the arch itself. The arrangement also contrasts with the uninterrupted ashlar above the outer sides of the arches which led into the north and south transepts, spaces which were undoubtedly covered with wooden roofs from the first.

The crossing tower rises for two full storeys above the nave and transept roofs (fig. 196). On each side of the first stage there is a centrally placed, round-headed window of two continuous orders. The inner order is plain, while the outer order has a broad chamfer. In the top stage each side has paired, round-headed belfry openings with a continuous hollow chamfer to the single order.

The small and rather simple plan would not have been unusual in the context of monastic planning among the female religious communities of medieval England and Wales. As archaeologist Roberta Gilchrist has asserted, nunnery churches rarely appear to have been designed with the same degree of complexity or architectural detailing as those of their male counterparts.[185]

The form of the east end must be considered in the context of nunneries and West Country Romanesque architecture. Apsidal east ends are known for major nuns' churches such as Barking (Essex) and Elstow (Beds.) but these are both late eleventh century.[186]

At Romsey (Hants.) around 1120 a squared eastern termination with ambulatory and a projecting eastern chapel was preferred. In the West Country, Whiteladies at Brewood (Staffs.) had a square-ended, aisleless presbytery, as did the Augustinian priory churches at Haughmond and Lilleshall (Salop), and in Wales at Benedictine Ewenny. It is very unlikely to be anything other at Usk. As to length, it would not be completely without parallel in the planning of nunnery churches to have a long eastern arm but almost certainly not in the twelfth century. St Radegund's at Cambridge had something similar, but there the presbytery was extended in the thirteenth century.[187] Similarly, the excavated plan of West Malling (Kent) shows an eastward extension in the thirteenth century.[188]

When considering the presbytery vault of St Mary's there are several good parallels for the surviving fragmentary voussoirs of the barrel. Similar evidence can be seen, for example, in the inner chapel of the north transept at Ewenny priory, and above the chancel arch of the circular chapel at Ludlow castle. The comparison of Usk with Ewenny extends to the use of a barrel vault in the eastern arm of the church. At Ewenny the eastern bay of the presbytery was covered with a four-part rib vault and it is possible that Usk was treated in a similar fashion. But even without such ribs, a plain barrel vault would have provided a permanent heavenly canopy in the manner of Kempley (Glos.) where the plastered finish of the architecturally unencumbered vault provided a perfect surface for the twelfth-century frescoes.[189]

The plain, round-headed arches seen in the crossing at St Mary's are of a form which occurs widely in the region, with good examples to be seen at Ewenny and in the former priory church at Leonard Stanley (Glos.).[190] They belong to a West Country Romanesque tradition, as seen in St Peter's abbey, Gloucester, the nave at Great Malvern priory, and the presbytery gallery and nave arcade at St John's, Chester. In Wales they appear in the naves of St Michael's at Kerry (Montgomery) (figs. 380–381), Sts Tysilio and Mary at Meifod (Montgomery) (fig. 348), St Woolos at Newport (Gwent) (fig. 216), and St Cadfan's at Tywyn (Merioneth) (figs. 345–347). Of these, Kerry and Meifod are especially interesting in that, like Usk, they are 'late' examples of this simple form: Kerry was rededicated in 1176, and Meifod was consecrated in 1156. For the moulding of the soffit of the eastern crossing arch with its broad central roll flanked by angular fillets and thinner angle rolls, a close parallel is in the paired version of this motif in the nave arcades of Malmesbury abbey probably constructed in the 1160s.[191]

In the crossing tower, the broad chamfer on the inner order of the windows, and the delicate hollow chamfer of the belfry openings accord well with a date in the 1170s or '80s. For the thin hollow chamfer there are the superimposed arcades on the west front of Malmesbury abbey. The broad chamfers seem to be best explained through Cistercian influence, initially at Fountains in the south transept arches to chapels and nave arcade and windows, at Kirkstall in the windows, in the crossing arches at Dore (probably after 1173), and in the west windows at Buildwas. Also starting in the 1170s chamfered arches are used consistently in the Augustinian priory at Llanthony (Gwent).

The strongly projecting circular stair turret at the north-west angle of the crossing tower is one of the distinct traits that betrays the ultimate Norman affiliations of the building.

Indeed, as one indication of the popularity of the form, there is the depiction of Edward the Confessor's Westminster abbey on the Bayeux Tapestry.[192] Comparisons may be drawn with the west towers of the Benedictine abbey church of Saint-Etienne at Caen, the northwest tower of the Benedictine church at Montivilliers (Seine-Maritime), and the crossing tower at Quillebeuf (Eure). The turret at Quillebeuf is particularly close to the form at Usk in that it clasps the corner rather than simply projecting from one side of the tower. Other parallels include Milborne Port (Somerset), where the vice was originally entered from the south transept next to the west respond of the south crossing arch. In this case, the turret is placed in the angle of the south transept and the south nave wall but it only projects on the south face of the crossing tower rather than clasping the angle as at Usk. Further parallels may be cited at Great Tey (Essex) at the north-west angle, and at the south-east angle at St Mary's, Hemel Hempstead (Herts.) where a date in the 1170s is likely.

Usk Castle

The twelfth-century keep at Usk is incorporated into the thirteenth century curtain wall of the castle (fig. 201).[193] At that time, according to the historian Jeremy Knight, the original first and second floors of the keep were incorporated into one, a large window was built in the west wall, and a new doorway constructed at the south end of the west wall, presumably as an enlargement of a twelfth-century predecessor.[194] Subsequently, the keep was heightened by about 8 feet in the fourteenth century, and the north wall was rebuilt in the fifteenth century, but the trapezoidal plan belongs to the original structure.[195] The exterior of the twelfth-century keep is devoid of any architectural detailing and ashlar is only used for the quoins. High on the south wall there are two round-headed, double-splay windows which, according to Knight, originally illuminated the second storey (figs. 201–202). They have rubble frames to the exterior but internally ashlar is employed. The openings themselves are cut into a screen-like partition in the wall. Knight considered that the round-headed doorway with a continuous chamfer in the south wall of the first floor was 'a renewal of the early thirteenth century, when the projecting latrine block to which

Fig. 201 Usk castle: the exterior of the gate tower from the south

Fig. 202 Usk castle: the interior of the gate tower looking south

it leads was added against the keep, but it may originally have served the stair to the upper floor of the keep and perhaps also an earlier latrine' (fig. 202).[196] Thus for Knight there were two storeys in the Norman keep above the basement, the first marked by the doorway to the later latrine turret and the adjacent large doorway in the west wall; the second, by the Norman windows.

On the exterior of the east wall to the left of the present entrance there is a massive sloping buttress which, towards the top, partially covers four ashlar voussoirs that spring toward the right (fig. 203). Reconstructing in the mind's eye the trajectory of this arch would result in a large Romanesque entrance arch to the ground floor of the tower similar to those in the tower gates at Ludlow and Sherborne castles (figs. 50 and 51). If this reconstruction is correct it precludes Jeremy Knight's idea of there having been a first and second storey in the Romanesque tower. Instead, there would have been the ground-floor entrance with a hall above to which the two windows in the west wall belong. This arrangement was then modified in the thirteenth century when the intermediate floor, marked by the doorway to the latrine turret, was introduced. It is unfortunate that the heavily remodelled west wall of the tower preserves no trace of any Romanesque masonry that might support or deny this tentative new reconstruction.

Fig. 203 Usk castle: detail of the springer of the former Romanesque arch entrance to the ground storey

Llanthony Priory (Gwent)

A monk's history, written in the late twelfth or early thirteenth century, records that, in the late eleventh century, one William, a household knight of Hugh de Lacy, abandoned his earthly profession and established a hermitage in the east bank of the Honddu where St David had earlier erected a small chapel.[197] Giraldus Cambrensis further states that the chapel was on the same site as St David's chapel.[198] About 1103 Ernisius, formerly chaplain to Matilda, wife of Henry I, joined William, and they gradually gathered around them a group of followers whose church was consecrated in 1108. By 1117–18 the community adopted the rule of St Augustine.[199]

The rebuilding of the church was funded by a series of land grants in Ireland by Hugh de Lacy and his son Walter between 1171 and 1205. At the death of Hugh de Lacy in 1186 these Irish revenues passed to the royal treasury and they were not restored until 1198. This suggests that the first campaign of work would have commenced after 1171 and continued until 1186. The break in funding may coincide with the break in design in the eastern responds of the nave. The second campaign would have continued after 1198. Details of the presbytery, crossing and transept accord happily with a start of construction soon after 1171, and if this is the case, Llanthony priory is one of the earliest examples of Brakspear's West Country School of masons.[200]

The ruins of the late twelfth-century fabric are sufficient to permit a virtually complete reconstruction of the church (fig. 204 and plate 13). The square ended presbytery has three aisleless bays. There is a crossing from which two-bay, aisleless transepts project to the north and south. From these there were two square-ended chapels to the east which were later remodelled into large single chapels; the arch to the one in the south transept is built of reused twelfth-century ashlar. Narrow doorways communicate between the west end of the presbytery and the inner chapels of both transepts. The nave comprised eight bays with aisles and twin western towers.

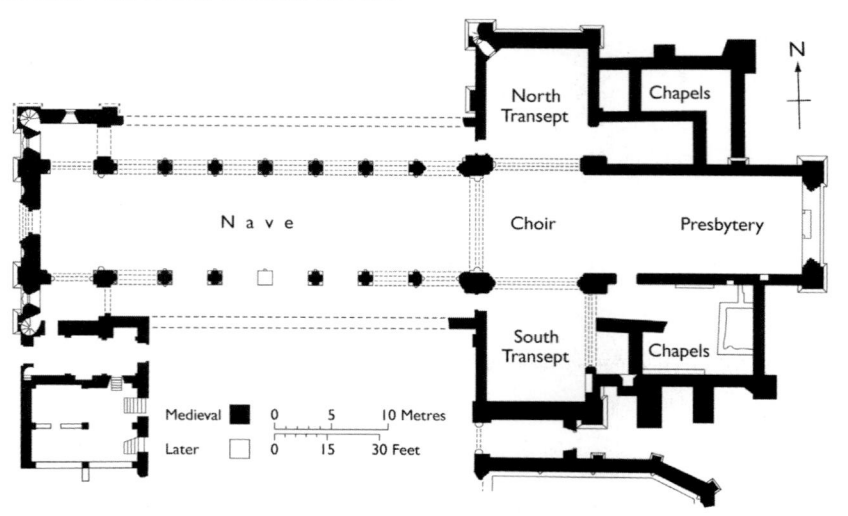

Fig. 204 Plan of Llanthony priory (Cadw)

CATHEDRAL, CASTLE AND MONASTERY POST 1120

Fig. 205 Llanthony priory from the north east

Fig. 206 Llanthony priory: the north-east interior of the presbytery

The church is built of rubble with ashlar dressings. The east wall of the presbytery, including the angle buttresses, has a tall sloping plinth with five angled steps below a string-course (fig. 205). The plinth is also preserved on the surviving buttress between the first and second bay on the north wall of the presbytery. There are string-courses at windowsill level on both the exterior and interior, and one at the top of the plinth on the east wall but the latter is not continued on the north and south walls. The best-preserved window is in the first bay of the north wall. It is tall, round-headed, without any internal articulation, and just a simple chamfer on the exterior. The east wall of the presbytery is not well preserved. The outer jambs of the lateral windows of the former stepped triplet survive (fig. 206). They retain an inner order of coursed masonry with a keeled roll between hollows at the angle without a base and rising to a squat moulded capital. The second order in the jamb has a moulded base with a coursed shaft with mid-shaft ring and trumpet-scallop capitals with round abaci. There is a thin rebate for glass, a feature continued throughout the church.

The articulation of the interior of the east windows is used in an iconographic sense to emphasize the importance of the place of the high altar in the sanctuary. Single coursed shafts in the eastern angles rise to trumpet-scallop capitals to carry the chamfered ribs of the high vault (fig. 206). This would have been a four-part vault over single bays as evidenced by the bay divisions in the presbytery. These are marked by triple stepped shafts — best preserved between bays one and two on the north side, and bays two and three on the south — on which the middle shaft is nibbed, that rise to large trumpet-scallop capitals with semi-octagonal abaci.

Fig. 207 Llanthony priory: looking west from the presbytery

In the south-west angle of the presbytery the springer of the high vault rib rests on a trumpet-scallop capital with round abacus atop a short shaft that rests on a cone corbel adjacent to the outer order of the eastern crossing arch (fig. 207). The simple chamfered profile of the rib matches that in the north-east angle of the presbytery, which indicates that there is uniformity in the rib profile over this space.

The crossing has pointed chamfered arches and is surmounted by a tower in which there are two superimposed wall passages (fig. 207). In each arch the inner order is carried on a capital above a stepped triple-shaft group with a nibbed central shaft that has just two courses of masonry above a foliage corbel. On the north and south crossing arches

Fig. 208 Looking east along the nave to the crossing tower

the two outer orders are continuous but, in the east and west arches, the second order sits on an elaborately moulded stepped corbel about halfway up the height of the pier. This arrangement facilitated the placement of choir stalls through the crossing.

The lower passage in the crossing tower was lit on all sides from the interior of the crossing by three round-head arches, each with two continuously chamfered orders. Aligned with these on the west wall of the crossing three plain, single-order arches opened into the space above the nave vault (figs. 207–208). In the south transept there is only a single, centrally placed arch at this level (fig. 209). The equivalent sections of wall above the former east and north crossing arches are destroyed. The jambs of the openings from the second passage into the crossing are preserved but not the arches. In each case on the outer wall there were lateral windows while the middle arch opened high into the roof space. There are paired shafts corbelled out between the

Fig. 209 The south crossing arch from the south

Fig. 210 The interior west wall of the south transept

openings in the crossing. The ashlar exterior superstructure of the tower was articulated with two-order chamfered arches that corresponded with these windows and adjacent blind arches to the outside.

The terminal wall of the south transept stands to almost its full height. There are large clasping pilaster buttress at the angles and two tall, round-headed windows with two continuously chamfered orders with a narrow rebate for glass at the mid-point of the wall. Placed centrally above these windows is an oculus also with two chamfered orders. On the west wall a broad pilaster provides a clear bay division but this is not reflected on the interior of the transept (fig. 210). In the south transept in the wall above the south crossing arch there is a distinct trace of the former high vault (fig. 209). The webbing of the vault would have been keyed into the channel and probably would have been of tufa, a point to which we will return below. Trumpet-scallop capitals with round abaci remain in the angles of the south transept for the ribs of the high vault, and in the middle of the west wall, one course above the string-course at windowsill level, there is the cone corbel that would have carried the triple vault shafts (figs. 209 and 210). The vault would therefore have had a quadripartite plan in each of the two bays. In the outer bay of the west wall the lower half of the south jamb of a window is preserved (fig. 210) The large number of putlog holes in the west wall may indicate that there was some substantial wooden furnishing abutted at this point.

The north transept is less well preserved than the south, although in the broad finger of masonry of the eastern section of the terminal wall there is the jamb of the window that suggest the pattern of fenestration matched that on the south transept. There is also a matching suture for the high vault and the north-east vault capital carried on a single shaft in the angle corbelled from just above the string course at the level of the windowsill. In the north-west angle there is the entrance to the spiral staircase.

There is a modification to the intended design in the east respond of the north nave arcade. Level with the foliage corbel for the inner order of the arch there is a similar foliage corbel in the angle between the chamfered orders of the respond on both the nave and aisle sides (figs. 211 and 212). Above these lateral corbels a roll moulding is used for just one course, above which it is abandoned. The corresponding section of the east respond of the south arcade is not preserved.

Also, the eastern bay of the nave differs from those to the west in that the inner order of the arch is carried on a foliage (foliated trumpet-scallop to the north-east) capital with

Fig. 211 The north-west crossing pier from the south-west

Fig. 212 The eastern bay of the north nave aisle, looking south-east

octagonal abacus atop a nibbed shaft, of just one masonry course in height, on a foliage corbel. Above the east respond the outer order of the arch towards the nave rests on a chamfered corbel (fig. 211). It has been suggested that this represented a change in plan to thicken the nave arcade. This may be true but had the outer order of the arch been carried down to the ground it would have stood in front of the inner faces of the crossing piers and thereby intruded into the space required for the choir stalls. In the second bay of the nave, and the other bays to the west, the corbelled inner order used in bay 1 is abandoned with the result that the soffit of the arch is much broader (figs. 208, 211, 213 and 214). The orders of the arch remain continuous but instead of just having chamfered stones, the modified design has a middle order of a continuous roll moulding to provide an alternating system to the orders of the arch and pier. The roll mouldings are used on both the nave and aisle sides of the piers and they sit on moulded bases.

Fig. 213 The eastern bays of the north nave elevation

The nave has a three-storey elevation with a giant order to link the triforium and clerestorey in all but the west bay (figs. 214 and 215). The triforium has paired pointed arches with continuous angle-roll mouldings set inside a chamfered second order that rises through to the clerestorey. Other than for the arched openings, rubble is used for the walls of the triforium and clerestorey in contrast to the ashlar of the nave arcades. In the two western bays there are passages in the triforium and the clerestorey but to the east of this there is no passage in the triforium. Above the nave arcade piers, two courses below the triforium string-course, there are cone corbels that carry triple coursed shafts that rise to trumpet-scallop capitals at the level of the triforium arches. These would have carried a quadripartite rib vault of wood rather than stone. The nave aisles were vaulted with stone quadripartite rib vaults.

Evidence for a wooden high vault is clearest in the two western bays where the stone arches of the high vault remain (fig. 215). The rubble masonry above the high vault

CATHEDRAL, CASTLE AND MONASTERY POST 1120

Fig. 214 The nave from the south-east

Fig. 215 The western bays of the north nave elevation showing the arches of the high vault

capitals is laid in regular horizontal courses and there are no signs of the webbing of a stone vault above the wall arches. Turning to the masonry above the western crossing arch, the rubble is laid in regular horizontal courses, and there is no indication of any disturbance caused by the removal of a masonry vault (fig. 2o8). This is in contrast to the chase left by the removal of the vault web above the south crossing arch (fig. 2o9).

Sources and affiliations:
Trumpet-scallop capitals are ubiquitous in the West Country in the late twelfth-century. To some extent they serve as a useful dating tool although, as with nearly all motifs, it is not an exact science

155

and there are usually exceptions to the 'rule'. Be that as it may, trumpet-scallops are used in the western bays of Worcester cathedral nave, commenced after the fall of the tower in 1175.[201] In an Augustinian context they occur at Keynsham Abbey (fd.1167)[202] and at Wigmore abbey (Herefs.), founded in 1172 and dedicated in 1179.[203]

The superimposed passages in the crossing tower belong to a tradition established at Saint-Etienne at Caen. The type is well represented in England after the Conquest at St Albans abbey, Norwich cathedral, and in the West Country at Tewkesbury abbey. The type continued in the early Gothic period at Wells cathedral.

The form of square-ended unaisled presbytery was used at Ewenny priory where there is also a crossing, aisleless transepts of two bays and two rectangular chapels. Also at Ewenny round-headed doorways connect the western bay of the presbytery with the inner transept chapels. For an Augustinian comparison of these planning elements, we may cite Lilleshall priory, founded in 1148.[204] Like Llanthony, Lilleshall was rib-vaulted throughout, and the same was true of the near-contemporary Augustinian St Frideswide's, Oxford. Communication between the nave aisles and the transept through low, round-headed arches is also related to Ewenny priory and the parallels cited there, and later at St Davids cathedral.

The steep plinth of the presbytery east wall and buttresses is paralleled in the west wall at Buildwas abbey and in the Lady Chapel of Glastonbury abbey. A less steep version appears on the exterior of the presbytery at Kirkstall, commenced in 1152, and at Lilleshall priory after 1148. Earlier, the motif was popular in secular architecture, as in the keep at Castle Hedingham and was used in Wales at Kenfig.

In the 1170s chamfered ribs were used in the western slype at Worcester cathedral and at the same time chamfered orders to piers and arches appeared at Dore abbey (Herefs.) and in the south nave arcade at St Mary's, Shrewsbury. Cone corbels for vault shafts are used in the 1160s in the chapter house at Buildwas abbey.

Tufa vault webbing has already been discussed in connection with the nave vault of Chepstow priory. Closer in date to Llanthony, tufa is used in the chapter house of Much Wenlock priory (1160s), the choir high vault of Canterbury cathedral (1175–84), Dover castle chapel (1181), in the two western bays of the south nave aisle at Worcester cathedral (post-1175), and Glastonbury abbey Great Church (post-1185).[205]

Wooden ribbed vaults were used frequently in the West Country in the late twelfth and first half of the thirteenth century.[206] There is the well-known documented example at Lichfield cathedral, and the early Gothic choir of Pershore abbey was almost certainly covered with a wooden rib vault.[207] Geographically and temporally closer to Llanthony, a good case can be made for a high wooden rib vault in the presbytery of Dore abbey.[208] The earliest surviving example (c.1260–80) is in the nave of Warmington (Northants.).

The documentation indicates that the first phase of construction that included the presbytery, crossing and transepts should be placed between 1171 and 1186. The consistent use of trumpet-scallop capitals and the limitation of foliage ornament suggest a starting date close to 1171. This is confirmed by the use of chamfered pointed arches at Dore, where construction probably commenced around 1173.[209]

4

Church Architecture and Sculpture for Norman Patrons

This chapter examines the smaller churches built for Norman patrons after 1120, and a large number of fonts also probably, but not certainly, commissioned by Normans. The work is arranged by county, not for any profound historical reason but rather for convenient geographical grouping. We start with Gwent/Monmouthshire, move to Glamorganshire, then to Breconshire, further north to Denbighshire and, finally, to Pembrokeshire.

GWENT/MONMOUTHSHIRE

Our investigation commences with the more ambitious churches in the county; the aisled naves at Newport and Caerleon, the central tower at Caldicot, the elaborate doorways at Christchurch (near Newport) and Whitson, and the richly decorated, but heavily restored, Over Monnow. We then consider a number of two-cell churches with aisleless naves and narrower square-ended chancels, a doorway at Llandenny, a single-cell church at Penterry, the wonderfully sited and eccentric Cwmyoy, and end with a variety of fonts.

Newport, St Woolos

St Woolos at Newport, now the cathedral, is one of the most interesting Romanesque churches in Wales. In 1093, the church was granted to St Peter's abbey, Gloucester.[1] It preserves a five-bay nave with north and south arcades and clerestorey windows, a west window and elaborate west doorway and a significant fragment of the Romanesque font. At the west end there is the site of the grave church (*Eglwys y Bedd*) of St Gwynllyw.

The nave arcades are round-headed with two plain orders on columns with a variety of scalloped capitals with square abaci (fig. 216). Round-headed clerestorey windows are set above the tops of the arcade arches. These are deeply splayed and the small exterior frames of the windows are constructed in ashlar with single-stone heads now seen from within the aisles. While the nave arcade columns are all cylindrical, the east and west responds are semi octagonal and are further differentiated from the columns in their plain capitals (fig. 217).

The west doorway has two orders both richly adorned with chevron in the arch (fig. 218).[2] On the inner order to either side of a thin angle roll, double-roll chevron projects from both the face and the soffit of the arch. On the left there are distinct traces of limewash and red paint. The outer order has triple chevron on the face of the arch and there is a hood mould with single billet. The inner order of the jamb has a narrow chamfer. The richly

Fig. 216 Newport, St Woolos: looking west along the nave

Fig. 217 Newport, St Woolos: semi-octagonal west respond with simple capital

carved capitals that carry the arch sit atop detached shafts on moulded bases and abaci (figs. 219–221, plate 14). The latter continue on to the plain jamb of the outer order. The capitals are based on the Roman Composite type in which the angle volutes derive from the Greek Ionic order while the foliage on the bell of the capital derives from the Corinthian order. The designs have gone a long way from their original models. The foliage bears little resemblance to the spiky thistle form of Greek acanthus; instead we find striated pointed projections from the capital. The capitals are figurated and it has been suggested that they are recut Roman.[3] The theory is reasonable in so far as the capital and shaft are carved from monoliths, a practice not known to me in Norman times.

On the west face of the north capital there is a centrally placed figure with arms raised to either side of his large head (fig. 219). A leaf largely hides his puny body but, in a remarkably acrobatic gesture, he seems to kick out his legs to either side of the top of the leaf. To the right of this central figure there is a smaller member of the same family. On the south face of the capital a bird perches awkwardly on the lower left leaf and pecks at a fruit or berry adjacent to the volute (fig. 220). There is a ball or orb immediately beneath the bird. In the centre of the capital is the upper half of a figure with arms raised in the same manner as on the west face of the capital. To the right there is what appears to be a richly decorated wing attached to an animal (ox?) head. The subject matter is not easy to determine but the gestures of the human figures suggest that torment is involved.[4] On the north face of the right capital, a hand emerges at the top left from a section of uncarved stone (plate 14). Beneath the hand there is a human head to the right of which, in the centre of the capital, is a frontally posed bird with large wings that arc down to either side of its body to frame two round objects.

Fig. 218 Newport, St Woolos: the west doorway into the nave

Figs. 219 and 220 Newport, St Woolos: north capital on the west doorway from the west (left) and south (right)

Next to the right wing there is a fish and it appears that another fish is partially hidden by the lower part of the bird's body. For C.O.S. Morgan, author of a late nineteenth-century article on St Woolos' church, this 'seems to be a representation of the Creation and the Trinity, the creating Father being represented by an open hand, the impersonation of the Son by a human face, the Holy Ghost by a dove, beneath which is an orb to represent the Spirit of God moving on the face of the waters'.[5] Unsophisticated as this carving may be, the juxtaposition of the fish with the Trinity suggests association with baptism. This is confirmed when we read the two round objects beneath the bird's wings as ampoules of holy oil used in the sacrament of baptism. This iconography is Carolingian, as seen in the Metz ivory casket (Brunswick Museum),[6] and is introduced into Anglo-Saxon England in the *Benedictional of St Aethelwold* (London, British Library, MS Add. 49598, fol. 25).[7]

Fig. 221 Newport, St Woolos: south capital on the west doorway from the west

The west face of the right capital has a centrally placed, apparently naked, figure with both arms raised, and carrying a sword in his right hand in front of a tree(?). To the right is a smaller naked figure also with arms raised. Morgan's reading of the scene as the Expulsion from Paradise would seem to be correct although, if I am right in seeing the central figure as naked, the sculptor has managed to conflate the figures of Adam and the angel who traditionally carries the sword.

The nave design is extremely ambitious with five bays and both north and south aisles. This is grander than Ewenny priory where there was just a north nave aisle. The variety between the nave columns and the responds follows the principle established in the nave of Chepstow priory and is paralleled in the choir of St Peter's, Gloucester, and the nave of Shrewsbury abbey. In other words, it is a feature normally associated with great-church architecture. Caröe associated the nave and the west doorway with the gift of the church to Gloucester in 1092, or shortly thereafter.[8] However, this seems too early. The right-angled chevron on the outer order of the west doorway is a more elaborate version of this motif in the nave triforium and clerestorey at St Peter's abbey, Gloucester (figs. 101 and 218). This may be as early as 1100 but the chevron to either side of the thin angle roll on the inner order of the Newport doorway is unlikely before the second quarter of the twelfth century. Both types of chevron could well have been executed much later and therefore it is important to determine how the capitals of the doorway fit into the equation. They are naïve both in terms of style and iconography, and yet if I am right about the reading of the baptism, then at some point there would have to have been some contact with an important centre of learning and/or artistic production. Seeing that St Woolos was given to St Peter's, Gloucester, the link may well have been there. Unfortunately, we do not have enough figurative sculpture from Gloucester for comparison with the Newport capitals, but when we consider that Kilpeck church was given to Gloucester in 1134, this suggests that accomplished figure sculptors were available in the region by the early 1130s. It follows that the work at St Woolos was completed before this time.

At St Woolos the font is located in the narthex of the church (fig. 222). Just the south-western sector of the font is original, while the remainder was restored in 1854 on the basis of the medieval work and repeated the motifs exactly. A large mask occupies the upper angle of the square bowl. It wears a plain skull cap from which long, pointed ears poke out from which in turn issue beaded stems that end in broad leaves that grow on to the underside of the bowl. The large almond-shaped eyes have bulbous pupils, the nose is badly damaged and the inflated cheeks are those of a trumpet player. Two broad, beaded stems issue from the mouth to the side of a central trilobe leaf. The stems arc to the side and terminate in single fleshy leaves to the side of the head. At the right edge of the original fragment, in the middle of the south side of the bowl, there is a trefoil leaf with damaged right lobe. The remaining lobes have a pronounced central vein characteristic of early stiff-leaf foliage. Below and to the right of this there commences the mirror image of the foliage pattern to the left that indicates that the original design was symmetrical and has been restored correctly.

The font has been associated with the Herefordshire School of sculpture but this is an erroneous suggestion.[9] The chubby cheeks and almond eyes of the mask, and the fleshy foliage are quite different from Herefordshire School work; contrast, for example, the

Fig. 222 Newport, St Woolos: the font from the west

masks on the Brecon priory font (figs. 145, 146 and 222). The fleshy quality of the foliage suggests a date late in the twelfth century and in terms of font decoration is analogous to the Aylesbury group not least Great Kimble (Bucks.).[10] The Great Kimble font probably dates from about 1180 and this would also suit the existence of the early form of stiff-leaf foliage on the south side of the font. Such forms occur in the earliest leaves in the capitals in the western bays of the choir at Wells Cathedral commenced about 1175.

Although there is no sign of Romanesque masonry in St Mary's chapel it may well be significant that the font is placed there. It is probably the site of the *Eglwys y Bedd* (grave church) of St Gwynllyw who was buried in the floor of the church,[11] and later effigies and tomb recesses indicate that it was continued as a place of burial. Burial close to a saint was always popular, and the west end of the church was frequently the location for a font, as in the late eighth-century *westwork* at St Riquier at Centula. A grave church is located at the west end of the parish church at Partrishow (Breconshire), and there was formerly one at Llangollen, which was destroyed in 1749.[12]

Fig. 223 Caerleon, St Cadoc: western bay of the south nave showing the remains of the Norman church

CAERLEON, ST CADOC

William Coxe, in *An Historical Tour In Monmouthshire* (1801), wrote:

> In its splendid days, Caerleon enjoyed the honour of being the metropolitan see of Wales. According to the annals of the church, Dubricius, the great opponent of the Pelagian heresy, was the first archbishop. He was succeeded by St David, called by bishop Godwin uncle of king Arthur, and son of Zanctus, a prince of Wales, who removed the see from Caerleon to Menevia, which from him was called St Davids. The reason for this translation, and the extraordinary accounts of his sanctity, are detailed by bishop Godwin:
>
> 'It seemeth he misliked the frequency of people at Caerlegion, as a means to withdraw him from contemplation; whereunto that he might be more free, he made choice of this place for a see, rather than for any fitnesse of the same otherwise. He fate long, to witte, 65 yeeres, and died at last ann. 642.'

Gerald of Wales wrote that 'in former times there were three fine churches in Caerleon', and that there was formerly a royal palace in the town.[13]

Caerleon may have been ecclesiastically less significant in the twelfth century but evidence remains for a church of reasonably high status. There survives a bay and a half of the south nave arcade of the Norman church (fig. 223). The rectangular, ashlar-faced pier has a modern plain, chamfered capital and it carries unmoulded, two-order, round-headed arches. The west respond has chamfered angles. There is a Norman clerestorey window in the spandrel above the west respond. The 'heavy square pillars and low arches' that survived until 1878 in the nave of the former cell of Glastonbury abbey at Bassaleg (Gwent) may have been related to the work at Caerleon.[14]

Mathern, St Tewdric

The west pier and arch of north nave arcade may be twelfth century (fig. 224).[15]

Fig. 224 Mathern, St Tewdric: possible twelfth-century west pier of the north nave arcade

Caldicot, St Mary

The central axial tower is Norman as evidenced by a small window in the south wall (fig. 225). The Norman chancel and nave are rebuilt but the original plan probably had a square-ended chancel and an aisleless rectangular nave. The plan was a fairly popular one in England and has been studied in detail in connection with the example at Studland (Dorset).[16] The tower served as a marker for the

Fig. 225 Caldicot, St Mary: from the south

ecclesiastical presence in the community and also for the importance of the internal space below, in which there was probably an altar. This view is reinforced by the existence of a barrel vault under the tower at Langford (Oxon) and a rib vault at Castle Rising (Norfolk) in churches that are otherwise roofed in wood.

CHRISTCHURCH (NEAR NEWPORT)
The church boasts a rich, round-headed, three-order Norman south doorway with alternating continuous and non-continuous orders (fig. 226). The inner order is continuous and has a narrow chamfer, while the outer order has chamfered jambs that change to a hollow chamfer in the arch. Between is the second order with nook shafts, scalloped capitals topped with a row of incised triangles and beaded imposts. The main order of the arch has right-angled chevron that is paralleled, less one middle, narrow roll, in a voussoir from Sarum cathedral (no. 81109706).

Fig. 226 Christchurch (nr. Newport): south doorway

WHITSON (DEDICATION UNKNOWN)
The two-order Norman south doorway has a segmental arch with a continuous inner order with a quadrant roll, and an outer order on coursed shafts, damaged capitals and a quadrant roll in the arch (fig. 227). The quadrant roll is in the tradition of the choir aisles at St Peter's, Gloucester, and this continues to the late twelfth century in the West Country School of masons as in the south doorway of Glastonbury abbey Great Church and the north doorway of St Davids cathedral. The left capital is a variant of a trumpet scallop with a wide recess at the top in the tradition of Reading abbey and, more directly, the west bays of the nave of Worcester cathedral. The right capital has upright leaves rather than the trumpets. The

Fig. 227 Whitson: south doorway

Fig. 228 Over Monnow, St Thomas: the priest's door in the north wall of the chancel

portal should be dated with reference to the west bays at Worcester cathedral, i.e. after 1175.

The church also boasts a contemporary font with a square bowl on a stem with three scallops on the underside and the north face carved with lattice work. The lattice may be compared with the same pattern on one of the grave slabs at Llanfihangel Abercywyn (Carmarthenshire) and thus associates baptism with death and rebirth.[17]

OVER MONNOW, ST THOMAS
St Thomas at Over Monnow is a heavily restored example of a late twelfth-century two-cell aisleless church. The chancel is square ended and of two bays with a priest's door set in a projecting gabled frame at the west end of the north wall. The doorway has a continuous plain inner order, and an outer order with furrowed chevron and a gorged angle roll in the arch carried on plantain-leaf capitals atop coursed shafts (fig. 228). Similar shafts and capitals articulate the outer angles of the frame. In the middle of the north nave wall there is a three-order doorway with completely renewed jambs but an essentially original, albeit very weathered arch (fig. 229). The inner order has a simple angle roll, the second order is plain, and order three has traces of chevron. The west doorway is by F. Mew and is dated to 1880.[18] However, its cavernous, multi-ordered form reflects that recorded in the 1830 plan by A.M. Wyatt, and in turn to the tradition of multiple-ordered west portals discussed in connection with Chepstow priory (fig. 230).[19] The responds of the chancel

Fig. 229 Over Monnow, St Thomas: the north nave doorway

Fig. 230 Over Monnow, St Thomas: the west doorway

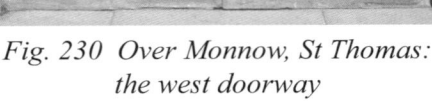

Fig. 231 Over Monnow, St Thomas: the chancel arch

arch are renewed but the arch itself is largely original (fig. 231). The inner order has an angle roll, order two has 90-degree chevron and there is a chevron hood mould.

The gabled frame of the priest's door may be traced in the West Country to the north portal of Lullington (Somerset) and is reflected in the west portal of Roscrea cathedral (Tipperary), Freshford and elsewhere in Irish Romanesque.[20] These examples probably reflect Sarum cathedral as remodelled by Bishop Roger (1102–39). The gorged roll on the priest's door suggests a date between 1170 and 1190.

The font at St Thomas, Over Monnow, has been related to the Herefordshire School (fig. 232).[21] In terms of the style of the mask on the bowl the Herefordshire analogy is appropriate but that it dates from the twelfth century is doubtful. Peter Lord, author of *The Visual Culture of Wales: Medieval Vision*, referred to two nineteenth-century illustrations of the interior of the church that 'clearly show a simpler unadorned font on a much heavier pillar'.[22] He suggested that it is unlikely that the present font was in the church prior to the 1835 restoration, and further that it may have come from Monmouth priory church. The form of the font, with the small bowl on a relatively tall, decorated stem and ornamented base, is quite unlike other twelfth-century work, and the sharpness of the carving seems to preclude over eight hundred years of use. It is surely a product of the nineteenth century.

PORTSKEWETT, ST MARY

The church was confirmed to Llandaff by papal privilege in 1128 and 1129.[23] There is a square chancel and a rectangular nave built of rubble limestone. The nave has north and south doorways and there is a Norman window in the north wall of the chancel. The north doorway has a lintel carved with an embossed Greek cross with concave-sided arms under a doubly outlined semi-circular arch, as if to create a miniature tympanum (fig. 233). The tradition of a cross above the entrance to the church goes back to early Christian times. It is described in 403 by Paulinus in his church at Nola: 'the sign of the Lord above the entrance, painted in the following form as indicated by the verse:

> Behold the wreathed cross of Christ the Lord
> Standing aloft above His courts with promises
>   of high rewards for hard work
> Take up the cross, ye who wish to carry off the
>   wreath.'[24]

Also, in early medieval churches in Ireland there is a carved cross on the lintel of the west doorway of St

Fig. 232 Over Monnow, St Thomas: the font

Fig. 233 Portskewett, St Mary: the north portal

Fig. 234 Portskewett, St Mary: the chancel arch

169

Fechain's at Fore (Westmeath), and immediately above the lintel on the west doorway at Clonamery (Kilkenny).[25]

The rubble-built chancel arch has plain jambs with chamfered imposts and a quadrant roll moulding in the arch (fig. 234). The latter motif indicates some architectural pretension in that it is used in Serlo's abbey church of St Peter at Gloucester, commenced in 1089.

RUNSTON, ST KEYNA[26]

The church has a square chancel and rectangular nave with robbed north and south doorways. There is a deeply splayed north nave window, a robbed south nave window, and robbed windows in north and south chancel walls. The chancel has no east window, as is the case in five Norman churches in neighbouring Gloucestershire.[27] The plain, round-headed chancel arch rests on imposts on plain jambs.

Of other evidence for Norman work in Gwent, at St John at Llandenny, the south doorway is set less than halfway down the aisleless nave and has a solid semi-circular tympanum (fig. 235). The surface of the tympanum has been badly scraped which suggests that it had been plastered and most likely painted; the relief of the tympanum is too shallow to suggest that it had ever been carved. In the north wall there is a small round-headed north window, which is heavily reworked and may not be original. The nave interior measures 45ft 10in x 15ft 2in, very close to a 1:3 proportion.

At St Andrew's, Tredunnock, there is a two-cell Norman church with a square-ended chancel to which a fourteenth-century(?) west tower has been added (fig. 236). There is a blocked Norman window in the north wall of the nave and a Norman window in the north and south walls of the chancel. The south doorway is located at the very west end of the nave, which suggests that the later tower occupies the western section of the original Norman nave. The relatively long chancel probably indicates a date in the late twelfth century.

At St Arvans there is a priest's doorway in the south wall of the

Fig. 235 Llandenny, St John: tympanum of the south doorway

Fig. 236 Tredunnock, St Andrew: from the south

chancel with an eccentrically shaped lintel, a tympanum of roughly coursed rubble and a poorly constructed arch (fig. 237). The lintel rests on chamfered imposts of which the one on the left is decorated with saltire crosses with pellets — some with a central hole — in the interstices. The date is not easily determined. Priests' doorways become more popular in the later twelfth century, but there is one at Weaverthorpe (Yorks.) between 1108 and 1114, and examples at Castle Frome (Herefs.), Heddon-on-the Wall and Warkworth (both Northumberland) probably date from the 1120s or 1130s.

Fig. 237 St Arvans, St Arvan: the south doorway into the chancel

The small, single-cell church of St Mary at Penterry is wonderfully isolated in a field above the Wye valley and preserves a Norman window in the north wall.[28] At St Mary's, Magor, there remains a fragment of chevron built into the wall near the south-east angle which probably indicates that there was a rather ambitious Norman church (fig. 238).

Fig. 238 Magor, St Mary: chevron fragment

St Martin's, Cwmyoy, is located on the east scarp of the valley just off the minor road that leads north-west from the A465 to Llanthony priory and over the Black Mountains to Hay-on-Wye. The angle of the west tower recalls the better-known example at Pisa, but Cwmyoy can also boast equally eccentric deviations from the vertical throughout the church. The nave is late twelfth-century as shown by a window with continuous roll mouldings in the north wall, and the quadrant moulding on the south doorway. The egg-cup-shaped font with roll lip and raised waistband is contemporary (fig. 239).

Fig. 239 Cwmyoy, St Martin: font

Fig. 240 Abergavenny, St Mary: font

Fig. 241 Goetre, St Peter: font

Fig. 242 Llansantffraed, St Bridget: font

Fig. 243 Llantilio Crossenny, St Teilo: font

FONTS

Numerous fonts provide further evidence of the Norman presence in Gwent. The variety of forms is considerable. At Abergavenny there is a circular bowl with radiating arcs on the underside above a thick rope moulding (fig. 240). Closely related fonts, almost certainly from the same workshop, are at Bettws Newydd, Goetre (fig. 241) — attributed to the same hand as Abergavenny and Bettws Newydd by Iltyd Gardner[29] — and Llansantffread (fig. 242).[30]

At Llantilio Crossenny the large (2ft 8in external diameter), granite, chalice-shaped bowl has a band of chevron ornament incised on the rim but otherwise is plain (fig. 243). It stands on a columnar pedestal and is a smaller version of the fonts at Bredwardine and Kilpeck (Herefs.).[31] A related example is found at Llanddew where only the bowl of the font is original. It has a deep plain frieze above a deeply splayed underside, and a 3ft 1in external diameter. Unlike the plain bowls of the related fonts, Llandew has a serpent incised in its western quadrant (fig. 244).

At St Bartholomew, Llanover, there is an elegant round bowl decorated with eleven roundels filled with a variety of symmetrically petalled flowers above a rope moulding at the bottom (fig. 245). Newman wondered if the decoration was later, but I see no reason to doubt a late twelfth-century date.[32]

The font at St Mable, Llanvapley, has a bulbous chalice-shaped bowl with a frieze of the simplest chip-carved chevron (fig. 246). It is set on a (later?) stem with a large central shaft and four minor attached shafts with capitals and bases. The squat, tapering bowl at Llanddewi Skirrid has incised chevron on the rim, considerable amounts of limewash and even distinct traces of paint: yellow ochre on the lip, and red ochre patterning on a white ground below (fig. 247).

Fig. 244 Llanddew, Holy Trinity or St David: font

Fig. 245 Llanover, St Bartholomew: font

Fig. 247 Llanddewi Skirrid, St David: font

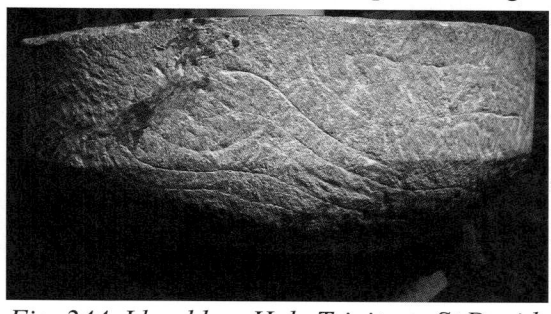

Fig. 246 Llanvapley, St Mable: font

At both Llangua and Rogiet there is a circular bowl on a thick circular stem, while at Wilcrick the circular bowl has a raised rim. There are basic tub-shaped fonts at Llanwenarth, Mitchell Troy, Pen-y-Clawdd and St Maughans. The latter has a narrow ring at the waist and is roughly finished but traces of limewash on the bowl almost certainly reflect the original finish and possibly that the font was painted, as at Llanddewi Skirrid. The fonts at Llanelly, Llanfair Cilgedin (second font) and Llanfihangel Pontymoile may also be Norman.

GLAMORGAN

The establishment of Norman authority in Glamorgan witnessed in the construction of Llandaff cathedral and the monastic houses of Ewenny and Margam and their associated castles at Ogmore and Kenfig, is also evident in a number of smaller churches in the county. And, as in Gwent, fonts also attest to Norman presence. While small in scale the churches are not without ambition, as in the south doorway at Marcross, which is associated with Llandaff cathedral, and the former chancel arch at Llandough, which relates to the work of Bishop Roger of Sarum (1102–1139). As in Gwent, Glamorgan also boasts a significant number of fonts, some of which are very elegant and incorporate sophisticated iconographic features.

St Bride's Major, St Bridget

The plain round-headed chancel arch is built of good-quality ashlar with plain jambs and imposts with multiple grooved mouldings on the underside (fig. 248). In *The Buildings of Wales, Glamorgan*, Newman compared these mouldings with Ewenny, but I know of nothing like this at Ewenny.[33] The north doorway has a plain tympanum on chamfered imposts and plain ashlar jambs. The church was given to St Peter's abbey at Gloucester before 1138.[34]

St Donats, St Donat

The chancel arch and the font remain from the Romanesque church. The single-order arch is quite plain and is of tufa. It sits on chamfered abaci atop simple volute capitals on coursed nook shafts with steep damaged bases all in Sutton stone (fig. 249).

The tub-shaped font sits on a squat stem, and is decorated with imbrication

Fig. 248 St Bride's Major: chancel arch

Fig. 249 St Donats: chancel arch   *Fig. 250 Kenfig, St Mary Magdalene; font*

(fish-scale pattern) on the bowl,[35] a simpler version of the fonts at Llantwit Major and Kenfig (fig. 250). Imbrication is used on late Antique sarcophagi, Anglo-Saxon hogback tombs, on the twelfth-century sarcophagus at Fordwich (Kent), and on the tomb shrine of St Lotharius at Saint-Loyer (Orne).[36] As for its appearance on fonts, some imbrication is used on the bowl of the font at Harpole (Northants) and at Lichtenhagen in Germany.[37] This speaks clearly of the iconographic connection between death and resurrection and their simulation in Baptism.[38]

MARCROSS, HOLY TRINITY

The Norman church at Marcross is a typical two-cell plan with a square chancel and rectangular aisleless nave, which preserves the south doorway and the chancel arch. The south doorway has a single order with a roll moulding in the arch carried on foliage capitals without abaci, nook shafts and moulded bases (fig. 251). The foliage has two-strand stems that terminated in roundels from which three striated leaves grow at right angles to each other. The hood mould has double billet and is terminated by head stops with huge eyes with drilled pupils. This is a very ambitious portal for a small parish church and one for which a sculptor from Llandaff cathedral has been recruited. The foliage on the capitals is comparable to the outer right and outer left capital of the east arch of the presbytery, and

Figs. 251 and 252 Marcross, Holy Trinity: south doorway (left) and chancel arch (right)

the interior capital of the presbytery second south arch (plates 5 and 6 and figs. 100 and 251).[39] The roll moulding in the arch and the lack of abaci on the capitals are also paralleled in the south presbytery windows at Llandaff (figs. 98–100 and 251). The quadrant form of the nook shafts suggest a knowledge of the nave aisle responds of St Peter's, Gloucester (figs. 38 and 251), and one label stop preserved at Gloucester shares a similar treatment of the eyes with those at Marcross.[40] The label stops should also be compared with a number of corbels at Kilpeck.[41]

The Marcross chancel arch has a single order with jambs chamfered with a raised ribbon that terminates in a laurel-like leaf at the top left and a volute at top right (fig. 252). There is a spear-like termination at the bottom, and a chamfered plinth. The imposts have a quirked-chamfer and there is an angle roll moulding on the west face of the arch that breaks out into five zigzags at the top. The form of the chevron is not exactly paralleled at either Llandaff or Gloucester but the basic idea of some chevron in the arch may well have been in emulation of the east arch of the presbytery at Llandaff. The raised-ribbon chamfer with a volute top on the right jamb is paralleled on the inner order of the chancel arch of the former Cluniac priory at St Clears (fig. 179), while the spear-like termination relates to the crossing piers at St Dogmaels priory (fig. 138). It has been suggested that Marcross church dates from the late twelfth century,[42] but this seems to be too late. Of the comparisons cited, Llandaff cathedral was started in 1120, Kilpeck was built around 1134, St Clears was founded between 1147 and 1184, and St Dogmaels was founded in 1113. The dates of Llandaff and Kilpeck are secure, and the chancel arch at St Clears probably dates soon after 1147. Therefore, a date in the second quarter of the twelfth century seems to be best suited to the work at Marcross. The tub-shaped font with a raised roll rim and neck may also date from this time.[43]

MONKNASH, ST MARY

Monknash is a complete, two-cell, Norman church with a square-ended chancel and aisleless nave. The chancel is constructed on small, roughly squared stones with larger blocks for the quoins while rubble is used for the nave (fig. 253). Towards the east of the north wall of the chancel there is a round-headed window which is distinguished by a continuous roll moulding that even returns along the sill on the exterior. Continuous mouldings are used for the wall arches of the presbytery aisles at Gloucester cathedral, and inside the east window at Kempley. Originally there were two doorways to the nave. The south doorway has been reduced in height although the Norman arch remains inside, as does the arch of the blocked north doorway (fig. 254). The chancel arch is narrow and has a single plain round-head on plain jambs and chamfered imposts of tufa.

In 1129 Richard de Glanville, who held the parish of Monknash gave the 'whole fee of Aissa with the church and all its belongings to Neath abbey'.[44] The date may be associated with the construction of the church.

Fig. 253 Monknash, St Mary: from the north

Fig. 254 Monknash, St Mary: looking west along the nave

Fig. 255 Wick, St James: font

Fig. 256 St Athan, St Tathan; font

To the north of St Donats, Marcross and Monknash there are three two-cell churches with square-ended chancels at Colwinston, Llandow and Wick.[45] As at Marcross the main entrance to these churches is through the south nave doorway located halfway down the nave, although only the plain, round-headed doorway at Llandow is original. This arrangement is paralleled in similarly scaled churches in Gloucestershire, as at Winson, and it may suggest that the western half of the nave would have been sectioned off as a baptistery. At Colwinston and Wick there are plain, round-headed chancel arches on chamfered imposts; they are more accomplished, larger and probably later than the chancel arch at Monknash. Continuing north across the A48, a similar chancel arch is reset in the north wall of the nave of St Mary Hill.[46] The slightly bulbous, tub-shaped font at Wick has a cable moulding at the top and a simple roll at the bottom of the plain bowl (fig. 255). It looks like a plain version of the imbricated example at Kenfig (fig. 250), and one wonders if similar decoration was originally executed in paint at Wick. The font at Llandow is also a plain tub, while at St Athan although the font is plain it takes on an elegant goblet shape (fig. 256), a form that suggests wine and, concomitantly, a link between baptism and the eucharist. The cylindrical form of the St Lythans' font may lack the elegant lines of the St Athan's goblet but it makes up for that with no less that six rows of chevron ornament.[47] A less exuberant display of chevron is found on the single-order, pointed chancel arch at Penmark (fig. 257). The arch sits atop human-headed chamfer stops, the naturalistic appearance of which along with the pointed arch, suggest a date not before the end of the twelfth century. To the north of the church at Penmark are the earthworks and a section of the curtain wall on the line of the Norman ringwork of the former castle. While no Romanesque stonework remains, the juxtaposition of church and castle is an excellent example of this sort of Norman pairing of ecclesiastical and secular.[48]

Prior to the 'restoration' of the church of St Dochdwy, Llandough, two miles north-west of Penarth, Samuel Lewis recorded the following in his *Topographical Dictionary of Wales*: 'the church, a very ancient structure, neatly fitted up, and kept in good repair, is evidently of a period anterior to the introduction of the English style of architecture, though some windows of that character have been inserted'.[49] This former *clas* church, known chiefly for the cross in the churchyard, has at the east end of the south aisle a neo-Norman arch that almost certainly replicates an original in the church (fig. 258).[50] This is indicated by the irregular sizes of chevron in the arch — especially just to the right of centre — and in the left jamb on which the rhythm of the ornament in the upper half is quite different from that in the lower half. The arch is of a single order with chevron on the face of the jambs and the arch. The plain impost blocks are likely to be the invention of the nineteenth century, and may have been intended for carving *in situ*. The chevron has two rolls separated by a

Fig. 257 Penmark, St Mary: chancel arch

Fig. 258 Llandough, St Dochdwy: former chancel arch reset at the east end of the south nave aisle

hollow roll framed by thin angle fillets, and there is a small step outside the outer roll. The arch is framed with a hollow chamfered hood mould.

Although Butler was not impressed by the quality of craftsmanship in the Llandough arch,[51] the richness of the decoration suggests that the church had a high status in the twelfth century. This is confirmed with reference to a close parallel for the profile of the chevron in the fragments from Sarum cathedral. On arch springer 8109789 (fig. 259) and voussoir 8109736 there is the same juxtaposition of roll-hollow-roll, albeit with two narrow steps rather than angle fillets to frame the rolls and hollow.

Various sorts of evidence remain for other small Norman churches in south Glamorganshire. At St Baruch's Chapel, Friars Road, Barry Island, Giraldus Cambrensis recorded the shrine of St Baruch, whose body was interred there in the year 700.[52] Leland recorded that 'there is no dwelling in the isle, but ther is in the middle of it at fair little chapel of St Barrok, wher much pilgrimage was usid'. Jeremy Knight's excavation revealed the original Norman apse which was replaced in the late thirteenth or early fourteenth century by a square-ended chancel.[53] The apse may have contained the shrine of St Baruch.[54] Evidence was found for the setting of the altar to the west of the chancel arch.[55] At Sully the footings of an apsidal chancel were observed during the restoration of 1833.[56] On the Gower peninsula the chapel at Burry Holms had an apsidal chancel. Also in Gower, the Norman two-cell church of St Illtyd at Oxwich was extended to the east and west in the fourteenth century, but there is still the plain narrow chancel arch (figs. 260 and 261). At Llanmadoc the chancel

Fig. 259 Sarum cathedral: chevroned arch springer no. 81109789, a parallel for the profile on the arch at Llandough

Fig. 260 Oxwich, St Illtyd: from the noth-north-east

arch is narrow, round headed and rendered,[57] while at Penrice the round-headed chancel arch has an angle roll. At Oystermouth, there is evidence for something grander. The square-ended chancel, long aisleless nave and west tower of the twelfth-century church is preserved to the south of the twentieth-century church.[58] Towards the east end of the south wall of the former chancel there is a reset pillar piscina with the bowl of a scalloped capital.[59] Also at Oystermouth there is a Norman font with a square bowl with scalloped undersides carried on a cylindrical shaft like a scalloped capital. Similar fonts occur in the Gower peninsula at Llangennith, Llanmadoc, Oystermouth and Reynoldston, and numerous examples further west in Wales. They are discussed below.

At St Fagans the core of the two-cell Norman church remains in the western half of the chancel and in the south wall of the nave.[60] In the north and south walls of the chancel there are blocked heads of the round-headed windows that would have lit the area of the high altar in the Norman church. In the south wall of the nave the inner arch of the Norman doorway is retained, and further east part of the Norman window frame is exposed to the right of its much larger, fourteenth-century replacement (fig. 262).

One of the great losses from the twelfth-century architectural heritage of Glamorgan is the nave of St Illtyd, St Wonno and St Dyfodwg at Llantrisant, which was rebuilt by J. Pritchard between 1872 and 1874.[61] The nave boasted five-bay north and south arcades with single order, round-headed arches on columns with plain capitals and square abaci.[62] The latter feature and the tall and slim proportions of the columns suggest a date in the second half of the twelfth century. Fortunately, the font was not replaced with

Fig. 261 Oxwich, St Illtyd: interior looking east

Fig. 262 St Fagans, St Mary: the nave looking south-west showing the blocked inner arch of the Norman doorway and part of a Norman window frame

the rebuilding. It is octagonal and each face is decorated with a roundel with chip-carved ornament. Newman related the font to those at Llanharry and Pyle and dated them to the fifteenth century.[63] While the affiliations are convincing, the chip carving is more at home in the twelfth, rather than the fifteenth century. This was the view expressed by J. Romilly Allen, although the octagonal form of the font led him to attribute it to the thirteenth century.[64] However, the Norman font at Mears Ashby (Northants.) provides a good analogue for the octagonal form and the decorated roundels at Llantrisant.[65]

At St Mary the Virgin, Rhossili, the reset, round-headed south doorway is of two orders, the inner chamfered and continuous, the outer with two rows of right-angled chevron in the arch carried on scalloped capitals atop nibbed shafts (fig. 263). Worn head stops carry a hood mould decorated with dog-tooth ornament on which there is an apex head. The scalloped capitals and chevron relate to the north and south nave doorways of Llandaff cathedral. The north doorway at Llandaff has a dog-tooth hood, an apex head and hood stops.

Fig. 263 Rhossili, St Mary the Virgin: south doorway

BRECONSHIRE

The county of Brecon cannot boast the Romanesque riches of either Gwent or Glamorgan. Other that the font at Brecon priory (now cathedral), discussed on pp.111–113, there is evidence for another high-status church in St Mary at Brecon, and there are two very interesting fonts, one at Partrishow, and another at Defynnog.

BRECON, ST MARY

The nave of St Mary at Brecon has a four-bay north arcade with single-chamfered pointed arches on columns probably of the thirteenth century (figs. 264 and 265). The middle support

Fig. 264 Brecon, St Mary: north nave arcade

of the arcade is quite different from the others in stone type, masonry and capital design. It has a sharply flared multi-scalloped capital clearly of the twelfth century. It is the only Romanesque feature in the church and if it is *in situ* it would represent the central column of a two-bay arcade. Given the rarity of arcade columns in Welsh Romanesque parish churches, it indicates that a church of considerable status existed here in the twelfth century, appropriate to a chapel of ease to the Benedictine priory.

Partrishow

The date of the Partrishow font has been the subject of considerable debate. An inscription on the rim records: '*Menhir me fecit i(n) te(m)pore Genillin*' (Menhir made me in the time of Genillin) (fig. 266). The paleographer and historian J.O. Westwood has associated Genillin with Genillin Voel, the only son and heir of Rhys Goch, who was Lord of Ystradyw, and Prince of Powys in the mid eleventh century.[66] Westwood also recorded that Partrishow church was consecrated in 1060 and therefore he suggested that the font was coeval with the dedication. Straightforward as this argument may seem, it is complicated by the nature of the foliage ornament that accompanies the inscription. In a footnote to Westwood's original article, the editor of *Archaeologia Cambrensis* observed that 'these foliated ornaments appear to us later than the period conjectured by Mr. Westwood. Their character seems not earlier than the end of the twelfth century'.[67] In the same footnote Westwood replied, with reference to a number of parallels for the foliage in Anglo-Saxon manuscripts. Welsh literary historian Rhys accepted the 1060 date while Francis Bond, in his book entitled *Fonts and Font Covers*, included Partrishow in his chapter on pre-Conquest fonts.[68] E. Tyrrell-Green, an early twentieth-century authority on fonts, observed that the 'inscription, however, is not free from difficulty', and that 'the ornamental border suggests a date after

Fig. 265 Brecon, St Mary: detail of middle column in the north nave arcade

Fig. 266 Partrishow, St Ishow: font

the Conquest'. He therefore suggested that the inscription and ornament may have been added later.[69] In his catalogue of *The Early Christian Monuments of Wales*, Nash-Williams opted for the rather broad date bracket of 1075–1199 without explaining why he chose to ignore the 1060 date.[70] Richard Haslam in his entry in *The Buildings of Wales, Powys*, gave the date of *c*.1055, while Lord accepted Westwood's suggestion of 1060.[71]

The debate is a familiar one in the realm of art history in which the evidence of an inscription or document is deemed to be at odds with the stylistic or typological evidence of the work of art. In this particular case we have to weigh the authenticity of the inscription against the typology of foliage in the eleventh and twelfth centuries. It seems to me that the Partrishow leaves are not sufficiently unusual to permit really close dating. In other words, their form could be paralleled in works from the mid-eleventh to the end of the twelfth century. For the inscription, to ignore the evidence for the 1060 date, proposed by Westwood, there needs to be a reason why it would be added at a later date. I cannot think of one, and therefore we must surely accept the inscription as authentic and date the font to 1060.

DEFYNNOG

The shallow round bowl of the font at Defynnog is decorated at the top with a row of large round beads set above a band of raised cross shapes separated by narrow vertical ovals (fig. 267). Below this the bowl tapers in sharply to sit on a bell-shaped stem banded in the middle. It flares in the lower half and sits on a square base with four trefoil leaves, one at each angle. On the rim is the inscription SIWVRD + GWLMER. It has been dated to the eleventh century, on the basis of comparison of the foliage on the base with that on the rim of the Partrishow font.[72] The parallel is hard to accept and the leaves at Defynnog recall nothing better than a single stiff-leaf characteristic of early Gothic capitals of the late twelfth and early thirteenth century. This would also suit interpretation of the raised diagonal crosses on the bowl as a flattened version of dog-tooth ornament.

Fig. 267 Defynnog, St Cynog: font

DENBIGHSHIRE

Like Breconshire, Denbighshire is not rich in Romanesque remains. However, the key monument, the church of St Mary at Chirk, presents some interesting archaeological problems.

Chirk, St Mary

The double-nave church of St Mary's, Chirk, has been variously interpreted in regard to the possible survival of any Romanesque fabric (figs. 268-270). The Royal Commission suggested that the original church consisted of the present south aisle and chancel, and that the present south wall of the church was built in the second half of the twelfth century.[73] In keeping with this, Mike Salter, author of *The Old Parish Churches of North Wales*, noted that the clasping buttress at the south-east angle of the church, and the blocked south doorway are 'Norman-looking'.[74] Ignoring the Royal Commission account, Hubbard's entry in *The Buildings of Wales, Clwyd*, recorded that the south wall was 'earlier' than the 'Late Perp', north nave, and that it had 'a series of shallow recesses, and a blocked round-headed doorway, which looks C17 and is obscured by a later buttress'.[75] The account of the church by the Clywd-Powys Archaeological Trust records that the 'nave and chancel on the south side are the earliest portion of the church'.[76] The account then notes that, 'a small round-headed window should indicate a 12thC date', and that the 'original south wall was perhaps taken down and rebuilt slightly further to the south with recesses holding the Perpendicular windows; built into this wall are the remnants of a round-headed door which could be 17thC, though its purpose is unclear'. Fortunately, things are not quite as complex as this review of the literature suggests.

While lacking any assessment of the detail, the Royal Commission was quite correct in seeing the south wall as that of the Romanesque church. Reading the exterior of the wall from west to east, to the east of the modern Gothic south-west-angle stepped buttress there is a Romanesque pilaster buttress with mixed ashlar and rubble, and a section of plain rubble wall (fig. 268). There are then ashlar quoins of a projecting section of wall that includes the blocked, single-order round-headed south doorway with a moulded impost preserved on the west but not on the east (figs. 268 and 269). The rough diagonal tooling on the voussoirs, the profile of the impost and the wide mortar joints, all speak

Figs. 268 and 269 Chirk, St Mary: the western end of the south wall from the south-west (top) and south-east

of Romanesque construction. A modern stepped buttress is built in front of the doorway. To the east of the projecting doorframe there is blocked round-headed window with the head cut from a single stone and then the lower section of another pilaster buttress below a rectangular late Gothic window (fig. 269). To the east of this there are Romanesque quoins to a section of wall that projects and then tapers towards the top of the wall. Also behind the south-east

Fig. 270 Chirk, St Mary: the south wall from the south-east

angle Gothic buttress the ashlar quoins are in keeping with a Romanesque pilaster buttress (fig. 270). The east wall provides no clues as to the Romanesque fabric.

The method of construction with the use of ashlar for the quoins, the doorway and window, and rubble for the remainder of the wall is common Romanesque practice and finds a close regional parallel at Heath Chapel (Salop). The setting of the doorway in a projecting frame that rises the full height of the wall reads as a plainer version of the more richly articulated group in Worcestershire, at Bockleton, Eastham, Knighton-on-Teme, Martley, and Stoulton.[77] What is more difficult to interpret is the section of wall that projects between the two Perpendicular windows. The quoins are Romanesque, so that the appearance is one of a massively wide pilaster buttress, but this quoining fizzles out at the top of the wall where the masonry runs interrupted with that to the left and right. A projecting section of wall like this is not likely to represent the whim of a quirky designer. Instead, it probably expresses a division within the church. There are no clues inside the church so analogues with other churches must be sought. The most plausible explanation is to read the feature in relation to aisleless Romanesque churches with an axial tower between the nave and chancel. While the increase in thickness of the wall at Chirk is hardly sufficient to carry a large masonry tower, it is reasonable to entertain the idea of a wooden tower, in the manner of Breamore (Hants.) or

Fig. 271 Orcop (Herefs.), St Mary: showing a timber tower of the type that may once have existed at Chirk

186

the west tower at Orcop (Herefs.) (fig. 271). The added weight of such a tower would help to explain the deformation of the wall and the consequent rebuilding, possibly when the Perpendicular windows were introduced.

There is no documentation to assist in interpreting the patronage of St Mary's, Chirk, but, if my interpretation of the fabric is correct, the inclusion of a tower, along with the use of a certain amount of ashlar, suggest high-level patronage of an important church.

PEMBROKESHIRE

Evidence for the Romanesque in Pembrokeshire comes primarily through a large number of fonts, although in his 1811 book, *A Historical Tour through Pembrokeshire*, Richard Fenton recorded the Norman cruciform church of St Michael, Pembroke, with a stunted crossing tower, the whole 'having no tendency to ornament of any kind'.[78] Unfortunately, the church is so heavily remodelled that there is no longer evidence of Norman work.

In smaller churches, plain round-headed chancel arches survive at Gumfreston, Lawrenny and Martletwy, while at Manorbier on the south side of the nave in the spandrel of the easternmost later pointed arcade arch is a Norman window that has been opened up. This may indicate that the entire nave is Norman.

The presence of the church in Pembrokeshire in the twelfth century is well recorded in the large number of fonts. The majority of them take on the form of a cushion or a scalloped capital, the latter usually articulating the underside of the bowl in the form of a square table top. Cushion-capital fonts are found at Bayvil,[79] Henry's Moat,[80] Lawrenny, Rosemarket and St Twynnels.[81] They are quite plain and are paralleled at Clovelly, Instow, Inwardleigh and Upton Hellions (Devon), and Kingston Seymour, Markbury and Weston-in-Gordano (Somerset). There is a variant of the type at Bosherston in which the angles of the cushion are given a broad chamfer. Links with fonts in the west of England are confirmed with the font at Castlemartin (fig. 272). This takes the form of a large cushion capital and rests on a squat shaft with moulded base and plain roll at the top. Unlike the plain cushion-capital fonts just discussed, Castlemartin is decorated with five scallops at the top. Each of the outer scallops is adorned with delicately fluted half palmettes and at the angle the stem of the leaf descends a short distance to a volute. This fusion of a cushion and volute capital is encountered in late eleventh-century work in the crypt at Lastingham priory and the nave clerestorey capitals of Blyth priory, and in Normandy at Cerisy-la-Forêt.[82] However, the delicate outlining of the scallops and the foliage on the font indicates a date much later in the twelfth

Fig. 272 Castlemartin, St Michael and All Angels: font

century. Most interestingly, Castlemartin shares a number of peculiar details with two fonts in Somerset at Chelwood and Hinton Blewett (figs. 272–273).[83] In addition to the basic cushion form on the stem, all three have scallops along the top and angle volutes. Moreover, at Castlemartin and Hinton Blewett the lateral scallops are carved with half palmettes, a detail that confirms Boak's attribution to the same workshop and further that the Castlemartin font was imported into Pembrokeshire.[84] The Welsh examples may have been imported from the west of England, a point that would be confirmed or disproved with investigation into the stone type(s). We may be fairly sure that these fonts would have been enriched with painted decoration.

By far the most common type is a bowl set in a square table top with three, four or five scallops on the underside, usually supported on a centrally set column. We have already encountered them in Glamorgan, and they appear in Cardiganshire and Carmarthenshire, as well as in Pembrokeshire. They are so numerous that they are simply listed below. There are three four and five scallops on each side, and in the case at Lamphey there is a frieze of six-petalled flowers set in rosettes at the top of the font bowl.[85] The font at Newport (plate 15) has traces of paint on its south face, likely an indication that all these fonts would have been painted, as was formerly the case with the font at St Philip and St Jacob, Bristol.[86] As with the Castlemartin font, the scalloped group finds parallels in the west of England, as at Molland (Devon).[87] At Llanreithan the three plain scallops on the font project in the manner of a trumpet-scallop capital.[88]

Fig. 273 Hinton Blewett (Somerset), St Leonard: font showing similarities to that at Castlemartin

List of Scalloped Table-top Fonts in Pembrokeshire

Ambleston, Amroth, Angle, Bayvil, Begelly, Brawdy,[89] Burton, Camrose,[90] Dinas, Freystrop, Haroldston West, Hayscastle, Herbrandston. Hodgeston,[91] Hubberston, Jeffreyston,[92] Johnston, Jordanston, Lambston, Lampeter Velfrey, Lamphey, Little Newcastle, Llandewi Velfrey, Llangwm, Llanhowell, Llanreithan, Llanstinian, Manorbier,[93] Marloes, Martletwy, Moylgrove, Nash, Nevern, New Moat, Newport, Nolton, Pembroke (St Mary),[94] Penally, Prendergast, Rhoscrowther, Roberston West, Rudbaxton,[95] St Brides, St Dogwells, St Florence,[96] St Ishmaels,[97] Solva, Spittal, Upton, Uzmaston, Walton East, Walton West, Wiston.

5

The Patronage of Gruffudd ap Cynan, Prince of Gwynedd

Of all the potential patrons of architecture and sculpture we encounter in our survey of the Romanesque in Wales, we are best informed about Gruffudd ap Cynan, Prince of Gwynedd (d.1137).[1] *The Chronicle of the Princes* recorded that he built many churches,[2] but we are more fully informed about him thanks to his twelfth-century biography, the *Historia Gruffud vab Kenan*.[3] Not that it provides specific details of his patronage to the effect that he built church 'x' or 'y', but it does tell us that he was a patron of architecture. We are told that 'Gruffudd, on his part made great churches for himself in his chief places, and constructed courts and [gave] banquets constantly and honourably. Wherefore he also made Gwynedd glitter then with limewashed churches like the firmament of stars'.[4] Also, at his death he bequeathed money to a number of churches, including twenty shillings to Christ Church, Dublin, 'where he was born and reared', and a similar amount to all the chief churches of Ireland. He also left twenty shillings to St Davids, 'the monastery [St Werburgh's] at Chester, and the monastery at Shrewsbury, and more than this to the church of Bangor'. Then ten shillings were left each to Holyhead, Penmon, Clynnog, Enlli (Bardsey), Meifod, Llanarmon, Dineirth, 'and many of the other chief churches'.[5]

In 1114 Gruffudd and Henry I had made peace,[6] a peace that Gruffudd maintained in 1121 when he was approached by the 'men of Powys' to support their cause against the king.[7] The peace continued and Gruffudd and Henry reigned for many years in friendship.[8] During this period Gruffudd essentially passed the leadership of Gwynedd to his two sons and he would therefore have had time to devote to matters of ecclesiastical artistic patronage, something that may well have been tied to concern for the future of his soul. The appointment of David the Scot, a former chaplain to the Holy Roman Emperor, Henry V, as Bishop of Bangor in 1120 is of the greatest significance in promoting Gruffudd on the European stage.[9] In 1107 Urban was the Norman appointment as Bishop of Llandaff with obedience to Canterbury, and in 1115 the process was repeated when Bernard became Bishop of St Davids. Gruffudd's appointment of David was with the approval of Henry I and the Archbishop of Canterbury consecrated the new bishop at Westminster.[10] These events, and the inclusion of Norman elements in the architecture of Bangor cathedral, may be read as signs of Norman influence in Gwynedd and/or a desire on Gruffudd's part to be associated with the Norman regime. A somewhat broader interpretation indicates that Gruffudd wished to be seen as the equal of the Normans. In this light it is significant that the historian C.P. Lewis has called David's appointment 'a statement that Gruffudd aspired to make Gwynedd a European principality'.[11]

Like Gruffudd himself, David may have been of mixed Welsh-Irish parentage or upbringing.[12] Most importantly, he had moved in the highest circles internationally. He taught at the cathedral school at Würzburg, and was the ambassador who accompanied the king's daughter, Matilda, to Germany for her marriage to the Holy Roman Emperor Henry V.[13] Henry V was charmed with his virtue and knowledge, and made him one of the imperial chaplains.[14] David accompanied Henry V to Rome in 1110 and for William of Malmesbury he was a panegyrist of the emperor.[15] It has been suggested that David may have been responsible for one recension of Ekkehard of Aura's *World Chronicle*, which was one of the main sources of the *Kaiserchronik*.[16] In the *Kaiserchronik* the notion of an unbroken continuity between the emperors of Rome to those of the German nation was contrived, and in this tradition the *Historia Gruffudd vab Kenan* traced the ancestry of Gruffudd from 'Locrinus son of Brutus' (great-grandson of Aeneas).[17]

Gruffudd's biography accords with this sense of worldliness:

> Gruffudd goverened for many years successfully and powerfully with moderation and peace, and enjoyed neighbourly relations in accord with the kings nearest to him, namely Henry king of England, Murchadh king of Ireland, and the king of the islands of Denmark; and he was known and prominent both in the kingdoms far from him and in those near him. Then every kind of good increased in Gwynedd and the people began to build churches in every part therein, sow woods and plant them, cultivate orchards and gardens, and surround them with fences and ditches, construct walled buildings, and live on the fruits of the earth *after the fashion of the men of Rome*' (emphasis mine).[18]

Emulation of Rome was of great importance for the Normans and Gruffudd was keen to follow this trend.

While the association between Gruffudd, Henry I and Bishop David established the climate for building, we have to ask about the iconography of the work and the recruitment of the masons. To what extent would the architecture and sculpture represent an extension of the indigenous tradition of Gwynedd versus the introduction of something new from England or even further afield? If inspiration came from outside Gwynedd then we must try to determine where the craftsmen were trained.

Our examination of the churches associated with Gruffudd starts with Bangor cathedral where building was commenced in 1120. We then explore the near-contemporary work at Penmon priory where Gruffudd's son, Idwal, was abbot. Aspects of the design and construction of Penmon are related to Ynys Seiriol (Puffin Island) while the rich articulation and sculpture at Penmon are explained with reference to Norman patronage in England and imperial patronage in Germany. Similar associations are suggested for the elaborate arch at the west of the nave of St Beuno at Aberffraw, probably Gruffudd's court church. Architectural fragments at several churches and a series of fonts are discussed in relation to indigenous artistic traditions and the work of Roger, Bishop of Salisbury (1102–39), one of the most munificent patrons in England. The chapter concludes with a brief investigation of some churches in which the plans reflect earlier medieval traditions, while others are allied to developments in Norman England.

Bangor Cathedral

About 546 Deiniol, the founder of the see of Bangor, was consecrated as bishop about twenty years after he had established the first cell on the site. Bangor was ravaged by the barbarians in 1073 but whether or not the cathedral was damaged is not known. In 1092, in an attempt to impose Norman authority on the church in north Wales, Hugh of Avranches, Earl of Chester, procured the election of Hervé, a Breton, as Bishop of Bangor.[19] With the failure of Norman rule in the region, Hervé was unable to live in his diocese, and it was not until the appointment of Bishop David (1120–39), under the auspices of Gruffudd ap Cynan and Henry I, that circumstances were conducive for the reconstruction of the cathedral. Work was sufficiently advanced for Gruffudd ap Cynan to be buried beside the high altar in 1137.[20]

Bangor cathedral does not retain a large amount of Romanesque fabric, just a pilaster buttress and a blocked round-headed window in the south wall of the presbytery, and short sections of the east and west walls of the south transept (figs. 274 and 275).[21] However, excavation has revealed the foundations of the apsidal east end of the presbytery, the crossing piers, a shallow eastern apse and parts of the terminal wall of the south transept, the west wall of the nave and the south wall of an axial western tower, and the south aisle wall of the nave.[22]

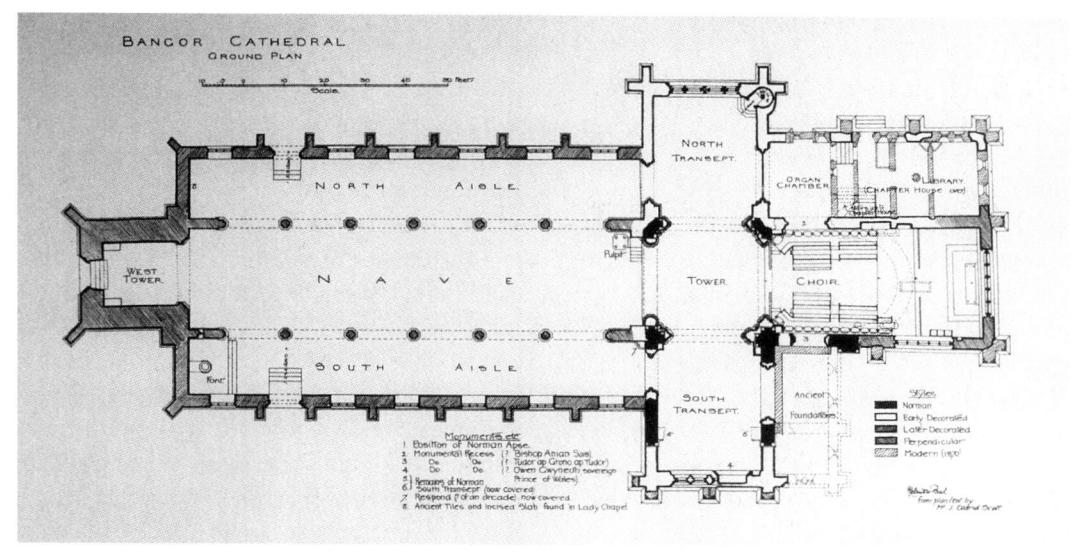

Fig. 274 Plan of Bangor cathedral from The Builder

Fig. 275 Bangor cathedral: south wall of the presbytery

The use of good-quality ashlar for the window and the buttress (fig. 275) immediately suggests a connection with in the finest English Romanesque buildings. The double step to the buttress is fairly unusual and as such is the sort of motif that might indicate a specific association for the master mason. Exactly this detail is used in the nave aisles at Shrewsbury abbey, a Benedictine house founded by Roger of Montgomery, Earl of Shrewsbury, in 1083, to which Gruffudd ap Cynan left twenty shillings at his death.

The cathedral is much smaller than its English contemporaries like Winchester, Durham, and Norwich, all of which take on the vast scale of the Constantinian basilicas of fourth-century Rome and the imperial cathedral of Speyer. A better comparison for the scale of Bangor is the former palace chapel built for King Henry I at Melbourne (Derbs.).[23] The two churches are also similar in plan with an apsidal east end beyond a square bay in the aisleless presbytery, a crossing and transepts with apsidal chapels, and an aisled nave. The Norman derivation of these elements is confirmed by comparison with Notre-Dame sur l'Eau at Domfront (Orne), although the use of a crossing tower and an axial western tower at Bangor recalls the Anglo-Saxon cathedrals of Winchester and Sherborne.[24] The same arrangement of towers was adopted after the Conquest at Hereford cathedral and Leominster priory, the latter founded as a cell of Reading abbey under the patronage of Henry I.[25] On a smaller scale, central and western axial towers were built at Petersfield (Hants.), probably under the patronage of Henry I. The plan follows one established in the late tenth/early eleventh-century First Romanesque church of St Vorles at Chatillon-sur-Seine (Côte d'Or).[26] It is also possible that the western tower at Bangor was an element deemed appropriate by Bishop David to suggest an association with the westwerks of imperial Germany. These affiliations are something new for Gwynedd and suggest that Bishop David and Gruffudd ap Cynan wanted the architecture of the new cathedral to have more than mere regional recognition. There is no evidence for the elevation at Bangor but it is most likely that it had two storeys, as at Llandaff cathedral and St Werburgh's at Chester.[27]

The elongated eastern responds of the nave arcades may reflect the Romanesque fabric and even retain the core of the twelfth-century work. Such responds were standard in West Country Romanesque, as at Gloucester and Tewkesbury, and this would imply that Bangor nave had aisles. Moreover, if the comparison of the *clas* church at Tywyn (Merioneth) with St Davids and Bangor cathedrals in the twelfth-century poem *Canu Cadfan* is taken at face value,[28] then, like Tywyn nave, the Bangor nave would have had a round-headed arcade carried on columnar piers. Columns were also used at Shrewsbury abbey and at St Werburgh's, Chester, two major Norman churches geographically close to Bangor.

The proportional system used in the plan for Bangor cathedral is a square for the crossing and transepts and one for the presbytery, then twice the diagonal of that same square for the length of the nave. Similarly, the width of the nave multiplied by the square root of 2 gives the width of the nave plus one aisle.

Just one piece of chevron ornament remains on a shaft fragment reset on the aisle side of the south-west crossing pier (fig. 276).[29] The elaboration of the multiple rolls on the chevron may be linked with entry into the sanctuary. Similar chevron shafts are used in the dado arcade of the west wall of the south transept at Penmon priory (Anglesey) (fig. 281).

Some other fragments preserved, at the time of writing, at the west end of the south nave aisle, are also of interest in connection with Gruffudd ap Cynan. One stone is carved with a rectangular panel of four-chord plaitwork on the upper section of both the front and back faces, damaged at the top (fig. 277). Nash-Williams dated it to the tenth century, while the Anglesey antiquary Harold Hughes simply claimed that it was 'pre-Norman'.[30] A second slab, not published by Nash-Williams, is carved on the upper half of both sides with a sort of elongated meander ornament. While one may be able to suggest a date in the tenth century for the ornament on the slabs, the shape of the stone and the application of the carving in a frieze-like manner on the upper section are difficult to account for. When we consider how the slabs might have functioned, one possibility is that they came from a screen.[31] If this was indeed the case then

Fig.276 Bangor cathedral: chevron shaft fragment reused on the south side of the south-west crossing pier

Fig. 277 Bangor cathedral: fragment from screen (?)

they were surely used in the twelfth-century cathedral. Whether or not they are tenth or twelfth century is likely to remain a moot point but, as we shall see with a number of fonts in Anglesey churches, there was a strong desire to boldly reflect the indigenous artistic heritage of the region in the twelfth century. Thus, whether the slabs were reused from an earlier church or carved two centuries later, they would have been happily integrated in the twelfth-century cathedral.

Attribution of Bangor cathedral to Gruffudd ap Cynan and Bishop David makes sense given the references to Gruffudd as a patron of church building in Gwynedd. The introduction of a new, more monumental style of architecture went hand in hand with the religious reform, and in this regard the achievement at Bangor parallels that elsewhere outside direct Norman rule.[32] In Munster the master mason of King Cormac Mac Carthaig's chapel at Cashel had a good knowledge of the work of Bishop Roger of Sarum, and in Gloucestershire and south Wales.[33] Yet details of some of the ornament, especially on corbel heads, bear witness to a regional heritage. In Scotland King David commenced Dunfermline abbey in 1128 with masons from Durham cathedral, but, as at Cormac's Chapel, heads and interlace on the north and south doorways reflect indigenous traditions.[34] In Orkney King Magnus began Kirkwall cathedral as a scaled-down 'copy' of Durham cathedral in 1137.[35] The same principle is encountered in Sweden where the Romanesque cathedral at Lund is a reduced version of the imperial cathedral of Speyer. The plan of the new cathedral at Bangor and the precise parallel of the buttress with Shrewsbury abbey suggest that Gruffudd and Bishop David used this very pattern of recruiting a master mason from England. At the same time, the ornament on the screen fragments spoke of the Hiberno-Welsh background of the patrons.

PENMON PRIORY

The religious community at Penmon was founded by St Seirol who was a contemporary of St Cybi (*c*.540), the founder of the church at Holyhead.[36] The community at Penmon was Augustinian by the 1220s, although how long before that date the canons had been established is not known. As a former *clas* church, Penmon is akin to the minster churches of Anglo-Saxon England. As part of the Norman reform of the English church, a significant number of the minster churches were refounded as Augustinian priories in the twelfth century, and it is possible that the change at Penmon happened in the time of Gruffudd ap Cynan.[37] Whatever the exact date of the introduction of the canons, the architecture of Penmon shows an awareness of some prestigious buildings in Norman England.

The cruciform church of Penmon preserves a significant amount of Romanesque fabric: the aisleless nave, crossing with tower, and south transept (fig. 278). The chancel dates from the thirteenth century, although it was rebuilt from above the level of the windowsills in 1855, in which year the north transept was rebuilt on Romanesque foundations, and the east wall of the south transept was built anew.[38] Local antiquary G.G. Holme tells us that 'until less than a century ago an altar stood in each of the transepts'.[39]

There are differences of opinion in the literature as to the chronology of the Romanesque work. Holme dated the church to the first half of the twelfth century.[40] Hughes

Fig. 278 Penmon priory: exterior from the north-west

placed the nave, transepts and crossing in the first half of the twelfth century and, later in the same article, attributed the nave to Prior Idwal, son of Gruffydd ap Cynan, *circa* 1130, a link previously made by H. Longueville Jones, author of an 1849 article on Penmon priory.[41] Against this the Royal Commission considered the nave to be around 1140–1150 'during the early years of the reign of Owain Gwynedd', while the central tower and south transept are placed somewhat later, between 1160 and 1170.[42] The latter interpretation is the one followed by Radford,[43] although ambiguously he attributed the south doorway of the nave to Gruffudd ap Cynan.[44] Lord also adopted an 1140–50 date for the nave 'in the time of Owain Gwynedd'.[45] National Museum of Wales curator, Mark Redknap, dated the tympanum of the south portal to the mid-twelfth century and indicated that the three-strand interlace on it reflected older artistic traditions.[46] Leask paralleled the arch moulding of the west doorway of St Flannan's Oratory at Killaloe (Clare) with the south doorway at Penmon and suggested a date somewhere between the late eleventh century and *circa* 1130.[47]

Careful examination of the fabric will allow us to establish a relative chronology for the church and to determine the most likely dates of execution. Technical aspects and especially details of the sculptural decoration will determine the training of the masons. We will also explore the motives behind the creation of a church that is far more lavish than at Ynys Seiriol on Puffin Island off the eastern tip of Anglesey, across from Penmon.

The arch to the chancel is plain, round-headed and of a single order on plain jambs with chamfered imposts (fig. 279). The arch to the south transept is also of a single order but, in sharp contrast to the chancel arch, it is larger

Fig. 279 Penmon priory: east crossing arch from the north-east

and lavishly decorated (fig. 280). There is a tall, plain, slightly tapered plinth. The bases have three rolls topped by a chamfered ring. On the east there is a semi-hexagonal shaft that is carved with chevron except for the very top section. On the west the shaft is plain.

Fig. 280 Penmon priory: south crossing arch

The capitals are an unusual blend of cushion and scalloped types. On the east the faces of the capital each have a single cushion with double cones with triangular wedges between. On the west, the inner face of the capital is a blend of a cushion shield with a scalloped underside, and the outer face has triple scallops. Both capitals have a chamfered abacus that continues through the thickness of the wall to carry the soffit of the arch. The arch soffit is plain and plastered but the front boasts a row of bead-and-reel ornament below a chevron pattern, except on the four lowest voussoirs on the west where chevron is used alone. The flat 'hood' is covered with a blend of countersunk chequers and billet ornament.

The interior of the south transept has dado arcades on the south and west walls, a feature normally reserved for churches of the highest status (fig. 281). On the face of each arch there are three rows of chevron each with a simple roll-moulded profile without any intervening hollows, steps or angle fillets. The capitals have double scallops with triangular wedges between the cones, except for the left capital of the south arcade where the capital is a plain cushion. The chamfered abaci are plain. Five of the shafts are decorated. On the south wall the second shaft from the left and the third shaft from the right both have annulets just below the middle of the shaft. On the west wall the southernmost shaft is spiralled while the one next to it and the northernmost shaft are chevroned. The bases are varied and range from quadruple stepped rolls to rolls surmounted by shallow hollows.

The west arch of the tower has two richly decorated orders (figs. 281–284). The inner order has two narrow rolls separated by a flat hollow on the face of the arch. On

Fig. 281 Penmon priory: interior of the south transept looking south-west

Fig. 282 Penmon priory: west crossing arch

Fig. 283 Penmon priory: detail of the north jamb of the west crossing arch

the second order there are narrow bands of various geometric incisions on the face and soffit of the arch, outside which there is two-roll chevron on the face towards the nave. The broad, flat label is carved with countersunk chequerboard. The abaci are all chamfered and have various ornaments on their faces. On the outer left there is chip-carved chevron, while on the inner left there are countersunk semicircles above a quirk (fig. 283). The latter motif also adorns the inner right abacus, but the inside of the outer right abacus is plain (fig. 284). There are two horizontal incisions on the angle of the outer right abacus while a row of S-shapes is gouged out of the face towards the nave. The shafts are monolithic with half cylinders for the outer order, angle rolls between flat faces on the inner left and a half octagon with an angle roll to the inside for the inner right shaft. On the outer left and inner right capitals the necking is scored with a series of diagonal incisions. The outer right capital is scalloped with rounded wedges between the cones, while the carving of the other three capitals is very difficult to interpret. The outer left capital has a deformed angle volute to the right of which a serpentine creature curls on to the right face of the capital and then back across both faces (fig. 283). Another serpent occupies the space below and to the right of the first. On the left face it is difficult to determine whether or not we have a stylized creature or an elementary geometric effort of a less-than-gifted sculptor. On the inner left capital a creature (bird?) with a bell-shaped body and no arms holds a serpent firmly with its two clawed feet (fig. 283). Details on the serpent are lacking but presumably it is the tail that curls up to the left while the upper body returns up the right side of the capital. The creature with the bell-shaped body has a tiny head from which hair (or a headdress?) grows prolifically to either side of the full length of the body. At this point things are most unclear. At the end of the hair on the left a raised arc connects to the edge of the capital, while on the right a flat tub is adjacent to the edge of the hair. A large arc covers the

Fig. 284 Penmon priory: detail of the south jamb of the west crossing arch

creature and this terminates on the left in what might be a crocodile-like head with an open mouth, and, on the right, in an upward extension of the flattened tub in which there is an irregularly shaped sunken oval. The carving seems to defy interpretation but it is perhaps worth noting a couple of potential parallels. First, the serpent recalls the one trodden on by David as warrior in the Durham *Cassiodorus* (Durham, Cathedral Library MS B.II 30, fol. 172v)[48] or more generally examples of Christ trampling the beasts. Secondly, the hair of the creature with the bell-shaped body reads as an extreme version of the Celtic tonsure worn by the image of St Matthew in the *Book of Durrow* (Dublin, Trinity College Library MS 57 [A.4.5], fol. 21v.).[49] The style of centrally parted long hair may also be allied to such works as the applique figures on the Breac Maodhóg in the National Museum in Dublin.[50] The hair of the Irish figures is far more detailed than at Penmon, but the principle of design is the same. It may also be significant that on the east capital of the chancel north doorway of St Bertoline at Barthomley (Cheshire) there is an angle head with three long fluted leaves that grow from the crown of the head to frame the face.[51] The treatment of the

Barthomley capital is more sophisticated that at Penmon but it is possible that the design of both reflect a common model from Chester. Quite what to make of these analogues, I am not sure, except to suggest that the scene is in some way associated with the idea of the triumph of good over evil. The abacus has a quirked chamfer and sunken semi-circles on the face, two to the left and one to the right.

On the right, the inner capital has a figure with a bowl-shaped head with simple features set on the corner with a small body and arms raised to the side of the head and seemingly draped with voluminous sleeves. The legs spread widely and extend across the sides of the capital to finish, on the left in an upturned animal head, and, on the right in a vertical serpent(?). The animal head attempts to bite the head of a stylized bird positioned between the leg and arm of the human figure.

Reset above and to the right of the western crossing arch is a corbel carved with what appears to be a mouth and tongue underneath a featureless face, to the sides of which are forearms and hands that grasp the sides of the face (fig. 285). Presumably the facial features were originally applied in paint. Above and to the left of the arch are two more reset stones (corbels?) carved with bland faces without either hair or ears (fig. 286). The heads are set in roundels, the one on the right seemingly held at the lower left by a human hand, while the stone on the left has a second frame that is split at the bottom and may have originally terminated here in small grotesque heads.

The crossing tower is built of roughly squared stones and is capped with a pyramidal stone roof (fig. 278). On each face of the tower there are paired belfry openings. Of these arches those on the south and west faces are renewed, although it is possible that the plain cushion capital without abacus of the west opening reflects the original. To the east and north the openings are original. The round-headed arches of the north openings are each cut from single stones, and there is a relatively massive, steep base that sits on a plain square sub-base (fig. 287). The cylindrical shaft and the cushion capital without abacus are cut from a single stone. The tower is without articulation except for

Fig. 285 Penmon priory: corbel reset above the west crossing arch

Fig. 286 Penmon priory: heads reset above the west crossing arch

chamfered string-courses that appear at the corners, just above the lower angles of the roof of each arm of the church.

The nave and south transept are rubble built except for ashlar at the corners, for windows, the south doorway and the angles of the pilaster buttresses (fig. 278). There is one pilaster buttress on both the north and south walls located to the east of centre. Their form is entirely in keeping with work in Norman England. However, it is unusual that they are not matched with buttresses at the western corners of the nave, and equally strange that they are not aligned with each other. The pilaster on the north wall is set further west than that on the south, and there is the same disjunction in the setting of the windows (fig. 288). Moreover, while the inside of the north window is plain, an angle-roll moulding frames the inside of the south window. Such a deviation from the symmetrical may indicate sloppy workmanship but I think that would be a cruel judgement on the master mason. Instead, it

Fig. 287 Penmon priory: north belfry opening in the crossing tower

Fig. 288 Penmon priory: the nave looking west

203

makes sense to place a screen in the space between the two windows to separate the (parochial?) nave from the canons' church. This interpretation accords happily with the placement of the moulded window frame in the liturgically more important area of the church.

The south doorway has a single order with plain, worn capitals and large, block-like abaci atop detached shafts supporting a roll and hollow moulding in the arch surrounded by a single-billet hood (fig. 289). A carved tympanum contains a quadruped with back-turned head attempting to bite its tail, with interlace below and above to the right. The difference in height in the placement of the two capitals is clumsy and may suggest that the doorway has been reconstructed. The interlace on the bottom of the tympanum tapers from left to right as if the design was taken from a cross shaft laid horizontally or was based on one taken from a tapering tomb slab. The interlace on the right has a different pattern to that along the bottom of the lintel and it stops just to the right of the centre of the arc. There is no corresponding carving on the left arc of the tympanum. The surface of the stone here is in the same plane as the animal's body and therefore there was never any carving on the left of the tympanum. Presumably a design was applied in paint. The rich articulation of the south and west tower arches, the south transept and south nave doorway at Penmon speak of contact with work in Norman England and careful examination will suggest specific associations for the details and a date of execution for Penmon.

Fig. 289 Penmon priory: south doorway

The plan of Penmon is most unusual amongst cruciform churches in that the crossing tower is narrower than the nave and transepts (fig. 278). In post-Conquest cruciform churches, the walls of the individual arms of the church continue those of the crossing, as at Ewenny priory, for example (fig. 118). In contrast, it was a hallmark of pre-Conquest cruciform churches to have a crossing tower with salient angles. The only parallel known to me for the arrangement at Penmon, with a nave wider than the crossing tower, is at Wootton Wawen (Warks.). Here the tower is pre-Conquest and the nave Norman. This analogue and the lack of parallels in churches elsewhere suggest that the tower pre-dates the nave and transepts. That the string-courses on the tower are largely covered by the roofs of the nave and transepts confirms this reading.

A further anomaly in the design of the crossing is that the east arch is plain and much smaller than either the south or west arch. The north arch dates from 1855 and there is no record of its form prior to this date. Moreover, the south and west arches are both richly decorated.[52] It seems likely that the eastern arch remains from the early tower and that the south and west arches are insertions into that fabric. Even so it seems unusual that the eastern arch was not remodelled in a richer mode, if it was the entry to a traditional chancel that housed the high altar. This raises questions as to the liturgical arrangement in the twelfth-century church. We have already referred to the record of there being an altar in each transept in the early nineteenth century. But what of the high altar? It seems likely that the low east arch would have led to a small, barrel-vaulted chamber as at Cormac's Chapel (fig. 290). At Cormac's Chapel the arch is considerably taller and wider than at Penmon, and the space into which it leads is simply an appendage to the richly articulated, rib-vaulted chancel. There is evidence for a similar barrel-vaulted room at Kilmalkedar (Kerry) but there the arch is wider than at Penmon and richly decorated, and the space opens directly into the nave of the church. Just how these spaces worked liturgically is not recorded but niche-like spaces are often associated with altars. Assuming that this was also the case at Penmon, the space beneath the tower would have functioned as the sanctuary space, in the manner of the rib-vaulted chancel at Cormac's Chapel. Had this been the case one imagines that the eastern arch would have received some painted decoration.

Normally in a cruciform church the high altar would be located in the eastern arm and would often be 'advertised' by a more richly articulated entrance arch into the space. Even if it is argued that the eastern arch is earlier than the south and west arches, it would still be difficult to account for the retention of such an inferior form as the entrance to the most important part of the church. It therefore makes sense to suggest that the high altar would have been placed under the crossing and that the space in the eastern arm would have been a subsidiary area for the clergy. I do not know of a parallel for this

Fig. 290 Cashel (Tipperary), Cormac's Chapel: the chancel looking east, showing a barrel-vaulted chamber similar to what may have existed at Penmon priory

arrangement in a cruciform church but at Castle Rising (Norfolk), Christon (Somerset) and Langford (Oxon), the central axial tower is the only part of the church to be vaulted. Given the frequent association of a vault with a permanent ciborium above an altar, this suggests that the high altar would have been located under the tower. Then there is the evidence excavated by Jeremy Knight at St Barruch's, Barry Island (Glamorgan), where he found evidence for an altar before the apse arch.[53] Something similar may have occurred at Studland (Dorset), and earlier medieval precedent may be cited at Reculver (Kent) and Raunds (Northants.).[54] It is possible that the pillar piscina, now set against the north wall of the nave towards the west end, might have accompanied an altar beneath the crossing.

The pyramidal stone roof of the crossing tower is related to Ynys Seiriol and Llaneilian (Anglesey), and Holme further observed that this form is common in eleventh and twelfth-century Normandy, and cited Matthew Bloxham's *Principles of Gothic Architecture* as a source.[55] Bloxham referred to the towers at Saint-Contest near Caen and Saint-Loup-Hors near Bayeux, but both appear to be later than Penmon.[56] However, the towers of Aiziers (Eure), Saint-Martin at Anguerny (Calvados), Saint-Georges at Basly (Calvados), Thaon (Calvados) and Ver (Calvados) are candidates, although to claim that any of them date from the eleventh century would be bold.[57] Of these Norman towers, Anguerny and Ver-sur-Mer are illustrated in cross-section by Ruprich-Robert, and he shows corbelled ashlar masonry for the roof construction.[58] Further examination of the masonry from within the towers would be necessary to determine whether or not the roofs have a corbelled construction as seems to be the case in Normandy or whether there are angled stones as at Ynys Seiriol.

In the north belfry opening of the Penmon tower, the form of the base recalls the bases of cross shafts, and the monolithic treatment of the shaft and capital looks back to the Eliseg Pillar.[59] It is continued in the twelfth century with a square shaft in the Corwen cross.[60] Such analogues are not a great help towards a precise date for the Penmon tower but there can be no doubt that it is earlier than the richly decorated work in the south transept and nave, and most likely contemporary with Ynys Seiriol, between 1100 and 1120.

Dado arcades are usually reserved for churches of the highest status. In the West Country School of Romanesque architecture dado arcades occur in the presbytery aisles of St John's, Chester,[61] in the south transept of Pershore abbey,[62] and in the nave of Ludlow castle chapel.

Fig. 291 Chester, St Werburgh's abbey (now cathedral): niches 1-3 in the cloister south walk

Between 1127 and 1134 they are used in both the chancel and the nave at Cormac's Chapel (fig. 290), a building closely related to West Country works, not least Ewenny priory.[63] Here we have a major collegiate church, a large Benedictine abbey, and a royal chapel named after Cormac Mac Cárthaig, King of Munster (1123–27). Three details of the Penmon dado are especially useful with regard to the determination of the source for the sculptors. First, the inclusion of the shaft ring is a rather unusual detail but one that is paralleled in both shafts of the east niche in the south wall of the cloister at St Werburgh's, Chester (figs. 281 and 291).[64] Second, the spiral and chevron shafts are paralleled in the second niche in the Chester cloister wall (figs. 280, 281 and 291). Third, the multiple roll bases of the northernmost shafts of the west dado arcade at Penmon are paralleled in the left base of the first niche at Chester, and the comparison extends to the arch to the south transept Penmon (figs. 280, 381 and 291). Details of the west crossing arch at Penmon confirm the association with St Werburgh's. The left shaft of the sixth niche at Chester is octagonal like the inner right shaft of the tower west arch at Penmon. The roll moulding on the face of the inner order of the west crossing arch is a slightly simplified version of the one on the face of the fourth niche in the south wall of the Chester cloister. At Chester the two rolls are clearly separated by a hollow roll framed with angle fillets. At Penmon the hollow is less clearly defined and indicates the work of a less accomplished hand. Be that as it may, there is no doubt that the forms belong together. The double-scallop capitals are also similar in both paces.

The link between Penmon and St Werburgh's, Chester, is substantiated with reference to the south doorway of St Michael at Shotwick (Cheshire).[65] The chevron ornament carved on the dado arcades at Penmon is identical to that on the second order of the Shotwick doorway. Moreover, the hood of the Shotwick doorway is carved with a countersunk chequerboard/billet as on the south and west tower arches at Penmon. The manor of Shotwick belonged to the monks of St Werburgh's, Chester,[66] and it is likely that the Shotwick doorway was executed by masons who had worked at the abbey. It is also a mark of the status of Penmon that this countersunk chequerboard motif also appears inside the presbytery windows of Llandaff cathedral (figs. 94 and 100).

Details of the work at St John's, Chester, help to confirm the artistic link between that city and Penmon. At St John's the west capital of the window in the west bay of the south choir aisle interior is a double scallop with triangular wedges between the cones, as in many of the Penmon capitals But there are two other details that are important. First, the pronounced angular outline of the scallops agrees with the outline of the cushion on the left capital of the south transept arch at Penmon. Secondly, the complex moulding on the abacus of this Chester capital suggests that the string-course above the south dado arcade at Penmon is a reduced version of this principle.

It may be that the rich decoration at Penmon was deemed appropriate for a chapel in a church of a princely patron, but I suspect it is something more than that. Gruffudd ap Cynan was buried at Bangor cathedral but it is possible that the Penmon transept was for the burial of his son, Idwal, abbot of Penmon. Historian Alan Thacker has suggested that Earl Hugh of Chester founded St Werburgh's, Chester, as a Benedictine family mausoleum, on the model of Roger of Montgomery's foundation of Shrewsbury abbey in 1083.[67] Ron Baxter, Director of the *Corpus of Romanesque Sculpture in Britain and Ireland*, has indicated that the cloister niches at St Werburgh's were probably intended to carry a series of tombs of members of the family of Hugh d'Avranches.[68] He cited parallels with the later tomb recesses in the north chancel wall at Carlisle cathedral, and in the choir aisles at Hereford cathedral. Closer in date to Chester would be the examples in the south nave aisle at Worcester cathedral.[69] There are also similar tomb recesses in the south cloister wall at Blyth priory and a single tomb recess to the east of the north portal at Cormac's Chapel, Cashel. It is also possible that the scheme at Penmon had imperial associations with the Emperor Henry IV's plan for a mausoleum of the Salian dynasty at Speyer cathedral.[70] Such a link may seem far-fetched but we must remember that Bishop David of Bangor moved in those very imperial circles prior to taking up the episcopacy at Bangor. An entry in a collection of genealogies made in the thirteenth century, *Achau Brenhinoedd a Thywysogion*, states that 'Idwal son of Gruffudd [ap Cynan] was abbot of Penmon and his grave is in Penmon'.[71] This establishes a specific connection with Gruffudd ap Cynan, and indicates that Penmon was of appropriate status for the prince's son to be the abbot and later to be buried there.

The roll-and-hollow moulding of the Penmon south doorway has been compared with the west doorway of St Flannan's Oratory at Killaloe.[72] They clearly belong to the same Norman world of forms but they are not identical nor does the parallel suggest that the Penmon carvers may have come from Killaloe. As architectural historian Richard Gem has shown, Killaloe represents the impact of Anglo-Norman forms in that part of Ireland. It is more likely that Penmon also reveals Anglo-Norman sources. It makes sense to start our search as close as possible geographically to Penmon for this is the area that would surely have been contacted by a patron in search of skilled craftsmen. Once again, St John's at Chester provides some analogues. Here the arch from the south transept to the south choir aisle is especially instructive in that the moulding on the west face of both orders of the arch is identical to that on the Penmon doorway. Moreover, on the capital of the inner order on the left of this Chester arch, we see the same sense of design ambiguity between the cones and the scallop faces as on the capitals of the arch to the south transept at Penmon (figs. 280 and 292).

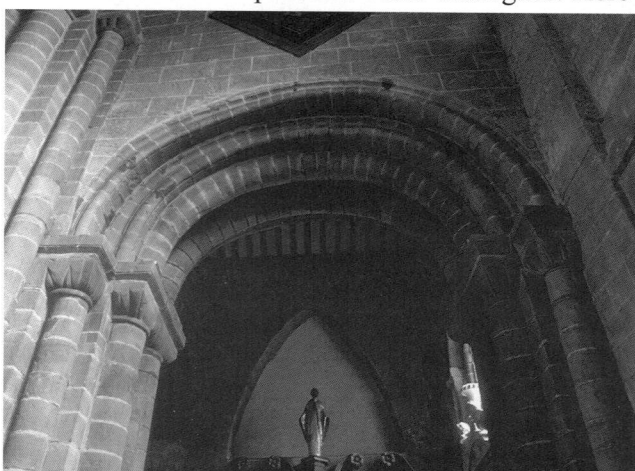

Fig. 292 Chester, St John the Baptist: arch from the south transept to the south choir aisle

A source for the Penmon craftsmen in Chester makes good sense in that it is geographically the closest Norman centre of major architectural and sculptural activity. At the time, work was in hand on both St Werburgh's abbey and the collegiate church of St John the Baptist. And the link with between Gruffudd ap Cynan and St Werburgh's is documented; Gruffudd left money to St Werburgh's at his death, and the prior of St Werburgh's was at Gruffudd's death-bed.[73]

We have already mentioned some associations between Penmon and Cormac's Chapel and these may be extended to some specific motifs. The multiple-roll bases in the south crossing arch and the south transept dado arcade at Penmon, are also used in the north portal of Cormac's Chapel. The inner left shaft of the west crossing arch at Penmon, which has angle rolls to either side of a flat central strip, relates to the responds of the inner order of the chancel arch at Cormac's Chapel. The variety in the types of shafts used at Penmon is akin to the chancel arch, north portal and doorway to the north tower at Cormac's Chapel. Both churches have portals with carved tympana, a very unusual motif both in Ireland and in Wales. These parallels are not sufficient to establish a link between the craftsmen at Cashel and Penmon but they demonstrate the strong desire of two patrons to create richly decorated churches that would vie with contemporary work in Norman England. In neither case was their desire to challenge the gigantic scale of some English churches, but in the use of masons from Sarum cathedral at Cashel, and from Chester at Penmon, the respective patrons aimed at smaller versions of the best buildings of the day.

Just as we have suggested that the interlace on the panels associated with the choir screen at Bangor cathedral provided visual reference to an indigenous artistic heritage, so the interlace on the Penmon tympanum tells the same story. The importance of the regional artistic tradition in the church is also witnessed in the font. The font is located at

Figs. 293 and 294 Penmon priory: the font from the south-south-west (left) and the north-east (right)

the west end of the nave and has a square bowl that tapers from bottom to top (figs. 288, 293–294). We are told by Francis Bond that it 'is the base of a rectangular cross, which lay in a stone-mason's yard (hence the weathering of the stone) till it was converted into a font, and removed to Penmon church in the middle of the last century'.[74] Nash-Williams recorded the following: 'Font of truncated pyramidal shape with a hollow basin in the top (? Cross-base reused. Cf no. 38, Penmon cross). Front (E) border of plain square T-fret pattern enclosing two plain triquetra-knots. Right face: Plain square T-fret pattern. Left, four interjoining squares of diaper key-pattern. Style similar to Penmon cross no. 37 to which the present base may have belonged'. He proposed a date of the late tenth or eleventh century.[75] For the Royal Commission the font originally served as a cross base and was dated *circa* 1000.[76]

Tapering is indeed a feature of cross bases but this does not necessarily mean that Penmon font originally served that purpose. A number of the Anglesey tub fonts also taper, as at Cerrig-Ceinwen and Newborough, on the plain fonts at Llanbabo and St Mary at Rhodo-Geidio,[77] and originally at Llanffinan, and at Pistyll (Gwynedd) (fig. 321). One side of the Penmon font is plain, a feature not associated with cross bases but found on fonts in Anglesey, at Cerrig Ceinwen, Llanbeulan, Llangwyllog, Llechcynfarwy, Newborough and Trefdreath. This may be explained either by the plain section being set against a wall, or that the plain section is where the priest stood to administer baptism.

The date of the Penmon font is not easily determined. On the one hand, parallels with Penmon cross no. 37 may indicate that the two works are contemporary. On the other hand, evidence will be presented below for the continuity or revival of such motifs on the twelfth-century fonts in the region. It may therefore be argued that the Penmon font is contemporary with the rich phase of work on the church in the 1120s and '30s.

Ynys Seiriol (Anglesey) Priestholm/ Puffin Island

Ynys Seiriol, also known as Ynys Lenach, Priestholm or Puffin Island, is a privately owned island off the eastern tip of Anglesey, across from Penmon.[78] The location is not exactly conducive to architectural-historical investigation. In the 1890s a plague of brown rats was recorded on the island, which subsequently succeeded in wiping out ground-nesting birds including all but twenty pairs of puffins.[79] A century later, in 1998, an exercise was mounted to exterminate the rats, which 'involved enlisting the help of the RAF who airlifted two-and-a-half tonnes of poison-treated wheat'.[80] Subsequent monitoring suggests that the rats have gone. And so have the rabbits, killed off by myxomatosis, which has allowed a ground cover of elder scrub to thrive,[81] thus making the prospect of walking with full camera equipment from the shore of the island to the church a rather uninviting one. This architectural historian has not taken up the challenge, and therefore the following account is based on antiquarian sources, most specifically that of Harold Hughes, and a report produced in connection with conservation work on the church undertaken by intrepid officers of Cadw in 1994.

Of the fabric of the Romanesque church, there remains the axial tower, plus the ruins of the nave to the west, and the former barrel-vaulted chancel to the east. Jones dated the tower to the early twelfth century while the Royal Commission attributed it to the middle of the twelfth century.[82] During excavations in 1896, the foundations of an earlier chancel were found within those of the thirteenth century.[83] This early chancel was about five feet square and had a stone barrel vault and a sharply pointed roof; the lines of both are visible against the east wall of the tower.[84] The plan is comparable with Cormac's Chapel at Cashel (fig. 360) and Kilmalkedar (Kerry), while the stone barrel vault with a steeply pointed stone roof has been compared with St Columba's House at Kells.[85] Most significantly, Ynys Seiriol provides the closest formal parallel for Penmon priory with a former low room entered through a simple round headed arch in the east wall of the tower.

The internal dimensions of the tower are 8ft 3in east to west, and 8ft 5in north to south.[86] It has two stages and a pyramidal stone roof. Hughes recorded that the east and west round-headed arches of the tower are 'formed of rough unwrought limestone'.[87] On the western arch there are square imposts with lower chamfers of the 'simplest Norman type'.[88] The imposts of the eastern arch are not extant. The ground floor of the tower was originally lit by a small round-headed window in the south wall, which was subsequently cut by a round-headed arch 'to give communication to a building situated southward'.[89]

There was a floor in the tower some thirteen feet from the ground and supported on wooden beams for which sockets remain on the east and west walls.[90] At belfry level there are single-round-headed openings located centrally in the east and north walls, and twin-headed openings in the south and west walls. In each case the arch heads are cut from single stones.

Hughes reported that the roof of the tower was constructed on wooden centering and that 'under the northern and eastern slopes the marks of the boards so employed, each about 7 ins. wide, are distinctly visible throughout'.[91] Gerard Baldwin Brown, former Watson-Gordon Professor of Fine Art at the University of Edinburgh, suggested that the roof of the tower is of corbelled construction and has been paralleled with such work in Ireland, although he did not mention specific examples.[92] However, an unpublished report in the Cadw office observed that 'perhaps the most significant constructional detail is the way the stones are laid. At the base of the pyramid the lowest courses are set horizontally but above this they pitch downwards from the face — i.e. not corbelled. However, towards the top a few original tufa blocks appear to survive *in situ* and these seem to be set on the horizontal, most notably the perforated stone'.[93] These observations help to place the construction in context. On the one hand, the use of tufa suggests knowledge of Anglo-Norman vault construction, as in the nave at Chepstow priory. Tufa is also used in the stone roof above the nave of Cormac's Chapel, Cashel although whether this is a reflection of traditional Irish practice or the fusion of Norman and Irish techniques is not known. On the other hand, the pitching of the stones relates to the south doorway at Capel Lligwy (Anglesey) (fig. 295), and to Irish vault construction, as illustrated by architectural historian Harold Leask.[94] I have not examined the Irish stone roofs in question first hand, except the one above the nave of Cormac's Chapel.[95] Interestingly the stones there are not corbelled out and they are of tufa, very much like Ynys Seiriol as described in the Cadw report. Earlier than this, radial stones are used above corbelled stones in St Columb's 'House' at Kells and in the nave of St Kevin's at Glendalough.⁹⁶ This is essentially the same in principle as at Ynys Seiriol but not with the use of tufa. The matter calls for further investigation and this should include examination of the pyramidal stone roof on the north tower of Cormac's Chapel.

It is possible that the structure of the Ynys Seiriol roof represents something that was already established in Wales. Capel Trillo at Llandrillo-yn-Rhos (Denbighshire) is a small rectangular structure that covers a holy well.⁹⁷ Unfortunately the original stone roof has been replaced by one of a lower pitch, but an illustration of 1855 depicts its more steeply pitched predecessor.⁹⁸ It shows a hole in the roof that reveals that the stones on the roof are not of corbelled construction but that they radiate more like voussoirs in an arch. In other words, they pitch downwards from the face of the roof like the roof of the Ynys Seiriol tower. The representation may simply follow artistic convention for the depiction of an arch, but Higgons Well, just north of Uzmaston (Pembrokeshire), preserves a barrel vault beneath a stone roof. It has been attributed to the thirteenth or fourteenth century, but in the absence of clearly datable architectural motifs the matter of the date is a difficult call.⁹⁹ The case is analogous to Capel Trillo where dates ranging from the sixth to the sixteenth century have been suggested but, as Edward Hubbard observed in *The Buildings of Wales, Clwyd*, 'There is no reason why it should not be early'.¹⁰⁰

Fig. 295 Capel Lligwy, Anglesey: south portal

The nave at Ynys Seiriol (measuring about 18ft x 12ft) is destroyed but part of the south wall is embedded in a modern wall and the rest of the nave is determinable from the foundations. The juxtaposition of the aisleless nave and axial tower is paralleled in a large number of churches in Norman England, as at Studland (Dorset), although in the English examples the cell to the east of the tower was significantly larger than at Ynys Seiriol.¹⁰¹ It has been suggested that at Studland the high altar was not located in the eastern arm of the church, while the exclusive use of vaults under the central axial towers at Castle Rising (Norfolk), Christon (Somerset) and Langford (Oxon), is likely to indicate that the high altar was placed beneath the tower in these churches. Whether the altar at Ynys Seiriol was beneath the tower or in the niche to the east is likely to remain a moot point, but my preference would be for the former.

Hughes observed that the Ynys Seiriol tower is of the same character as the tower at Penmon, and is probably of similar date.[102] However, the unornamented character of the stonework suggests that Ynys Seiriol pre-dates the richly articulated work in the south transept and north and south arches of the tower at Penmon priory. Therefore the period 1100–20 would suit the work at Ynys Seiriol.

Aberffraw (Anglesey), St Beuno

In his Presidential Address to the Cambrians on 'The Ancient Churches of Anglesey', Harold Hughes observed on the south wall of Aberffraw church, 'mutilated remains of a string course, apparently of Norman character and date contemporaneous with the arch' at the west end of the south aisle.[103] Today the string-course in question is badly weathered but an illustration in the Royal Commission inventory of Anglesey monuments suggests that Hughes was correct in the Norman attribution.[104] The wall would therefore have been the south wall of the aisleless nave of a Norman church before the present nave was built to relegate the Norman space to an aisle.

Inside the west wall of the aisle is a richly carved, two-order arch that is now blocked (fig. 296). The inner order sits on plain jambs and chamfered imposts that continue as abaci of the capitals of the second order. On the right there is a cushion capital with recessed shields, while a cushion capital with outlined shields is on the right. The detached monolithic semi-cylindrical shafts rest on moulded bases. The arch is capped with a quirked-chamfered hood mould. The inner order of the arch is carved on the face with chevron composed of two quirked rolls with a hollow between them, and sits on a chamfered impost atop plain jambs (fig. 374). The chevron is a more accomplished version of that on the tower west arch at Penmon, where there are two rows of rounded-section separated by a channel (fig. 350). The second order comprises twenty-six stones each carved with various beasts' heads and interlace. Except at the lower left of the arch there is an alternating pattern of frontal heads and frontal foliage (figs. 374-382). The former are characterized by framed, rectangular foreheads, eyes that are either delineated

Fig. 296 Aberffraw, St Beuno: blocked west arch in the nave

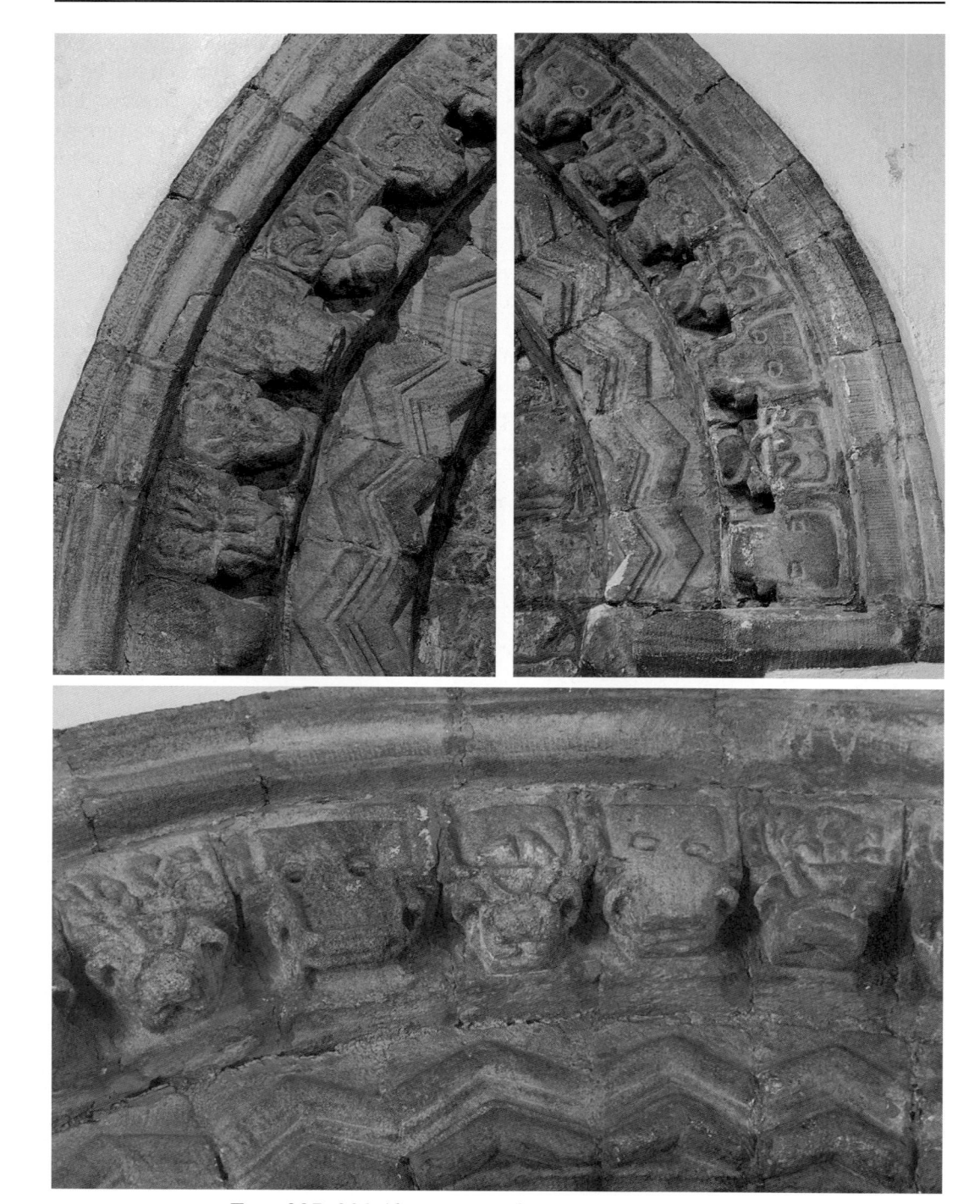

*Figs. 297–301 (this page and opposite top and centre)
Aberffraw, St Beuno: details of the blocked west arch in the nave*

by drilled holes or as if they were two discs pressed into clay, and a broad snout. Their stylized mouths bite on rods or stems of foliage, or have protruding geometric tongues. In some cases stems issue from the mouth and grow to the sides and above the head. The alternate voussoirs are carved with interlacing foliage patterns that grow from two stems that issue from the mouth of strangely stylized heads at the inner edge of the voussoir. These heads have a pronounced muzzle and large drilled eyes, and on the alternate voussoirs they are integrated with the creatures with rectangular foreheads so as to create an interlocking play between the two heads.

The heads on the Aberffraw arch are not traditional beakheads nor are they easy to parallel.[105] There is a family resemblance with heads on the south portal of St Cuthbert at Great Salkeld (Cumbria) and the west portal of the Nuns' church at Clonmacnois (fig. 302).[106] The former is not dated

Figs. 302 Clonmacnois (Offaly), Nuns' church: detail of the west portal showing similar heads to those on the Aberffraw blocked arch

but it is probably of the third quarter of the twelfth century, while the Nuns' church at Clonmacnois was completed in 1167.[107] The interlacing foliage above some of the Aberffraw heads may also suggest Irish associations but I have not found precise parallels that would indicate a direct connection. For interlace and heads there are two Scottish doorways with associations, the south portal of St Cuthbert at Dalmeny (Lothian) and the west portal of Dunfermline abbey. In both instances three-dimensional heads alternate with single voussoirs carved either with interlace or animals at Dalmeny, or heads and interlace and geometric pattern at Dunfermline. Dalmeny is not dated by any documentary evidence, but Dunfermline abbey was commenced by King David of Scotland in 1128 and the church was consecrated in 1150.[108] The projecting heads on the west doorway at St Bees (Cumbria) relate to Dalmeny and Dunfermline.[109] Heads on the reset south doorway at Killaloe cathedral provide a close parallel for the central head at St Bees and the south doorway at Great Salkeld.[110] There are allied heads loose at St Finn Barre's cathedral, Cork, and in the chancel of Cormac's Chapel (fig. 290).[111] There are also three-dimensional heads on the west portal of the chapel of St Oran on Iona, but they are very worn and later in date.[112] To this may be added the simplicity of the heads on the south portal of St James at Kilkhampton (Cornwall) where the stumpy snouts are sometimes flanked by stylized leaves just as various ornaments flank some of the snouts of the Aberffraw heads (fig. 303). These comparisons may suggest that the works share a common Celtic heritage but they are hardly close enough to indicate that the Aberffraw arch was executed by any one of these workshops.

Instead, as at Penmon priory, there is strong evidence to suggest that the sculptors were recruited from Chester. The form of the chevron is precisely paralleled on the second order of south choir aisle window bay 2 at St John's, Chester (figs. 297, 298). This is not an especially common profile of the ornament and serves to link the two works very closely. This is reinforced by the form of the cushion capital with the recessed shields, as on the west capital of bay 2, south choir aisle window at St John's, Chester. Most interestingly, an angle mask on a fragment of an impost at St John's, Chester, has the same treatment of the beady eyes as in the Aberffraw heads in which the plain eyes are simply created with a circular incision. The tusks of the Chester head grow to a simple spiral on the left and more intricate interlace on the right like in a way that foreshadows the Aberffraw designs. Also, the drilling of the cavities from which the tusks grow on

Fig. 303 Kilkhampton (Cornwall), St James: detail of the south portal

the Chester head is allied to the treatment of the eyes on the inside heads at Aberffraw. The west doorway of the Norman chapel at Prestbury (Cheshire) is also of interest in this connection, even if its very weathered condition precludes judgment on questions of style quite as exact as one would like.[113] Each voussoir of the inner order of the arch is carved with a head from which stems issue from the mouth to grow up the side of the head and burst into symmetrical leaves above. To either side of the heads there are incised straps just as on the impost head from St John's, Chester. Then, the manner in which the foliage is arranged in a box-like frame above the head recalls alternate voussoirs on the Aberffraw arch where foliage becomes interlace, as appropriate to the artistic tradition of Gwynedd. The heads on the outer south capital of the chancel arch of St Mary at Bruera (Cheshire) are also of interest in this connection. The centre and left heads are finished off almost square at the top like many of the Aberffraw heads and the simple carving of the eyes is the same in both places, except that at Aberffraw the incised eyebrows of the Bruera heads are dropped.

Two details at Penmon should also be related to Aberffraw. First, the semi-cylindrical monolithic jamb shafts on the south and west tower arches at Penmon are set against the side rather than the face of the jamb exactly as in the Aberffraw arch (figs. 280, 296). Secondly, the stylized lips and protruding tongue of the corbel head above the west tower arch at Penmon are allied to some of the Aberffraw heads (figs. 285, 300).

The position of the Aberffraw arch on the inside of the west wall of the south aisle of the church requires explanation. It has been suggested that it was formerly the chancel arch of the Romanesque church and was subsequently moved to its present position.[114] If this was the case then it must be asked when the move took place? It would have to have been done when the present arcades were being built in the sixteenth century because there is no place in the later medieval structure to fit the arch.[115] While many English Romanesque portals were reset in later aisle walls, I do not know of a resetting of a chancel arch in this way. We must therefore consider the possibility that the arch is *in situ*. In his *Topographical Dictionary of Wales* Samuel Lewis recorded that 'the tower of the church was demolished many years ago, but there is a handsome pointed arch, formerly leading into it from the church, still in a very perfect state of preservation'.[116] The reference is interesting for, although the arch is not pointed, Lewis sometimes made mistakes on matters of description, as at Kerry, where he refers to eight bays of a Norman north arcade where the western four bays are twelfth century but the four to the east are Perpendicular. He called the Aberffraw arch 'handsome', which would be strange if the arch was not exceptional in some way. Thus, if it is in its original position, the rich decoration suggests that the tower was a very important part of the Romanesque church.[117] Richly moulded arches leading into west towers are used in pre-Conquest churches in England, as at St Benet's, Cambridge, and Barnack (Northants). After the Conquest there are examples at Corringham (Lincs.), Morcott and Tixover (Rutland).[118] In each case it seems likely that the richness of the arch announced entry into the baptistry. On a larger scale there is the three-order arch to the west tower at St Peter's, Northampton, on which there is a variety of chevron in the arch, carved capitals, and ornamented shafts.[119] Unfortunately the ecclesiastical status of St Peter's in the twelfth century is not known, but the sophisticated articulation of the church that includes the alternation of major and minor supports in the nave arcades suggests that it was a high ranking church. Pevsner asked, 'Is the ambitious conception of St Peter connected with its situation close to the castle?'[120] The answer must surely be affirmative, which leads us to consider the situation and patronage of use of the church of Aberffraw.

Aberffraw had long been the principal seat of Gwynedd and Gruffudd ap Cynan held his court there.[121] Given the documentation that Gruffudd built 'large churches in his own major courts', there can be little doubt that Lloyd and Radford were quite correct to suggest the Aberffraw arch is the work of Gruffudd ap Cynan.[122] The church would therefore have been a palace chapel for the prince, within which an elaborate western arch suggests associations with the tradition of *westwerks*. Of course, integral with the *westwerk* is a tribune, and other than Lewis's mention of a tower at Aberffraw, there is no evidence for this. Be that as it may, it is worth mentioning that Henry I's contemporary chapel at Melbourne (Derbs.) had a tribune above a large arch at the west end of the nave. Affiliations with the German imperial tradition of the *westwerk* may be explained through Bishop David of Bangor.

In regard to the nature of the decoration itself, it is significant that arches carved with animal heads came into vogue in England in the 1120s with the patronage of King Henry I and Bishop Roger of Salisbury. Henry's work at Reading abbey is well known for the introduction of the classic beakhead ornament.[123] Beakheads also appear at Old Sarum cathedral and Sherborne castle for Bishop Roger of Sarum where other animal head types were also used.[124] Thus it would seem that Gruffudd ap Cynan wished to emulate this great royal patron and that of his justiciar.[125]

Certain fragments of sculpture at St Cybi at Holyhead, Penmynydd, Llanbabo, and Heneglwys, and a number of fonts in Anglesey churches plus one at Pistyll on the Lleyn peninsula, may be associated with the patronage of Gruffudd ap Cynan and/or followers who wished to emulate his work.

HOLYHEAD (ANGLESEY), ST CYBI

St Cybi founded his church at Holyhead in the sixth century within the old Roman fortress later known as Caer Cybi.[126] Hughes recorded 'two or three stones with Norman chevron reused as ordinary building material in the walling of the south transept. Whether these belonged to the former church on the site of St Cybi's, or that occupied by Capel Llan-y-Gwyddel, is uncertain'.[127] He further noted that the chevron is similar to that at Llanbabo.[128] Gruffudd ap Cynan left money to the church at Holyhead and it may be that he either initiated or inspired the rebuilding there.

PENMYNYDD (ANGLESEY)

Three chevrons are reused in the exterior south and east walls of the church.[129] They have triple rolls that relate to closely to the chevron on the dado arcades in the south transept at Penmon (figs. 281 and 304). The *Canu Tysilio* refers to Penmynydd as St Tysilio's

Fig. 304 Penmynydd, St Gredifael: chevron reset in the exterior east wall of the chancel

(d.640) place of retreat.[130] St Tysilio is specifically connected with the church at Meifod (Montgomery) to which Gruffudd ap Cynan left ten shillings in his will. This association, and the stylistic relationship of the chevron with Penmon, may indicate that Gruffudd was responsible for the work at Penmynydd.

LLANBABO (ANGLESEY)

The single-cell church at Llanbabo preserves a Romanesque double-splay south nave window with the head cut from a single stone and some interesting Romanesque sculpture reset above the south doorway (fig. 305). The head of the doorway is a segmental brick lintel but to the side and above is Romanesque work. Hughes informs us that 'amongst the illustrations made by the Rev. John Skinner, in connection with his "Ten Days' Tour through Anglesey in December, 1802," is a sketch of a round arched doorway in the south wall of the nave, with chevron voussoirs forming the arch. The doorway has been altered and slightly enlarged, probably in the first half of the last century, to enable coffins to be

Fig. 305 Llanbabo, St Pabo: detail of the south doorway

brought into the church with less difficulty than of old.'[131]

The sculpture above the south doorway consists of a large, oval, Celtic-shaped head with a small mouth in a roughly circular frame to the left (fig. 306), a smaller head, also encircled, on the right, and a large, flat head at the apex of the arch with four chevron voussoirs each to the left and right. The chevron has three rope-like lines and an irregular pattern. The heads are all weathered. Hughes suggests that the heads may represent the three persons of the Trinity.[132] There is another head reset at the apex of the inside of the doorway. The chevron is of the same type as in the blind arcade of the south transept at Penmon priory and the fragments at Penmynydd (figs. 281 and 305), whilst the encircled heads recall those above the west crossing arch at Penmon (figs. 286, 305 and 306). These parallels suggest that the work was undertaken in the time, and perhaps under the patronage, of Gruffudd ap Cynan.

Fig. 306 Llanbabo, St Pabo: detail of the eastern head

Heneglwys (Anglesey)

The church was originally dedicated to the Irish saint, Caibre.[133] Above the doorway to the south porch there is a reset stone from the apex of an arch carved with a triple-roll chevron atop a simple stylized mask (fig. 307). The chevron takes the place of the hair for the mask. The creature is without a defined nose, and the mouth is simply implied on the underside of the stone, while volutes provide the ears. A similar stone is reset above the north nave doorway (fig. 308). Apex masks are popular in West Country Romanesque architecture. Perhaps the most celebrated example is from Bishop Roger's Sarum cathedral and contemporary with it is one in the west bay of the Romanesque north nave arcade at St Peter's abbey, Gloucester.[134] There are

Fig. 307 Heneglwys, St Llwydian: label mask above the door to the south porch

Fig. 308 Heneglwys, St Llwydian: label mask above the north nave doorway

allied examples at Elkstone, Forthampton, Kempsford, Little Barrington, Siddington, Upleadon (all Glos.), Bolstone (Herefs.), Great Durnford and Malmesbury abbey (Wilts.) and Cormac's Chapel at Cashel. It is quite possible that Bishop Roger's work at Sarum would have been known to Gruffudd ap Cynan through Bishop David of Bangor because Roger was present at David's consecration at Westminster.[135] The stylization of the Heneglwys heads recalls certain heads on the Aberffraw arch where we find close parallels for the drilled eyes and the stylized mouths (figs. 300, 307 and 308). The chevron is of the same type as the Penmon south transept dado arcades, Penmynydd and Llanbabo (figs. 281, 292–294, 307 and 308). Hughes has also compared two stones with billet ornament reset in the east gable at Heneglwys to the arch to the south transept at Penmon.[136] With these parallels we are dealing with sculptors who worked for Gruffudd ap Cynan so it is not unreasonable to suggest that he was also the patron at Heneglwys. This would fit happily with the association with Bishop Roger of Sarum and is confirmed with reference to the Heneglwys font.

The round bowl of the font is carved with a band of meander above a round-headed arcade below which there is a frieze of lozenge chevron (fig. 309). Both the chevron and meander may be interpreted in two ways. The lozenge pattern of the chevron is closely paralleled on a hogback tomb in Gosforth (Cumbria) (figs. 309 and 310). Such an association would serve to emphasize the importance of an indigenous insular tradition, and the simulation of death and resurrection with baptism. But the chevron is also a progressive

Fig. 309 Heneglwys, St Llwydian: font

221

motif in near-contemporary Anglo-Norman Romanesque architecture, the lozenge type first appearing at Hereford cathedral, commenced between 1107 and 1115. More specifically it occurs on the arch of the window in bay 2 of the south choir aisle at St John's, Chester, the very window that provides the precise parallel for the chevron on the Aberffraw arch. The handling of the motif on the Chester window is more three dimensional, not least with the pellets between the chevrons, but this may be accounted for by the difference in stone type. The Chester sculpture is in sandstone and much easier to carve than the gritstone of the Heneglwys font.

Fig. 310 Gosforth (Cumbria), St Mary: hogback tomb showing similar lozenge carving to the font at Heneglwys

The meander ornament is, on the one hand, a continuation of a traditional form of ornament used on earlier crosses, as at Penmon (fig. 280). On the other hand it relates to Sarum cathedral.

So how are we to decide the question of the date of the font? The literature presents a confusing state of affairs. The second Penmon cross has been linked with the fonts at Heneglwys and Llanbeulan, and it has been suggested that 'the Penmon artefacts and some of the fonts came from a single workshop and were produced in the first half of the eleventh century'.[137] Against this, the Royal Commission attributed the Heneglwys font to the mid-twelfth century, and the one at Llanbeulan to the late twelfth century.[138] For Hughes the arcades and lozenge chevron represented Norman influence.[139]

Crucial for the dating of the Heneglwys font is the detailing of the arches of the arcade in which the sculptor creates a subtly curved roll moulding and a hollow between the extrados of the arch and the curved triangles in the spandrels. The juxtaposition of roll and hollow is very much in the repertoire of the Romanesque architect and its appearance on the font is most readily explained if we see the font and heads at Heneglwys as products of the same time and patron. Association with Gruffudd ap Cynan happily explains the lozenge chevron and meander as both a reference to traditional ornament, and one that will link him with the most prestigious contemporary patrons like Bishop Roger of Sarum.

Fonts

Closely related to the Heneglwys font is the one at Llanbeulan, which, however, is unique amongst the Anglesey examples in being rectangular (figs. 311 and 312). The east, north and west faces are carved but the south side is plain, like the west side of the Penmon font. The upper angles of the font are articulated with shafts that sit on ledges above roll mouldings. On the north face there is an arcade of six round-headed arches set above a lozenge-chevron frieze (figs. 311–312). The frieze extends beyond the limits of the arcade and the spaces at the ends of the arcade are occupied with a plain strip that returns around the ends and bottom of the chevron, and unornamented shafts at the angles of the font. The strip to the left of the arcade is ornamented with a simple incised chevron. The juxtaposition and detail of the arcade and lozenge chevron is the same as on the Heneglwys font except that the arches of the arcade have a more fully rounded section like a truly architectural roll moulding in an arch. Such a detail speaks more clearly of Norman rather than Anglo-Saxon associations and surely precludes Lord's dating of the font to the late tenth to eleventh century. On the west face at Llanbeulan the lower frieze has fret ornament as on the upper frieze at Heneglwys, while the main decoration is countersunk chequerboard (fig. 312). As with the lozenge chevron and meander, the

Figs. 311 and 312 Llanbeulan, St Beulan: font from the north-east and north-west (top)

countersunk chequerboard reflects earlier work, as on the seventh-century Bewcastle (Cumbria) cross. But it also appears in a purely twelfth-century context on the west arch of the tower and arch to the south transept at Penmon priory (figs. 280, 283 and 284). It is also used on the book shrine of the Stowe Missal, a mid- to late-eleventh-century oak box decorated with silver plates.[140] The motif appears in Normandy in the eleventh century; a particularly good example is on the lintel of the south doorway at Beaumais (fig. 20). The east face of the font has an equal-armed cross, superimposed on a doughy circle in the middle of the composition (fig. 311). The shape of the cross-head is like the Penmon crosses nos. 37 and 38, and Diserth (Flintshire) no. 185. Nash-Williams dated the Diserth cross and the conical cross base (no. 186) to the twelfth/thirteenth century. To the lower left and right are raised plain semi-circles while the upper rim has lightly incised linear chevron, and the strips to the side have a flattened cable. The close similarities between the Heneglwys and Llanbeulan fonts indicate that they come from the same workshop and even the same hand. Therefore it is most unlikely that they are separated in time as suggested by the Royal Commission.

Like the Heneglwys and Llanbeulan fonts, that at Llanddeusant (Anglesey) is also arcaded (9 bays), but it is unique in having a series of circular and oval depressions on the capitals and beneath the arches that may have connections with metalwork (fig. 313). The un-architectonic shape of the capitals indicates that they were created with the depressions in mind. Beneath six of the arches there is a single depression in the centre of the bay, but under the western arch a Latin cross is formed with a large circular sinking with oval depressions set above, below and to either side. In the arch to the left there are three vertically set ovals, while to the right five depressions are arranged in the form of a St Andrew's cross. For Hughes the more elaborate panels 'may possibly have represented the Trinity, the Cross and the Five Wounds respectively'.[141] He also suggested that the depressions may have been 'filled with metal or some distinctive substance', or that they were set with pebbles.[142] Whatever the material of the fillings, we should imagine that they were painted in imitation of precious stones to give the font the appearance of metalwork. Three analogues make the point clearly. First, the late eleventh-century 'Krodo Altar' preserved in Goslar museum which is pierced by holes, like the sinkings on the Llanddeusant font, which

Fig. 313 Llandeussant, St Marcellinus and St Marcellus: font from the south-east

originally would have been filled with semi-precious stones and coloured glass in imitation of gems.[143] Second, the pre-1014 pulpit of the Holy Roman Emperor Henry II in Aachen cathedral is encrusted with gems and some large bosses as well as sunk enamels.[144] On a smaller scale, the Ardagh chalice, in the National Museum of Ireland, is enriched with bosses, and comparison of the font with a chalice serves to connect the sacraments of baptism and Eucharist.[145]

The propensity to imitate the art of the metalworker in other materials was common in the Middle Ages and was often associated with the very highest levels of patronage. On the Gero Crucifix in Cologne cathedral, so named after the patron, Archbishop Gero (969–76), wood is painted in imitation gems on Christ's cruciform halo. The late 1130s sculpture of the west portals of the abbey church of Saint-Denis, commissioned by the famous Abbot Suger, abounds with imitation gems and pearls, and many further references to the art of the metalworker are seen in Suger's limestone Apostle Relief.[146] For font design there is the celebrated case of the late twelfth-century Aylesbury group in which the fluted, chalice-shaped bowls were probably based on a great gold chalice made for Abbot Simon of St Albans (1167–83).[147] And, of particular interest in relation to Llandeussant, the bowl of the Romanesque font at Crick (Northants.) is covered with three rows of hemispherical projections carved against moulded circular frames in imitation of gem settings.[148]

Decorative bosses are also found on the Llanbadrig font but here they are carved directly onto the bowl, one beneath each of the eleven arches of the arcade (fig. 314). Here the capitals and the articulation of the arcade recall the Heneglwys font, although the arches themselves lack any degree of plasticity and the bases have been omitted. The bosses look like elementary versions of the 'ice-cream-whirl' paterae of the triforium of the west bays of the nave at Worcester cathedral (after 1175) and in the dado arcades inside the Lady Chapel at Glastonbury abbey (1184–86/89).[149] This does not mean that the Llanbadrig font necessarily dates from the late twelfth century. Wall bosses were used by Bishop Roger's masons at Sarum cathedral and the motif was taken up in Cormac's Chapel before 1134. Given the associations of aspects of the sculpture at Heneglwys with the work of Bishop Roger, it seems reasonable to suggest that the inspiration for the bosses on the Llanbadrig font may have been taken from the work of that great English patron.

A simpler, square version of an arcaded font is at Llanfechell (Anglesey) with two arches on each side

Fig. 314 Llanbadrig, St Padrig: font

(fig. 315). Here the rough finish of the stone makes one think of the application of a thin film of plaster and paint and the possibility of figures painted beneath the arches, as on Romanesque fonts in the Rhineland.[150]

A much smaller arcade is used in the lowest of three ranges of ornament on the Llaniestyn Rural (Anglesey) font (figs. 316–319). The bowl takes the form of an oval with flattened ends, and the execution of the carving is less accomplished than on the fonts examined so far. The arches

Fig. 315 Llanfechell: font

are both round headed and segmental. In the middle is a layer of three-strand chevron with truncated points. At the top on the west side there is a panel of countersunk chequerboard on the left, and countersunk lozenge to the right (fig. 316). On the south-west corner the countersunk chequerboard reappears, followed by a knot on the south face and an equal-armed cross with flared ends and irregular raised rectangles in the interstices on the south-east corner (figs. 317 and 318). A straight-sided spiral on the east face spreads to the north-east corner (fig. 318). An interlaced cross is carved on the north face (fig.

Figs. 316 and 317 Llaniestyn, St Jestyn: font from the west-south-west (left) and the south (right)

*Figs. 318 and 319 Llaniestyn, St Jestyn:
font from the east (left) and the north-north-west (right)*

319). The countersunk chequer-board clearly belongs with the Llanbeulan font and the Penmon arches (figs. 280, 283, 284 and 320). The chevron is similar to that on the single ornamented band at Tregaian (Anglesey) (fig. 320). A more involved and somewhat unruly variant of the chevron is on one face of the font from Tal-y-lyn chapel at Llanbeulan.[151]

Just as there is significant difference of opinion as to the date of the Penmon and Heneglwys fonts, so other fonts on Anglesey and the allied example at Pistyll (Gwynedd) (fig. 321), across the straights from Anglesey on the north coast of the Llyn peninsula, have been variously dated and interpreted. Lord has dated the ring-chain pattern on the Pistyll font to the late tenth or eleventh century, while the Royal Commission saw it as a product of the late twelfth century.[152] The ring-chain pattern is related to that on the second Penmon cross and the shaft of Gaut's Cross, Kirk Michael, Isle of Man, which, according to Kermode, is one of eighteen examples on Manx crosses.[153] The parallel may be extended to the Gosforth cross.[154] These are generally dated to the

Fig. 320 Tregaian: font

tenth or early eleventh century so it is important to record that the patterns on the Romanesque fonts at Vänge and Mårdaklev in Sweden come close to Pistyll.[155] C.S. Drake, a leading authority on Romanesque fonts, suggested that such patterns would be more easily comprehended if the separate elements were shown in different colours. He also cited Danish examples on which there is good evidence for the painting of fonts.[156] A good example of the application of colour on a stone is the panel carved with a large animal caught in the coils of a serpent found in the neighbourhood of St Paul's churchyard in London, now preserved in the Museum of London.[157]

Two links of the ring chain pattern on the Pistyll font are repeated on the font at Llangristiolus (Anglesey) where the ornament is set in an architectural frame with pilasters that support a four-arched corbel table (figs. 321 and 322). This is most important in terms of the date of the font. The motif of the arched corbel table is most frequently associated with First Romanesque architecture in northern Italy, the Pyrenees, the Rhone valley and Burgundy, and contemporary Ottonian and allied buildings like St Pantaleon, Cologne, which was consecrated in 980 (fig. 53). Its life continued in Second Romanesque architecture and in terms of the architecture of the British Isles it is a motif of the later eleventh and twelfth century. Therefore the Llangristiolus font should be dated to the twelfth century, as suggested by Radford.[158] Lord has attributed the Llangristiolus font to the same workshop as the font

Fig. 321 Pistyll, St Beuno: font

Fig. 322 Llangristiolus, St Christiolus: font from the north-east

Fig. 323 Cerrigceinwen, St Ceinwen: font

at Cerrigceinwen (Anglesey) (fig. 323),[159] and has further paralleled one interlaced panel on the Cerrigceinwen font with the central front and rear panel of the second Penmon cross.[160] On the basis of this he suggested a tenth to eleventh-century date for both the cross and the font. Against this Nash-Williams and the Royal Commission suggested a twelfth-century date for the Cerrigceinwen font.[161] My preference would be for the latter.

A variant on the Cerrigceinwen interlaced panel occurs on the font at Trefdraeth (Anglesey) where it is accompanied by four panels each with a saltire cross, and one plain panel (fig. 324). Here it is interesting that the raised elements in the design have a curved surface in the manner of the lozenge chevron on the Heneglwys and Llanbeulan fonts (figs. 309, 311 and 324). A further variant, in which the cross interlace is combined with a two-strand circle, appears on the Newborough (Anglesey) font (fig. 325). This allies it to two panels on the Llangristiolus font where the arched corbel table dates it firmly to the twelfth century (fig. 326).

The motif of the saltire cross on the Trefdraeth font (fig. 324) appears on three other Anglesey fonts: Llangaffo, Llechcynfarwy and Llanfair-yn-Neubyll. At Llangaffo the recut round bowl has five rectangular panels filled

Fig. 324 Trefdraeth, St Beuno: font

Fig. 325 Newborough, St Peter: font

Fig. 326 Llangristiolus, St Christiolus: font from the west-north-west

with saltire crosses (fig. 327). There are subtle differences in the treatment of the individual panels that illustrate the interest of the sculptor in subtle variety in design. A simpler version of the theme is encountered on the font recorded at the former church of St Mary at Llanfair-yn-Neubyll. The church is now de-consecrated and enquiries have not determined the whereabouts of the key, meaning that the following observations are based on the account in the Royal Commission.[162] There are seven square panels created with simple incisions filled with an incised saltire cross with a single incised chevron in each quadrant. Also with incised design is the font at Llechcynfarwy two-strand St Andrew's crosses in square panels to north-east, south-east and south-west, then blank, then to the north-north-west there are four lines from top right to bottom left but only two lines top left to bottom right (fig. 328).

The lower half of the Llanfinnan font has been cut back to facilitate its setting on a later square stem, but the upper section of the bowl remains in good condition (fig. 329). The pronounced taper on the bowl is most closely allied to Pistyll where the ring-chain motif seems to be the inspiration for the simplified version at Llanfinnan (figs. 321 and 329). The meandering ribbon interlace lacks the sense of order found in the works considered so far and it seems fair to attribute the Llanfinnan font to a lesser hand.

Another five Romanesque fonts in Anglesey stand apart from those considered so far and may have been

Fig. 327 Llangaffo, St Caffo: font

Fig. 328 Lechgynfarwy, St Cynfarwy: font

Fig. 329 Llanfinnan, St Finnan: font

Fig. 330 Llanfair yn Cwmwd: font

Fig. 331 Llangefni, St Cyngar: font

executed later in the twelfth century or in the early thirteenth century. At Llanfair yn Cwmwd the contracted oval bowl sits on a projecting square frieze atop a modern stem (fig. 330). The bowl has a thin moulded rim and a projecting cross on the cardinal axes. Human heads occupy the four corners of the frieze and a fifth head is carved in the middle of the north side. Here there are additional crosses between the central and angle heads while on the east side there is a loosely defined chevron-like ribbon. The simplicity of the heads recalls those at Penmon and Llanbabo but the lack of clearly defined stylistic details makes it difficult to assess the significance of such analogues. Rather more telling is the introduction of human heads at the angles of the font, something that is encountered most readily in Cornish fonts of the late twelfth century.[163] The Llanfair yn Cwmwd font is probably contemporary with these works. At Llangefni the disused font, now in the west porch of the church, has a plain, chalice-shaped bowl with a simple incised chevron frieze (fig. 321). The chalice shape, rather than the tub, is probably indicative of an advanced date in the twelfth century. The Llangwyllog font is especially interesting (figs. 322–323). On the one hand, the tub shape is in keeping with many of the Anglesey fonts examined so far and the uncarved section of the bowl relates to Cerrig Ceinwen, Llanbeulan,

Fig. 332 Llangwyllog: St Cweyllog: font from the north-west

231

Llechcynfarwy, Newborough and Trefdraeth, as well as to one side of the square font at Penmon. To the left of the plain area there is an unfinished section of carving in a square panel in which a saltire cross is a recognizable element in the design (fig. 332). This may be related to a number of the fonts examined so far, from the simple designs at Trefdreath, Llangaffo and Llelchgynfarwy (figs. 324, 327–328 and 332), to more involved patterns at Penmon, Cerrigceinwen and Newborough (figs. 293, 323, 325 and 332). On the other hand, the next design to the left has a circumscribed cross and quatrefoil with stylized leaves in the interstices. Then, the remainder of the bowl is carved with interlocking triangular groups of stylized trefoil leaves that grow alternately from stems that form semicircular frames for the leaf triangles at the top and the bottom of the bowl (fig. 333). These are quite different to any of the designs we have met so far on the Anglesey fonts. The last pattern is repeated on the Llantrisant font[164] and looks forward to the designs on the fonts at Llangeinwen and Llanidan (figs. 334 and 335). The Royal Commission attributed the fonts at Llangwyllog, Llantrisant and Llanidan to the thirteenth century,[165] but the typologically earlier foliage forms at Llangwyllog and Llantrisant would be more at home in the last third of the twelfth century. For Llangeinwen and Llanidan the foliage patterns are best compared with work at Valle Crucis abbey, a Cistercian house founded from Strata Marcella in 1201 (figs. 333–337). The capitals of the south doorway at Llanfair Caer Einion (Montgomery) are also related and, like those at Valle Crucis, may reflect work Strata Marcella.[166]

Lord's dating of some of the Anglesey fonts to the tenth or eleventh

Fig. 333 Llangwyllog: St Cweyllog: font from the east

Fig. 334 Llangeinwen, St Ceinwen: font

Fig. 335 Llanidan, St Idan: font

Fig. 336 Valle Crucis abbey: south corbel on the south crossing arch

Fig. 337 Valle Crucis abbey: north capital in the north window of the interior east wall of the presbytery

century prompts me to emphasize the case for a date in the twelfth century. While not all the fonts include motifs that are peculiar to the Romanesque period, it is important to stress that the dating of the group should be made with reference to the latest motifs. As we have seen, the arcades and the arched corbel table belong to the twelfth century. Moreover, to have such a large group of fonts earlier than the twelfth century would be unusual, even unique, in European terms. While there are examples of pre-Conquest fonts in England — Deerhurst (Glos.) is probably the best-known — the vogue for fonts begins in earnest in the twelfth century.[167] In terms of Anglesey, the start of this trend should be attributed to the patronage of Gruffudd ap Cynan. The location of the fonts is interesting in that in most cases they are found in churches that boast an early Christian foundation. Llanbadrig is so named after the dedication of the church to St Patrick, and was reputedly founded in 440 by Patrick himself when he stopped in Anglesey *en route* from Pope Celestine in Rome to Ireland.[168] Cerrigceinwen was founded around 450 and Llanbabo in 460.[169] Llangristiolus was founded about the year 550,[170] whilst Llantrisant dates from 570.[171] Llaniestyn was founded towards the end of the sixth century.[172] Llanbeulan, dedicated to St Peulan who lived in the early sixth century, was founded in 630.[173] Llangaffo, named after St Caffo, is from the sixth century,[174] and Llangeinwen was originally built in the sixth century.[175] Penmon was founded in the sixth century by Maelgwyn Gwynedd.[176] Llaneugrad was built about 605,[177] and Llanidan was founded in 616.[178] Llanfinnan dates from the early seventh century.[179] Llechgynfarwy and Rhod-geidio were founded about 630.[180] Llangadwaladr, was founded or built by Cadwaladr, the last of the Welsh kings of Britain, in 650.[181] The foundation of Newborough is not recorded but it was the location of one of the palaces of the princes of Gwynedd.[182] The use of traditional insular motifs on the fonts celebrates the history of Christianity in the region, while the reference to current Romanesque vocabulary indicates a more worldly approach to artistic patronage. The fonts therefore provide the perfect compliment to the architectural ambitions of Gruffudd ap Cynan at Bangor cathedral, Penmon priory and Aberffraw.

With the exception of the fonts here attributed to the late twelfth and early thirteenth century, the range of motifs used fits quite happily in the time of Gruffudd ap Cynan. However, the dating is not absolute and it is entirely possible that some of the fonts were produced in the time, and perhaps under the patronage, of Gruffudd's son, Owain Gwynedd (1137–70).

OTHER ANGLESEY CHURCHES

While the plans of Bangor cathedral and Penmon priory depend on Norman precedent, elsewhere a tension between tradition and innovation is witnessed in the plans, and presumably the liturgical arrangements, of several churches. At Capel Lligwy the single-cell church has a south doorway with one order of non-radiating voussoirs. Llanbabo and Pistyll both have single-cell plans with the distinction of retaining small, twelfth-century windows; on the south side to the east of the main portal at Llanbabo, and towards the east end of the north wall at Pistyll (fig. 338). Both Capel Lligwy and Pistyll boast beautiful coastal settings but for spectacular coastal isolation there is nothing quite like Llangwyfan, which is accessible only at low tide (fig. 339). The Royal Commission claimed that the south wall of the church is twelfth century.[183] This may be correct even though I could not detect any traits in the fabric peculiar to that time. Whatever the date may be, we experience the isolation of the church and the continuity of the single-cell plan inherited from an early medieval tradition. There is no church fabric in Wales that is unequivocally early medieval. However, in Ireland there remain a significant number of single-cell churches from the tenth and eleventh centuries. The tradition of the *damliac*, or stone church, goes back to the eighth century,

Fig. 338 Pistyll, St Beuno: from the north-north-west

Fig. 339 Llangwyfan, St Cwyfan: general view from the south-east

and a particularly fine example is Clonmacnois cathedral, which was erected about 909.[184] The rectangular plan measured 18.8m by 10.7m internally, and although the church has been subsequently remodelled and is now roofless, the walls of the church stand to an impressive height. There can be little doubt that 'in the eastern part of the church' a screen would have provided a liturgical division between the nave and the sanctuary, as described in St Bride's church at Kildare in the mid-seventh century.[185]

Other single-cell rectangular churches are much smaller, as at Teampall Chiaráin at Clonmacnois, which measures 3.8m by 2.5m internally.[186] It has been suggested that these small examples are tomb churches and that it is in the tradition of funerary architecture that lies behind the *damliac*[187] This concept would also seem to work for Wales where the *eglwys* or *capel y bedd*, the grave church, would represent the start of this tradition. The chapel of St Cybi at Holyhead is a simple rectangular structure located in the churchyard south-south-west of the parish church (fig. 340). The chapel is built next to, and in line

Fig. 340 Holyhead, St Cybi: general view from the east

with, the Roman wall that defines the perimeter of the churchyard, and is on a different axis to the main church.[188] It therefore seems likely that the grave church marks the site of the burial of St Cybi. There is a similar separate grave chapel at Llaneilian (Anglesey) located to the south-east of the church, and at Clynnog Fawr (Gwynedd) the grave of St Beuno is marked by a huge fifteenth-century tower to the south-west of the church to which it is connected by a passage.[189] Something similar it also witnessed on the island of Iona where the mortuary chapel of St Oran is located at the south-west angle of the abbey church.[190]

At Llaneugrad we see something quite different, a two-cell plan with round-headed chancel arch that belongs to the Anglo-Norman tradition (fig. 341).[191] Unfortunately the exterior has been rendered with roughcast but at least the proportions of the twelfth-century church can still be appreciated. Norman influence was also evident at Llanfairpwllgwyn where an apsidal chancel was excavated.[192]

Fig. 341 Llaneugrad, St Eugrad: view from the south-east

Fig. 342 Llanfairgynghornwy: looking east

The nave at St Mary at Llanfairynghornwy measures 27ft 6in by 13ft 10in (internal measurement), a 1 to 2 proportion, with a plain, single-order, round-headed chancel arch which is set back slightly on its jambs (fig. 342).[193] Entrance is through later west doorway. The chancel arch is not set symmetrically within the east wall of the nave, for there is 2ft 9¼in of walling to the north but only 1ft 9½ in to the south. The deflection from centre is not as extreme as at Pennant Mellangell but it may suggest placement of relics to the north-east of the chancel arch.

On a larger scale at Llaneilian the west tower is Romanesque and has three stages each slightly set back from the one below in a pre-Conquest tradition, as at Earls Barton (Northants.) and carried on in major English tower design after the Conquest (fig. 343). The

Figs. 343 and 344 Llaneilian, St Eilian:
the west tower from the north (left) and arch from the nave into the west tower (right)

exterior is completely rendered and without distinguishing architectural features. However, the tall proportions of the round-headed window in the second stage of the north wall suggest a date towards the end of the twelfth century. This accords happily with the pointed arch from the nave to the tower (fig. 344). This has completely plain jambs, chamfered imposts and a narrow chamfer in the arch. There is no west doorway to the tower and this indicates that the space was probably used as a baptistry. The Romanesque west towers at Market Weighton (Yorks. E.R.) and Great Shefford (Berks.) house contemporary fonts, a placement that seems to reflect that encountered in Carolingian *westwerks* as at St Riquier at Centula and elsewhere.[194]

Comclusion
The nature of the patronage of Gruffudd ap Cynan clearly emulates that of King Henry I and Bishop Roger of Sarum. While our prince of Gwynedd could not compete with these patrons in terms of architectural scale, the choice of motifs in his churches and on his fonts display an awareness of the latest trends in the most prestigious work in England. But far from being satisfied with mere copies of English works, Gruffudd created monuments

that fused Anglo-Norman features with elements that proudly proclaimed his Hiberno-Welsh heritage. Executed by masons recruited from Chester, works such as Penmon priory and Aberffraw have associations with the Holy Roman Empire that vie with analogous imperial links in Anglo-Norman architecture and may have been inspired by Bishop David of Bangor's time in the court of the Emperor Henry IV.

6

Church Architecture, Shrines and Fonts for Welsh Patrons

Under Norman control in Ceredigion, in 1111/16 the church of Llanbadarn Fawr was given to the Benedictine monastery of St Peter at Gloucester.[1] Unlike Ewenny priory, which was also given to St Peter's, Gloucester, around that time, there is no evidence for construction of a Norman church at Llanbadarn Fawr. The present grand cruciform edifice dates from the early thirteenth century, which implies either that nothing was built in the twelfth century, or, if it was, then it was not a very large building. This would accord with the view expressed by Gerald of Wales, who, on his visit in 1188, found that the church of Llanbadarn Fawr was 'reduced to a sorry state'.[2] While it is not absolutely clear that this applies to the condition of the fabric, there is no doubt that it refers to the customs of the church. Gerald wrote, 'a remarkable fact that this church, like so many others in Ireland and Wales, has a layman as what is called its abbot'.[3] His account is most informative in regard to the continuation of the tradition of the pre-Norman *clas* church, and what he saw as a corrupt practice.

> There has come about a lamentable use and custom by which the most powerful people in the parish have been appointed by the clergy as stewards in the first place, or rather as patrons and defenders of the churches. In the process of time their greed has grown greater and they have usurped full power, in their impudence appropriating all church lands and assuming secular possession, leaving the clergy nothing but their altars, with their tenths and oblations. Even these last they have made over to their sons and other relations who are actually in the church. These so-called defenders of the churches, who are really bent on destroying what they should protect, have taken the name of abbots, presuming to attribute to themselves not only a title but also lands to which they have no right.[4]

He contrasted this with the Norman practice: 'In the reign of King Henry I, when the English were still in control of Wales, Saint Peter's monastery in Gloucester administered this church in peace and tranquility. After Henry's death the English were driven out and the monks expelled. As I have explained, laymen took forcible possession of the church and brought in their own clergy'.

The gloomy picture painted of Llanbadarn Fawr by Gerald suggests that there would be little hope for artistic activity in the traditional *clas* church. But clearly this proved not to be the case. Abbot Morfran of Tywyn in the 1140s was praised for his patronage and he is almost certainly responsible for the construction of the Romanesque church there. And there is good evidence to suggest that architectural ambitions ran even higher at Meifod.

Our investigation of Welsh patronage in this chapter commences with the important *clas* churches at Tywyn and Meifod. We move on to consider the patronage of Rhys ap Gruffudd, The Lord Rhys of Deheubarth (d.1197) at the Cistercian abbey church at Strata Florida. It is suggested that some fine fonts in Cardiganshire may be products of the patronage of The Lord Rhys and his circle, and this vogue for fonts in the late twelfth century is paralleled in adjacent counties. Churches in Powys and Gwynedd are examined against both Welsh and English backgrounds and crosses and fonts are similarly explored. Finally, we investigate the reconstructed shrine at Pennant Melangell and allied fragments in nearby churches that suggest the shrines like the one at Pennant Melangell housed the relics of other local saints in the vicinity.

TYWYN (MERIONETH), ST CADFAN

Of the important twelfth-century cruciform *clas* church of St Cadfan at Tywyn, there remains the west wall of the north transept and three bays of the nave north and south arcades, with round-headed clerestorey windows above the arcade spandrels.[5] On the exterior the rubble construction of the walls is fully exposed and is without any articulation (fig. 345). In contrast, the interior is plastered and lime-washed (figs. 346 and 347). Before 1692 there were four bays in the nave but in that year the crossing tower fell and was replaced by a low west tower within the church that occupied most of the former western

Fig. 345 Tywyn, St Cadfan: the exterior from the north-west

Fig. 346 Tywyn, St Cadfan: the interior looking east

bay.[6] This tower was pulled down in 1848.[7] The present crossing, south transept, and sanctuary date from the nineteenth century, but the Royal Commission suggested that the chancel was probably built upon the original foundations.[8] It seems likely that this is also true for the crossing and transepts.

The plain, single-order, round-headed arches of the nave arcades rest on squat columns except at the east end where the responds are square-ended and extend like a spur wall to the west of the crossing piers (figs. 346 and 347). The columns do not have fully articulated capitals but simply flare out at the top. The elongation of the east responds of the nave arcades is paralleled in the great south-west midlands abbey churches of Gloucester and Tewkesbury, and the nave of Bangor cathedral. The ledge created level with the tops of the arcade responds probably provided support for the rood screen. The columns also belong in the West Country Romanesque orbit, with analogues in the nave at Great Malvern priory, and in Wales in the north nave arcade at Ewenny priory (fig. 126) and both nave arcades at St Woolos at Newport (fig. 216). Ewenny also supplies a parallel for the setting of the clerestorey windows above the nave arcade spandrels rather than above the arches. The flaring at the top of the column is unusual but may have been the result of the reluctance to create a cut-stone neck for the capital. On the other hand, capitals without necking become fairly popular in the West Country school in early Gothic buildings of the late twelfth century. It is therefore possible that the design at Tywyn is simply an earlier example of that trait.

Fig. 347 Tywyn, St Cadfan: the interior looking west

The Royal Commission proposed a date between 1150 and 1200 for the construction of the church at Tywyn but Peter Lord's suggestion of the 1140s is infinitely more convincing.[9] He refers to a poem by Llewelyn Fardd, probably written shortly after 1147, which praised the beauty of the church of Tywyn and its relics of St Cadfan, the sixth-century founder of the church, that included a crozier.[10] The poem praises Abbot Morfran of Tywyn, a layman, for the civilized life at Tywyn under the abbot and the *clas* of resident clergy. In addition to being Abbot of Tywyn, Morfan was steward of the castle of Cynfael. Admittedly, the poem may well have been commissioned by Morfan to enhance the fame of his church and to ensure favour with his new lord, Cynan ab Owain Gwynedd, who took control of Merionnydd in 1147.[11] In the poem Tywyn church is compared with the cathedral churches at both St Davids and Bangor,[12] and whilst the poem is self-promotional, the comparison is most significant at a number of levels. In the first place, Abbot Morfan's traditional Welsh *clas* church is put on a par with two cathedral churches. Secondly, both St Davids and Bangor had been constructed under the auspices of Norman-appointed bishops and were subject to the authority of Canterbury. In spite of the protests of the incumbent *claswyr* at St Davids, Bernard, a Norman, was appointed bishop by Henry I in 1115 and remained in office until 1148. He rebuilt the cathedral, which was consecrated in 1131. David was bishop of Bangor from 1120 until 1139, and his new cathedral was sufficiently advanced for Gruffudd ap Cynan to be buried next to the high altar in 1137. For Morfan's church at Tywyn to be considered the equivalent of two 'Norman' cathedrals was to state quite clearly that the traditional organization of the *clas* church was working perfectly well. Thirdly, the poem celebrates the 'renowned relics' of St Cadfan, especially,

> The fair precious crozier of new miracles,
> which prevents an enemy from killing his opponent (lines 51-52).[13]

At a time when the cult of saints was so important in religious culture, the possession of relics of the patron saint was, of course, a clear sign of superior status. And, in this context, it must be recalled that the relics of St David had been stolen from St Davids in 1079. That was unfortunate, but what happened at Bangor may even be regarded as relic mismanagement. In 1120 Bishop David and Gruffudd ap Cynan agreed to the removal of the body of St Dubricius (Dyfrig) from Bardsey island to Llandaff cathedral. This was good for Urban and Llandaff but it left Bangor in an inferior position to Tywyn in the patron-saint-relic department. Fourthly, from the architectural point of view, Tywyn church was considered to be cathedral-like. While medieval notions of 'similarities' between buildings are not always the same as ours, features like a cruciform plan with crossing tower, and a nave flanked by two aisles and lit by clerestorey windows, may be taken as hallmarks of a 'great church', features that Tywyn shared with Bangor cathedral. With the parallel with Bangor in mind, it is also worth recalling the suggestion that the present square chancel at Tywyn was built on twelfth-century foundations. That would result in a square-ended version of the apsidal east end at Bangor, but it is possible that by the 1140s something grander might have been attempted by the ambitious Abbot Morfan. At Ewenny priory, which shared the cruciform plan with crossing tower and aisleless transepts with Tywyn, there is a three-bay eastern arm, and in the early thirteenth century a long chancel is built at the great *clas* church of Llanbadarn Fawr. Only excavation would determine the answer for Tywyn.

The rebuilding of Tywyn church in a manner akin to that of the Normans should not be interpreted as a sign of submission to the would-be ecclesiastical invaders, but rather as a bold assertion of independence by an equal, or should one say 'superior', Welsh organization.

Meifod (Montgomery), St Tysilio and St Mary

Meifod church is set in a 2.2-hectare, 5.44-acre, circular churchyard,[14] a legacy of its high status as a *clas* church.[15] St Tysilio was the second son of Brochfael Ysgythrog (*c.*502–560/70), King of Powys. He entered the church at Meifod where he studied under Gwyddfarch, and after spending seven years as a hermit on Anglesey, where he established his church on Ynys Tysilio — church island, in the Menai Straits — he returned to become abbot of Meifod.[16] By the mid-twelfth century he was regarded as the principal saint of Powys. The ode written to Tysilio by Cynddelw, court bard to Madog ap Maredudd, prince of Powys (d.1160), focuses on Meifod.[17]

Of the Romanesque north nave arcade there remain one and a half bays at the west end of the present nave, and similar remains of the former south arcade are immured in the

Fig. 348 Meifod, St Tysilio and St Mary: the nave looking north-west

south nave wall (figs. 348 and 349). The arches are round-headed and those of the north arcade have two plain orders. They are carried on a column with a 'Doric' capital and a matching east respond. There are distinct traces of limewash on the column and respond with some on certain stones in the arch but there is no sign of painted decoration. In both arcades the western arch is cut back to about half its original size in the later remodelling of the west end of the church. At this time the arch to the west tower reused the shafts of two Romanesque responds, which are taller versions of the east respond of the Romanesque north nave arcade. The north arcade was discovered in 1871 when 'workmen began to make an aperture in the wall to receive the monument (previously in the chancel), a large mass of masonry fell, when the Norman column and arch were brought into view'.[18] The plain, two-order arches and short columnar piers relate happily to a

Fig. 349 Meifod, St Tysilio and St Mary: the nave south exterior

246

number of Welsh churches, such as St Woolos at Newport and Ewenny priory, both of which belonged to St Peter's abbey, Gloucester, and, outside the realm of Norman control, the nave of Tywyn (figs. 126, 216 and 346–348).

Interpretation of the fabric of Meifod church is not a straightforward matter. It is possible that there were two other churches on the site, 'ruins of which Mr Pryce of Llanvyllin, in a letter to Mr Babington, dated April 12th, 1701, acknowledges to have seen, but from their contiguous situation, an opinion has been entertained, that they were probably only portions, or a subsequent enlargement of the original building, dedicated respectively to their several founders, and forming distinct chapels in the same church'.[19] The first church was in honour of St Gwyddvarch, a local anchorite, the second which was contiguous to the first was dedicated to St Tysilio. The church of St Mary was reputedly founded by Madoc ab Meredydd, prince of Powys, and *The Chronicle of the Princes* records the consecration of this church in 1156.[20] In 1159 Madoc ab Meredydd was buried in the church of St Tysilio, the burial place of his ancestors and of most of the princes of the races of Mervyn and Conwyn.[21] The Royal Commission equated the start of the present church with the 1137 bequest of Gruffudd ap Cynan.[22]

In the entry on Meifod in the *Topographical Dictionary of Wales*, Lewis observed that the present church is in the Norman style 'and seems to have been once much larger than it now is: on the north side are evident traces of the foundation of a transept, which may probably have been either the church of St Tysilio, or a portion of the original building in honour of that saint'.[23] Benjamin Ferrey, the architect responsible for the restoration of the church, recorded that 'the ruins of a transept, extending northwards from the spot where the fragments (of the north nave arcade) have been discovered, were distinctly traced out about thirty or thirty-five years ago, when the north aisle was added to the present church. It is believed that the foundation walls of that transept are existing, though they are not visible at present'.[24] This would result in a rather unusual plan with a transept at the west end of the church that was separated from the nave with regular arcades rather than a larger arch that would normally be used in conjunction with a transept. Unusual as the arrangement might have been, Ferrey's association with Augustus Welby Pugin (1812–52), champion of the Gothic revival and the accurate observation of medieval detail, would seem to suggest that Ferrey's account would be accurate.

The existence of both north and south arcades at Meifod makes it virtually certain that the northern transept would have been matched to the south. In spite of the truncated state of the western bay of both arcades, the report of the proximity of the transept foundation makes it probable that the arcade was originally of two bays. For the form of the Romanesque nave to the east there is no evidence. It may have been aisleless, although given the princely patronage of the church, an aisled plan, like that at the near-contemporary Twywn, seems more likely. Aisled or unaisled, the inclusion of a western transept suggests association with *westwerks* of the Holy Roman Empire. It is true that the relatively thin walls at Meifod preclude a stone structure of great height, although a taller wooden superstructure must remain a possibility. However, it is significant that a formal parallel for the two-bay arcades at Meifod is found in the *westwerks* at St Saviour,

247

Werden (*ca* 920–43);[25] St Pantaleon, Cologne (984–91);[26] and at Munstereifel (*c*.1050).[27] *Westwerks* are often associated with baptism and burial, as at St Riquier at Centula, where the founder, abbot Angilbert, was buried in the vestibule of the *westwerk* in 799.[28] At St Pantaleon, Cologne, the construction of the *westwerk* is associated with the donation of the relics of St Albini in 984 by the Empress Theophanou.[29] Following her death in 991, Theophanou was buried in the *westwerk* to the west of the altar of St Albini.[30] On a smaller scale there is the Benedictine abbey church of Kornelimunster, near Aachen, in which there were burials in the *westwerk*.[31] In the discussion of Penmon priory, reference was made to the remodelling of the transepts of Speyer Cathedral by Emperor Henry IV to create an imperial mausoleum.[32] A link between Gruffudd ap Cynan and the German emperor was documented through Bishop David of Bangor.[33] There is a further link to Meifod through Gruffudd ap Cynan who left ten shillings to the church, possibly in commemoration of St Tysilio's time in Anglesey.

Closer to home, the idea of burial in a space adjacent to the nave of the church may be associated with the church of St Peter and St Paul at Canterbury. There, in the seventh century, the archbishops of Canterbury were buried in the north porticus and King Ethelbert and Queen Bertha were buried in the south porticus.[34] Bede recorded that Bishop Tobias of Rochester (d.726) was buried in a chapel (*in porticu*), which he had built for that purpose, and in 721 John of Beverley was buried 'in the porticus of St Peter in his monastery'.[35] These burials reflect the practice in the Roman church as it would have been introduced with the mission of St Augustine in 597. Architecturally it could be expressed through the subdivision of aisles as described by Paulinus in his church at Nola.[36] Alternatively, there are chapels attached to basilican churches in the manner of the mausoleum of Galla Placidia and the church of S. Croce, Ravenna.[37]

The tradition of burial at the west end of the church should also be seen in the context of the Celtic church. The mortuary chapel of St Oran is located at the south-west angle of the abbey church of Iona.[38] In Irish texts from 825 to 1156 the term *erdam* is of significance.[39] This may refer to a free-standing structure or to a porticus, and perhaps most interestingly in the present context, it has been interpreted as a modest version of a *westwerk*.[40]

The responds of the tower arch at Meifod are clearly reused from the Romanesque church. Their greater height than the arcade columns indicates that they came either from a crossing or from the arch to an earlier western tower. The latter possibility is intriguing in connection with a *westwerk*, as at Werdun, or at Aberffraw.

Without excavation of the site the form of the early church(es) at Meifod must remain a matter of speculation. Be that as it may, the surviving arcades and the record of the foundations of the transept indicate that Madoc ab Meredydd was an ambitious patron of architecture who wished to create a building worthy of his princely status that may even have aspired to imperial associations. It is significant that Cynddelw records that Gwyddfarch was granted a vision of Rome at Meifod.[41] This must surely be read as a strong statement in favour of the *clas* church, in that Meifod was associated with Rome without any Norman intermediary to impose or supervise Gregorian reform. Architecturally it was intended to vie with Norman-influenced churches in Wales and, if the reading of an elaborate *westwerk* is correct, to surpass them.

RHYS AP GRUFFUDD, PRINCE OF DEUHEUBARTH

In 1164, with Cistercian monks from Whitland, Robert fitz Stephen established a small colony on the banks on the Fflur brook. A year later, Rhys ap Gruffudd (d.1197), prince of Deuheubarth, claimed lands from the Norman usurpers and became an enthusiastic supporter of Strata Florida. It was probably under his auspices that fonts were introduced into a large number of churches in the region.

STRATA FLORIDA

Exactly when the community moved the two miles to Strata Florida, on the south bank of the Teifi above Tregaron Marsh, is not recorded but Lord Rhys's charter of 1184 recorded that he had 'begun to build the venerable abbey entitled Stratflur'.[42] In 1201 the *Chronicle of the Princes* recorded that 'the community of Strata Florida went to the new church on the eve of Whit Sunday; after it had been nobly and handsomely built'.[43]

The plan of the church follows a well-established Cistercian tradition, with a square-ended aisleless presbytery, transepts with square chapels and an aisled nave (fig. 350).[44]

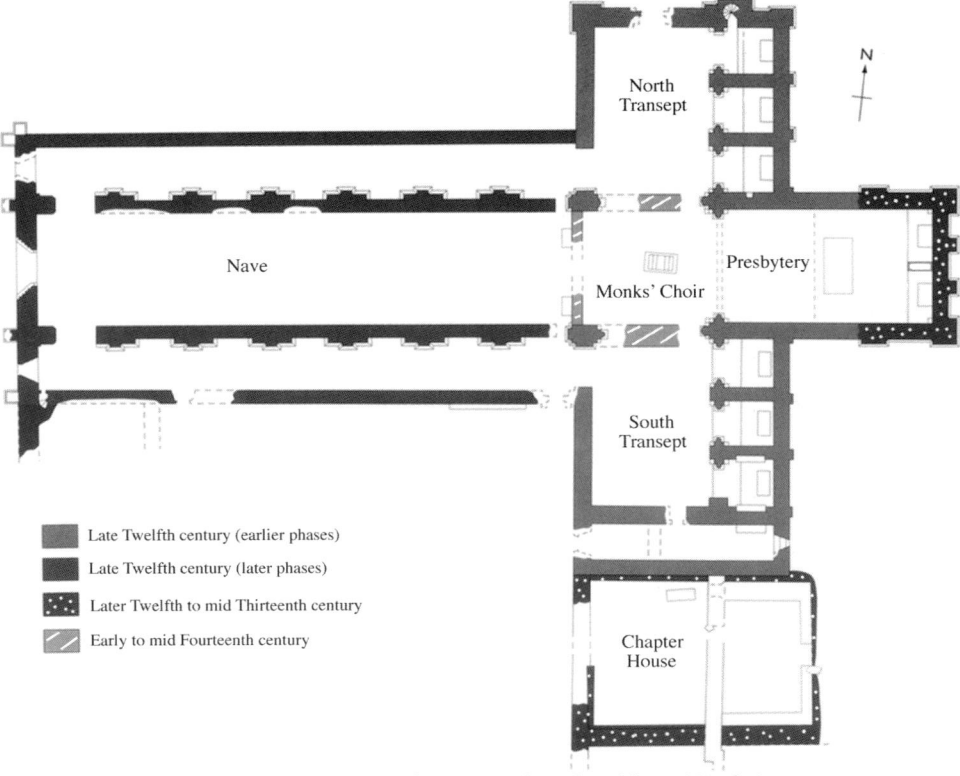

Fig. 350 Plan of Strata Florida abbey (Cadw)

Fig. 351 Strata Florida abbey: the presbytery (right) and north transept

Fig. 352 Strata Florida abbey: 'domino' rib fragment

Fig. 353 Strata Florida abbey: capital

However, instead of two chapels off each transept, as at Whitland, Strata Florida has three. The arches to the transept chapels had two orders of which the lower parts of the coursed shafts and the moulded bases remain (fig. 351). The northeast and south-east crossing piers are similarly articulated. The initial plan was for a two-bay presbytery but this was expanded to three bays and an elaborate rib vault was introduced, with a unique 'domino' pattern on the ribs (fig. 352). Fragments of a wide range of capital sculpture survive. There are trumpet-scallops with foliage on the scallop faces and upright trefoil leaves between the cones (fig. 353). Variants on waterleaf and plantain-leaf types are preserved in which the waterleaves take on an unusual succulent quality (fig. 354). Then there are tightly curled fronds that generally seem allied to stiff-leaf but lack the characteristic clusters of trefoil leaves (fig. 355). The

Fig. 354 Strata Florida abbey: capital fragments

Fig. 355 Capital

Fig. 356 Fragments

Fig. 357 Fragment

Fig. 358 Vault boss

capital illustrated is carved in deep purple Caerbwti stone and Stephen Williams, who undertook the excavations at Strata Florida, indicated that the juxtaposition of this stone with yellowish-white sandstone provided a polychrome treatment to the walls. Other foliage sculpture appears to be unfinished, as here illustrated in a damaged capital and a fragmentary relief (figs. 356 and 357). It seems most likely that the foliate details would have been finished in paint. There are numerous chevron voussoirs with two distinct patterns that may have come from the north transept doorway, from which there is also a fragment of hood mould decorated with shuttlecock ornament.[45] Most unusually, there are foliage bosses from the groin vaults of the transept chapels from which oil lamps probably hung (fig. 358).

Fig. 359 Strata Florida abbey: looking west down the nave

The nave and aisles were separated by a low wall about five feet in height upon which eight main arcade arches were constructed (figs. 350 and 359). The appearance is visualized best with reference to the naves of the Irish Cistercian churches at Baltinglass (Wicklow) and Jerpoint (Kilkenny) where the state of preservation is better than at Strata Florida.[46] Roger Stalley has also pointed out a remarkably close parallel between one of the decorated scalloped capitals at Baltinglass with Strata Florida, and has observed that 'it is not impossible that ideas moved both ways across the Irish sea'.[47] With this in mind, it is worth noting that at Baltinglass, and in the three eastern piers of the Jerpoint nave, there is an alternating system of round columns and square piers, but the fourth and fifth piers at Jerpoint introduce more complex plans. The starting point for each design is a

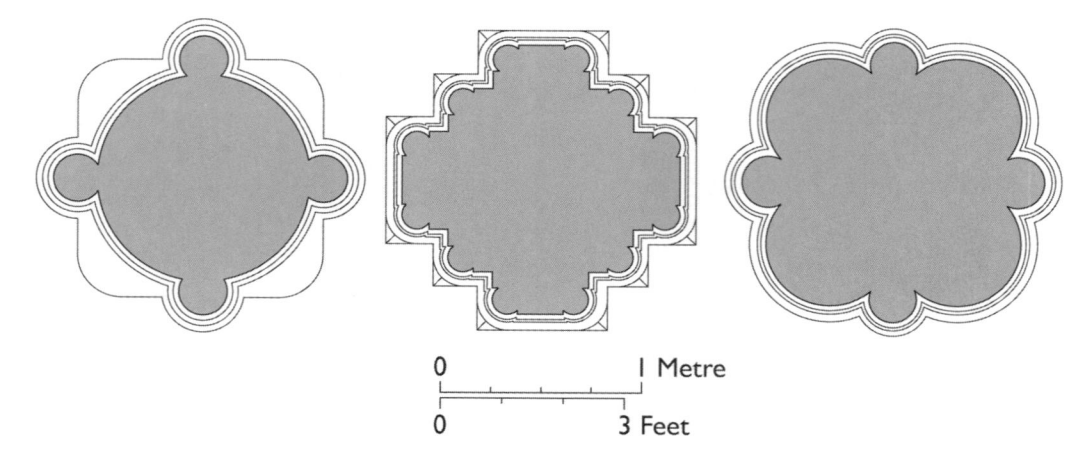

Fig. 360 Strata Florida abbey: reconstruction of nave piers (Stuart Harrison)

square pier, but in pier 4 at Jerpoint the angles are chamfered and thin shafts attached. Pier 5 represents a variation on this design in which the corner shafts are larger and are flanked by hollow mouldings.[48] In the nave at Strata Florida the variation in pier design becomes more complex. Architectural historian Stuart Harrison has demonstrated that at least three different pier types were employed in the Strata Florida nave (fig. 360).[49] One has a large cylindrical core with a shaft attached on the each of the main axes, a so-called pilier cantonné, which is adapted in the extant west respond of the south arcade. A second has a symmetrical compound design based on a square with narrow attached shafts at the angles, to which a pilaster with angle shafts is added on each side. The third is a quatrefoil plan with intervening shafts on the main axes which also serves as the model for the west respond of the south nave arcade (fig. 361).

The round-headed west doorway is elaborate and preserves five of the original six orders (fig. 362). Each order has a continuous roll moulding and is punctuated with binding ties that sprout foliage scrolls on the outside. The only window to survive is at the west end of the south nave aisle and is a simple lancet with a continuous chamfered moulding. However, on the inner face of the wall above the west doorway there are the lower sections of the jambs of two windows which preserve their shaft rings.

Strata Florida abbey
Fig. 361 (left) West respond in the south nave arcade; Fig. 362 (right) The west portal

The dates of construction of Strata Florida have obviously been determined with reference to the historical documentation. However, the 1201 reference to the entry of the monks into the new church 'after it had been nobly and handsomely built' has not been taken to mean that the church was completed by that date. It has been suggested that work on the nave continued for the next twenty or twenty-five years,[50] reference to a huge fine of £800 imposed on the abbey by King John in 1212 being cited for the slow progress of construction.[51] It is true that there are cases where medieval documentation of 'completed' churches refers not to the entire fabric but just to the sanctuary and choir. In such cases the church could be said to be liturgically 'complete', and for the monks of Strata Florida this would have meant the presbytery, transepts and chapels and the liturgical choir that occupied the crossing. Where architectural historians suggest that construction of a church continued after it had been 'completed', reference is usually made to features in the building which are taken to indicate a later date. Thus at Strata Florida, Radford tells us that the nave, 'where the ornament is of a more advanced character, may be attributed to the following twenty-five years' (after 1201).[52] It has also been suggested that the extension of the presbytery and the construction of its high vault also took place in the early thirteenth century, along with the construction of fully articulated crossing with tower.[53] Quite frankly I find the suggestion that construction continued well past 1201 difficult to comprehend. It seems to me that the range of motifs used at Strata Florida provides nothing inconsistent with a 1201 completion of the entire church. The base mouldings of the crossing piers and transept chapels are typologically earlier than the water-holding base that is so characteristic of early Gothic (fig. 363). The chevron ornament is remarkably conservative in that it shows none of the three-dimensional qualities so often found in the late twelfth century. This is surprising enough in the 1180s and would be very antiquated in the thirteenth century. The shuttlecock motif has been discussed in connection with Margam abbey in the 1180s.[54] The domino motif is unique to Strata Florida but such encrustation of decoration of the ribs has more in common with a Romanesque chevron tradition than it does with early Gothic articulation of the rib with a series of delicate roll-and-hollow mouldings. It is also worth noting that a variant of the motif appears in the arch of the fourth bay of the south nave arcade at St Davids cathedral in the 1180s. The continuous roll mouldings of the west portal and the string course inside the west front, not to mention the round head of the doorway are all more at home before, rather than

Fig. 363 Strata Florida abbey: north respond in the middle chapel in the north transept

Fig. 364 (left) Wells cathedral: capital in the south choir arcade
Fig. 355 (right) Strata Florida abbey: capital showing similarity of design

after, 1201. Here we may contrast the east processional doorway at Valle Crucis abbey (fd.1201) in which each of the three orders of the pointed arch has triple-roll mouldings, and the triplets reflecting the articulation of the responds.[55] The trumpet-scallop capitals with stylized acanthus carved on the faces of the scallops and upright trefoil leaves between the cones are paralleled in the nave of St Davids cathedral. The spiralling form and somewhat bulbous volutes of the foliage capitals find some of their closest parallels in the earliest capitals in the choir of Wells cathedral, commenced around 1175 (figs. 355 and 364).[56] One such fragment carved in Caerbwti stone is especially instructive in that the leaves are of the multi-petalled stylized acanthus rather than the trefoil stiff-leaf. It also has slightly hollowed facets on the bell of the capital that reflect northern French experiments with foliage capitals in the third quarter of the twelfth century. Typological divisions between these capital forms and leaf details are not absolute but it is fair to say that the features at Strata Florida are more readily paralleled in twelfth- rather than thirteenth-century work.

Similarly, with the nave piers, the pilier cantonné is paralleled in Wales in the nave of St Davids cathedral but appears earlier in the West Country in the nave of St James's priory, Bristol. It is also used in the crypt of York Minster under the patronage of Archbishop Roger of Pont l'Évêque between 1154 and 1181. I do not know of an exact parallel for the stepped pier with minor nook shafts but it belongs to the tradition established in the nave of Jerpoint. The quatrefoil pier with minor shafts on the main axes finds a parallel in the nave of Rochester cathedral and in the west responds of the presbytery main arcades at St Davids cathedral. Less massive but still with a quatrefoil form are the piers of the south nave arcade at Aymestrey (Herefs.) which Pevsner thought may come from Wigmore abbey (fd.1171).[57] The capitals of the St Davids' responds, and others in the crossing there, parallel the succulent waterleaf and plantain leaf capitals at Strata Florida. It is with these last two comparisons that the case for the 1201 date for the completion of the church at Strata Florida hits a snag, in that the comparative details at St Davids date after the fall of the crossing tower in 1220. While there can be no denying the absolute date of this work at St Davids, there is considerable room for debate as to when the designs were conceived. As we shall see in our detailed examination of St Davids, the post-1220 rebuilding, and the subsequent one after the 1247/8 earthquake, are both amazingly conservative and, I believe, self-consciously antiquarian in their approach. With that in mind, along with the pier forms being more at home in the twelfth century, we must consider the form of the capitals. The waterleaf capital is introduced into England in the 1150s, had its greatest popularity between 1160 and 1180, and was just about a spent force by 1200. It never caught on in the West Country to anything like the extent it did in the north but it may be significant that they do appear in the Cistercian abbey churches at Buildwas and Dore. A striking parallel for the Strata Florida capitals is provided by the central capital of the north respond of the north chapel of the north transept at Boyle abbey (Roscommon), dated around 1170 by Roger Stalley.[58]

When considered in the context of the patronage of the Lord Rhys it makes sense to see the work on the church of Strata Florida solely in connection with his patronage with the view that the completion of the church was achieved with funds left on his death in 1197.

Strata Marcella

The Cistercian abbey of Strata Marcella was founded in 1170 from Whitland by Owain Cyfeiliog, prince of southern Powys.[59] He became a monk late in life and was buried in the abbey in 1197. His son, Gwenwynwyn (d.1216) was a generous benefactor to the house. Nothing remains above ground but aspects of the plan and details of foliage capitals are recorded plus a capital reused as the font at Buttington church.[60] The pier forms excavated by Williams have more in keeping with early Gothic designs of the late twelfth and first half of the thirteenth centuries, although a number of the sculptural details relate to Strata Florida and St Davids cathedral.[61]

Cardiganshire Fonts

The font at Llanarth has been pronounced the finest in the county (fig. 365).[62] The square bowl tapers down to the base and has broad triangular chamfers at the angles that create an octagonal plan to the bottom of the bowl. Around the base are four lions carved in three dimensions but unfortunately they have lost their heads. The font is unique in Wales but analogues for lions at the base of fonts are found at Hereford cathedral, Shobdon (Herefs.), Sutton (Herefs.) and St Mary's, Stafford.[63] The Mosan *calcaire bleu* font at

Fig. 365 Llanarth, St David: font

Furneaux also has four lions at the base,[64] and this regional association may be important in light of Mosan analogues for other Cardiganshire fonts discussed below. To interpret the meaning of the lions is not straightforward. On the one hand, a sinister meaning is supported with reference to the late twelfth-century font at St Mary's, Stafford, which also has lions carved on the stem.[65] An accompanying inscription reads: DISCRETUS NON ES SI NON FUGIS ECCE LEONIS ('You are not wise if you do not flee from the lions'). On the other hand, the *Bestiary* informs us that 'when the lioness brings forth her cubs, they come into the world dead. She watches over them for three days, until on the third day the father comes, blows in their faces, and awakens them to life. In the same way the Almighty Father awoke our Lord Jesus Christ from the dead on the third day'.[67] Thus the lions provide a link between the sacraments of Eucharist and Baptism.[67]

Fig. 366 Bettws Bledrws, St Bledrws: font

Fig. 367 Henfynyw, St David: font

Fig. 368 Henfynyw, St David: font

The frieze at the top of the Llanarth font is almost totally obscured by a metal tie, but on the north face (left side in fig. 365) traces of rosettes and pellets are seen above the tie. This ornament also adorns the square-top fonts at Bettws Bledrws (fig. 366) and Henfynyw (figs. 367–368), and the rectangular example at Llansantffraed, which have been considered as products of the 'same school of masons, if not by the same hand'.[68] The rosette friezes on the font bowls are instructive in regard to the mode of operation of the craftsmen. For example, on the east frieze at Henfynyw the spandrels between the first, second and third rosettes, and also the fifth and sixth rosettes, are carved with pellets (fig. 367). These are not used in the other spandrels. Then, on the top of the font, two of the corners have rosettes and two do not (fig. 368). As a piece of sculpture, the work is unfinished but perhaps we should think of 'finished' parts as guidelines along with the incised elements as instructions to the painter for the completion of the work. We have something analogous to the incised tympana discussed in relation to the tympanum at Chepstow castle. Tyrrell-Green suggested that the craftsman came from the Cistercian abbey church at Strata Florida.[69] The idea is an attractive one although difficult to prove. A fragmentary trumpet-scallop capital at Strata Florida is decorated with half rosettes, not unlike the rosettes on the fonts, although more deeply carved (figs. 353, 367–368). Arguments based on the depth of carving may not be that pertinent in that the form of the font bowls, with their triangular angles an incised articulation, is the same as at Llanarth where we have the most three-dimensional lions encircling the base (figs. 365–368). Moreover, the sculpture from Strata Florida displays a similar range. On the one hand, we encounter the deep relief as in the decorated scalloped and acanthus capitals. On the other hand, there are boldly outlined leaves with flat surfaces interrupted only by the simplest incisions (figs. 356 and 357). Technically this is the same as on the fonts and would have likely been finished with a more detailed design in paint.

Fig. 369 Llanwenog, St Gwenog: font

Fig. 370 Cenarth: font from St Tysilio, Llandyssiliogogo

Fig. 371 Silian, Sy Sulian: font

The stylized rosette ornament on the fonts is allied to Llandaff cathedral, which in turn we have linked with the work of Bishop Roger of Salisbury. Such associations imply an ambitious patron, someone who would wish to be linked with the artistic elite. For this region, one immediately thinks of the Lord Rhys. While it may not be him directly who ordered the fonts, he was the person who set the inspiration for and high standard of artistic patronage of the day. It had to be every bit as good as Norman work.

The font from Lampeter, now in the chapel of ease of St Mary at Maestir, has a square bowl carved at the angles with anthropomorphic demi-figures of the symbols of the evangelists.[70] Evangelist symbols also appear on the font at St Mary, Llanfair Clydogau, but they lack the quality of the Maestir work.[71] I do not concur with Lord's attribution of this font to the carver of the font at St Gwenog, Llanwenog (fig. 369).[72] There the bowl is ringed with eleven mask-like heads and the treatment of the facial features has little in common with the head of St Matthew at Maestir.

The shallow bowl of the font at Cenarth, from St Tysilio, Llandyssiliogogo, is carved with three single heads and one pair of heads, equally spaced within an undulating scroll (fig. 370).[73] Allied work is found on the font at Llanllwchaiarn, which originally had four heads of which one remains with a loop beneath, and there are two arched loops adjacent to the right.[74] At Silian the twelfth-century round font bowl is carved with four projecting heads and is on the floor of the church next to its nineteenth-century replacement (fig. 371). These fonts with circular bowls and four projecting heads are paralleled in the Mosan region of Belgium where there are a number of fonts with plain bowls with four projecting heads, as at Soulme.[75] As with the 'copies' of the Tournai marble fonts, such a connection suggests great ambition of the patron. Outside Cardiganshire, similar fonts carved with four heads are found at Rhayader (fig. 372) and St Harmon (Radnorshire) (fig, 373) Llanwrthwl (Breconshire) (fig. 374) and Pencarreg (Carmarthenshire) (figs. 375 and 376). Of the group,

Fig. 372 Rhayader, St Clement: font from the south

Fig. 373 St Harmon, font from the north-east

the Royal Commission suggested that they date 'from the second half of the twelfth century, and they may possibly be connected with the sphere of influence of the able and enlightened prince Rhys ap Gruffydd'.[76] The theory is an appealing one, especially for the fonts around Rhayader where Lord Rhys built a castle in 1177.[77] However, although Lord Rhys may well have been responsible for starting the vogue for these fonts, details of certain heads at Llanwrthwl and Pencarreg suggest a somewhat later date. The hairstyle of the north-west head at Llanwrthwl with a curled roll below the level of the ears would be more in keeping with the first half of the thirteenth century. At Pencarreg there is a clear differentiation between the heads that includes a king at the north-west corner, and a lady wearing a pill-box hat to the south-east (Fig. 516). This speaks of the sort of individuality met in the label stops and corbels in The Elder Lady Chapel at St Augustine's, Bristol (1218–22), and Salisbury cathedral (commenced 1220).[78]

Table-top fonts with scalloped undersides that were so popular in Pembrokeshire, also appear in Cardiganshire. A list of them is given at the end of this chapter. Further north, in Merioneth there is also an example of this type of font at Llanfihangel-y-Pennant (fig. 277), while at Llanegryn scallops are applied to the underside of a round bowl (fig. 378). At Llanymawddwy

Fig. 374 Llanwrthwl, St Gwrthwl: font

Fig. 375 Pencarreg, St Patrick: font

Fig. 376 Pencarreg: lady with pillbox hat on font

Fig. 377 Llanfihangel-y-Pennant, St Michael: font

Fig. 378 Llanegryn, St Egryn: font

Fig. 379 Llanymawddwy, St Tydecho: font

(Merioneth) the font has an octagonal sandstone bowl with raised single scallops at the top of each side and a middle band on a granite base (fig. 379). This has been dated to the fourteenth century but the scallops indicate that the twelfth century is more likely as in the associated design at Til-Châtel (Côte d'Or).[79] This would better suit the tub shape of the font and also the simple raised middle band.

CHURCHES IN POWYS AND GWYNEDD

KERRY (MONTGOMERY), ST MICHAEL

The church of St Michael at Kerry, which was consecrated by Giraldus Cambrensis in 1176, has a Romanesque north nave arcade of four, two-order, round-headed arches carried on squat cylindrical piers (figs. 380 and 381). During the restoration of the church in 1883, a similar column and parts of the bases of two other columns were found during the rebuilding of the south wall.[80] The bases are now visible on the outside of the south wall in their original position that corresponds to the columns of the north arcade. They indicate that the twelfth-century church had a nave flanked by both north and south aisles, as at Tywyn. The account written by V. Cotterill Scholefield, clerk of works for the restoration, tells of more of the former twelfth-century fabric and is worth quoting at length:

Other portions of the Norman work were found built into the walls. Thus in the east jamb of the chancel door, but hidden in the wall, is a portion of a capital and stringcourse with the tan and dentil mouldings and rough carving, and in the lower part of the east pier of the nave arcade is a portion of the base of a window pier or mullion. Another portion of the same character was found in the south wall, together with large quantities of red sandstone re-used from the old church. The existence of this portion in the pier indicates that the arcade of what is now the chancel was rebuilt. [This arises from the custom of lengthening the churches eastwards, which commenced in the latter part of the twelfth century.] This is also indicated by the character of the work, and by the use of a different sort of stone; the different jointing and shape of the last column in the nave, and a bend in the last arch of the nave arcade to narrow the chancel.[81]

Scholefield believed that the nave arcade and the tower 'with its walls over six feet thick', 'dated from about the latter part of the eleventh century'.[82] The tower has no identifiable Romanesque features and the north nave arcade accords more happily with the 1176 consecration.[83] Of this arcade, the outer order is plain, and the inner order is chamfered in the upper sector of the arch. The only ornament is a simple chip-carved zigzag on the abacus of the west respond (fig. 382). Capitals are simple 'Doric' and belong to a West Country Romanesque tradition as in the nave of Shrewsbury abbey.

Fig. 380 Kerry, St Michael: interior looking east

Fig. 381 Kerry, St Michael: north nave arcade

The east column of the north nave arcade is unusual in a number of respects (fig. 383). The moulded capital is only on the western quadrant of the column, and in this respect it is a mirror image of the west respond of the arcade (figs. 383–383). Also, just to the east of the capital there is a break in the coursing of the ashlar on both the north and south sides of the column, as Scholefield

262

Fig. 382 Kerry, St Michael: detail of capital on west respond in north nave arcade

Fig. 383 Kerry, St Michael: east column in the north nave arcade

Fig. 384 Kerry, St Michael: bases on the east respond in the north nave aracde

noted. This suggests that originally the capital and western sector of the column were part of a respond that was remodelled into a column in the fourteenth century when the chancel was extended.

On the east side of the east Romanesque bay of the north arcade there are moulded Romanesque bases to either side of a plain section of the same stone, immured beneath the fourteenth-century octagonal column (fig. 384). The detailing of the bases is quite different. On the left there are cones as if from an upturned scalloped capital; on the right, a base with a roll moulding surmounted by two shallow hollow mouldings. It is hard to agree with Scholefield's interpretation of the stone as a portion of the base of a window pier or mullion. Given the difference in the base mouldings, in conjunction with Scholefield's record that 'another portion of the same character was found in the south wall', it is tempting to place them as responds of a lost chancel arch.

The work is generally dated with reference to the rededication of the church in 1176. Parallels with the late eleventh-century work at Tewkesbury and Gloucester may suggest that this is unlikely. However, the use of angle chamfer stops at about ten and two o'clock on the inner order of the arcades accords happily with this date.

Llandrinio (Montgomery), St Trinio, St Peter and St Paul

Of the fabric of the twelfth-century church at Llandrinio, there remains the south doorway, the blocked western bay of the former nave north arcade, a window in the north wall of the chancel, and the font. The round-headed south doorway has plain jambs with quirked-chamfered imposts that carry the two plain orders in the arch (fig. 385). The inner order has a very thin chamfer and the arch is surmounted with a plain hood mould. The arch of the remaining bay of the north nave arcade is also plain and round-headed (fig. 386). To the west it rests on a squared respond with a thin chamfered capital. To the east the support is columnar, as at Meifod and Tywyn, but here the capital is different — it splays out to a square top and is carved at the north-west angle with a weathered foliage(?) crocket (fig. 387). The use of a column at this point and the springing of the extant arch from just the western half of the capital indicate that originally the arcade would have continued further east. It is possible that it continued for the entire length of the nave, marked by the vertical joint just to the east of the eastern Gothic nave window. This marks the division of nave and

Fig. 385 Llandrinio, St Trinio, St Peter and St Paul: the south portal

Llandrinio
Fig. 386 (above) north nave arcade with
Fig. 387 (right) detail of eastern column

Fig. 388 Llandrinio: northern impost at junction of nave and chancel

Fig. 389 Llandrinio: font

Fig. 390 Llanfechain, St Garmon: view from the south

chancel. Continuing to the east, a Gothic piscina bears witness to a former chapel at this point that would have been at the end of the north nave aisle. Then there remains a single narrow round-headed north chancel window from the Romanesque church. Inside, the only discernible Romanesque architectural feature is a chamfered impost in the north wall at the junction of nave and chancel (fig. 388). It is heavily limewashed but abstract foliage patterns can still be seen on the flat face. Its shallow projection from the wall indicates that there was no masonry division between the nave and chancel; the impost would just have 'supported' the lintel of a wooden screen. Also from the twelfth century is the partly recut cylindrical font (fig. 389). It is articulated with twelve segmental arches with two roll-moulded orders that sit on 'Doric' capitals and half-columns that are joined with inverted segmental arches at the bottom.

The form of the north nave arcade capital complete with the boldly projecting crocket indicates a date in the late twelfth or even the early years of the thirteenth century.

LLANFECHAIN (MONTGOMERY), ST GARMON

This is a relatively large, rectangular single-cell church measuring 72ft 10in by 17ft 8in internally, built of rubble with ashlar dressings (fig. 390). In the east wall are two small, round-headed windows with continuous chamfers, and, above, a similarly scaled rectangular window (fig. 391). There is a round-headed priest's door in the south wall,

*Fig. 391 Llanfechain, St Garmon:
east wall of the chancel*

*Fig. 393 Llanfechain, St Garmon:
south doorway*

*Fig. 392 Llanfechain, St Garmon:
looking east along the nave*

which, like the east windows, has a continuous thin chamfer, plus a chamfered hood mould. The door now opens immediately to the west of the choir screen but originally it would have given direct access to the chancel (fig. 392). The south doorway has a single order with a quadrant roll moulding in the jambs and arch, and chamfered imposts at the springing of the arch (fig. 393). The quadrant roll of the south doorway is a motif that is used in the late eleventh-century work at St Peter's, Gloucester. It becomes most popular, however, in the late twelfth century, when chamfered orders for doorways and windows were also in vogue.

LLANBADARN FAWR (RADNORSHIRE), ST PADARN

The south doorway of the nave of St Padarn, Llanbadarn Fawr, boasts a carved tympanum, a distinction otherwise only matched in Wales in the south doorway of Penmon priory (figs. 394 and 395). The doorway has two orders of chevron in the arch. The inner order is a double row to either side of a thin roll set at right angles to the wall; the outer order, a flat triple design with chunky triangles in the angle as in the works of the Dymock School of sculpture.[84] The arch rests on sculptured abaci; to the left a twisted serpentine creature with a crested head, and to the right two rows

Fig. 394 Llanbadarn Fawr, St Padarn: south doorway

Fig. 395 Llanbadarn Fawr, St Padarn: tympanum to south doorway

of chip-carved lozenges on the upright and spheroids on the chamfer (figs. 396 and 397). One crudely carved capital each side sits atop a coursed shaft. On the left, the outer face has a standing figure with its right arm raised and short left arm reaching down to a large head at the angle of the capital (fig. 396). On the inner face a standing figure with head in profile, with a long, torpedo-like tail of hair, reaches up to the angle of the capital while holding its left arm limply to the side. The scene has been interpreted as the Temptation of Adam and Eve.[85] The inner face of the right capital is inhabited by a dragon with huge head that turns towards the upper corner of the capital and has its small body in a c-shaped curve towards the lower angle (fig. 397). Here the end of the tail is bitten or sniffed by a nondescript quadruped with long upright tail. There is foliage to the upper right of the capital. The lintel is decorated with an incised joggled pattern and is carried on two corbels. On the left it is disfigured but on the right there is a male head with long, pencil moustache and small goatee beard. The tympanum is truncated and does not fill the space laterally (fig. 395). The clean stones above and to the sides of the tympanum are the product of restoration but even with their removal and juggling the placement of the tympanum in the mind's eye do not suggest an alternate setting. In the centre is a sparsely leafed tree that grows from the top of a cat's head. It is possible that the tree originally extended upwards on to another stone in the manner of the Pauntley (Glos.) and Kilpeck tympana.[86] To the left of the cat's

Fig. 396 Llanbadarn Fawr, St Padarn: west capital on the south doorway

Fig. 397 Llanbadarn Fawr, St Padarn: east capital on the south doorway

head is a disc with an eight-pronged star pattern. To the right of the tree there is a lion and to the left a lioness, both of whom appear to be ready to eat from the tree, interpreted by Charles Keyser in his book on *Norman tympana and lintels*, as the Tree of Spiritual Life and Knowledge.[87] Both creatures have a tail that passes between their hind legs above the body to end in a trefoil. Their 'floating' legs, huge eyes and gaping mouths relate them to creatures throughout the Herefordshire School. The lioness, complete with the trefoil-ended tail, is of the same breed as the one on the panel behind the dragon's head at the south-west corner of the Kilpeck nave.[88] The lintel is scored with a joggled pattern, a more complex, fictive version of the lintel of the north doorway at Hatfield (Herefs.) (figs. 23 and 395).

Two Romanesque corbels are reset in the inside of the east wall, a sheila-na-gig and a janus.

OLD RADNOR (RADNORSHIRE), ST STEPHEN

Tyrrell-Green suggested that the large font (3ft 10in external diameter) at Old Radnor (Radnorshire) 'appears to have been fashioned from a Druidical altar' (fig. 398).[89] Lord dated it to the eighth century but that is difficult to substantiate.[90] Also at Old Radnor there is a fragmentary trumpet-scalloped capital reset in the Easter sepulchre in the north chapel of the church (fig. 399). On the underside of the capital there is a segment of necking that shows the capital originally topped a columnar pier as in the north nave arcade at St Mary's, Brecon (fig. 264).

LLANDDEWI YSTRADENNI (RADNORSHIRE), ST DAVID

A blocked Romanesque priest's doorway is reset in the south nave wall of the 1890 church (fig. 400). There is a heavy roll moulding in the soffit of the arch and two plain stepped orders. The jambs have

Fig. 398 Old Radnor, St Stephen: font

Fig. 399 Old Radnor, St Stephen: capital reset in Easter sepulchre

single reset shafts on each side, a fourteenth-century foliage capital on the left and a rounded moulded impost on the right.

ABERDARON (GWYNEDD), ST HYWYN

The original twelfth-century *clas* church of St Hywyn at Aberdaron was rectangular, measuring about 58ft by 19ft, without a separate chancel and without north or west windows (fig. 401).[91] This church is preserved in all but the eastern quarter of the north wall and is now the north nave of a double-nave church. The rough, rubble construction is unrelieved by any articulation. The round-headed west doorway has three plain orders, originally chamfered but now almost worn away (fig. 402). There are worn moulded capitals and a renewed moulded label. For a west doorway with three plain orders we may compare the west portal at Clun (Salop), although in the Clun doorway chamfers are not used in either the jambs or arches. The chamfers and the moulded capitals suggest a date in the late twelfth century.

Towards the east end of the north wall there is the blocked head of a narrow, chamfered, round-headed arch. Originally this would have served as the priest's doorway at a time when the ground level was considerably lower than it

Fig. 400 Llandewi Ystradenni, St David: blocked doorway in south nave wall

Fig. 401 Aberdaron, St Hywyn: view from the north-east

Fig. 402 Aberdaron, St Hywyn: west portal

270

is today. To the east of the doorway there is a vertical break in the masonry, to the east of which is walling of uncertain date. The two modern steps that cross the church immediately to the west of the former priest's door mark the division between nave and chancel, and almost certainly retain the twelfth-century division, which would have been accompanied by a screen.

If we are correct in assigning a late-twelfth-century date to the church, then we have a good example of the continuity of the tradition of the single-cell plan, as represented in Ireland by Clonmacnois cathedral.[92] However, as the Royal Commission observed, 'the original form of the E end is unknown, but the comparatively short extension of the oldest portion eastwards is perhaps slightly in favour of an apsidal rather than a square end'.[93] If this was indeed the case, then it was to emulate Bangor cathedral and, ultimately Norman models.

CROSSES AND FONTS

The production of churchyard crosses that was such an important aspect of the pre-Romanesque artistic culture in Wales, diminishes significantly in the twelfth century. However, the form is not entirely lost. The standing pillar is well represented in the mid-twelfth century by an example in the churchyard to the west of the church at Llanfihangel-y-Traethau (Merioneth) (fig. 403). This roughly quadrangular pillar-stone marks 'the tomb of Wleder, the mother of Odeleu, who first built this church in the time of King Owain'. There is no other record of Wleder or Odeleu, but Owain was king of Gwynedd between 1137 and 1170, a date that agrees with the epigraphic evidence.[94]

In the churchyard south-west of the church at Corwen, stands a square, tapering cross shaft with angle roll mouldings, topped by a cushion capital the faces of which are carved with interlace (fig. 404).[95] The motif of the cushion capital has attracted much attention from architectural historians. On the one hand, it is suggested that the motif was introduced into England after

Fig. 403 (left) Llanfihangel-y-Traethau, St Michael: pillar
Fig. 404 (above) Corwen, St Mael and St Sulien: detail of cross shaft

the Conquest.[96] On the other hand, it has been compared with that on Eliseg's Pillar, located about 500 yards north of Valle Crucis abbey (Denbighshire), dated by inscription to the first half of the ninth century (fig. 405).[97] Then, there are also pre-Conquest examples of cushions at Gosforth and Beckermet St Margaret (Cumbria), and at Clulow (Cheshire) and Stapleford (Notts.).[98] Nash-Williams reported that the capital of the Corwen cross has a 'small oblong socket above (? for the attachment of a separate cross-head)'. The Corwen cross differs from all these crosses in having a square rather than a round shaft, and Nash-Williams considered the form 'is more consistent with that of a medieval churchyard cross', and suggested a date in the twelfth century. On the east face of the pillar just below the capital is a Latin cross that tapers towards the bottom in the manner of a sword blade. Each of the faces of the capital is carved with a pair of double-headed interlinked rings, the south face being the best preserved. Carved cushion capitals become a feature of Romanesque architecture in England in the late eleventh century and continue to be popular through the twelfth century. The earliest dated examples are in the arch to the south transept chapel at Worcester cathedral, a building commenced in 1084 and consecrated in 1089. The motif then flourished with its use in the crypt of Canterbury cathedral starting in 1096. The use at Corwen almost certainly post-dates the introduction of Anglo-Norman forms into north Wales in the time of Gruffudd ap Cynan in the 1120s. The font at Corwen is also twelfth century and boasts a bold cable moulding at the bottom of the stem.

Reset inside the west end of the nave at Diserth (Flintshire) there are a free-standing slab-cross and a truncated conical cross base (figs. 406–409). The former has been dated to the ninth or tenth century by the Royal Commission, while Nash-Williams suggested twelfth/thirteenth century for both pieces.[99]

Fig. 405 Eliseg's Pillar

Fig. 406 Diserth, St Fraid: cross

Diserth, St Fraid
Fig. 407 (top left) detail of cross;
Fig. 409 (bottom) cross base;
Fig. 408 (top right) detail of cross base

For Nash-Williams the decoration was 'degenerate' and therefore 'late', while the cusped wheel head was also cited in support of his dating of the cross. 'Degenerate' forms are not the most accurate guide to the date of a work of art; they can, after all, occur at any time during the production of a particular art form or tradition, in the hand of a copyist or lesser-skilled practitioner. The use of cusps in the wheel head, on the other hand, is rather more useful as a determinant of date. The motif is introduced in French Gothic architecture in the 1150s and 1160s, as in the exterior of the transept clerestorey at Noyon cathedral and the apse gallery tympana at Saint-Germer-de-Fly (Oise). From France the motif is imported into England in the choir gallery tympana at Ripon Minster, executed for Roger of Pont Évêque, Archbishop of York (1154–81).[100]

By the early thirteenth century cusps were firmly entrenched in the repertoire of English masons, as in the Galilee porch of Ely cathedral or the tomb of William Marshal (d.1206) at Exeter cathedral. Their appearance in the head of the Diserth cross is unlikely to be before the late twelfth century. In north Wales a particularly fine example is on the so-called tomb chest of Llywelyn ab Iowerth in St Grwst at Llanrwst (Denbighshire), *circa* 1240.[101] The evidence of the cusps for the dating of the cross is significant in connection with other motifs on the cross. The lattice decoration on the bottom panel on the east face is paralleled on a late-twelfth/early-thirteenth-century grave slab at Llanfihangel Abercywyn (Carmarthenshire) and on a coped grave slab at Llantwit Major (Glamorgan).[102] Lord dated the latter to the late eleventh or early twelfth century but the naturalistic head sculpture on the tomb precludes a date much before 1200. The second panel from the bottom on the east side of the Diserth cross does not add any precision to the date of the work (fig. 407). However, it is worth noting that its design evolves from a St Andrew's cross and as such may be seen as continuing a tradition established on some of the Anglesey fonts (figs. 324 and 327–328). With this in mind, when we turn to the Diserth conical cross base, further analogues with Anglesey fonts may be cited, like the ring-chain/interlace patterns in relation to the panels on the Llangristiolus font (figs. 322, 342, 408 and 409). Quite what this means for the relative dates of the Anglesey fonts and the Diserth cross and base is likely to remain a moot point. Be that as it may, there is good evidence to attribute at least some of the fonts to the time of Gruffudd ap Cynan, while the evidence of the cusps precludes a date before the late twelfth century for the Diserth cross.

Gwaunysgor (Flintshire), St Mary

The late-twelfth or early thirteenth-century table-top font at Gwaunysgor is supported on five renewed stems (figs. 410 and 412). The bowl is decorated with single leaves with five hollowed lobes that grow down from heart-shaped stems that frame individual leaves. There is a small head at the north-west angle. The basic form of the font with the square

Fig. 410 Gwaunysgor, St Mary: font

Fig. 411 Gwaunysgor, St Mary: font

bowl supported on five stems derives from the black Tournai marble type imported into England by such munificent patrons as Henry of Blois, Bishop of Winchester (1129–71), and either Bishop Alexander (1123–48) or Bishop Robert Chesney of Lincoln (1148–56).[103] The basic foliage pattern is a cross between that on the south corbel of the east crossing arch at Valle Crucis abbey and the left capital of the central east lancet window at Valle Crucis abbey (fd.1201) (figs. 336 and 337).

EFENECHDYD (DENBIGHSHIRE), ST MICHAEL

The wooden font at Efenechdyd is a particularly rare survival (fig. 412). It is cut from a single piece of oak and is dated by the Royal Commission to the fourteenth or fifteenth century.[104] However, Tyrrell-Green compared the tub shape of the font with the Romanesque font at Tangmere (Sussex),[105] and the fourteen bulbous knobs on the neck suggest a Romanesque design. Fluted fonts are popular in the twelfth century, as in the well-known Aylesbury group from which Eydon (Northants.) and Flitwick (Beds.) provide the closest form to Efenechdyd.[106] There are also examples in Devon, as at Abbotsham, and fluted fonts were popular in Sweden in the twelfth century.[107]

Fig. 412 Efenechdyd, St Michael: font

SHRINES

PENNANT MELANGELL (MONTGOMERYSHIRE), ST MELANGELL

The church of St Melangell at Pennant Melangell holds a very important place in the study of Romanesque churches not just in Wales but throughout Europe. While it is architecturally unspectacular it houses the reconstructed shrine of the patron saint, a particularly rare treasure. While there is likely to be debate over the exact form of the reconstruction of the shrine, it is sufficient to be content that it has been put together from fragments into an entirely plausible form (fig. 413).

The nave-cum-chancel measures 60ft x 16ft 6in, to the east of which there is a reconstructed semi-circular apse. The entrance arch to the apse is offset to the north, which suggests that it did not function in the traditional manner as either the space for the high altar or as a separate space for priests (fig. 413). Instead it suggests that something would have been placed against the southern half of the wall, and there has been debate as to whether the saint's grave or shrine would have occupied this space (fig. 414).[108] The evidence seems to favour the arrangement as reconstructed with the shrine set immediately behind the high altar. This disposition accords well with that of St Cuthbert at Durham as recorded in the *Chapters concerning the Miracles and Translations of St Cuthbert:*

Fig. 413 Pennant Melangell, St Melangell: the sanctuary looking east

The reliquary-coffin of the incorrupt body was to be lifted up higher behind the altar on a stone, diligently wrought by the hand of craftsmen for the purpose of sustaining such a burden, which nine columns raise higher above the ground, as befits its size.

A similar location behind an altar is found in the shrine of St Sylvanus in the crypt of Saint-Sylvain at Ahun (Creuse), where the shrine shares the same steeply pitched gable with Pennant Melangell.[109] The shrine of the patron saint in the crypt of the church of St Radegunde at Poitiers (Vienne) also provides an analogous instance of the shrine elevated above a crawl space for the pilgrim.

The capitals, arches and gables of the Pennant Melangell shrine were encrusted with foliage scrolls, which Radford and Hemp, in their account of the

Fig. 414 Pennant Melangell, St Melangell: grave and shrine from the east-north-east

church and shrine, related to Valle Crucis abbey (fd.1201) (fig. 415).[110] In this connection the left capital of the round-headed arch to the slype at Valle Crucis is decorated with foliage that is a more three-dimensional rendition of the Pennant Melangell foliage carving (fig. 416). The right capital of the Valle Crucis slype arch is also carved with a foliage scroll but here it is significant in that the individual leaves are closer to the trefoil design associated with Early English stiff-leaf foliage (fig. 417). This suggests that the Valle Crucis sculpture is later.

While the details of the foliage on the Pennant Melangell capitals may find parallel at Valle Crucis, the form of the capitals is quite different. The block form of the shrine capitals has been related to the cloister capitals from Reading abbey and to capitals at Leominster priory, works of *circa* 1130 and *circa* 1140 respectively. This form is entirely different to the chalice or inverted bell-shape at Valle Crucis that ultimately derives from a classical Corinthian capital. Chalice forms, whether plain, foliated or trumpet-scallops, come into vogue in the last quarter of the twelfth century, which suggests that the typologically earlier form of the Pennant Melangell capitals are unlikely to be later than the third quarter of the twelfth century.

Fig. 415 Pennant Melangell, St Melangell: shrine, showing detail of the south arcade

Fig. 416 Valle Crucis abbey: north capitals on the slype doorway

Fig. 417 Valle Crucis abbey: south capitals on the slype doorway

Radford and Hemp have also drawn attention to fragments that relate to the St Melangell shrine at Llanrhaeadr-ym-Mochnant and Llangollen.[111] The former preserves one stone from a shrine gable now set on a windowsill in the south nave aisle (fig. 418). Like the Pennant Melangell gables, the Llanrhaeadr-ym-Mochnant fragment sports foliage crockets the individual leaves of which are more finely finished than at Pennant Melangell. At Llangollen two carved stones are reset in the exterior east wall of the vestry of the church (fig. 419). The symmetrical foliage patterns and specific details of stems and leaves are intimately related to Pennant Melangell, but the Llangollen stones are different in being simple rectangular blocks. The stone on the left would have extended further to the left because the foliage pattern is unfinished but the integrity of the other two foliage patterns on the block suggests that the height of the stone is original. The right stone gives a different impression in that both the right side of the stone has been cut back and the foliage design to the top right would have been truncated. It is therefore possible that this stone originally had some arched shape like those in the arcades at Pennant Melangell. The stones may have come from the shrine of St Collen whose grave was located in a building known as 'the old church' that adjoined the west end of Llangollen church but was demolished in 1749.[112] There is also a related fragment of foliage sculpture built into the exterior

Fig. 418 Llanrhaeadr-ym-Mochnant, St Dogfan: fragment of shrine

Fig. 419 Llangollen, St Collen: fragments of shrine(?) reset in exterior east wall of the vestry

Fig. 420 Llantysilio yn Ial, St Tysilio: fragment of shrine(?) reset in west jamb of north nave window

right jamb of the easternmost north nave window at Llantysilio yn Ial (Denbighshire) (fig. 420).

The gables of the Pennant Melangell shrine and the related fragment at Llanrhaeadr-ym-Mochnant have been allied to steeply pitched gables surmounting a number of Romanesque doorways in Ireland, most specifically the west portal of Clonfert cathedral (figs. 415, 418 and 421).[113] Here it has been suggested that an enhanced version of the border decoration would come close to the Pennant crockets. This line of investigation may be taken further to produce an interesting and perhaps a surprising result. Medievalist Roger Stalley, of Trinity College, Dublin, has convincingly related the gabled west portal at Roscrea with the north portal at Lullington (Somerset), and suggested that both probably reflect the work of Roger, Bishop of Salisbury (1102–39) at Sarum cathedral.[114] Examination of the stones from Sarum cathedral preserved in the English Heritage stone store at Salisbury reveals a number of gabled stones, one of which (no. 81109824) is decorated with a damaged crocket (fig. 422). More stones of this type are recorded in the report on the excavation at Sarum.[115] The Sarum gabled stones were excavated outside the south transept and probably came from the façade of that transept rather than from a shrine, but the analogue for Pennant is significant in two respects. First, it associates the motif of the decorated gables at Pennant with the work of one of the greatest patrons of architecture and sculpture in

Fig. 421 Clonfert cathedral: west portal

Fig. 422 Sarum cathedral, Salisbury: fragment of gable (no. 81109824) in English Heritage stone store

the twelfth century. Secondly, the gable motif appears on all the tabernacles that surmount the figures on the west front of Wells cathedral and it has often been remarked that this façade has a shrine-like quality. It now appears that such an inter-relationship between shrines and architecture extends back into the Romanesque period.

There remains one other related fragment, hitherto unpublished and kindly drawn to my attention by Aimee Pritchard. It now forms the west face of the belfry at St Foddhyd or St Trillo at Clocaenog (Denbighshire) and like one of the arches from the Pennant Melangell shrine is cut from a single stone (fig. 423). It is now cracked and rather weathered, but preserves a symmetrical foliage pattern that grows into the spandrels from above the apex of the arch. The foliage is too worn for detailed comparison but it is significant that the broad, flattened stems are incised with single lines near each edge. Also the stems curl over to couch large leaves as at Pennant Melangell and even more clearly in the Llangollen fragments (fig. 419).

Fig. 423 Clocaenog, St Foddhyd or St Trillo: belfry

APPENDIX
Table-top fonts with scalloped undersides in Cardiganshire:
LLANFIHANGEL YSTRAD — square with three scallops on each side supported on a stem.[16]
MYNT — square with three scallops on each side supported on a stem.
PENBRYN — font in the porch with three scallops to each side of the square bowl with
    angle fillets between the undersides of the scallops.
SARNAU — scalloped underside of bowl related by Tyrrell-Green to Mynt and Tremain.[117]
TREMAIN — 'almost identical' to the font in the adjoining parish at Mynt.[118]

Other Cardiganshire fonts:
LLANGOEDMORE — a plain cushion capital on a stem, which Tyrrell-Green compared
    with Clovelly (Devon), Kingston Seymour (Somerset), St Twynnels
    (Pembrokeshire), Weston-in-Gordano (Somerset) and Dearham (Cumbria).[119]
ABERPORTH — A plain square bowl on a stem illustrated by Tyrrell-Green outside
    the porch.[120]

7
St Davids Cathedral

When one thinks of spectacular views of cathedrals, it is usually those with a hilltop location, like Durham or Lincoln, which come to mind, an image in which the building is the dominant feature on the skyline. The setting of St Davids cathedral couldn't be more different, hidden away from the town at the bottom of a steep hill. Yet to approach the cathedral from the town through the east gateway to the close, the Porth y Twr, is almost to simulate arrival by helicopter to be given a spectacular aerial view of the building. A less dramatic vista, but one that more closely recreates the experience of a medieval traveller who had arrived by boat to the harbour at Porth Clais, is to approach the cathedral from the south-west (fig. 424). From the car park, located some 300 yards away from the cathedral, the visitor walks over a narrow bridge to delight in the vista across the fields to the massive church beyond. If, at this moment, time travel to the Middle Ages proves too much, at least it might be imagined that John Constable had moved from Salisbury cathedral to paint St Davids.

    The inclusion of St Davids cathedral in a book on Romanesque architecture and sculpture in Wales requires some explanation. The present fabric was commenced in 1182, some years after the Gothic choir of Canterbury cathedral, begun in 1175, or the

Fig. 424 St Davids cathedral from the south-west

establishment of early Gothic in the West Country in Wells cathedral in 1175 or 1176. Moreover, it is over a quarter of a century after northern French Gothic elements were introduced in the choir built by Archbishop Roger of Pont l'Évêque at York Minster (1154–81).[1] Yet there are many aspects of the design of St Davids that preserve a strong link with the Romanesque, so much so that Roger Stalley concluded that, 'In many respects St Davids was the last great expression of English Romanesque, and perhaps deliberately so'.[2] Thomas Lloyd *et al* in the introduction to the Pembrokeshire volume of *The Buildings of Wales*, assert that St Davids is 'one of the last great Romanesque churches of Britain, barely aware of the Gothic then well underway elsewhere.[3] In the detailed account of St Davids cathedral in the same volume, Stalley reiterated boldly that 'St Davids was more Romanesque than Gothic'.[4]

Whilst there has been little agreement amongst architectural historians about the chronology of the fabric, there is consensus that it belongs in the West Country School of masons, as defined by Sir Harold Brakspear.[5] Indeed, St Davids cathedral is a key work for understanding this school that encompassed the west of England, the midlands as far north as Chester, Wales and Ireland. In the school traditional Romanesque elements were fused with progressive early Gothic motifs derived either directly or indirectly from northern France. As we shall see, at St Davids there was a strong desire to enrich the building with a wealth of ornament frequently found in works associated with the most munificent patrons of architecture and the most prestigious churches of the twelfth century.

The present church replaced an earlier one constructed between 1115 and 1131 by the Norman-appointed Bishop Bernard. It is possible that there are some remains from that church in the present fabric. These are a double-billet string course that faces the crossing

Fig. 425 Wall above the eastern face of the west crossing arch

above the western crossing arch, and five fragments of intersecting arcade ornament above this, two reused as voussoirs in a retaining arch and three in the right spandrel of this arch (fig. 425). On the other hand, these stones may have come from the 1180s church in the rebuilding after the fall of the crossing tower in 1220. If the latter case is the correct one, then the motifs are traditional and are best explained as references to continuity with the earlier fabric. Either way, they suggest that the early twelfth-century cathedral was richly decorated — something to be expected given that Llandaff cathedral was probably trying to rival the opulence at St Davids. For reasons discussed in relation to the church at Tywyn,[6] Bishop Bernard's church probably had a cruciform plan and an aisled nave.

Documentation

The documentation that relates to the present building provides an essential framework for our analysis of the building and yet, as is so often the case, it supplies so little of the detail we crave to know. The *Annals of Wales* record that in 1182 the church of St Davids was destroyed and work on the present cathedral church was commenced.[7] In 1188 Baldwin, Archbishop of Canterbury, said mass at the high altar during his tour of Wales.[8] This may be taken to mean that either part of the old cathedral was still in use or that the sanctuary of the new church was completed. In 1189, the papal legate, John of Anagni, granted Gerald of Wales and Bishop Peter de Leia release from their vows to join the crusade, on condition that they contributed to the rebuilding (*reparationem*) of the church of St Davids.[9] This indicates that building was still ongoing. In 1197 Lord Rhys of Deheubarth was buried in the cathedral. In 1198 Bishop Peter de Leia died and his obit records that he began (*incoepit*) the new work on the cathedral,[10] and so implying that the church was not finished. In 1220 the new tower collapsed.[11] This has been taken universally to refer to the crossing tower and, as shall be seen, there is strong archaeological evidence in favour of this interpretation. In 1248 an earthquake damaged 'a great part' of the church.[12]

The plan of the 1182 church has come down to us in its entirety, with the addition of the retrochoir and Lady Chapel to the east (fig. 529). There is an aisled presbytery of four bays, and a crossing tower under which there is the liturgical choir. The transepts have three bays, are aisleless and communicate with the nave aisles through doors. The nave itself is of six bays. The chronology of the church has been variously interpreted and there is no consensus as to whether construction progressed from west to east or, along traditional lines, from east to west.

Historiography

The historiography of St Davids cathedral is complex. The foci have been on the chronology of the building, whether or not it was vaulted in whole or in part, and its affiliations with other buildings, especially those of the West Country School and, concomitantly, its place in the history of architecture. For the sake of clarity it is best to keep these areas separate.

In their classic 1856 study of the cathedral, Jones and Freeman attributed the nave with the western crossing arch and the west wall of both transepts to the 1180s campaign of construction.[13] The north, south and east crossing arches, the terminal and east walls of

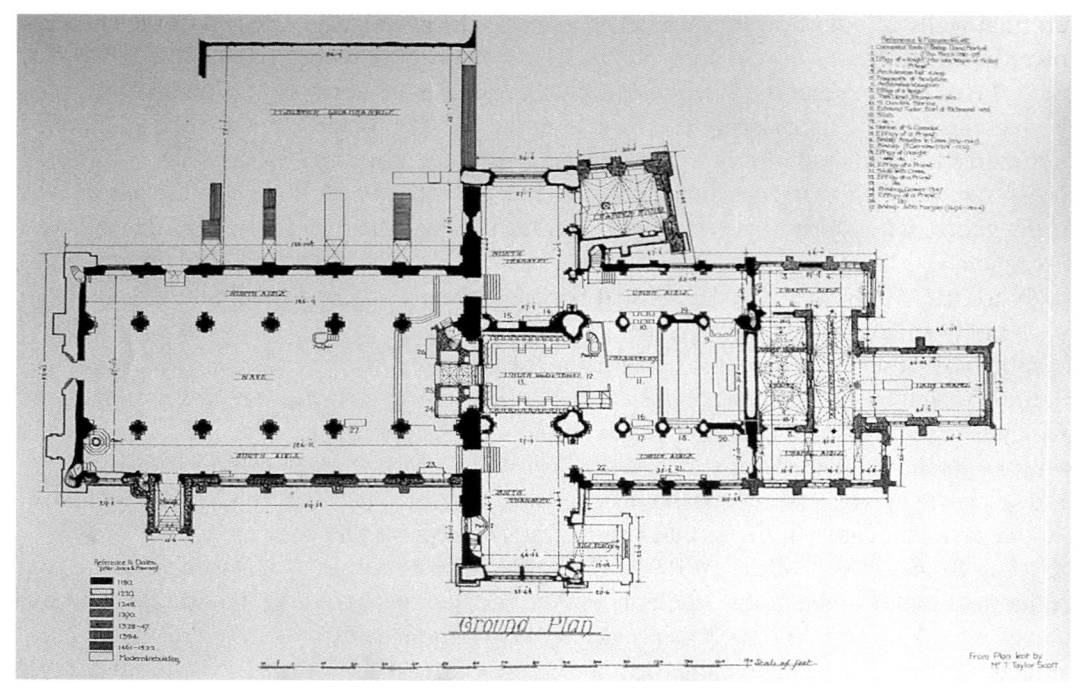

Fig. 426 Plan of St Davids cathedral (from The Builder*)*

both transepts, the choir arcades, east wall and inner face of the north choir aisle they dated to after the 1220 fall of the tower.[14]

The chronology adopted by George Gilbert Scott, the restoration architect of the cathedral, followed Jones and Freeman but not without certain reservations:

> The extent to which the Choir and Transepts were reconstructed after this misfortune [the fall of the crossing tower] is anything but clear. That they underwent very considerable change is quite certain; but so much pains seem to have been taken to avoid diversity of style, that it is a very difficult task to define exactly which parts belong to the first and which to the second period. It may, however, be assumed (I think) generally, that the Choir owed its general design, as now exhibited, to the reconstruction after 1220, and that the same extended to a considerable degree to the eastern side of the Transepts. The difficulty of exact definition is rendered the greater by a second general reparation having been rendered necessary through the effects of an earthquake which occurred in 1248.[15]

In Taylor Scott's plan in *The Builder*, the nave, western crossing arch, west walls of the transepts, the south aisle wall and the south respond of the arch from the south transept to the south choir aisle, the north choir aisle wall (except for the third bay), the east walls of both choir aisles, and the east respond of the north choir arcade, are all attributed to the 1180s build (fig. 426).[16] The east wall and arcades of the presbytery, and the east and terminal walls of both transepts are all ascribed to the period after the fall of the crossing tower in 1220.

Lovegrove presented a very complex sequence of construction and argued that work commenced 'in the usual way, by setting out and building the outer walls'.[17] He then considered that the west wall of the nave was constructed, followed by the aisle walls of the nave.[18] 'Next, a beginning was made at the east end of the choir, followed by the outer walls of the choir aisles. When the outer walls of the choir were completed, the building of the nave piers was begun, and operations were confined to the western area until the nave was ready for use'.[19] Lovegrove believed that Bishop Bernard's choir remained in use until the nave had been completed. Lovegrove then summarized the pre-1220 sequence of building as follows: 'west tower piers (in part); nave arcades; west tower arch; nave triforium and clerestory; transepts, with the eastern chapel now destroyed; eastern tower piers; east responds of the choir'.[20] Work on the choir piers was only commenced around 1215, initially with the intention of vaulting the aisles, which idea was abandoned during construction.[21] The sequence of work after the fall of the crossing tower in 1220, was 'entirely conjectural', and, to save the reader further confusion, will not be repeated here.[22]

In *English Art 1100–1216* T.S.R. Boase followed Lovegrove in starting the building at the west end,[23] while architect Geoffrey Webb dated the nave *c*.1180 and the choir and transepts *c*.1190.[24] He observed that the nave 'is distinguished for the intricacy and variety of its enrichment'.[25] In the reconstruction of the presbytery after the 1220 fall of the tower he saw 'a somewhat later character, as the new eastern wall seems to show in the use of banded shafts between the lancets. These seem to be due to an influence from outside the western region'.[26]

Archaeologist Tim Tatton-Brown placed the nave and the western parts of the crossing and transepts in the last twenty years of the twelfth century and stated that in many ways they reflect the high Romanesque style — round-headed arches with 'some fine decoration carved on them'.[27] Most recently, Roger Stalley placed the nave between 1182 and 1200, the original design of the presbytery 'perhaps *c*.1190', and the transepts 'slightly later in date' than the nave.[28]

On the question of vaulting, Jones and Freeman believed that vaults were constructed in the choir aisles but not in the nave and nave aisles, although they contended that a sexpartite vault was planned for the nave.[29] Scott believed that the entire building was planned for stone vaults, chiefly sexpartite, but added that, 'it would not appear that any part of the vaulting was actually carried into execution'.[30] King, Robson and Lovegrove all adopted this viewpoint.[31] Francis Bond believed that a sexpartite vault over single bays was intended in the nave but made no comment on whether he thought it was built.[32] Lovegrove considered that a sexpartite vault over the nave 'would have been impossible to construct, and the design would be artistically unsatisfactory',[33] instead suggesting that, 'Probably a wooden roof with curved wall ribs from principal to principal was intended'.[34] Boase suggested that the nave was possibly intended for a sexpartite vault over each bay, but that it was unlikely that this was carried out. In this he is followed by Evans.[35] Webb saw that 'Short vaulting shafts are provided between each clerestory window, as though for a sexpartite system, but whether any stone vaulting was ever contemplated is open to question'.[36] Tatton-Brown stated that 'The twelfth-century roof was clearly of timber', although whether this meant a wooden vault, a ceiling or open timber roof is not clear.[37] Hearn and Thurlby, and Draper opted for a wooden vault in imitation of stone.[38] Jean Bony suggested that in the nave 'a sexpartite vault was planned and probably built' over single bays and this probably reflected a lost prototype in the northern part of the Ile-de-France.[39] Most recently the present author argued that stone vaults were built in the aisles and over the main span of the nave.[40]

Scott's report on the state of the fabric and the restoration of the cathedral, placed St Davids in the context of the beginnings of Gothic architecture in England and suggested a 'very direct relationship' between Glastonbury abbey as rebuilt after the fire of 1184'.[41] He further observed,

> Remote as was the site of your Cathedral from the more active scenes of this great [early Gothic] artistic movement, it is most interesting to observe, that it in no degree falls short of contemporary structures in the grandeur of its conception, or the beauty and refinement of its details. It lingers in some degree behind many of them in the extent to which the pointed arch has supplanted the round, but this was probably owing rather to a desire to avoid undue height, than to any actual want of advancement; for in all the details, and especially in the carved foliage, the skill and taste exhibited is of first-rate order, and the execution of the ornamental masonry could hardly be excelled. Its architect, indeed, seemed determined to plant, in the furthest extremity of our island, the standard of the utmost advancement of this art, at the period of its most determined progression. These facts render the building a wonderfully interesting and valuable landmark in architectural history, taking, in the extreme west, a position parallel to that held by Canterbury in the extreme east of the island.

In spite of Scott's positive assessment of the architecture of St Davids cathedral, for the most part the fabric has not been rated highly by architectural historians. Instead it has been seen as one of the also-rans of the West Country School of masons, a design not in the same league as the progressive Gothic of the near-contemporary Wells cathedral. Lovegrove stated that 'the master builder was a bad engineer'.[42] Brakspear opined that there 'were undoubtedly lesser lights of the school, one of whom was employed on the earlier work at St David's, but in this the whole design is clumsy and devoid of originality. The later work in the transepts there is entirely different and characteristic of the school; it assimilates so closely to that at Slimbridge in Gloucestershire that it was probably the same hand'.[43] Boase said that 'There are in fact several indications that the enterprise of the builders somewhat outran their skill, but of the high standard of the decorative carvers that Bishop Peter brought to his remote cathedral there can be no question'.[44]

Recently, this negative reading of St Davids has changed, and both Peter Draper and Roger Stalley have indicated that St Davids deserves a place in the architectural mainstream of the late twelfth century.[45] In order to achieve as accurate an assessment as possible, it is first important to try to unravel the archaeology of the building and to determine which parts belong to the 1182 design, or to the post-1220 rebuilding, or work done after the 1248 earthquake.

The Archaeology of the Fabric
Given that the crossing tower is the only part of the building that can be specifically associated with the documentation, it makes good sense to start with it. This will allow us to identify features that are specific either to the 1180s or to the 1220s. The western crossing arch is round headed, in contrast to the pointed arches to the north, south and east (fig. 425). The west arch has three orders to both the east and the west but the two sides are differently treated: it is plain towards the east but is richly articulated towards the nave (figs. 427–429). To the east the capitals are all trumpet-scallops; those supporting the second and third orders are without necking while the capitals in the western angles of the crossing have necking (figs. 427 and 428). The shafts are all nibbed. The plain soffit is carried on trumpet-scallop capitals without necking above stepped triple shafts separated by deep hollows (figs. 429–430). The middle shaft is nibbed but the lateral shafts are plain. The north capitals have plain scallop faces and a single trefoil leaf sprouts between the western and central capital. In contrast to this the south capitals have trefoil leaves growing on and between their cones, while the scallops have almost completely dissolved into symmetrical foliage (figs. 427and 429). The next order is continuous and has a triple roll at the angle with a central nib, flanked by deep hollows and narrow rolls (figs. 429–430). In contrast to the equivalent order on the east side of the responds, this order has no base whereas on the east side the nibbed shaft sits on a water-holding base (fig. 430). This base contrasts with the pre-water-holding bases of the adjacent triple shafts of the inner order of the arch (fig. 430). Returning to the west side of the arch, in classic West Country School fashion the first three orders are non-continuous, continuous and non-continuous, and there follows a non-continuous order (fig. 429).[46] In the arch there is an angle group of two gaping chevrons flanked by a narrow roll and a further row of the same elaborate chevron.

Capitals at St Davids cathedral.
Fig. 428 Northern capitals on the western crossing arch

The order is carried on nibbed shafts and capitals without any necking, a trumpet-scallop on the north, and two rows of upright stylized acanthus leaves — some with serrated edges — on the south. Next to these capitals there is one more trumpet-scallop for the ribs of the high vault.

The north, south and east crossing arches are also of three orders. Unlike the west crossing arch, the north and south arches are the same on both sides; the soffit is flat with a narrow edge roll, order two has a narrow chamfer and the third order is plain (figs. 431 and 432). The inner order is carried on a foliage capital on the east responds and on trumpet-scallop capitals on the west respond, all atop triple stepped shafts, the central one of which is filleted. The other orders also sit on a variety of foliage and trumpet-scallop forms atop filleted shafts. The east crossing arch is fundamentally the same except foliage or foliated trumpet-scallop capitals are used throughout, and the second order in the arch is enriched with chevron (figs. 433 and 434).

Capitals at St Davids cathedral.
Figs. 429 and 430 South capitals on the western crossing arch

The differences between the west and the other crossing arches illustrate changes between the 1180s and post-1220 work. The changes are: from round-headed to pointed arches, from sharp nibs on the shafts to fillets, from some capitals without necking to the consistent use of necking, and from deeply cut and projecting mouldings to shallow mouldings and simple chamfers. There is also a change from deep to shallow carving in the capitals

Fig. 430 Northern bases of the western crossing arch

Capitals at St Davids cathedral.
Figs. 431 and 432 Eastern capitals on the north and south crossing arch respectively

which is especially noticeable in the foliated trumpet-scallop types in the north, south and east arches.

Towards the east above the west crossing arch there are eight pointed arches with single chamfers carried on trumpet-scallop and foliage capitals (fig. 425). The capitals alternate between foliate and trumpet-scallop except at the north end where there are two trumpet-scallops together. The foliage capitals have the same slim, chalice-shape, and upright leaves that range between plantain and stylized acanthus. Under arches two, four, five and seven there are lower pointed arches with a continuous unmoulded order. The capitals have no necking and square moulded abaci with narrow chamfers at the angles to correspond with the chamfers in the arches. This arcading is dissimilar to the other three walls of the crossing (fig. 435). Here there are four arches per side that open into a wall passage. The arches have three orders that alternate non-continuous and continuous in the tradition of the west face of the western crossing arch. The details are very different. The non-continuous orders are carried on heavy trumpet-scallop capitals with round abaci

Capitals at St Davids cathedral.
Figs. 433 and 434 North and south capitals respectively on the east crossing arch

Fig. 435 Arcade above the north crossing arch

rather than square abaci in the 1180s work. The inner order of each arch has a filleted shaft below the capital and this motif is also used in the centre of the outer arcade. But the other outer orders are carried on hook corbels beneath the capitals. The capitals are trumpet-scallops but, unlike those encountered so far, they have squatter proportions and rounded abaci instead of square or octagonal. In the arch the inner and outer orders have a hollow chamfer while the middle order is a roll with a fillet towards the outer edge. In the north arcade the central pier used alternating polychrome masonry, and some random limestone is also used in the central pier of the south arcade.

The capitals of the east crossing arch and the east responds of the north and south crossing arches are significantly different from the examples examined so far. Three types prevail. First, there are variants on the trumpet-scallop in which the scallop faces dissolve into an S-shaped scroll and contain highly stylized foliage, while the cones have collars with spear-like forms between (figs. 431–433). Secondly, there are what might be described as superimposed waterleaves (fig. 434). Here the classic waterleaf form with the inward turning volute shares that volute with a bulbous and larger under-leaf that sprouts volutes to the side. Thirdly, there are foliage scrolls with winding and interlacing stems (figs. 431–433). It is also worth noting that nibs are reserved for the shafts in the eastern angles of the crossing and that otherwise the fillet is here the more popular form of shaft adornment, with a broad one on the central shaft of the eastern arch. There is a significant difference between the abaci of the western crossing arch and the nave arcade piers on the one hand, and, on the other hand, those of the eastern crossing piers (figs. 427–429 and 431–434). The former has a simple hollow chamfer beneath a quirk and a straight upper stone. The latter present a bolder and more complex profile. The differences observed between the capitals of the western crossing arch, and those of the eastern crossing arch and adjacent responds of the north and south crossing arches, are fundamental in our study of the cathedral. They provide the clearest way of differentiating between the work of the 1180s and that executed after the 1220 fall of the tower.

Fig. 436 The north side of the nave from the south-west

Fig. 437 The west end and part of the north side of the nave

The Nave

In the nave we find close analogues for the motifs in the western crossing arch, as well as other details that are compatible with a date in the 1180s.

The nave is divided into six bays with wide, round-headed arches except in the narrower west bay where the arch is pointed (front cover and figs. 436–437). The floor slopes down from east to west and the side walls have rotated outwards, a point especially evident on the north aisle wall. The relatively squat columns alternate between round and octagonal and have attached shafts on the cardinal axes — the pilier cantonné which we have met in the nave at Strata Florida, and which was to enjoy popularity in French architecture after their use at Chartres cathedral after 1194. The detached shafts of the west responds are exceptional (fig. 438). On the aisle side of the piers there are stepped triple shafts with capitals and abaci that project beyond the plane of the wall as if to support the ribs of an aisle vault (fig. 439). The arches have three orders, of which the inner one is plain with hollow chamfers. The second order towards the nave is adorned with rich chevron ornament, which changes in detail from bay to bay, and which is framed by a segmental roll moulding. There is no decoration to the second order on the aisle side but there is an interesting detail in the south aisle that gives a clue as to constructional practice. The lowest voussoirs in the arch — between seven and nine

Fig. 438 West respond of the south nave arcade

voussoirs, depending on the size of the blocks — just have a plain broad chamfer but above which there is a narrow channel at the outside edge. The change probably represents the point at which centering was introduced for the construction of the arch. The outer order on the aisle side is plain, but towards the nave there are two roll mouldings, the inner one of which is nibbed. In the western bay of the north arcade the chevron in the left arc of the arch does not match that on the right and there is an awkward junction between the two at the apex (fig. 440). There is a set back at the triforium sill to facilitate the placement of vault shafts; a triplet above the columns and a single shaft above the middle of the main arcade arch (figs. 436 and 437). The upper half of the nave elevation appears to link a triforium and clerestorey under a single giant arch carved with chevron or meander ornament that changes from arch to arch. In fact there is no division within the passage between triforium and clerestorey (fig. 441). The triforium arches are sharply pointed and have two continuous orders, the inner with a quadrant roll, the outer with a roll moulding. Between the heads of the arches there is

Fig. 439 Looking west along the south nave aisle

Fig. 440 Detail of the chevron on the wetsren bay of the south arcade showing an awkward junction

Fig. 442 The north capital on the inside of the western portal showing symetrically arranged foliage patterns

a pierced roundel with a variety of carved detail. The inside arch of the west doorway is round headed and has a single order carried on shafts and capitals carved with symmetrically arranged foliage patterns (fig. 442).

The west front is the product of Scott's restoration and as such is an interesting advertisement for his knowledge of West Country School motifs. Perhaps we might view it as an exercise in how Scott saw himself as master mason of the cathedral in charge of designing the new building. However, as a reflection of the actual 1180s design it must be used with caution and in conjunction with pre-restoration photographs and antiquarian drawings.[47] All aspects of detail must be dismissed but some broad outlines do follow the original (fig. 424). The clear framing of the nave and aisles with flat buttresses that carried turrets, the central doorway and round windows in the upper walls of the aisles fronts, are all supported in the antiquarian evidence. The nook shafts to the buttresses, the triple, round-headed windows above the doorway, and the quintuplet

Fig. 441 South triforium in the nave, looking east showing the integration of the traditional triforium and clerestorey passages in one

above, and the use of blind arches on the central buttresses above the lower storey likewise find authority in antiquarian sources.

The south doorway dates from the fourteenth century but the north doorway is contemporary with the rest of the nave (fig. 443). It is round headed and has three orders. The inner order is continuous and has a quadrant roll moulding. Orders two and three both have chevron in the arch and are carried on capitals atop nibbed shafts and moulded bases. The chevron is not well preserved but enough remains to determine that on order two it took on an overall lattice pattern while in order three it was a saw-tooth form with outer and central thin roll mouldings. The two left, and the outer right capitals have remnants of foliage decoration. The inner right capital is very badly damaged but it is possible to discern that it took the form of a grotesque mask, the pointed ears and edges of the bulbous cheeks being most recognizable. The hood mould is carved with shuttlecocks and has a mask at the apex and damaged dragon's head stops.

The doorway from the south nave aisle to the south transept has two orders, the inner one continuous with a quadrant moulding, the outer on a steep base, nibbed shafts and trumpet-scallop capitals (fig. 444). In the wall above the doorway there is an arced set off that starts on the left from a trumpet-scallop capital and marks the trajectory of the former aisle vault.

Fig. 443 North doorway to the nave, which is contemporary with the nave

Fig. 444 The south aisle looking east with the arced outline of the former vault

The doorway from the north nave aisle to the north transept also has a continuous inner order with a quadrant moulding but there is a trefoil head to the arch. The outer order has an angle roll in the round-headed arch carried on foliage capitals atop nibbed shafts and steep bases (fig. 445). There is also a vault trace but it has been tidied up in restoration.

There was a remodelling of the nave aisles in the time of Bishop Gower (1328–1347) when the walls were heightened and larger windows inserted. However, the walls up to the string-course at windowsill level and the triple-shafted vault responds up to the level of the nave arcade capitals belong to the 1180s build. At the west end of the south aisle below the rose window there is part of the lower frame of its predecessor (fig. 439). The abandonment of the lower window and the subsequent rebuilding at a higher level may have been precipitated by damage caused in the 1248 earthquake.

Fig. 445 North nave aisle looking east

The capitals of the main arcades boast a wonderful array of different designs from standard trumpet-scallops to richly foliated and even figured versions of the type, to a range of foliage forms that includes experimental varieties of stiff-leaf. Some of the capitals atop the attached shafts are without necking but on the core capital necking is used. On the south capital of the easternmost pier of the north arcade (N1S) there are foliage crockets at the angles and in centre of each side of the capital (fig. 446). Where the trefoil leaves are well preserved, as on the left in fig. 446, we see that the stem tapers towards the top and disappears into a hollow in the central lobe of the leaf. In the central crocket on the right there is a berry cluster. The large backing leaves on both sides have what is called a plantain notch, in other words a step out just above the short, broad stem. The lower tier of symmetrical leaves has narrow, pointed upper fronds that betray their ultimate derivation from classical acanthus foliage. These details will be of crucial importance when we come to determine the source of this sculpture. On N2S there is another example of the plantain notch but with a completely different leaf than on N1S (figs. 446 and 447). On N2W there

Fig. 446 North nave arcade capital N1S with foliage crockets that have stems tapering into the central lobe of the leaf

Fig. 448 North nave arcade capital N3N with plantain notches and a ring beneath the abacus

Fig. 447 North nave arcade capital N2SW from the south-east showing fusion of the trumpet-scallop and stiff-leaf ornamentation on the left

is a brilliant fusion of the trumpet-scallop and stiff-leaf types (fig. 447). In between, on the core capital a pair of feet is all that remains of a former angle figure, and above this there is a ring beneath the abacus, another detail that ultimately harks back to the classical Corinthian capital. The latter detail is prominent on N3N on which the plantain notch is again in evidence (fig. 448). On N3E single acanthus leaves to the north and east are flanked by the simplest pointed leaves that ultimately derive from stylized French models (fig. 449).

Fig. 449 North nave arcade capital N3SE (RIGHT?); acanthus leaves flanked by simple pointed leaves

Fig. 450 North nave arcade capital N4S, with figures on the scallop faces

Fig. 451 North nave arcade capital N4S from the east, with a figure on the scallop face

N4S provides a sequel to N2W but here lively figures inhabit the scallop faces, and the one on the east proudly asserts his masculinity (figs. 447, 450 and 451). S1E presents a somewhat fussier variant of the fusion between trumpet-scallop and foliage capitals while the adjacent capital to the south (S1S) provides more excellent examples of plantain notches. Throughout the nave the abaci remain consistent with a quirked hollow chamfer beneath a flat top.

The capitals atop the interior shafts of the west doorway are quite different from any encountered in the nave arcades. On the north capital we find symmetrically arranged stems with a beaded binding tie at the angle and somewhat under-nourished, flat acanthus leaves (fig. 442). Similarly, on the doorway from the north nave aisle to the north transept, the north capital belongs to the tradition of flatter foliage designs but one that is exquisitely detailed with fine drill holes and the most delicate beading (fig. 452).

Before discussing the question of vaulting in the aisles and nave, it will be well to take stock of the parallels between the details in the nave and the western crossing arch. The triple shaft groups on the aisle side of the nave arcade piers, in which plain shafts flank a nibbed shaft, are a more compact version of the responds of the soffits of the west crossing arch (figs. 427–428 and 448). The abaci of the main arcade capitals are the same as on the west crossing capitals. The capitals without necking in the nave arcades and atop the single high-vault shafts are used throughout the western crossing responds (figs. 427–428, 436–437, 445–448 and 450). Trumpet scallops with a clear separation between the individual elements, richly foliated scallops, and upright trefoil leaves with a gorged central lobe that grow from the bell of the capital, are also common to the nave and western crossing arch (figs. 427–429, and 448–449). Gaping chevron is common to the westernmost clerestorey arch on the north side of the nave and the west face of the west crossing arch (figs. 446 and 453). Finally, the stepped roll moulding with

Fig. 452 Northern capital on the doorway from the north aisle to the transept showing fine detailing

Fig. 453 North nave clerestorey, bay N6 showing gaping chevron

Fig. 454 North nave clerestorey, bay N2E, showing the uper half of the formeret

Fig. 455 Glastonbury abbey: the north-east vault springer in the eastern chapel of the south transept showing formerets with varying degrees of surviving vaulting

a central nib on the western face of the west crossing arch appears in reduced form on the outer order of the nave arcades (figs. 429, 446, 447 and 449).

As indicated above, the nature of the original covering of the main span of the nave has been, and will probably continue to be, a matter of debate amongst architectural historians. The alternation of triple shafts above the main arcade piers with single shafts above the centre of the bay indicates that a six-part vault over single bays was intended. The set-back above the main arcades to create a sill for the triforium and vaulting shafts (figs. 436 and 437) confirms the intention to vault. Where such set-backs occur in English Romanesque architecture, as in the presbytery and transepts of Durham cathedral, the nave of Lindisfarne priory, the nave of St Peter's, Gloucester, and the presbytery of Malmesbury abbey, high vaults were always constructed.[48] Of these churches, the nave of Gloucester may well have been the point of departure for the St Davids scheme. But was the St Davids nave high vault ever constructed, and, if so, was it built of wood or stone? Detailed examination of the condition of the wall arches or formerets of the high vault provides the answer. The evidence in question concerns the appearance of the wall arches of the putative high vault. In the western half of the nave — bays 4 to 6 — the formerets that define the edge of the vault are chiselled back (fig. 453). However, in the eastern half of the nave, bays 1 to 3, the removal of the formerets has been far less thorough. For

304

our purposes it is most important to record that above both clerestorey arches in bay N2 the upper half of the formeret survives, that is between about 10 and 2 o'clock in terms of a clock face (fig. 454 and 561). Why were the formerets completely removed in some bays but not in others? Their partial removal may suggest that the modification took place when the present sixteenth-century ceiling was erected. However, this does not explain why the formerets were entirely removed in the western bays where the ceiling does not encroach on the formerets. The answer must be that there was something present in addition to the formeret, and that could only have been the masonry web of a high vault. This evidence may be contrasted with the formerets in the nave at Llanthony priory which remain in near-perfect condition after the removal of the former wooden high vault.[49] Indeed, the label stops of the arches are even preserved. On the other hand, the remains of vaults in the Great Church of Glastonbury abbey provide a more involved picture. Figure 455 illustrates the north-east angle of the vault of the south transept chapel in the Great Church at Glastonbury abbey. Above and to the left of the formeret the stones of the vault web — limestone below and tufa above — are intact. The same is true for the limestone springer and the first two pieces of tufa above the right formeret, but above this the vault web has fallen away and thus the formeret stands alone. Such differentiation is commonplace in the ruins of medieval vaults and simply indicates that some sections of mortar were stronger than others used at the junction of arch and vault web. At St Davids it would seem that the mortar used for the high vault was for the most part very good. It held the vault web in place next to the wall in the three western bays so that when the time came to remove the remnants of vault web it was deemed easier to chisel it off complete with the formerets. In the eastern bays, however, sections of the web next to the wall either fell down in the earthquake of 1248 or were easily removed without damaging the formeret.

Association of the damaged formerets in the nave with the removal of a masonry high vault is supported by evidence in the western bay of the presbytery. Here the springers of the formerets have been chiselled back like those in the nave (fig. 456). Immediately above these truncated wall arches there are trefoil-headed niches which were probably

Fig. 456 Vault capital and springer above the western pier of the north arcade at St Davids cathedral, showing chiselled back formerets

introduced with the remodelling of the clerestorey after the collapse of the high vault in the 1248 earthquake. It would therefore appear that, just as in the nave, removal of the formeret has been conditioned by the necessity to remove the attached vault web.

Roger Stalley is quite correct to suggest that the nave high vault would have been domed.[50] This can be visualized today with reference to the west crossing arch or to the large, round-headed arch on the inside of the west wall that encloses the windows of the west front (front cover and fig. 437). The capitals of these arches are at the same level as the capitals of the high vault, while the head of the arch disappears behind the present ceiling.

The only stone that could have been used for the webbing of the high vault is tufa. In spite of Stalley's reservation as to the daring of the masons about trying to build a high vault, even in lightweight tufa, there is such a good tradition of tufa vaults in the West Country that such a bold move should come as no great surprise.[51]

Reconstruction of a high stone vault in the nave of St Davids strongly suggests that aisle vaults were also built. This is confirmed by the offset on the east wall of the nave south aisle, by the triple shafts on the aisle side of the main arcade piers and the responds against the aisle walls (figs. 439 and 440). Be that as it may, it must be admitted that there is no compelling archaeological evidence in the aisles to support the claim that

Fig. 457 West pier and arch in the south nave arcade at St Davids cathedral

Fig. 458 Llanthony Priory: vault springer in the north nave aisle, separate from the main aracde arches

vaults were erected there. The stonework above the vault capitals shows no sign of the removal of vaults (fig. 457). Is it possible that the remains of masonry vaults could have been so completely cleaned up after the 1248 earthquake? Indeed it is, for at Tewkesbury abbey the trace of the former Romanesque barrel vault above the south crossing arch is marked only by fire damage that cuts across otherwise unmarked ashlar.[52] One might expect that the springer blocks of the aisle vaults would have been bonded into the wall above the capitals. Moreover, the space for the St Davids aisle-vault springers is unusually narrow (fig. 457). Perhaps surprisingly, regional parallels can be found for both traits. The ashlar springers of the nave aisle vaults of Llanthony priory are quite separate from the main arcade arches (fig. 458). Here the space between the arcade arches is wider than at St Davids but a narrower version occurs in the slype at Llanthony where the four-part rib vault is still extant (fig. 459). Here it will be observed that each rib is cut from a different stone all distinct from the wall arch. There is a further parallel in the south nave aisle of Dore abbey (Herefs.). Here the springers of the arcade arches are set as close together as at St Davids, and concomitantly the vault springer was set on a separate stone atop the capitals at the back of the arcade.[53]

Fig. 459 Llanthony priory: slype vault showing narrower separation of the vault arch springers and the main arcade arches

Associations for the Western Crossing Arch and the Nave

All aspects of the western crossing arch and the nave are closely related to West Country School architecture, with some elements that reflect a well-established Romanesque tradition while others indicate first-hand knowledge of the most progressive designs. The continuous quadrant roll on the inner order of the nave north doorway is ultimately derived from the wall arches in the late eleventh-century presbytery aisles of St Peter's, Gloucester. The motif was especially popular in the later twelfth century in the area around Worcester, so much so that Lovegrove labelled it the '"Worcestershire" sunk roll'.[54] In the west bays of the nave, and in the arch from the cloister to the western slype at Worcester cathedral, nibbed shafts and either trumpet-scallop or foliage capitals are used alongside an order with a continuous quadrant roll.[55] This work at Worcester probably dates immediately after the fall of the 'new tower' in 1175. Earlier candidates for this arrangement are the

Fig. 460 Dublin's Christ Church cathedral: doorway to the south transept

east processional doorway at Flaxley abbey (fd.1151), and the responds of the arch from the south nave aisle to the south transept at Keynsham abbey (fd.1167). The continuous order on the west face of the west crossing arch at St Davids is far more complex than the simple quadrant roll on the north doorway (fig. 429). A larger version of the triple roll on the angle of the order there is used on the first and third orders of the south transept portal of Christ Church cathedral, Dublin (fig. 460). Here we also find a simpler variant of the biforkated chevron on the St Davids west crossing arch. Biforkated chevron is also used on the arch to the north porch at Bredon (Worcs.) where the inner order has a single nibbed roll flanked by deep hollows. The Christ Church, Dublin, and Bredon roll mouldings therefore parallel the elements for the profile of the St Davids moulding. Roger Stalley has placed the start of Christ Church, Dublin, to 1186 and therefore it is too late to have influenced St Davids.[56] Bredon is undated but the manor belonged to the Bishop of Worcester and therefore the work there may be attributed to masons from Keynsham and/or Worcester. In his study of the late twelfth-century work at Worcester cathedral, Christopher Wilson suggested that Worcester masons were responsible for work at St Mary's, Shrewsbury.[57] This is significant because the arch moulding of the second order of the doorway in the terminal wall of the north transept at St Mary's is remarkably close to the continuous order towards the nave in the St Davids west crossing arch (figs. 429 and 461). Add to this the stylized flowers on the faces of the scallops of the right capital on St Mary's doorway in relation to the capital of the second order of the east side of the south respond of the west crossing arch at St Davids (figs. 427 and 461). Quadrant rolls are used for the continuous orders on all the late twelfth-century doorways at St Mary's, and the label of the south doorway is decorated with shuttlecock as on the north nave doorway at St Davids.

Other aspects of the north nave doorway at St Davids betray a West Country Romanesque background. The label mask has been discussed in relation to Heneglwys (Anglesey), and the dragon's head label stop in connection with Llandaff cathedral and Ewenny priory. In addition, the shaft-swallowing-mask capital appears at Malmesbury, Monkton Farleigh (Wilts.), Abbotsbury (Dorset), Elkstone, Siddington and South Cerney

Fig. 429 (above) Arch moulding on the west crossing arch and stylsied flowers on the faces on the scallops on the capital on the right, show similarities to the arch moulding on the second order and supporting capital on the doorway in the terminal wall of the north transept at St Mary's, Shrewsbury (Fig. 461, right)

(all in Glos.), and Beckington (Somerset). Also from the West Country Romanesque tradition is the use of doorways from the nave aisles to the transepts as at Ewenny priory and Llanthony priory. In the nave arcades of St James' priory, Bristol (fd.1144), the pilier cantonné with scalloped capitals is used to carry round-headed arches with a plain inner order and a moulded second order without any vertical articulation in the spandrels, all of which foreshadows the St Davids nave arcades (front cover and figs. 427 and 462). The pilier cantonné at St James, Bristol, only use a cylindrical core rather than the alternating system of cylindrical and octagonal at St Davids. However, the easternmost column of the south nave arcade at St James is a plain octagon. The pilier cantonné appears earlier in the West Country in the presbytery gallery of St Peter's, Gloucester, and if wall arches were used in connection with the Romanesque high vault in the nave there, then they would

Fig. 462 St James, Bristol: north nave arcade

have encompassed the triforium and clerestorey as in the St Davids nave. The vogue for rich chevron ornament is also established in the Gloucester nave. A number of different chevron types are found in the Herefordshire School of sculpture, and no less than eighteen different types of chevron were used in Bishop Roger's work at Sarum cathedral. A great variety of rich forms of chevron are used in the second half of the twelfth century as in the chapter house and the gatehouse of St Augustine's, Bristol. It is on the southern arch of the St Augustine's gatehouse that we find the 'gaping' chevron as on the western crossing arch and the east window of the west bay of the north nave clerestorey (figs. 105 and 429). Moreover, the plain inner order of the arch to the west range at St Augustine's has the unusual motif of a hollow chamfer as on the inner order of the main arcade arches at St Davids. Various patterns of lozenge and biforkated chevron are paralleled at Keynsham abbey and in the Lady Chapel at Glastonbury abbey (1184–86/9). An amazingly wide variety of chevron is also encountered in Christ Church cathedral, Dublin. This is not peculiar to the West Country School but seems to have been regarded as the mark of a superior aesthetic. This is illustrated in the hospital church of St Cross at Winchester, built for Henry of Blois, bishop of Winchester (1129–71) and abbot of Glastonbury (1126–71), one of the most munificent patrons of architecture of the third quarter of the twelfth century. A direct reflection of this is witnessed in the nave of the collegiate church at Steyning (Sussex), and analogous obsession with the inclusion of many different types of chevron in a single space is witnessed in the fragments from the choir of Archbishop Roger of Pont l'Evêque's York Minster.[58] These parallels make it clear that St Davids was to vie with the buildings of the most prestigious patrons of the time.

Fig. 463 Keynsham abbey: capital showing scallops mutating into foliage

The capitals are either trumpet scallops or foliage chalice capitals or some sort of fusion of the two. Elementary versions of the trumpet-scallop capital already appear between 1084 and 1089 in the crypt of Worcester cathedral. However, it is not until the 1160s that the motif comes into its own. It is found at Keynsham abbey and is the most popular form in the west bays of Worcester cathedral. One capital from Keynsham is especially instructive in that it supplies a close parallel for the central south capital of the west crossing arch at St Davids in which the scallops begin to mutate into foliage (figs. 427, 429 and 463). A few foliage capitals are used in the late twelfth-century work at Worcester but none supply models for the St Davids foliage capitals. For these we must look elsewhere. Some fragments at Wigmore abbey are instructive, for in addition to a trumpet-scallop capital there is one with plantain notches and a ring beneath the abacus very similar to St Davids nave N3N (figs. 448 and 464). In these capitals we are dealing with an early stage in the development of the foliage capital that was ultimately derived from the classical Corinthian capital, and more immediately from examples from the third quarter of the twelfth century in northern France. These capitals represent something radically different to the cushion or scalloped capital in that their basic form is an inverted bell, or chalice-shape, as opposed to a block shape with the lower angles cut as segments of a sphere. Aesthetically the cushion appears squat, heavy and bulbous, whereas the concave shape of the new capital is lighter and more elegant. For the details of the foliage at St Davids, the left capital of the doorway from the north nave aisle to the north transept is typologically the earliest (fig. 452). The multi-lobed, fleshy leaf forms with fine beaded decoration belong with those in the spandrels of a blind arcade on a fragment at Glastonbury abbey (fig. 4655). This is probably from the work done for Abbot Henry of Blois before 1171. The foliage on the capitals of the western crossing arch and the nave arcades are most instructive because they include specific details that are both unusual and can be dated with some degree of accuracy with reference to comparative work at Wells cathedral and the Great Church at Glastonbury abbey. At Wells in the eastern arcades and chapels of the transepts, and the eastern crossing arches, we find elegant capitals often without necking as at St Davids, with plantain notches and upright leaves that blossom into profuse crockets.

Fig. 464 Wigmore abbey: capital with a ring beneath the abacus

Fig. 465 Glastonbury abbey: fragment of blind arcade showing decoration akin to that at St Davids on a capital in the doorway between the aisle and north transept

In the capitals illustrated here from the eastern arcade of the Wells north transept we notice some very specific parallels for details in the St Davids capitals (fig. 466). There are trefoil leaves with a gouged middle lobe, trefoil leaves that grow from just above the necking of the capital, and even a small cluster of berries on one of the crockets (figs. 427, 429, 446 and 448). It should be emphasized that these details are quite different to the foliage related to the work of Henry of Blois at Glastonbury. They represent the beginnings of the so-called stiff-leaf capital, which was to become one of the hallmarks of Early English Gothic. The one inhabited capital at St Davids, N4S (figs. 450, 451 and 467), may be generally related to those in the western arcades of the Wells transepts and a fragment from Keynsham abbey,

Fig. 466 Wells cathedral: northern capitals on the eastern aracde of the north transept

Fig. 467 Figure on capital N4S on the north nave arcade at St Davids cathedral

Fig. 468 Keynsham abbey: fragment of a figure

Parallels with Glastonbury abbey Great Church.
Fig. 448 (left) North nave arcade capital N3N at St Davids cathedral
Figs. 469 (centre) and 470 (right) Capitals from the north and south transepts to the choir aisles at Glastonbury

although the setting of the figures on the trumpet-scallop faces is unique to St Davids.[59] A fragmentary figure from Keynsham also supplies a close parallel for the naturalistic drapery of the figure on the west side of the St Davids capital (figs. 467 and 468). Like the details of the stiff-leaf foliage, this figurative naturalism is a mark of the most innovative artists of the 1180s, as is well illustrated in the sculpture of the Lady Chapel of Glastonbury abbey.[60] The comparisons with Wells are instructive in that they demonstrate that the St Davids workshop was aware of motifs used in what is generally considered to be the most progressive building of its time in the West Country School. Yet, other progressive motifs at Wells, like finely moulded pointed arches and clustered piers, were not favoured for the St Davids nave. The reasons for this will be examined below, but first our comparative study must be extended to the great church of Glastonbury abbey. Remarkably close parallels for St Davids capital N3N, including details like the ring beneath the abacus, plantain notches, and individual trefoil leaves on the lower part of the capital, are found in the arches from the transepts to the presbytery aisles in the great church (figs. 448, 469 and 470). In addition it should be noted that like St Davids, but in contrast to Wells, the Glastonbury arches are encrusted with chevron.

The large, upright trefoil leaves on the lower half of capital N2W at St Davids are not easily paralleled at either Wells or Glastonbury, but a similar form occurs on the only remaining early Gothic nave high vault capital at St Mary Redcliffe, Bristol (figs. 447 and 471). It will also be noticed that the central shaft is nibbed and that the hollows between the shafts approach those on the western crossing arch responds at St Davids (figs. 430 and 471).

What are we to conclude from these parallels for the work at St Davids? In the first place, the details accord happily with the start of St Davids in 1182. Secondly, the

Fig. 471 (left) St Mary Redcliffe, Bristol. The early Gothic north nave high vault capital, the large, upright trefoil leaves on which bear comparison with those on the north nave arcade capital N2SW at St Davids cathedral (Fig. 431, right)

parallels have been made with some of the most prestigious works created by the West Country School of masons. This indicates that there was a desire to have the very best for the new cathedral. But what can we decide about the recruitment of the masons? Parallels have been made with buildings from Shrewsbury to Bristol, east of Bristol at Keynsham, south of Bristol at Wells and Glastonbury, and across the Irish Sea in Christ Church, Dublin. Diverse as the group may seem geographically, when we think in terms of water transportation, the links are clear. The Severn connects Shrewsbury, Worcester and Bristol, Keynsham is reached from Bristol via the Avon, and the Axe links the coast with Wookey, close to both Wells and Glastonbury. In this regard the link between St Davids and the West Country School parallels that of Irish buildings like Christ Church, Dublin.[61] The details of the hiring of the masons are unknown and are likely to remain so given the paucity of documentary evidence and the loss of many potentially key buildings. The use of some Dundry stone at St Davids means that contact must have been made with that quarry, just south of Bristol. Perhaps masons could be hired directly from the quarry or information gathered as to the whereabouts of major building activity so that employers might be approached about the loan or release of masons. The many close comparisons between the late twelfth- and early thirteenth-century work at Wells and Glastonbury strongly suggests that a number of the same masons were engaged on both buildings at the same, or approximately the same, time. Then there is the precious survival of a letter from the Abbot of St Augustine's, Bristol, to the dean of Wells, written around 1218–20, requesting the loan of 'your servant L' — probably the mason Adam Lock — to design the Elder Lady Chapel at St Augustine's.[62] The close comparison between the architectural and sculptural details at Wells cathedral and the Bristol Elder Lady Chapel makes it clear that the dean acceded to the request. The parallel between the 'gaping' chevron at St Davids and the gatehouse of St Augustine's, Bristol, was highlighted by Roger Stalley.[63] One wonders what other building might have been going on in Bristol in the 1170s and 1180s? Perhaps the completion of the church of St Augustine's, and certainly the large and prestigious St Mary Redcliffe from which we have just the one high vault capital.[64] Perhaps it was at Bristol that the St Davids masons were recruited.

Attention must now be turned to the presbytery to see to what extent 'early' features can be identified there, and to what degree it was rebuilt after the fall of the tower in 1220.

The Presbytery

Roger Stalley's characterization of the four-bay aisled presbytery as 'a curious and frustrating piece of architecture', is entirely appropriate in that it presents us with some of the most complex archaeological problems of any medieval church.[65] In light of this, the following account will of necessity reflect this complexity but it will attempt to decipher the work from the three different campaigns — post-1182, post-1220 and post-1248 — and, for the first time, to offer a plausible reconstruction of the 1182 design.

The elevation now comprises two storeys, a pointed main arcade surmounted by pointed clerestorey windows (figs. 472–473). The main arcade is carried on columns that alternate between round and octagonal and there are triple vault shafts on the front of the piers that extend through to capitals intended to carry the ribs of a high vault. There are similar shafts on the aisle side of the columns that rise to trumpet-scalloped capitals as if to support vault ribs (figs. 474 and 475). Curiously, however, they are set three courses below the capital of the main arcade and, therefore, the present system could never have accommodated aisle vaults. The main arcade capitals are all trumpet scallops. The main arcade responds take on quite different forms. The east responds are compound and have an inner order of stepped triple shafts, the middle one of which is nibbed, and hollows between the shafts as on the responds of the

Fig. 473 Presbytery at St Davids cathedral looking north-west

315

Fig. 472 *The presbytery looking west*

Fig. 473 The presbytery looking south-east

*Fig. 474 Eastern bay
of the north presbytery aisle*

*Fig. 475 Eastern bays of the south
presbytery arcade seen from the aisle*

western crossing arch (figs. 427, 466–469). The second order has a single nibbed shaft and a foliage capital with a rounded abacus, while the outer order is a nibbed roll set between hollow mouldings and continues directly to the abacus. The west responds have a similar form to the west respond of the south nave arcade at Strata Florida, with two large half cylinders with stepped triple shafts between them and on the south respond are topped with succulent waterleaf capitals (figs. 470 and 471). This is an important detail for the capitals are paralleled in the post-1220 crossing capitals rather than in the 1180s work (figs. 431, 434 and 471). The bases also overlap those to the left and right from the 1180s and therefore the responds must be larger than in the 1180s work (fig. 470). The 1180s responds may, however, just have had a slimmer version of what is there now. The main arcade arches have three orders (figs. 472–473). The inner order has a flat soffit with keeled angle rolls. Order two has chevron towards the presbytery but is just chamfered on the aisle side (figs. 474 and 475). Order three is plain on the aisle side but has a nibbed angle roll towards the presbytery.

At the east end of the aisles there are now doorways that lead to the later retrochoir (figs. 474 and 476). They are set in much larger pointed arches with a chamfered inner order set on moulded capitals and detached shafts in the south aisle, and foliage capitals

Fig. 476 Eastern bay of the south presbytery aisle

Fig. 477 Penultimate western bay of the north presbytery aisle showing traces of the vault approximately two--thirds of the way up each pillar

in the north aisle, and a continuous outer order with a hollow chamfer. The arch in the south aisle has random polychrome of grey sandstone and Dundry limestone. Above the pointed arches there are round-headed wall arches. In the south aisle this arch is carried on a trumpet-scallop capital with a square abacus to the north but is suspended to the south. In the north aisle it is suspended to the outside and rests on a trumpet-scallop capital with a round abacus on the inside. These capitals are set at a lower level than the capitals of the main arcade and yet are at the same height as the capitals atop triple shafts at the back of the main arcade piers. The wall arches and the capitals at the back of the arcade piers are normally associated with the intention to vault the aisles. However, the placement of the capitals of the main arcade just three courses above the 'vault' shafts at the back of the piers has suggested to most commentators that the vaults were never built. Be that as it may, in the penultimate west bay of the north aisle there is further evidence of at least the intention to vault (fig. 477). Here the scars of the junction of the putative vault are preserved in the restored pointing above and to the outside of a former round-headed window. To the east the scar descends to the side of a triple-shaft vault respond at which point there is a significant change. Below the junction there is a hollow to either side of the respond but this feature is lacking above. The change marks the original setting of the vault capital, while the present position of the capital dates from Bishop Gower's heightening of the aisle wall. In the north-west angle of the western bay north aisle there is a single vault shaft and capital for the putative vault and above it enough space for the springing of the vault (fig. 478). There is even a fragment of a wall arch at about ten o'clock on the aisle wall.

The seemingly insoluble problem of the original aisle vault can be resolved if we accept that the main arcade capitals and the vault capitals below them come from two separate builds. This agrees happily with the difference in the mouldings of the abaci (fig. 479). The more complex moulding is used for the main arcade capitals while the quirked hollow chamfer tops the aisle capitals. This is the very differentiation noticed in the abaci of the crossing capitals, the quirked hollow chamfers on the western crossing arch of the 1182 build, and the more complex moulding used in the post-1220 work (figs. 427–430 and 431–434). It follows that the presbytery aisle vault capitals belong to the 1180s while the main arcade capitals date from post-1220 rebuilding. The vault capitals comply with the regular coursing of the piers and therefore do not mark an earlier level of a main arcade capital (fig. 479). Rather, the section of the column towards the presbytery would have continued above the level of the aisle vault capitals in the manner of a giant order, as at

Fig. 478 Western bay to the north, north presbytery aisle, with a single column and capital in the corner for the putative vault

Fig. 479 Eastern pier of the northern arcade in the presbytery, seen from the aisle, with vault pier and capital

St Frideswide's, Oxford (figs. 480 and 481). Like Oxford, the arches at St Davids would have been round-headed, as indicated by the trace of the round-headed wall arch in the presbytery aisle. It is also interesting that in the nave at Oxford there are alternating round and octagonal columns as in the St Davids presbytery. Whether this indicates a direct connection between Oxford and St Davids is a moot point, not least because the columns in the presbytery and transepts at Oxford are all cylindrical. Be that as it may, the alternating system should be seen as a reflection of Canterbury cathedral where it is used in the present choir as a reflection of its Romanesque predecessor. The giant order was formerly used in the presbytery of Tewkesbury abbey and with royal patronage in the abbey churches at Romsey, Reading and Jedburgh.[66] After 1185 it appears in the Great Church at Glastonbury (fig. 482) possibly as a reflection of the Romanesque church there.[67] This would provide an iconographic association for St Davids because St David himself is reputed to have built an extension to the east of the *Vetusta Ecclesia* (the old church).[68] How the rest of the St Davids presbytery elevation was finished cannot be determined except to say that there would certainly have been a clerestorey and, given the preparation for a high vault in the nave, there must have been one in the presbytery.

Fig. 480 Penultimate western bay in the north arcade of the presbytery showing traces of the vault also seen in fig. 477

Fig. 481 St Frideswide's, Oxford: the nave showing how the elevation at St Davids may have looked

The east wall of the presbytery is dominated by three richly ornamented, graduated lancet windows each with four orders, three of which are continuous and are framed by the outer order on shafts and capitals (fig. 482). The inner order has a simple angle roll while the next two have varieties of 'gaping' chevron (fig. 483). The outer order has a filleted shaft flanked by thin rolls, a trumpet-scallop capital and thin filleted rolls and hollow mouldings in the arch. The outer jambs and the lower half of the two intermediate supports are of local grey sandstone, while in the upper half of the intermediate supports and the arch heads local sandstone and Dundry stone are used to give an irregular polychrome effect (fig. 482). Moreover, the intermediate shafts and the lower halves of the outer shafts are detached, filleted and have multiple shaft rings, while the upper halves of the outer shafts are coursed and are without rings. The capitals atop the outer shafts are trumpet scallops with square abaci while the intermediate capitals are stiff-leaf and have round abaci (plate 16). These detail differences suggest that the windows are not the product of a single build. The 'gaping' chevron to either side of a roll moulding on the outer order of the windows is precisely the same as on the western crossing arch (figs. 429 and 483). This suggests that the windows belong in part to the 1180s, which would agree with the attribution of the east responds of the presbytery arcades to the first campaign of construction. Confirmation of this reading is supplied by the ornament on the string-course beneath the windows. Here the meander ornament may be compared with the east window in the west bay of the north nave clerestorey, where it is used next to the 'gaping' chevron in the west window. As has been discussed in connection with the Anglesey fonts, meander ornament has a good pedigree in West Country Romanesque architecture as at Sarum cathedral and Malmesbury abbey. Below the meander on the east wall of the presbytery is a row of intersecting arches like those on the hood of the north arch of the gatehouse at St Augustine's, Bristol (fig. 105). It will be recalled that that the St Augustine's gatehouse also used 'gaping' chevron.

The random polychrome is also used on the exterior of the east windows of the presbytery at St Davids (now the west wall of the Trinity Chapel). The central window

Fig. 483 Northern capital and arch of the northern window on the east wall of the presbytery, showing the varieties of 'gaping' chevron

Fig. 482 The east end of the presbytery

Fig. 484 The niche in the east wall of the presbytery

Fig. 485 The northern bay of the presbytery showing the eastern clerestorey

was replaced in order to facilitate construction of the vault of the Trinity chapel but the frames of the north and south windows survive, albeit in damaged condition. They have a continuous inner order with a roll moulding that returns across the sill. The outer order is also continuous and is carved with an unusual chevron that takes the form of individually contained and deeply undercut pyramidal forms. Of the outer order, the lower sections of coursed filleted shafts on bases remain, but the upper sections of the jambs and the arch heads are not extant. Below the refaced central window there is a small pointed niche with a continuous nibbed angle roll on pre-waterholding bases that now contains a casket with remains of saints David and Justinian, and possibly St Caradog (fig. 484). At the back of the niche there is a pierced roundel ornamented with beaded semi-circles and stylized flowers in which there is a cross-shaped opening through which one can see into the presbytery.

    To the north of the windows there is a doorway, the sill of which is level with that of the blocked windows. This is an unusual place for a doorway but it probably provided access to small wooden balcony from which activities at the niche could be observed. Here it was probably not just a matter of looking into the church as today but rather at relics placed immediately to the east of the high altar.

Fig. 486 The north wall above the penultimate western pier in the presbytery

Fig. 487 The south wall above the penultimate western pier in the presbytery

Returning to the interior, above the triple lancet windows, the four pointed clerestorey windows with a wall passage are the product of Scott's restoration and replace a single, large Perpendicular window at this point (figs. 482 and 485).[69] However, Scott indicated in his Second Report that the jambs of the Early English windows were extant, and that he located many fragments of the original windows which he incorporated into his reconstruction. He pointed out that the design is incompatible with a high vault and he therefore dated the windows after the 1220 fall of the tower in which build he believed that no high vault was contemplated for the presbytery.

Our attribution of the pointed arches of the main arcade of the presbytery to the post-1220 build indicates that the clerestorey must belong with it or be after 1248. Close examination clarifies the matter. The two eastern bays on the south side are anomalous in that they have a passage, whereas the jambs of all the other windows are solid (fig. 473). This immediately suggests that the two types are not contemporary, which hypothesis is confirmed with reference to the high vault capitals. Above the westernmost columns on both the north and south sides, the high vault capitals are of the same type of decorated scallop as on the eastern side of the crossing (figs. 431–433, 456, 486 and 487). The distinct differences between this capital type and those used in the 1180s work makes it clear that the vault capitals belong with the post-1220 rebuild. Above the two high-vault capitals are the damaged remains of wall arches and space for the springing of the vault, on either side of which there is the clerestorey string-course. There is similar evidence for a high vault in the south-west and north-west angles of the presbytery. Above the westernmost column on the north side, a large trefoil niche interrupts the lines of the high vault, while at approximately the same point on the south side there is a change of masonry from ashlar below to rubble above (figs. 486 and 487). Clearly the high vault and the niche are incongruous and this must be explained by the removal of the high vault, presumably after the 1248 earthquake, and the subsequent introduction of the niche. Niches are used between the clerestorey windows throughout the north side but they are not used on the south (figs. 471–473). Thus the three eastern bays of the north clerestorey date from the post-1248 removal of the high vault. This is confirmed by the clerestorey string-course which continues without interruption from east of the wall arch in the penultimate western bay to the north-east angle of the presbytery (figs. 473 and 482). It will be noticed that the high vault capitals are below this string-course and there are no wall arches or any other signs of a high vault. The same is true of the south elevation, which suggests that the three eastern bays of the clerestorey date after 1248. Why there is a clerestorey passage here, but not on the north side, is a moot point. It is especially strange that the sill of the opening is higher than the sill of the window, which would make it difficult to use. It is unlikely to be a hangover from the 1220 build because the western bay — in which there is the evidence for the post-1220 high vault — there is no wall passage. Be that as it may, there is a passage in the east clerestorey where the lateral windows are too high to accommodate a high vault. It follows that this range of windows must date after 1248.

Before concluding our investigation into the chronology of the presbytery, it is important to examine one aspect of the exterior. The south aisle wall was completely

Fig. 488 Presbytery and crossing tower from the north-east, showing two of the original buttresses

rebuilt in the fourteenth century at which time new windows were inserted into the north aisle. However, the original buttresses were retained, two of which are seen in fig. 488. The former north-east angle of the north aisle is marked by a pilaster buttress with nook shafts set on a stepped plinth (this is to the right of the doorway in fig. 488). The next buttress to the west is a simple, unadorned pilaster. For the nook-shafted buttress there are parallels in the nave aisles of Malmesbury abbey and the Lady Chapel of Glastonbury abbey. For the plain pilaster we simply have to look to the Romanesque tradition. When these observations are added to the form of the eastern responds in the presbytery, the evidence for the aisle vaults and the details of the chevron on the east windows, it must be concluded that we have here elements from the 1182 design. Given that the form of the east responds and the chevron go with the western crossing arch, it is difficult, if not impossible, to decide whether construction of the nave preceded the presbytery. What is clear is that in 1220 the fall of the crossing tower caused major damage in the presbytery, so much so that the main elevation had to be rebuilt from just above the level of the aisle vault capitals. This was achieved, complete with a high vault, and in a remarkably conservative style in which details like trumpet-scallop capitals and chevron ornament conformed to the design vocabulary of the 1180s, even if the chevron of the main arcade arches generally lacked the gusto of that in the nave. Perhaps even more amazingly, this antiquarian attitude prevailed in the subsequent reconstruction following the 1248 earthquake.

The transepts must now be considered to see if the details there are closer to those in the nave or those in the presbytery. This will allow the determination of a relative chronology.

The Transepts

As is often the case, the design of the east and west walls of the transepts seem to have little to do with each other. On the east there are three richly articulated, pointed arches in both arms while the west wall is plain, broken only by the plain surrounds of the doorways to the nave aisles and, in the north transept, a blocked window and adjacent blind arch above a door to the outside (figs. 489–491). The difference is simply to do with function, the rich east arches either mark entry into the presbytery aisle, frame an altar, or, in the case of the northern arch in the north transept, lead to a chapel. In each case the arches have three orders but the manner in which they are articulated varies from bay to bay.

Fig. 489 The eastern wall of the north transept

Fig. 491 *The western wall of the north transept*

Starting with the north transept, the north arch now leads to the later St Thomas Becket chapel, but the design of the arch indicates that it always communicated with a chapel in contrast to the middle arch, which was always just a niche. There are alternating continuous and non-continuous orders arranged in a very inventive fashion (figs. 492 and 493). The unmoulded inner order of the pointed chamfered arch is carried on capitals atop triple shafts with the central one nibbed, as in the responds of the western crossing arch. The shaft group is set into an arced recess, a deeper version of the motif in the presbytery aisle responds (figs. 481, 492 and 493). The capitals have no necking, and, on the south side, the cones of the trumpet-scallop capital have damaged foliage decoration. On

Fig. 490 *The eastern wall of the south transept*

Fig. 494 Capital between the Becket chapel and the central niche in the eastern arcade in the north transept

Figs. 492 and 493 North (top) and south (bottom) responds for the arch to the Becket chapel in the north transept

the north side the capital has lost its symmetrically set foliage crockets but retains the plantain notches of the central leaf that recall the nave capitals (figs. 448 and 492). To either side of the inner order there is a continuous nibbed roll. Inside the chapel, and on the outside to the north, this is followed with a trumpet capital without necking atop a plain nook shaft. To the outside, the south capital, which is also without necking, is carved with alternate single trumpet scallops and upright trefoil leaves. This is a simpler version of nave capital N4 (figs. 450 and 494). The shaft is distinguished with fillets to the north and south and a nib to the west, in contrast to the plain shaft in the equivalent position on the north (figs. 492-494). Like the arch to the St Thomas chapel the one to the central niche has three orders with chamfers to the otherwise plain arches of the first and third orders (fig. 489). However, in contrast to the continuous nibbed roll and hollows in the second order of the Becket chapel arch, the second order of the centre niche has capitals and nibbed shafts and a triple roll moulding in the arch. This juxtaposition is repeated in the arch to the north presbytery aisle but here further delight in juggling detail is witnessed in the highly original south respond (fig. 489). Here a large column of the type we have met in places like the north nave arcade at Ewenny priory, grows out of a plinth-like

Fig. 495 Capital of the triplet of piers on the north transept arch to the presbytery aisle

Fig. 496 Capital between the window and blind arch on the west wall of the north transept

projection to the north of the north-east crossing pier. The ashlar of the column and the plinth courses are without any variation which demonstrates that they were built together. On the north respond of this arch the inner triplet has the same separation of the shafts with deep hollows as on the responds of the western crossing arch and the east responds of the presbytery arcades (fig. 494). The capital of the triplet has very unusual ribbed leaves that curl over at the top to grow down in front of the backing plantain leaf, just as on nave capital N2S (figs. 447 and 495). The outer shaft that doubles as the outer shaft of the arch of the central niche has the same arrangement of lateral fillets and frontal nib as on the shaft between the niche and St Thomas's chapel.

On the west wall of the north transept there is the segmental head of the arch from the north nave aisle and, to the right, another doorway that formerly came from the outside but now communicates with the song school (fig. 491). Above this doorway are two blocked round-headed arches, formerly a window to the left and a blind arch to the right. The capital between the two arches has damaged upright leaves but is of greatest interest because the shaft is enriched with three nibs and is set into a shallow recess in the wall (fig. 496). Although the capital is badly damaged the plantain notch is still in evidence on the central leaf, as in nave capital N3N (figs. 430 and 496). Thus at once we find foliage like the nave capitals, as opposed to the post-1220 capitals of the crossing; the shallow recess for the triple shafts as in the vault responds in the north presbytery aisle; and a variant of the fillet-nib-fillet articulation of the shafts to either side of the central arch on the opposite side of the transept.

In the south transept, the north arch that communicates with the south presbytery aisle has a broadly chamfered outer order carried on trumpet-scallop capitals without necking (fig. 490). The articulation essentially matches that of the equivalent arch in the north transept except that the roll mouldings of the middle order are executed in Dundry stone (figs. 489 and 490). The south respond of the arch is also a match for the equivalent in the north transept, although here on the capitals of the triplet there are single trefoil leaves on the lower bell as in the western crossing capitals and nave capital N3N (figs. 430–433, 448 and 497). The shaft between the arch to the south presbytery aisle and the central niche is an intriguing variant on the theme of the nib. Here instead of a single central nib, there are two nibs, one to the south-west and a matching one to the north-west (figs. 497 and 498). As if this was not playful enough, the next shaft takes up the theme but with the nibs applied to the west and south. To contrast with this the inner shaft is plain. The outer capital has a plantain notch to the central leaf. The south respond of this arch repeats this disposition of the shafts and has foliage capitals to the inner and outer orders to either side of a trumpet-scallop capital. The central arch is the most adventurous outing into polychrome met with so far (fig. 490). In the inner and middle orders there is a random alternation of grey sandstone and creamy limestone. The lower sections of the outer order are of sandstone but the upper part of the arch is all limestone.

On the north respond to the southern chapel the inner shaft is plain and the second shaft has a nib on the diagonal (fig. 499). These features and the scalloped capitals are repeated on the south

Fig. 497 South respond on the south transept arch to the presbytery aisle, showing nibs protruding on the shafts

Fig. 498 Capitals between the northern and middle arches of the eastern arcade in the south transept

respond where the outer shaft has a quadrant form. The arch repeats the disposition of chamfered outer and inner orders and a triple roll moulding in the middle. The inner and outer orders are sandstone but the middle order alternates limestone and sandstone.

There is one round-headed window in the west wall of the south transept and, like the north transept, there is no clerestorey, nor is there any attempt at a middle storey. The wooden high vaults in both transepts are the product of Scott's restoration but may well reflect the original scheme. The vault is carried on a variety of capitals atop alternating single and triple shafts — the central one nibbed — and foliage corbels.

The details of articulation of the shafts in the transepts with multiple nibs or fillets provide further clues as to the associations of the St Davids masons. I know of only two other instances of the use of three nibs on a single shaft: on the responds of the eastern crossing arch at Wells cathedral and in the nave piers at Slimbridge (Glos.). This is important because Slimbridge offers a number of parallels for the work at St Davids. Most specifically, on the detail illustrated on the capitals of pier N2, we notice plantain notches, clusters of trefoil leaves some with gouged central lobes, a cluster of berries, and the absence of necking, all details encountered in capitals in the St Davids nave (figs. 446, 448 and 500). On the central capital of the east respond of the north arcade at Slimbridge there a simple, upright, tapering leaves as on N3E in the St Davids nave (figs. 449 and 501). The south doorway at Slimbridge is round headed in contrast to the pointed arches of the contemporary nave and chancel arch (fig. 502). The inner order has large trefoil leaves like those on St Davids nave capitals N2W and N4S, while the outer order is a continuous roll with a fillet, a variant on the continuous nibbed roll on the entrance arch to the Becket chapel at St Davids (figs. 447, 450, 493 and 502). Finally, capital S3W at Slimbridge is a trumpet scallop with widely separated trumpets that were popular at St Davids (figs. 427–428, 449 and 503). Unfortunately, there is no documentation

Fig. 499 North respond in the south niche of the eastern arcade in the south transept with nibs protruding from the shafts

Fig. 500 (above) St. John, Slimbridge (Glos.): capitals from pier 2 in the north nave arcade.
Fig. 446 (right) North nave arcade capital N1S at St Davids cathedral. The capitals contain carvings of plantain notches, clusters of trefoil leaves, some with gouged central lobes, and a cluster of berries

Fig. 501 St. John, Slimbridge (Glos.): capitals on the east respond in the north nave arcade

Fig. 449 Norh nave arcade capital N3SE at St Davids

The central capital at St John, Sl;imbridge, and N3SE at St Davids both have simple, upright, tapering leaves

to assist with the dating of Slimbridge. However, it is important that the triple-nibbed shafts are paralleled in the responds of the eastern crossing arch at Wells. Moreover, many of the singular aspects of the varied foliage capitals are otherwise only found in the western bays of the choir and the eastern arcades of the transepts at Wells. This suggests that Slimbridge should be dated in relation to this section of Wells, which was in hand between 1175 and 1184.

Brakspear believed that the designer of the Slimbridge nave was also responsible for the St Davids transepts, and that the latter were 'entirely different' from the work in

*Fig. 502 (left) St John, Slimbridge (Glos.):
the south doorway*

*Fig. 450 (above) Capital N4S in the north
nave arcade at St Davids cathedral
The large trefoil leaves on the capital are
similar to those on the inner order of the arch
surrounding the door at Slimbridge*

St Davids nave.[70] Of the connection between Slimbridge and St Davids there can be no doubt, but the nature of the differences between the nave and transepts at St Davids is open to an interpretation other than Brakspear's. On the one hand, it is true that there are many differences between the nave, transepts and the 1180s design for the presbytery. If I am correct in the reconstruction of a giant order with round-headed arches in the presbytery, then this is far removed from the round-headed main arcade and linked triforium and clerestorey in the nave. And quite apart from the elevation, the wide bays of the nave are in sharp contrast to the narrow bays of the presbytery. The transepts provide yet a further alternative with the use of pointed arches in the eastern arches, no chevron ornament, and no clerestorey. On the other hand, the many detailed similarities we have cited between the 1180s presbytery, the nave and the transepts at the very least demonstrate some continuity of personnel in the masons' yard. Then, if differences in elevation and articulation are read in conjunction with the different functions of the separate parts of the church, rather

*Fig. 503 St John, Slimbridge (Glos.):
capitals on pier 3 in the suth nave arcade
showing use of widely spaced trumpet
scallops, a design used often on the capitals
at St Davids cathedral*

than assuming that they are the products of different designers, an alternative interpretation of the building may be offered.

The narrow bays of the presbytery allowed for a four-bay design in a relatively restricted space. Four bays would have been deemed desirable so as to conform to the tradition established in Anglo-Norman great churches at St Augustine's abbey, Canterbury (1070), and then St Albans (1077). The four-bay arrangement then became common for great churches as at Winchester, Ely, London, Durham, Norwich and Peterborough cathedrals, and was also adopted by Bishop Roger of Salisbury when he rebuilt the eastern arm of Sarum cathedral. It was never the norm in the south-west Midlands or West Country and therefore St Davids represents a first in this regard, and clearly a feature to be equated with a sense of superiority for the Welsh cathedral. For the much larger space of the nave, the use of bays the same size as the presbytery would have resulted in a cluttered appearance dominated by the masses of masonry of the main arcade piers and arches. As it is, massive nave piers were deemed essential for a vaulted building but the dramatically wide bays impart a degree of openness that is entirely lacking in the presbytery. Add to this the rich variations in the capital design and the chevron both at arcade and triforium-clerestorey levels, then the public area of the church was to be by far the most opulent in Wales and to vie with the most prestigious churches in England. The transepts were not the place for such lavish displays. Their primary purpose was to house subsidiary altars for the canons and therefore rich displays of decoration deemed appropriate for location of the high altar in the presbytery, or in the public area of the nave, would have been excessive for the secondary liturgical spaces. Be that as it may, the different chevron patterns in the nave are matched by the variety in the shafts and arch designs of the eastern arcades the transepts.

The flat east end of the presbytery is relatively unusual. The only absolutely certain antecedent is the hospital church of St Cross at Winchester, although York Minster as rebuilt by Archbishop Roger of Pont l'Evêque (1154–81), Jervaulx abbey and the collegiate church of New Shoreham (Sussex) are contenders. It may also be seen as an adaptation of Sarum cathedral, a building worthy of emulation because of Bishop Roger's status as second only to King Henry I.

The aisleless transepts belong to a tradition in the West Country School dating back to the late eleventh century, as at Worcester cathedral, the Benedictine abbey churches of Gloucester, Pershore and Tewkesbury, and later at Sherborne and Malmesbury. The transept façades with angle turrets relate to Gloucester, Hereford and the west front of Worcester cathedral. They may also be compared to the west façades at Bredon (Worcs.), Bishop's Cleeve (Glos.) and Ledbury (Herefs.).

The arches that framed altars in the transept east walls may be seen as smaller-scale versions of those in the transept at Exeter cathedral.[71] A closer, near-contemporary parallel occurs in the eastern aisles of the transepts at Wells cathedral.

The shafts recessed in the responds of the entrance arch to the Becket chapel wall adapt a motif that has a long history in West Country Romanesque. It is used in the entrance to the north transept chapel at St Peter's, Gloucester; and appears subsequently in the responds of the east crossing arch at Malmesbury abbey, throughout the crossing at Leonard Stanley (Glos.), and in the chapter houses of the Cistercian abbeys at Forde and Bindon (Dorset).[72] Shallow recesses, like those of the presbytery aisle responds at St Davids, are used in the Lady Chapel at Glastonbury abbey.

Two aspects of the west front follow West Country precedent and specifically the façade of Hereford cathedral.[73] The plain lower storey and the use of pilaster buttresses topped by turrets to articulate the outer angles of the aisles and the division between the nave and aisles are common to both façades.

Use of the Building
The basic divisions of the cathedral offer no surprises. The high altar is located at the east end of the presbytery, the liturgical choir is under the crossing and is separated from the nave by the later screen. The nave altar is in the east bay of the nave. What does require some explanation is the strange deflection to the north of the alignment of the St Thomas chapel to the east of the north transept. Wyn Evans has suggested that the chapel may reflect the alignment of an earlier structure, possibly the original sixth-century church.[74] A number of other factors tend to support the idea of the chapel being one of particular veneration. In the first place, the portal in the west wall of the north transept is an unusual feature and may be explained as an entrance for pilgrims visiting the chapel. I do not know of an exact parallel for this but it is worth recording that shrines are located in the north transept at St Frideswide's, Oxford, and Whitchurch Canonicorum (Dorset), and were probably at Bampton (Oxon) and Steyning (Sussex). It may also be significant that the angle of deflection recalls that of the Old Minster against the Norman cathedral at Winchester.

Conclusion
With reference to the extravagant range of twenty-two different forms of chevron ornament at St Davids, Roger Stalley observed that the 'ostentatious display was evidently seen as a way of asserting the prestige of the cathedral at a time when the clergy still harboured ambitions for archiepiscopal status'.[75] Separation from Canterbury had been on the agenda of Bishop Bernard and, although it was not subsequently the official episcopal position, the canons of St Davids boldly revived the claims in 1176.[76] A lavish rebuilding programme as an integral part of the promotion of a see would not have been unique to St Davids at this time. Between 1160 and 1162 St Andrews cathedral-priory in Scotland began a massive new church in connection with their campaign for metropolitan status and independence from York.[77] The rebuilding of Wells is almost certainly associated with the claim to have the seat of the bishopric returned there form Bath.[78] While St Andrews and Wells opted for very progressive designs, at St Davids is witnessed something that is embraces the traditional richness of the Romanesque great church. To apply the label 'Romanesque' might be seen as condemnation of the building as old fashioned, yet the nature of the work is remarkably close philosophically to the 'early Gothic' rebuilding of the choir

of Canterbury cathedral after the fire of 1174.[79] It is well to recall Scott's assessment of St Davids as 'a wonderfully interesting and valuable landmark in architectural history, taking, in the extreme west, a position parallel to that held by Canterbury in the extreme east of the island'.

It is clear from the contemporary account and analysis of the rebuilding of Canterbury after the fire, written by the monk, Gervase, that progressive elements in the new design were highly regarded. While Gervase did not discuss any of the ornamental details that derived from a Romanesque tradition, it is equally clear from his account of the monks' reluctance to destroy any of the old building, that reverence for the past was an important consideration in the design of the new building. The alternation of the choir arcade columns at Canterbury repeated that feature in Anselm's choir. What is so often overlooked at Canterbury is the use of chevron ornament and the single billet from a purely Romanesque tradition to which is added dog-tooth, a northern French detail that fuses so happily with the aesthetic of surface enrichment that we associate with late Romanesque. This is one side of the aesthetic of the new St Davids cathedral, something that would at once proclaim the history of the site and its status equal to that of Canterbury. This traditional aspect could only be enhanced with reference to Sarum cathedral and St Cross at Winchester, and Glastonbury abbey, products of the most munificent patrons of the day. The other side of the coin was the progressive one. Gervase seems to have been awestruck with the three triforia in the new work at Canterbury as opposed to one in the Romanesque cathedral. While there will always be debate as to the definition of 'triforium', there can be little doubt that at least in part Gervase was referring to passages in the thickness of the wall, that is double-skin or hollow-wall construction. This is precisely what we have in the hollow wall of the nave triforium/clerestorey at St Davids. The building was vaulted throughout, as in the new work at Canterbury, and throughout St Andrews and Wells. Moreover it is the sexpartite pattern of vaulting that is used both at Canterbury and St Davids. While the main arcade at Canterbury uses pointed arches, as opposed to the round-headed arches at St Davids, round-headed transverse arches are used throughout the aisles vaults, and in the arches from the aisles to the eastern transepts at Canterbury. Round-headed arches were also used in connection with the progressive design of the Galilee chapel at Durham cathedral, and in the castle hall at Oakham (Rutland), $c.$1180–90. It is perhaps most significant that both round-headed and pointed arches, and lavish chevron ornament, are used in both the Lady Chapel and the great church at Glastonbury abbey, commenced two and three years respectively after the start of St Davids.

To read the rebuilding of St Davids in light of the status of the cathedral raises the question of the patronage of the work. Bishop Peter de Leia is credited with the patronage in contemporary documents, but what of the role of the canons? Peter Draper has argued that the canons were the prime motivators,[80] but if they were responsible for the new church then why is the eastern arm of the building less that half the size of the nave? Whatever their role in the administration of the new operation, it is most unlikely that they had the deciding vote on the relative scale of parts of the church. Whether or not this means that the bishop contributed the majority of the funds is difficult to decide, and, in the absence of documentation, is likely to remain a moot point. Then, the burial of Lord Rhys of Deheubarth at St Davids in 1197 raises the distinct possibility that he was a major benefactor for the rebuilding.

8
Epilogue

Our survey of Romanesque in Wales has covered almost two hundred years, from the great tower of Chepstow castle around 1070 to the rebuilding of St Davids cathedral after the earthquake of 1247/8. That period is significantly narrowed when we appreciate that the thirteenth-century work at St Davids is in many respects conditioned by what was built as part of the 1182 design of the cathedral. Be that as it may, to have Romanesque in the 1180s is a testament to the longevity and popularity of this style introduced into Wales by the Normans.

The visual impact of the new Norman style at Chepstow in the form of the great hall and the priory church must have been even greater than in England. While it is true that Anglo-Norman churches were generally larger than their Anglo-Saxon predecessors, it must be remembered that Archbishop Lanfranc's cathedral at Canterbury (1070–77) was no larger than the Anglo-Saxon cathedral it replaced. There was nothing in Wales that could even come close to the monumentality of the new Norman work, except the Roman ruins at Caerleon. As the name suggests, Romanesque is a style that looks back to Rome and this association carried with it the idea of a revival of imperialism. Rome was much admired and offered much to be emulated, not simply in terms of architecture but also for society as a whole. This was true for the Normans and in turn for the Welsh princes, as documented with Gruffudd ap Cynan.[1] Aside from the emulation of Rome in the large scale of the castle and priory church at Chepstow, the use of tufa in the former vaults of the priory church reflected Roman constructional practice. The revival of chip-carving on the early lintels discussed in chapter 2 was probably inspired by near-contemporary work in Normandy, but it must also be remembered that close parallels for the technique and specific patterns are found in Roman sculpture, as on the altar preserved in the south porch of All Saints at Lanchester (Co. Durham).

While Llandaff cathedral, as built in the 1120s, was not large by the standard of English cathedrals like Winchester and Durham, it was vast by comparison with the earlier church there. It is built of ashlar and has rich sculptural decoration in keeping with Hereford cathedral and St Peter's abbey church at Gloucester. In constructing this monumental new edifice, Bishop Urban emphatically advertised Norman control of the ecclesiastical realm. The spread of Norman authority is similarly witnessed at Ewenny priory where it is accompanied on the secular front by the proud ruins of Ogmore castle. Later, under the patronage of Robert, Earl of Gloucester and his son, William, further castle building is witnessed at Kenfig and Bridgend, while the introduction of Cistercian monks is represented in nave of Margam abbey. Smaller churches are aisleless and have a two-cell plan with a square-ended chancel and rectangular nave, similar to those in the neighboring counties of Gloucestershire and Herefordshire. We also find occasional examples of rich decoration, like the south doorway at Marcross, or the fonts at Kenfig and St Donats. All these aspects provide clear visual evidence for the Normanization of south Wales, just as in England, albeit at a slower pace.

In Gwynedd, works commissioned by Gruffudd ap Cynan and his followers were intended, on the one hand, to reflect patronage at the highest level in England and, on the other hand, to advertise the indigenous Celtic tradition. The latter is especially evident in the Anglesey fonts, so much so that some examples have been dated much earlier than I have suggested. While it is likely that the debate will continue on the question of dating individual fonts carved with traditional Welsh motifs, there can be no doubt that motifs associated with the work of Bishop Roger of Salisbury are to be explained through the ambitious patronage of Gruffudd ap Cynan and his desire to be seen on a par with the most munificent patrons in England. In this regard his achievement is paralleled in King Cormac Mac Carthaig's chapel at Cashel, a building much smaller than royal works in England but one that is very richly decorated and closely connected to the work of Bishop Roger of Salisbury. And, just as German connections have been cited for Cormac's Chapel, the imperial link in Gwynedd is documented with the presence of Bishop David at Bangor cathedral, and may well account for aspects of the design of Gruffudd ap Cynan's church at Aberffraw, and the richly articulated interior of the south transept at Penmon priory.

The desire for Welsh leaders to be seen as players on the European stage of architectural patronage is also evident at Meifod, while the churches at Tywyn, Kerry and Llandrinio, were clearly meant to rival works of Norman lords like Ewenny priory. Elsewhere, the architectural tradition of the single-cell *clas* church is apparent, as at Aberdaron and Pistyll.

Just as in England, the promotion of local saints was an important aspect of ecclesiastical culture in Wales. In terms of tangible physical remains the shrine of St Melangell at Pennant Melangell is of European importance. Just as with works in Anglesey, this shrine advertises knowledge of high-level patronage in England while incorporating traditional indigenous motifs appropriate for the shrine of a local saint. Yet would appear from the fragments at Clocaenog, Llangollen, Llanrhaeadr-ym-Mochnant and Llantysilio yn Ial that the shrine of St Melangell was far from being an unusual phenomenon.

Robert, Earl of Gloucester's patronage of the Cistercians at Margam was matched by Lord Rhys of Deheubarth with the establishment of Strata Florida abbey. Although poorly preserved, enough remains to indicate that the church was lavishly conceived. The use of deep purple Caerbwti stone in contrast to the creamy limestone may be viewed in two ways. First, the use of alternating colours in coursed masonry was established in West Country Romanesque architecture, as at Worcester cathedral with green and white sandstone, or in the south doorway at Stockton-on-Teme (Worcs.) with red and white sandstone. Secondly, the fine texture and purple colour of the Caerbwti stone are related to the blue lias used by Bishop Henry of Blois at Glastonbury abbey (1129–71), and more generally to his use of Tournai and Purbeck marbles in his palace at Wolvesey palace and the hospital church of St Cross at Winchester. Purbeck and others marbles were then used extensively in the rebuilding of the eastern arm of Canterbury cathedral (1175–84), while polished blue lias played a similar role in the Lady chapel of Glastonbury abbey (1184–86/9). Variety in pier form in the nave at Strata Florida along with the 'domino' ribs of the vault and even the use of chevron ornament are related to the most prestigious buildings of the time in England. We have also seen that details of certain capitals at Strata Florida are closely paralleled in Irish Cistercian churches, while others find direct analogues in the progressive work at Wells cathedral after 1175. Lord Rhys's architectural patronage was therefore every bit as adventurous as the most prestigious work in England and yet details like the spiraling terminations to the annulets on the west doorway at Strata Florida speak clearly of a regional heritage.

To a certain extent the rich detailing of Strata Florida paves the way for St Davids cathedral as commenced in 1182. Here the goal seems to have been to combine the best of the rich decoration of the Romanesque tradition, especially aspects of variety in chevron ornament, with the most progressive elements like the daring hollow wall in the nave trforium-cum-clerestorey, and the stiff-leaf capitals. The latter are closely connected with the eastern arcades of the transepts at Wells cathedral where the work must have been undertaken before the start of St Davids.

Around this time, lavish late Romanesque forms are also in evidence in the north and south nave doorways at Llandaff cathedral. This seems to have been part of a scheme to extend or finish Bishop Urban's nave of the 1120s. The scheme was abandoned with the arrival of Bishop Henry of Abergavenny in 1193 under whose patronage the present choir, nave and west front of the cathedral were erected. Early Gothic replaced Romanesque. Pointed arches were used throughout the new work and chevron was abandoned in favour of a complex interplay of delicate roll and hollow mouldings. A similar overthrow of the vestiges of Romanesque is witnessed in the former nave of the Cistercian abbey Cwm Hir, part of which now forms the the north nave arcade of Llanidloes (Powys). Here the complex nave piers relate to the main arcades of Wells cathedral and presage the choir of Pershore abbey. On a smaller scale there is the rebuilding of the former *clas* church at Llanaber (Gwynedd). Here the elaborate south portal boasts four moulded orders on stepped triple shafts that relate to the main arcade piers at Cwm Hir. Inside, the columnar piers of the nave arcade retain the conservative form of Romanesque churches like St Woolos at Newport or St Cadfan at Tywyn but the capitals have upright leaves and the arches are pointed. In secular architecture innovative elements are evident under the patronage of the William Marshall in the 1190s with the construction of the lower bailey and the twin-towered outer gatehouse at Chepstow castle. Then, as earl of Pembroke (1199–1219), William, constructed a round keep at Pembroke and this was followed at Skenfrith by Hubert de Burgh, probably between 1219 and 1232. The great hall built for Hubert de Burgh at Grosmont castle between 1201 and 1204/5 is allied to the contemporary early Gothic 'Gloriette' erected for King John at Corfe castle and in both cases the detailing relates to near-contemporary ecclesiastical work. The change from Romanesque to Gothic is most vivid in the remodeling and addition of the third storey to the great hall at Chepstow, probably by William Marshall II after 1219. Here details of arch mouldings and stiff-leaf capitals, and especially the use of detached marble shafts, relate to the contemporary work on the west front of Wells cathedral and the Elder Lady Chapel at St Augustine's, Bristol (1218–22). With these works the Gothic style was well firmly established and Romanesque long forgotten.

Glossary

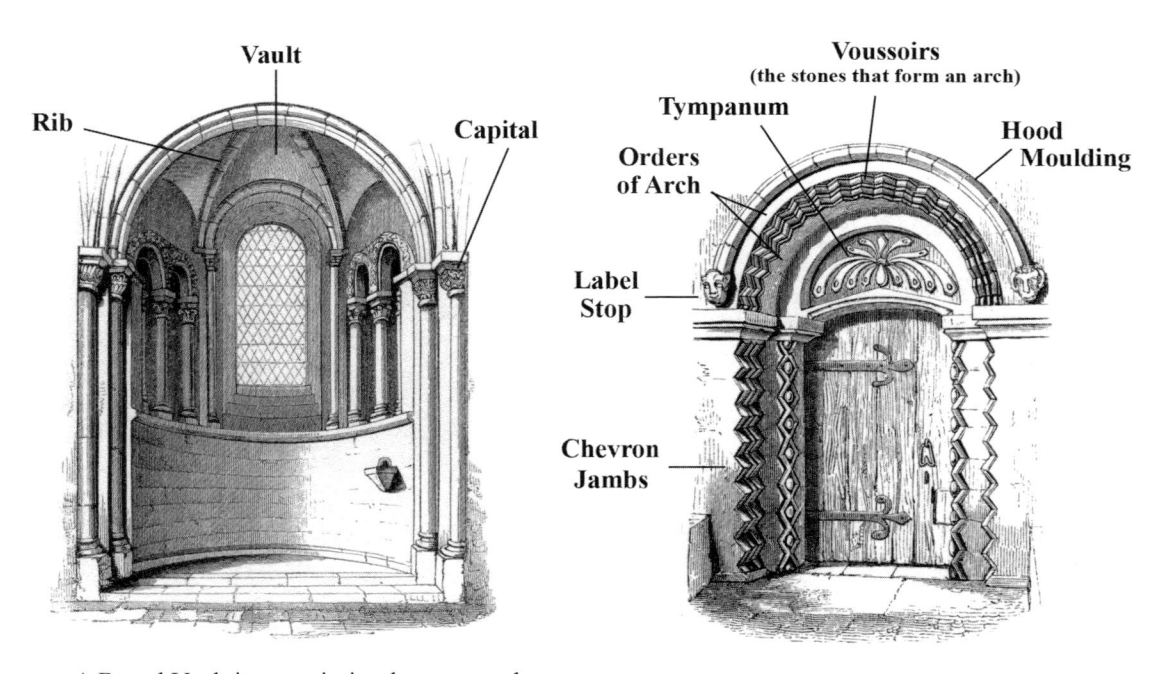

Apse
Corbel Table
String Course

Vault
Rib
Capital

Voussoirs (the stones that form an arch)
Tympanum
Orders of Arch
Hood Moulding
Label Stop
Chevron Jambs

A Barrel Vault is a semi-circular or tunnel vault; a Groin Vault is the angle produced by the intersection of two barrel vaults or various conical elements of a vault

Romanesque Architecture and Sculpture in Wales

Blind Arcade

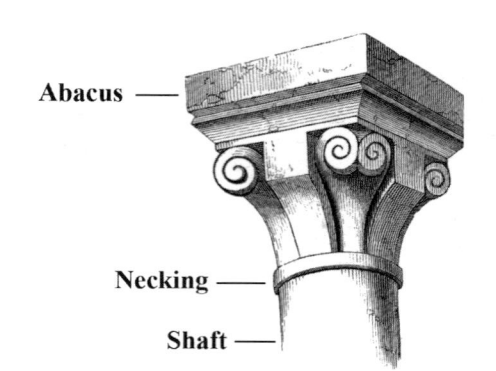

Intersecting Blind Arcade

Abacus

Necking

Shaft

Volute Capital

Acanthus Capital

Cushion: Capital:
a block-shaped capital with flat, semi-circular sides and the lower surfaces rounded off to join a shaft

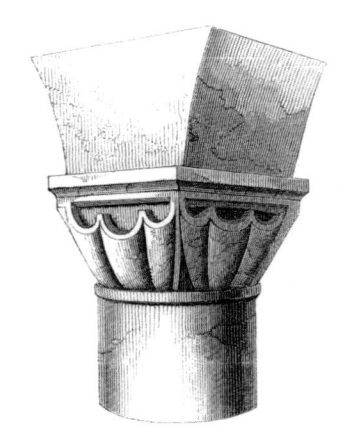

Scalloped Capital
(Trumpet Scallop is a scalloped capital in which the cones flare out)

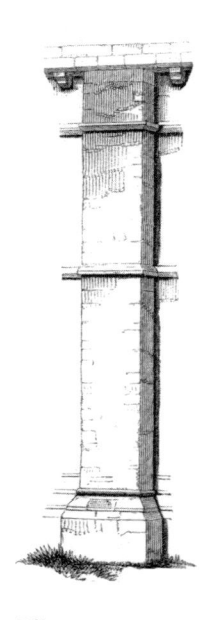

Pilaster Buttress

Glossary

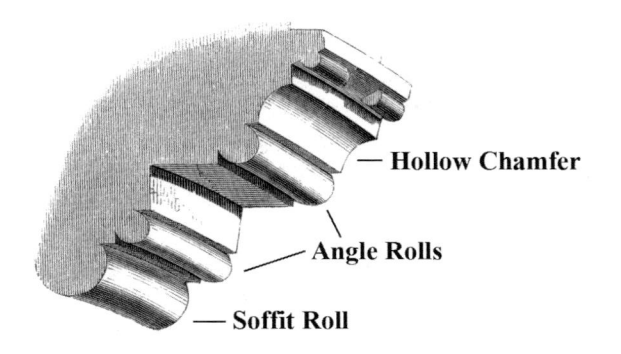

Hollow Chamfer
Angle Rolls
Soffit Roll

Two examples of Star or Saltire Cross Ornament

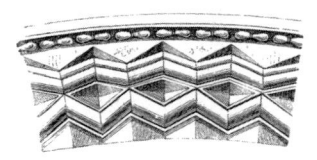

Zig Zag or Chevron Moulding
(Biforkated Chevron is where two chevrons are splayed at different angles from the same base; Furrowed Chevron is where there is a channel or hollow in the chevron)

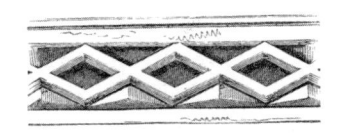

Lozenge Moulding
(Lattice is undercut lozenge-shaped chevron)

Cable Moulding

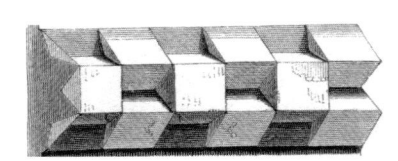

Chip Carving

Billet Ornament

Other Terms used:

Annulet:	a shaft ring
Apex mask:	a mask at the apex of a label or hood mould of an arch
Articulation:	emphasis of the joints or links within elements of architecture
Ashlar:	cut stone with square edges
Aumbry:	a cupboard for sacred vessels or books
Battered plinth:	inclined stones at the bottom of a wall
Beakhead ornament:	a bird or animal head with a beak biting a roll moulding
Binding tie:	a short strip that links two ornamental motifs
Cushion:	a block-shaped capital with flat, semi-circular sides and the lower surfaces rounded off to join a shaft
Chamfer:	an angle — usually 45-degree — cut at the edge of a stone

347

Ciborium:	a canopy above an altar or shrine
Clasping buttress:	a buttress that envelops the corner of a building
Clerestorey:	a row of windows in the upper storey of a church
Crocket:	a small volute at the end of a symmetrical, stylized leaf
Dog-tooth:	an ornament in the shape of a pyramid with undercut sides
Entablature:	the horizontal upper part of a Classical Order comprising architrave, frieze and cornice
Filleted shaft:	a shaft carved with a narrow raised ribbon
First Romanesque:	Romanesque architecture of the tenth and eleventh centuries in the Pyrenees, southern France, the Rhone valley, Burgundy, Switzerland and northern Italy. Built of small, roughly squared stones, rubble or brick, the exterior walls are articulated with pilaster strips and arched corbel tables, while interior spaces may be covered with barrel and/or groin vaults
Formeret:	a wall arch
Fret:	an ornament of upright and horizontal lines carved in the form of a band; also known as Greek key or meander
Galilee:	a chapel or vestibule at the west end of a church
Gorge:	a narrow channel cut into a roll moulding
Greek key:	see Fret
Imbrication:	fish scale pattern
Impost:	bracket in a wall, usually formed of mouldings, on which the ends of an arch rest
Jamb:	the side of a doorway or window
Joggled stones:	a jigsaw-like jointing of stones
Keeled roll:	a roll moulding with a pointed section like the keel of a ship
Label mask:	see Apex mask
Lintel:	the horizontal stone above a door or window
Narthex:	a low porch at the west end of a church
Nibbed shaft:	similar to a keeled shaft but with a reverse, or ogee, curve to either side of the keel, like the nib of a pen
Nook shaft:	shaft set in the angle of a pier, respond or wall, or the angle of the jamb of a window or doorway
Oculus:	a small round opening
Ogive:	a rib of a vault
Palmette:	a fan-shaped leaf
Pilier cantonné:	a large column with shafts on the cardinal axes
Piscina:	a small basin in a niche for washing Communion vessels after the Mass
Porticus:	a low, transept-like space projecting from the main body of a church
Quadrant roll:	an angle-roll moulding in the form of a quarter circle
Quirk:	a fine V-shaped incision in or between mouldings
Respond:	a half-pier bonded into a wall and carrying one end of an arch
Reticulated masonry:	lozenge-patterned masonry
Second Romanesque:	Romanesque architecture in Europe starting around 1020 and continuing in some regions to the early thirteenth century.

Glossary

	The most prestigious buildings are built on a larger scale than their First Romanesque counterparts, and are faced with ashlar masonry, while rubble-built structures use ashlar for quoins, piers and arches, and elements like half shafts, pilasters and string courses. The latter motifs provide rich articulation for the buildings and are accompanied by moulded orders to arches, and, in many cases, rich architectural sculpture.
Spandrel:	a curved triangular area of wall between arches
Springing (of arch):	the point at which an arch starts above its support
Stepped triple roll:	a triple roll moulding arranged in a stepped pattern
Stilted-arch:	an arch with its springing line raised above the level of the imposts
Trabeated:	a system of building with upright and horizontal elements
Tribune:	a gallery
Triforium:	an arcaded passage or a low arcade below a clerestorey and above an arcade or gallery
Triplet:	see Stepped triple roll
Vice:	a spiral staircase
Water-holding base:	a base with a hollow moulding deep enough to hold water
Westwerk:	a large western block with a low entrance hall and a room above open to the nave

Bibliography

Abbreviations:

AAAT:	*Anglesey Archaeological Association Transactions.*
ANS:	*Anglo-Norman Studies.*
AC:	*Annales Cambriae*, ed. John Williams (London 1860).
Antiq. J.:	*Antiquaries Journal.*
Arch. Camb.:	*Archaeologia Cambrensis.*
Archaeol. J.:	*Archaeological Journal.*
BAA CT:	*British Archaeological Association Conference Transactions.*
Baxter, 'Barthomley':	Ron Baxter, 'St Bertoline, Barthomley, Cheshire', www.crsbi.ac.uk/frchsites
Baxter, 'Chester Cathedral':	Ron Baxter, 'Chester Cathedral, Chester, Cheshire', www.crsbi.ac.uk/frchsites
Baxter, 'Prestbury':	Ron Baxter, 'St Peter?, Prestbury Norman Chapel, Cheshire', www.crsbi.ac.uk/frchsites
Baxter, 'St John's, Chester':	Ron Baxter, 'St John the Baptist, Chester, Cheshire', www.crsbi.ac.uk/frchsites
Baxter, 'Shotwick':	Ron Baxter, 'St Michael, Shotwick, Cheshire', www.crsbi.ac.uk/frchsites
B/E Essex:	Nikolaus Pevsner, *The Buildings of England, Essex* (Harmondsworth 1954).
B/E Gloucestershire:	David Verey, *The Buildings of England, Gloucestershire: The Vale and the Forest of Dean:* 2nd edn (Harmondsworth 1976).
B/E Northumberland:	Nikolaus Pevsner and Ian Richmond, *The Buildings of England, Northumberland* (Harmondsworth 1957).
B/E Shropshire:	Nikolaus Pevsner, *The Buildings of England, Shrophire* (Harmondsworth 1958).
B/E Wiltshire:	Nikolaus Pevsner, *The Buildings of England, Wiltshire*, 2nd edn. rev. by Bridget Cherry (Harmondsworth 1975).
B/W Clwyd:	Edward Hubbard, *The Buildings of Wales, Clwyd (Denbighshire and Flintshire)* (Harmondsworth 1986).
B/W Glamorgan:	John Newman, *The Buildings of Wales, Glamorgan* (Harmondsworth 1995).
B/W Gwent/Monmouthshire:	John Newman, *The Buildings of Wales, Gwent/Monmouthshire (*Harmondsworth 2000).
B/W Pembrokeshire:	Thomas Lloyd, Julian Orbach and Robert Scourfield, *The Buildings of Wales, Pembrokeshire* (New Haven and London 2004).
B/W Powys:	Richard Haslam, *The Buildings of Wales, Powys* (Harmondsworth 1979).
ByT:	T. Jones, *Brut y Tywysogyon or The Chronicle of the Princes* (Cardiff 1955).
CDF:	*Calendar of Documents preserved in France illustrative of the History of Great Britain and Ireland, I, A.D. 918-1206*, ed. J. Horace Round (London 1899).
Cong. Arch.:	*Congrès archéologique de France.*
DB Cheshire:	*Domesday Book, Cheshire,* ed. John Morris (Chichester 1978).
DB Gloucestershire:	*Domesday Book, Gloucestershire,* ed. J.S. Moore (Chichester 1982).
DB Herefordshire:	*Domesday Book, Herefordshire,* ed. F. and C. Thorn (Chichester 1982).
DB Kent:	*Domesday Book, Kent,* ed. Philip Morgan (Chichester 1983).
DB Worcestershire:	*Domesday Book, Worcestershire,* ed. F. and C. Thorn (Chichester 1982).
DNB:	*Dictionary of National Biography.*
Hist. et Cart. Glouc.:	*Historia et Cartularium Monasterii Sancti Petri Gloucestriae*, 3 vols, ed. W.H. Hart, Rolls Series (London 1863-1867).
JBAA:	*Journal of the British Archaeological Association.*
JSAH:	*Journal of the Society of Architectural Historians.*
Monasticon:	William Dugdale, *Monasticon Anglicanum*, 6 vols. (London 1818-30).
Mon. Ant.:	*The Monmouthshire Antiquary.*
Mont. Coll.:	*Montgomeryshire Collections.*
Oxford *DNB*:	*Oxford Dictionary of National Biography.*
PDANHS:	*Proceedings of the Dorset Archaeological and Natural History Society.*
PSANHS:	*Proceedings of the Somerset Archaeological and Natural History Society.*
PSAS:	*Proceedings of the Society of Antiquaries of Scotland.*
RCHME:	Royal Commission on Historical Monuments (England).
RCAHMW:	Royal Commission on Ancient and Historical Monuments in Wales and Monmouthshire.
TBGAS:	*Transactions of the Bristol and Gloucestershire Archaeological Society.*
TCAS&AR:	*Transactions of the Cardiganshire Antiquarian Society and Archaeological Record.*
THSC:	*Transactions of the Honourable Society of Cymmmrodorion.*
TTS:	*Transactions of the Thoroton Society.*
TWAS:	*Transactions of the Worcestershire Archaeological Society.*
WANHM:	*Wiltshire Archaeological and Natural History Magazine.*

Alexander, J.J.G. 1978. *Insular Manuscripts, 6th to the 9th Century*. London.
Allen, J.R. 1888. 'Pre-Norman Sculptured Stone and Thirteenth Century Sepulchral Slab at Llanrhidian, Gower, Glamorgan', *Arch. Camb.*, 5S, V, 173-76.
Allen, J.R. 1896. 'Font in Llantrisant Church, Glamorgan', *Arch. Camb.*, 5S, 13, 268-69.
Apted, M.R., Gilyard-Beer, R. and Saunders, A.D. (eds) 1977. *Ancient monuments and their interpretation: essays presented to A.J. Taylor*. Chichester.
Bailey, R. and Cramp, R. 1988. *Corpus of Anglo-Saxon Stone Sculpture, II, Cumberland, Westmorland and Lancashire North-of-the-Sands*. Oxford.
Baker, D. 1969. 'Excavations at Elstow Abbey, Bedfordshire, 1966-68: second Interim Report', *Bedfordshire Archaeological Journal*, 4, 27-41.
Banks, R.W. (ed.) 1882. 'Cartularium Prioratus S. Johannis Evang. de Brecon', *Arch. Camb.*, XIII, 275-308.
Banks, R.W. (ed.) 1883. 'Cartularium Prioratus S. Johannis Evang. de Brecon', *Arch. Camb.*, XIV, 18-49, 137-68, 221-36 and 274-311.
Barber, R. 1993. *Bestiary: Being an English Version of the Bodleian Library, Oxford. MS Bodley 764*. Woodbridge.
Barker, P. 1987. 'Hen Domen revisited', in Kenyon & Avent (eds.), 51-54.
Barker, P. 1994. *A Short Architectural History of Worcester Cathedral*. Worcester.
Barlow, F. 1979. *The English Church 1066-1154*. London.
Barral I Altet, X. 1989. *Belgique romane* (La Pierre-qui-Vire [Yonne]).
Barrow, Julia (ed). 1998. *St Davids Episcopal acta, 1085-1280*. Cardiff, South Wales Record Society.
Bartrum, P.C. 1966. *Early Welsh Genealogical Tracts*. Cardiff.
Baylé, M. 1979. *La Trinité de Caen: sa place dans l'histoire de l'architecture et du décor romans*. Geneva.
Baylé, M. 1991. *Les origines et les premiers developpements de la sculpture romane en Normadie: Art de Basse-Normandie*, no. 100. Caen.
Baxter, R. and Harrison, S. 2002. 'The Decoration of the Cloister at Reading Abbey', in *Windsor: Medieval Archaeology, Art and Architecture of the Thames Valley: BAA CT, XXV*, ed. Laurence Keen and Eileen Scarff, 302-12.
Baylé, M. ed. 1997. *L'architecture normande au moyen age*, 2 vols. Caen.
Bazeley, Revd. Canon. 1908. 'Early Connections between Glamorgan and Gloucestershire', *TBGAS*, XXXI, 40-51.
Bilson, J. 1928. 'Notes on the Earlier Architectural History of Wells Cathedral', *Archaeol. J.*, 85, 23-68.
Binns, Alison. 1989. *Dedications of Monastic Houses in England and Wales 1066-1216*. Woodbridge.
Birch, W. de G. 1897. *A History of Margam Abbey*. London.
Birch, W. de G. 1912. *Memorials of the See and Cathedral of Llandaff*. Neath.
Blair, J. 1985. 'Secular Minster Churches in Domesday Book', in *Domesday Book: a Reassessment,* ed. Peter Sawyer (London), 104-42.
Blair, J (ed.) 1988. *Minsters and Parish Churches: The Local Church in Transition 950-1200*. Oxford.
Blair, J. 2002. 'A Saint for Every Minster? Local Cults in Anglo-Saxon England', in Thacker and Sharpe 2002, 455-94.
Bloxham, M.H. 1859. *The Principles of Gothic Architecture*, 10th edition. London.
Boase, T.S.R. 1953. *English Art 1100-1216*. Oxford.
Böker, H. 1998. 'The Bishop's Chapel of Hereford Cathedral and the Question of Architectural Copies in the Middle Ages, *Gesta*, XXXVII/1 (1998), 44-54.
Bond, C.J. 1988. 'Church and Parish in Norman Worcestershire', in Blair 1988, 119-58.
Bond, F. 1908. *Fonts and Font Covers*. London.
Bond, F. 1912. *The Cathedrals of England and Wales*. London.
Bond, F. 1913. *An Introduction to English Church Architecture from the Eleventh to the Sixteenth Century*. London.
Bony, J. 1949. 'French Influences on the Origins of English Gothic Architecture', *Journal of the Warburg and Courtauld Institutes*, 12, 1-15.
Bony, J. 1958. 'La chapelle épiscopale de Hereford et les apports lorrains en Angleterre après la conquête', in *Actes du XIXe congrès international d'histoire de l'art*, Paris, 36-43.
Bony, J. 1981. 'Durham et la tradition saxonne', *Études d'art médiéval offertes a Louis Grodecki*, Paris, 80-92.
Bowen, E.G. 1956. *The Settlements of the Celtic Saints in Wales*. Cardiff.
Bradley, J. and King, H.A. 1985. 'Romanesque Voussoirs at St Fin Barre's Cathedral, Cork', *Journal of the Royal Society of Antiquaries of Ireland*, 115, 146-51.
Brakspear, H. 1931. 'A West Country School of Masons', *Archaeologia*, 81, 1-18.
Bramley, K.A. (ed.) 1994. *Gwaith Llywelyn Fardd I ac Eraill o Feirdd y Ddeudegfed Ganrif*. Cardiff.
Brewer, J.S. 1861. *Giraldus Cambrensis Opera*, Rolls Series, London.
Britnell, W.J. *et al*, 1994. 'Excavation and Recording at Pennant Melangell Church', *Mont. Coll.*, 82, 41-102.
Britnell, W.J., and Watson, K. 1994. 'Saint Melangell's Shrine at Pennant Melangell', *Mont. Coll.*, 82, 147-65.
Brooke, C.N.L. 1963. 'St Peter of Gloucester and St Cadoc of Llancarfan', in *Celt and Saxon: Studies in the Early British Border*, Cambridge, 258-322.
Brooke, C.N.L. 1986. *The Church and the Welsh Border in the Central Middle Ages*. Woodbridge.

Brown, G.B. 1903. *The Arts in Early England, Anglo-Saxon Architecture*. London.
Bulmer-Thomas, I. 1985. 'Some Churches of Gwynedd', *Transactions of the Ancient Monuments Society*, N.S. 29, 63-80.
Butler, L.A.S. 1971. 'Medieval Ecclesiastical Architecture in Glamorgan and Gower', in Pugh 1971, 379-415.
Butler, L. 1984. 'Neath Abbey', the Twelfth-Century Church', *Arch. Camb.*, 133, 147-51.
Buttress, D.R. 1966. 'Llandaff Cathedral in the Eighteenth and Nineteenth Centuries', *Journal of the Historical Society of the Church in Wales*, 16, 61-76.
Caerwyn Williams, J.E. 1996. 'Meilyr Brydydd and Gruffud ap Cynan', in Maund 1996, 165-86.
Cameron, N. 1994. 'The Romanesque Sculpture of Dunfermline Abbey: Durham versus the Vicinal', *Medieval Art and Architecture in the Diocese of St Andrews, BAA CT*, XIV, ed. John Higgitt, Leeds, 118-23.
Carley, J. 1988. *Glastonbury Abbey: The Holy House at the Head of the Moors Adventurous*. Woodbridge.
Caröe, W.D. 1924. 'Llanfilo (St Beilio), Breconshire', *Arch. Camb.*, ser. 7, 4, 291-98.
Caröe, W.D. 1933. 'Church of St Woollos [Newport]', *Arch. Camb.*, 88, 388-92.
Carr, A.D. 1982. *Medieval Anglesey*. Llangefni.
Carr, A.D. 1995. *Medieval Wales*. Basingstoke.
Cartwright, J. (ed.) 2003. *Celtic Hagiography and saints cults*. Cardiff.
Chierici, S. and Citi, D. 1979. *Piemont-Ligurie roman*. La Pierre-qui-Vire (Yonne).
Chester, G.I .1890. 'Notice of Sculptures of Oriental Design at Bredwardine and Moccas, Herefordshire', *Archaeol. J.*, 47, 140.
Clapham, A.W. 1913. 'The Benedictine Abbey of Barking', *Essex Archaeological Transactions*, 12, 69-89.
Clapham, A.W. 1921. 'St Dogmael's Abbey', *Arch. Camb*, 208-11.
Clapham, A.W. 1930. *English Romanesque Architecture before the Conquest*. Oxford.
Clapham, A.W. 1934. *English Romanesque Architecture after the Conquest*. Oxford.
Clark, G.T. 1876. 'Tretower, Blaen, Llyfni, and Crickhowel Castles', *Arch. Camb.*, ser. 4, 7, 276-83.
Clark, G.T. 1884. *Mediaeval Military Architecture in England*. 2 vols. London.
Clark, G.T. 1881-2. 'Chepstow Castle', *TBGAS*, 6, 51-74.
Coffman, P. 1994. 'The Romanesque Rib Vaults of Southwell Minster', *TTS*, 98, 38-48.
Coffman, P. 2001. 'Eadburg of Repton and Southwell Minster: Norman Shrine-Church for a Saxon Saint?' Proceedings of the St. Michael's College Symposium, *Saints and the Sacred* (25-26 February 2000) (Ottawa), 105-22.
Coffman, P. and Thurlby, M. 2001. 'Blyth Priory: A Romanesque Church in Nottinghamshire', *TTS*, 105, 57-72.
Colchester, L.S and Harvey, J 1974. 'Wells Cathedral', *Archaeol. J.*, 131, 200-14.
Collier, E.V. 1925-1926. 'Whitland Abbey Excavations: Interim Report', *Transactions of the Carmarthenshire Antiquarian Society*, 19, 63-65.
Colvin, H.M. 1963. *The History of the Kings Works*. 2 vols. London.
Cone, P. (ed.) 1977. *Treasures of Early Irish Art 1500B.C. to 1500A.D.* New York.
Conway Davies. J. 1943-4. 'Ewenny Priory: some recently found records', *National Library of Wales Journal*, III (1943-4), 107-137.
Conybeare, W.D. 1849. *Memoir on the History and Architecture of the Cathedral-Church at Llandaff*. Tenby.
Coplestone-Crow, B. 1998. 'The Foundation of the Priories of Bassaleg and Malpas in the Twelfth Century', *The Monmouthshire Antiquary*, XIV (1998), 1-13.
Coplestone-Crow, B. 2000. '[Ludlow Castle] From Foundation to Anarchy', in Shoesmith and Johnson, 21-34.
Coppack, G. 2000. ' The Round Chapel of St Mary Magdalene', in Shoesmith and Johnson 2000, 145-154.
Courtney, P. 1994. *Report on the Excavations at Usk 1965-76: Medieval and Later Usk*. Cardiff.
Cowley, F.G. 1968. 'Llangenydd and its priory', *Glamorgan Historian*, 5, 220-227.
Cowley, F.G. 1971. 'The Church from the Norman Conquest to the Beginning of the 14th Century' in Pugh 1971, 87-135.
Cowley, F.G. 1977. *Monastic Order in South Wales 1066-1349*. Cardiff.
Cowley, F.G. 1998 'Margam Abbey 1147-1349', *Morgannwg: the journal of Glamorgan history*, 42, 8-22.
Coxe, W. 1801. *An Historical Tour of Monmouthshire illustrated with views by Sir R.C. Hoare, Bart*, 2 vols. London.
Cramp, R. 1992. 'Schools of Mercian Sculpture' in *Studies in Anglo-Saxon Sculpture*, 174-216. London.
Crook, J. 1994. 'The Architectural Setting of the Cult of St Cuthbert in Durham Cathedral (1093-1200)', in *Anglo-Norman Durham 1093-1193*, ed. David Rollason, Margaret Harvey and Michael Prestwich, 235-50. Woodbridge.
Crook, J. 2000. *The Architectural Setting of the Cult of Saints in the Early Christian West, c.300-1200*. Oxford.
Crook, J. 2002. 'The Enshrinement of Local Saints in Francia and England', in Thacker and Sharpe 2002, 189-224.
Crosby, S. McK. 1972. *The Apostle Bas-Relief at Saint-Denis*. New Haven.
Crossley, P. 1987. "English Gothic Architecture', in *Age of Chivalry: Art in Plantagenet England 1200-1400*, ed. Jonathan Alexander and Paul Binski, London, 60-73.
Crossley, P. 1988. 'Medieval architecture and meaning: the limits of iconography', *Burlington Magazine*, 130, 116-21.
Crouch. D. (ed.) 1988. *Llandaff Episcopal Acta 1140-1287*. Cardiff.
Cunliffe, B. 1977. *Excavations at Portchester Castle, III, Medieval, the outer bailey and its defences*. London.
Cunliffe, B. and Munby, J. 1985. *Excavations at Portchester Castle, IV, Medieval, the inner bailey*. London.

David, H.E. 1929. 'Margam Abbey, Glamorgan', *Arch. Camb.*, 84, 317-24.
Davies, E.T. 1956. 'John Wood's Italianate Temple', *Journal of the Historical Society of the Church in Wales*, 6, 70-81.
Davies, J. Conway (ed. and trans.) 1946-8. *Episcopal Acts and Cognate Documents Relating to Welsh Dioceses, 1066-1272*, 2 vols. Cardiff.
Davies, J.R. 2002 'The Saints of South Wales and the Welsh Church', in Thacker and Sharpe 2002, 361-95.
Davies, J. R. 2003. *The Book of Llandaf and the Norman Church in Wales*. Woodbridge.
Davies, R.R. 1987. *Conquest, Coexistence, and Change: Wales 1063-1415*. Oxford.
Davis-Weyer, C. 1971. *Early Medieval Art 300-1150: Sources and Documents*. New York.
Decaëns, H. 1979. *Itinéraires romans en Normandie*. La Pierre-qui-Vire [Yonne].
D'Elboux, R.H. 1923. 'The Benedictine Priory of St Mary, Cardiff', *Arch. Camb.*, ser. 7, 3, 114-25.
De Lozendio, L-M. and Rodriguez, A 1966, *Catalogne romane*, II. La Pierre-qui-Vire (Yonne).
De Paor, M. 1977. 'The Viking Impact', *Treasures of Early Irish Art 1500 B.C. to 1500 A.D.*, Metropolitan Museum of Art, New York, 144-86.
Deshman, R. 1995. *The Benedictional of Aethelwold*. Princeton.
Dimock, J.F. 1853. 'Architectural History of the Church of the Blessed Virgin, of Southwell,' *JBAA*, VIII, 265-303.
Doble, G.H. 1971. *Lives of the Welsh Saints*. Cardiff.
Drake, C.S. 2002 *The Romanesque Fonts of Northern Europe and Scandinavia*. Woodbridge.
Draper, P. 1995. 'Interpreting the Architecture of Wells Cathedral', in *Artistic Integration in Gothic Buildings*, ed. V. Raguin, K. Brush and P. Draper (Toronto), 114-31.
Draper, P. 1999. 'St Davids Cathedral: provincial or metropolitan?', in *Pierre, lumière, couleur: Études d'histoire de l'art du Moyen Âge en l'honneur d'Anne Prache*, ed., Fabienne Joubert and Dany Sandron. Paris, 103-16.
Drewett, P.L. and Stuart, I.W. 1975/6. 'Excavations in the Norman Gate Tower, Bury St Edmunds Abbey', *Proceedings of the Suffolk Institute of Archaeology*, 33, 241-52.
E.L.B. 1880. 'Welsh Fonts', *Arch. Camb.*, 4S, XI, 214-217.
Edwards, N., (1986); 'Anglesey in the early middle ages: the archaeological evidence', *Trans. Anglesey Antiq. Soc.*, 19-41.
Edwards, N. 1994. 'Holy Wells in Wales and Early Christian Archaeology', www.bath.ac.uk/lispring/sourcearchive/ns1/ns1ne1
Edwards, N. 1997. *Landscape and Settlement in Medieval Wales*. Oxford.
Edwards, N. 2002. 'Celtic Saints and Early Medieval Archaeology', in Thacker and Sharpe 2002, 225-65.
Edwards, N. & Lane, A. (eds.)1992. *The Early Church in Wales and the West*, Oxford.
Ellis, P.C. 1855. 'Penmon Priory', *Arch. Camb.*, ser. 3, 1, 36-42.
Ellis, W.J. 1951. 'The Church of Saint Hywyn, Aberdaron', *Transactions of the Caernarvonshire Historical Society*, II, 5-35.
Elliston-Erwood, F.C. 1931. 'The apse in Kentish church architecture', *Arch. Cant.*, 43 (1931), 247-54.
Enlart, C. 1895. *Monuments religieux de l'architecture romane et de transition dans la région picarde. Anciens diocèses d'Amiens et de Boulogne*. Amiens.
Evans, A.C. 1989. *The Sutton Hoo Ship Burial*. London.
Evans, D.H. *et al*, 1982-1984. 'Further Excavation and Fieldwork at Llanthony Priory, Gwent', *Mon. Ant.*, V pts 1 & 2, 1-61.
Evans, D.H. 1995. *Valle Crucis Abbey*. Cardiff.
Evans, D.S. 1977. (ed.) *Historia Gruffudd vab Kenan*. Cardiff.
Evans, D.S. (ed. and trans.) 1990. *A Medieval Prince of Wales: the Life of Gruffudd ap Cynan*. Llanerch.
Evans, E. 2000. 'Medieval Churches in Wales: the Welsh Historic Churches Project', *Church Archaeology*, 4, 5-26.
Evans, J.W. 1992. 'The Survival of the *Clas* as an Institution in Medieval Wales: Some Observations on Llanbadarn Fawr', in Edwards and Lane 1992, 33- 40.
Evans, J.W. 2003. 'St David and St Davids: some observations on the cult, site and buildings', in Cartwright 2003, 10-25.
Evans, W. & Worsley, R. 1981. *St Davids 1181-1981*. St Davids.
Fairweather, F.H. 1933. *Aisleless Apsidal Churches of Great Britain*. Colchester.
Fenton, R. 1811. *A Historical Tour through Pembrokeshire*. London.
Fernie, E. 1983. *The Architecture of the Anglo-Saxons*. London.
Fernie, E. 1986. 'The Effect of the Conquest on Norman Architectural Patronage'*, ANS*, 9, 72-85.
Fernie, E. 1993a. *An Architectural History of Norwich Cathedral*. Oxford.
Fernie, E. 1993b. 'The Romanesque Churches of Dunfermline Abbey', *Medieval Art and Architecture in the Diocese of St Andrews, BAA CT*, XIV, ed. John Higgitt, Leeds, 25-37.
Fernie, E. 2000. *The Architecture of Norman England*. Oxford.
Fernie, E. 2003. 'The Architecture and Sculpture of Ely Cathedral in the Norman Period', in Peter Meadows and Nigel Ramsey (eds), *A History of Ely Cathedral* (Woodbridge), 94-111.
Ford, P.J. 1970. 'Llywarch, ancestor of Welsh Princes', *Speculum*, 45, 442-50.
Fox, C. 1933. 'Llancarfan', *Arch. Camb.*, 88, 400.

Freeman, E.A. 1850a. *Remarks on the Architecture of Llandaff Cathedral*. London & Tenby.
Freeman, E.A. 1850b. 'On the Architectural Antiquities of Gower', *Arch. Camb.*, NS, I, 41-64.
Freeman, E.A. 1851a. 'Chepstow Priory Church', *Arch. Camb.*, 2nd ser. 2, 1-8.
Freeman, E.A. 1851b. 'On Architectural Antiquities in Monmouthshire', *Arch. Camb.*, 2S, II, 99-113.
Freeman, E.A. 1854. 'The Churches of Brecon', *Arch. Camb.*, 2S, V, 148-81.
Freeman, E.A. 1856. 'The Ecclesiastical Architecture of Wales and the Marches', *Arch. Camb.*, 3S, II, 218-48.
Fryer, A.C. 1899. 'Ancient Fonts in Gower', *JBAA*, NS 5.
Galbraith, V.H. and Tait J (ed) 1950. *Herefordshire Domesday circa 1160-1170*, Pipe Roll Society Publications, NS 25.
Gardner, A. 1956. *Wells Capitals*. Wells.
Gardner, I. 1917. 'Some Fonts of Gwent and Hereford', *Arch. Camb.*, ser. 6, 17, 235-17.
Gardner, S. 1982. 'The Nave Galleries of Durham Cathedral', *Art Bulletin*, LXIV, 564-80.
Garton, T. 1981. 'A Romanesque Doorway at Killaloe', *JBAA*, 134, 31-57.
Garton, T. 2001. 'Masks and Monsters: Some Recurring Themes in Irish Romanesque Sculpture' in *From Ireland Coming: Irish Art from the Early Christian to the Late Gothic period and its European Context*, ed. Colum Hourihane (Princeton), 121-40.
Gem, R.D.H. 1975. 'Bishop Wulfstan II and the Romanesque Cathedral Church of Worcester,' *Medieval Art and Architecture at Worcester Cathedral: BAA CT*, I, ed. G. Popper, 15-37.
Gem, R. 1981. 'Chichester Cathedral: When was the Romanesque Church Begun?', *ANS*, 3, 61-64.
Gem, R. 1983. 'The Romanesque Cathedral of Winchester: Patron and Design in the Eleventh Century', *Medieval Art and Architecture at Winchester Cathedral: BAA CT*, VI, ed. T.A. Heslop and V. Sekules (Leeds), 1-12.
Gem, R. 1985. 'Holy Trinity Church, Bosham', *Archaeol. J.*, 142, 32-36.
Gem, R. 1986. 'The Bishop's Chapel at Hereford: the Roles of Patron and Craftsman', in Sarah Macready and F.H. Thompson (eds), *Art and Patronage in The English Romanesque*, London, 87-96.
Gem, R. 1987. 'Canterbury and the Cushion Capital', a Commentary on Passages from Goscelin's "De Miraculis Sancti Augustini" in N. Stratford, ed., *Romanesque and Gothic: Essays for George Zarnecki* (Woodbridge), 83-105.
Gem, R. 1988 'The English Parish Church in the 11th and early 12th Centuries', in Blair 1988, 21-30.
Gem, R. 1989. 'Melbourne Church of St Michael and St Mary', *The Nottingham Area Proceedings of the 135th Summer Meeting of the Royal Archaeological Institute*, 24-29.
Gem, R. 2000. 'Romanesque Architecture in Chester, c. 1075-1117', in *Medieval Archaeology, Art and Architecture at Chester: BAA CT*, ed. Alan Thacker (Leeds), 31-44.
Gerald of Wales, 1978. *The Journey through Wales/The Description of Wales*, trans. Lewis Thorpe. Harmondsworth.
Gethyn-Jones, E. 1979. *The Dymock School of Sculpture*. Chichester.
Gilchrist, R. 1994. *Gender and Material Culture: the Architecture of Religious Women*. London.
Glascodine, C.H. 1920. 'Llanrhidian' – Swansea Meeting Report, *Arch. Camb.*, 6S, 20, 310-13.
Glass, D. 1991. *Romanesque Sculpture in Campania: Patrons, Programs, and Style*. University Park, PA.
Goodall, J. 2001. *Richmond Castle*. London.
Graham, R. 1929. 'Four Alien Priories of Monmouthshire', *JBAA*, N.S., XXXV, 102-21.
Green, C.A.H. 1906. *Notes on the Churches in the Diocese of Llandaff: I, The Cathedral Group*. Aberdare.
Green, C.A.H. 1907a. *Notes on the Churches in the Diocese of Llandaff: II, The Conventual Group*. Aberdare.
Green, C.A.H. 1907b. *Notes on the Churches in the Diocese of Llandaff: II, The Manorial Group*. Aberdare.
Gresham, C.A. 1968. *Medieval Stone Carving in North Wales: Sepulchral Slabs and Effigies of the Thirteenth and Fourteenth Centuries*. Cardiff.
Grose, F. 1786. *The Antiquites of England and Wales*. 8 vols. London.
Haddan, A.W. and Stubbs, W. 1869. *Councils and Ecclesiastical Documents Relating to Great Britain and Ireland*, vol. 1. London.
Haddan, A.W. and Stubbs, W. 1964. *Councils and Ecclesiastical documents relating to Great Britain and Ireland*, 3 vols (Oxford).
Hague, D.B. 1971. 'The Castles of Glamorgan and Gower', in Pugh 1971, 417-48.
Hague, D.B. 1984. 'Ewenny Priory', *Arch. Camb.*, 133, 183.
Halsey, R. 1985. 'Tewkesbury Abbey: Some Recent Observations', in *Medieval Art and Architecture at Gloucester and Tewkesbury: BAA CT*, VII, ed. T.A. Heslop and Veronica Sekules. Leeds, 16-35.
Halsey, R. 1986. 'The earliest architecture of the Cistercians in England', in Norton and Park, 65-85.
Harrison, J.P. 1890. 'Anglo-Norman ornament compared with designs in Anglo-Saxon MSS', *Archaeol. J.*, 47, 143-53.
Harrison, S. 2004. 'Keynsham Abbey: an analysis of the loose stonework and reassessment of the buildings', *PSANHS*, forthcoming.
Harrison, S. and Barker, P. 1999. 'Ripon Minster: An Archaeological Analysis and reconstruction of the 12th-Century Church', *JBAA*, CLII, 49-78.
Harrison, S. and Thurlby, M. 1997. 'An Architectural History', in *A Definitive History of Dore Abbey*, ed. Ron Shoesmith and Ruth Richardson (Logaston), 45-62.

Harvey, J. 1984. *English Medieval Architects: A Biographical Dictionary down to 1550*. Gloucester.
Hearn, M.F. & Thurlby, M. 1997. 'Previously Undetected Wooden Ribbed Vaults in Medieval Britain', *JBAA*, 150, 48-58.
Heaton, R.B., and Britnell, W.J. 1994. 'A Structural History of Pennant Melangell Church', *The Montgomeryshire Collections*, 82, 103-26.
Heitz, C. 1963. *Reserches sur les rapports entre architecture et liturgie à l'epoque carolingienne*. Paris.
Henken, E.R. 1987. *Traditions of Welsh Saints*. Woodbridge.
Henken, E.R. 2003. 'Welsh hagiography and the nationalist impulse', in Cartwright, J 2003, 26-44.
Henry, F. 1965. *Irish Art in the Early Christian Period, to 800 A.D.* London.
Henry, F. 1967. *Irish Art during the Viking Invasions, 800-1020 A.D.* London.
Henry, F. 1970. *Irish Art in the Romanesque Period, 1020-1170 A.D.* London.
Henry, F. and Zarnecki, G. 1957-1958. 'Romanesque Arches Decorated with Human and Animal Heads', *JBAA*, 3rd ser., 20-21, 1-35.
Hensley, E.J. (Rev.). 1890-92. 'Chepstow Church', *Transactions of the Woolhope Naturalists' Field Club* (1890-92) [1894], 331-32.
Herity, M. 1993. 'The forms of the tomb-shrine of the founder saint in Ireland', In R.M. Spearman and J Higgitt (ed.) *The Age of Migrating Ideas*, Stroud, 188-95.
Heslop, T.A. 1991. 'Orford Castle, nostalgia and sophisticated living', *Architectural History*, 34, 36-58.
Higham, R. and Barker, P, 2000. *Hen Domen, Montgomery: a timber castle on the English-Welsh border: a final report*. Exeter.
Hiscock, N. (ed.) 2003. *The White Mantle of Churches: Architecture, Liturgy and Art Around the Millennium* (Turnhout [Belgium]).
Hoey, L. 1989. 'The Design of Romanesque Clerestories with Wall Passages in Normandy and England', *Gesta*, 28, 78-101.
Hoey, L. and Thurlby, M. 2004. 'A Survey of Romanesque Vaulting in Great Britain and Ireland', *Antiq. J.*, 84, 117-84.
Hoftun, O. and Franceschi, G. 2002. *Stavkirkene: og det norske middelaldersamfunnet*. Copenhagen.
Hogg, A.H.A. and King, D.J.C. 1963. 'Early Castles in Wales and the Marches', *Arch. Camb.*, 112 (1963), 77-124.
Hogg, A.H.A. and King, D.J.C. 1967. 'Masonry Castles in Wales and the Marches', *Arch. Camb.*, 116, 71-132.
Hogg, A.H.A. and King, D.J.C. 1970 'Castles in Wales and the Marches: Additions and Corrections to lists published in 1963 and 1967', *Arch. Camb.*, 119, 119-24.
Hohler, E.B. 1999. *Norwegian Stave Church Sculpture*. 2 vols. Oslo.
Holme, G.G. 1926. 'The "Confessio" and Penmon Church', *AAAT* (1926), 24-30.
Holme, G.G. 1930. 'Llaneilian and Penmon Church Towers, *AAAT* (1930), 54-59.
Hope, W. St J. 1913-14. 'Report on the Excavation of the Cathedral Church of Old Sarum', *Proceedings of the Society of Antiquaries*, 2nd ser., XXVI, 100-17.
Hughes, H.H. 1901a. 'The Architectural History of the Cathedral Church of St Deiniol, Bangor', *Arch. Camb.*, ser. 6, 1, 179-204.
Hughes, H.H. 1901b. 'Ynys Seiriol', *Arch. Camb.*, ser. 6, 1, 85-108.
Hughes, H.H. 1913. 'The Cathedral Churches of Bangor and St Asaph', in *Memorials of Old North Wales*, ed. E. Alfred Jones, London, 1913, 55-65.
Hughes, H.H. 1922. 'Early Christian Decorative Art in Anglesey', *Arch. Camb.*, ser. 7, 2, 61-79.
Hughes, H.H. 1923. 'Early Christian Decorative Art in Anglesey', *Arch. Camb.*, ser. 7, 3, 53-69.
Hughes, H.H. 1923b 'Oswestry Meeting Report', *Arch. Camb.*, ser. 7, 3, 403.
Hughes, H.H. 1924. 'Early Christian Decorative Art in Anglesey', *Arch. Camb.*, ser. 7, 4, 39-58.
Hughes, H.H. 1930a. 'Church of St Cybi, Holyhead, *Arch. Camb.*, 85, 355-65.
Hughes, H.H. 1930b. 'The Ancient Churches of Anglesey: Presidential Address', *Arch. Camb.*, 85, 237-66.
Hughes, H.H. 1930c. '[Penmon Priory]', *Arch. Camb.*, 85, 446-47.
Hughes, H.H. 1933. 'Miscellanea [The Font in St Mary's Chapel, Talyllyn (Anglesey)]', *Arch. Camb.*,88, 108-09.
Impey, E. 1999. 'The Buildings on the Motte at Kilpeck Castle, Herefordshire', *Arch. Camb.*, CXLVIII, 101-08.
Impey, E. 2002. 'The *Turris Formosa* at Ivry-la-Bataille, Normandy',in Merrion-Jones *et al*, 189-210.
Jalabert, D. 1931. 'La première flore gothique aux chapiteaux de Notre-Dame de Paris', *Gazette des Beaux-Arts*, ser. 6, 5, 283-304.
Jalabert, D. 1932. 'La flore gothique: ses origines, son évolution du XIIe and Xve siècle', *Bulletin Monumental*, 91, 181-246.
Jalabert, D. 1965. *La flore sculptée des monuments du moyen age en France*. Paris.
James, J.H. 1929. *A History and Survey of the Cathedral Church of Llandaff*. 2nd edn. Cardiff.
Jones, A. (ed. and trans.) 1910. *The History of Gruffydd ap Cynan*. Manchester.
Jones, F. 1992. *The holy wells of Wales*, 2nd edn. Cardiff.
J[ones], H.L. 1849. 'Penmon Priory', *Arch. Camb.*, 4, 44-60, 128-34, and 198-204.
Jones, N.A. and Morfydd, E. 2003. 'Twelfth-century Welsh hagiography: the *Gogynfeirdd* poems to saints', in Cartwright, J. 2003, 45-76.

Bibliography

Jones, W.B. & Freeman, E.A. 1856. *The History and Antiquities of Saint David's*. London & Tenby.
Jordan, A. 1911. 'Norman Doorway, Llanbadarn Fawr, Radnorshire', *Arch. Camb.*, ser. 6, 11, 250-51.
Kendrick, T.D. 1949. *Late Saxon and Viking Art*. London.
Kenyon, J.R. & Avent, R. (eds.) 1987. *Castles in Wales and the Marches: Essays in Honour of D.J. Cathcart King*. Cardiff.
Kenyon, J.R.. and Spurgeon, C.J. 2001. *Coity Castle, Ogmore Castle and Newcastle (Bridgend)*. Cardiff.
Kenyon, J.R. 2002. *Kidwelly Castle*. Cardiff.
Kermode, P.S.C. 1907. *Manx Crosses*. London (reprinted Balgarvies, Angus, 1994).
Keynes, S. 1988. 'Regenbald the chancellor [sic]', *ANS*, 10, 185-222.
Keyser, C.E. 1911a. 'An Essay on the Norman Doorways in the County of Gloucester', in *Memorials of Old Gloucestershire*, ed. P.H, Ditchfield. London.
Keyser, C.E. 1911b. 'Llanbadarn Fawr Church', *Arch. Camb.*, ser. 6, 11, 84-86.
Keyser, C.E. 1927. *A list of Norman tympana and lintels, with figure or symbolical sculpture still or till recently existing in the churches of Great Britain*, 2nd rev. edn. London.
Kidson, P. and Murray, P. 1962. *A History of English Architecture*. London.
Kidson, P. 1996. 'The Mariakerk at Utrecht, Speyer and Italy, in *Utrecht: Britain and the Continent, Archaeology, Art and Architecture, BAA CT*, XVIII, ed. Elisabeth de Bièvre, 123-36.
King, D.J.C. 1970. 'Manorbier Castle, Pembrokeshire', *Arch. Camb.*, 119, 83-118.
King, J.F. 1990. 'The Old Sarum Master: A Twelfth-Century Sculptor in South-West England', *WANHM*, 83, 70-95.
King, J.F. 1995. 'The Parish Church of Kilpeck Revisited', in *Medieval Art, Architecture and Archaeology in Hereford: BAA CT,* XIV, ed. David Whitehead (Leeds), 82-93.
King, J.F. 1996. 'Sources, Iconography and Context of the Old Sarum Master's Sculpture', *Medieval Art and Architecture at Salisbury Cathedral: BAA CT*, ed. Laurence Keen and Thomas Cocke, XVII, 79-84.
King, J.F. 2002. 'The Tournai Marble Baptismal Font of Lincoln Cathedral', *JBAA*, 155, 1-21.
King, R.J. 1873. *Handbook to the Cathedrals of Wales*. London.
Knight, J.K. 1976-78. 'Excavations at St Barruc's Chapel, Barry Island, Glamorgan', *Cardiff Naturalists' Society Transactions*, 99, 28-65.
Knight, J.K. 1977. ' Usk Castle and its Affinities', in Apted, Gilyard-Beer and Saunders, 139-54.
Knight, J.K. 1991. *Chepstow Castle and Port Wall*. Cardiff.
Krautheimer, R. 1942. 'An Introduction to an "Iconography of Medieval Architecture"', *Journal of the Warburg and Courtauld Institutes*, 5, 1-33.
Knowles, W.H. 1928. 'The Church of St Nicholas, Ashchurch', *TBGAS*, 50, 97-102.
Kubach, H.E. and Verbeek, A. 1976. *Romanische Baukunst an Rhein und Maas*, 2 vols. Berlin.
Lasko, P. 1972. *Ars Sacra 800-1200*. Harmondsworth.
Leask, H. 1951. *Irish Castles and Castellated Houses*. Dundalk.
Leask, H. 1955. *Irish Churches and Monastic Buildings, I, the First Phases and the Romanesque*. Dundalk.
Lefèvre-Pontalis, E. 1894. *L'architecture religieuse dans l'ancien diocèse de Soissons au 11e et 12e siècle*. Paris.
Lefèvre-Pontalis, E. 1908. 'Les clochers du Calvados', *Cong. Arch*, 75, 652-84.
Leland, J. 1964. *The intinerary of John Leland in or about the years 1535-1543*, ed. Lucy Toulmin Smith. London.
Lewis, C.P. 1988. *The Herefordshire Domesday*, London.
Lewis, C.P. 1996. 'Gruffud ap Cynan and the Normans' in Maund 1996, 61-78.
Lewis, D. 1975. *The History of Llantrisant*. Pontypridd.
Lewis, S. 1845/1855. *A Topographical Dictionary of Wales*, I, London 1845; II London 1855.
Liddiard, R. (ed.) 2003. *Anglo-Norman Castles*. Woodbridge.
Lloyd, J.E. 1912. *A History of Wales from the Earliest Times to the Edwardian Conquest*. 2 vols. London.
Lord. P. 2003. *The Visual Culture of Wales: Medieval Vision*. Cardiff.
Lovegrove, E.W. 1922. 'St. David's Cathedral', *Arch. Camb*. 7S, 2, 360-82.
Lovegrove, E.W. 1926. 'The Cathedral Church of St. David's', *Arch. J.* 83, 254-83.
Lovegrove, E.W. 1929. 'The Cathedral Church of Llandaff', *JBAA*, NS, XXXV, 75-90.
Lovegrove, E W. 1933. 'Llandaff Cathedral', *Arch. Camb*., 88, 365-67.
Lovegrove, E.W. 1942-3. 'Llanthony Priory', *Arch. Camb.*, 97, 213-29.
Lovegrove, E.W. 1946-7. 'Llanthony Priory', *Arch. Camb.*, 99, 64-77.
Lowe, B.J. *et al*. 1987. 'Keynsham Abbey: Excavations 1961-1985', *PSANHS*, 131, 81-156.
Lundgren, K. and Thurlby, M. 1999. 'The Romanesque Church of St Nicholas, Studland (Dorset)', *PDANHS*, 121 (1999), 1-16.
Lynam, C. 1905. 'Notes on the Nave of Chepstow Parish Church', *Archaeol. J.*, LXII, 270-78.
Mackie, G. 2003. *Early Christian chapels in the west: decoration, function and patronage*. Toronto.
Malone, C.L.M. 1973. 'West English Gothic Architecture 1175-1250', unpublished Ph.D. dissertation, University of California, Berkeley.
Malone, C.M. 2004a *Facade as Spectacle: Ritual and Ideology at Wells Cathedral*. Leiden and Boston, 2004.

Malone, C.M. 2004b. 'Cistercian Design in the Choir and Transept of Wells Cathedral' in *Perspectives for an Architecture of Solitude: Essays on Cistercians, Art and Architecture in Honour of Peter Fergusson*, ed. Terryl Kinder (Turnhout [Belgium]), 351-67.
Marschall, H-G. and Slotta , R. 1984. *Lorraine romane*. La Pierre-qui-Vire (Yonne).
Marshall, G. 1918-20. 'Remarks on a Norman Tympanum at Fownhope and Others in Herefordshire', *Transactions of the Woolhope Naturalists' Field Club*, vol. for 1918, 1919 & 1920, pt 1, 52-59.
Marshall, P. 1998. 'The Twelfth-Century Castle at Newark', in *Southwell and Nottinghamshire: Medieval Art, Architecture and Industry, BAA CT*, XXI, ed. Jennifer S. Alexander, 110-25.
Marshall, P. 2002. 'The Great Tower as Residence', in Merrion-Jones *et al*, 27-44.
Maund, K.L. (ed.) 1996. *Gruffudd ap Cynan*. Woodbridge.
Maund, K. 2000. *The Welsh Kings: The Medieval Rulers of Wales*. Stroud.
Maylan, C.N. 1992. 'Excavations at St Mary's Priory, Usk', *Mon. Ant.*, 8, 29-42.
McAleer, J.P. 1983. *The Romanesque Church Facade in Britain*. New York.
McCann, W.G. 1991. 'The Welsh View of the Normans in the 11th and 12th Centuries', *Transactions of the Honourable Society of Cymmrodorion*, 39-67.
McKenna, C. 1996. 'The Hagiographic Poetics of *Canu Cadfan*', in Kathryn A. Klar, Eve E. Sweetser and Claire Thomas (eds.), *A Celtic Florilegium: Studies in Memory of Brendan O Hehir* (Lawrence, Mass.), 121-37.
McLees, D. 1993. 'Llandaff Cathedral', *The Cardiff Area: Proceedings of the 139th Summer Meeting of the Royal Archaeological Institute, Supplement to the Archaeological Journal*, 150, 51-53.
Mein, A.G. 1986. *Norman Usk: The Birth of a Town*. Usk.
Mein, G. 1992. 'Usk Priory: an unrecorded excavation', *Mon. Ant.*, 8, 43-45.
Meyer, R. 1997. *Frühmittelalteliche Kapitale und Kämpfer in Deutschland*, 2 vols. Berlin.
Merrion-Jones, G.; Impey, E and Jones, M (eds). 2002. *The Seigneurial Residence in Western Europe AD c.800-1600*. Oxford.
Meyrick, S.R. 1808. *The History and Antiquities of the County of Cardigan*. London.
Moore, C.H. 1912. *The Medieval Church Architecture of England*. New York.
Moore, D. 1996. 'Gruffudd ap Cynan and the mediaeval Welsh polity' in Maund 1996, 1-60.
Morey, A. & Brooke, C.N.L. 1967. *Letters and Charters of Gilbert Foliot*. Cambridge.
Morgan, C.O.S. 1885. 'St Woollos' Church, Newport, Monmouthshire', *Arch. Camb.*, ser. 5, 2, 279-91.
Morris, R. 2000. ''The Architectural History of the Medieval Cathedral Church', in *Hereford Cathedral: A History*, ed. G. Aylmer and J. Tiller (London), 204-40.
Morgan Willmott,. E.C. 1907. *The Cathedral Church of Llandaff*. London.
Musset, L. 1974. *Normandie Romane, II, La Haute-Normandie*, La Pierre-qui-Vire (Yonne).
Musset, L. 1975. *Normandie romane, I, La Basse-Normandie*, 2nd edn., La Pierre-qui-Vire (Yonne).
Muthesius, A. 1997. *Byzantine Silk Weaving AD400 to AD1200*. Vienna.
Nash-Williams, V.E. 1950. *The Early Christian Monuments of Wales*, Cardiff.
Nelson, L.H. 1966. *The Normans in South Wales 1070-1171*. Austin, TX & London.
Nicholas, T. 1874. *The History and Antiquities of Glamorganshire and its Families*. London.
Nicholl, L.D. 1936. *The Normans in Glamorgan, Gower and Kidwelli*. Cardiff.
Nichols, S. and Thurlby, M. 1985. 'Notes on the Romanesque Capitals from the East Arch of the Presbytery of Hereford Cathedral', *The Friends of Hereford Cathedral Fifty-First Annual Report*, 14-26.
Nordenfalk, C. 1977. *Celtic and Anglo-Saxon Painting*. New York.
North, F.J. 1957. *The Stones of Llandaff Cathedral*. Cardiff.
Norton, C. and Park, D. (eds.) 1986. *Cistercian art and architecture in the British Isles*. Cambridge.
O'Keeffe, T. 1994. 'Lismore and Cashel: reflections on the beginnings of Romanesque architecture in Munster', *Journal of the Royal Society of Antiquaries of Ireland*, 124, 118-51.
O'Keeffe, T.1998. 'Architectural traditions of the early medieval church in Munster', in M.A. Monk and J. Sheehan (ed.), *Early Medieval Munster* (Cork), 112-24.
O'Keeffe, T. 2000. 'Romanesque as metaphor: architecture and reform in early twelfth-century Ireland', in *Seanchas : studies in early and medieval Irish archaeology, history and literature in honour of Francis J. Byrne*, ed. Alfred P. Smyth (Dublin), 313-22.
O'Keeffe, T. 2003. *Romanesque Ireland: Architecture and ideology in the Twelfth Century*. Dublin.
Ollivant, A. 1860. *Some Account of the Condition of the Fabric of Llandaff Cathedral*. 2nd edn. London.
Ó Riain-Raedel, D. 2000. 'German influence in Munster church and kings in the twelfth century', in *Seanchas : studies in early and medieval Irish archaeology, history and literature in honour of Francis J. Byrne*, ed. Alfred P Smyth (Dublin), 323-30.
Ormerod, G. 1861. *Striglensia: Archaeological Memoirs relating to the district adjacent to the confluence of the Severn and the Wye*. London.
Orrin, G. 1988. *Medieval Churches of the Vale of Glamorgan*. Cowbridge.

Parsons, D. 1995. 'Early Churches in Herefordshire: Documentary and Structural Evidence', *Medieval Art, Architecture and Archaeology at Hereford: BAA CT*, XV, ed. David Whitehead, Leeds, 60-74.
Paine, S. and Stewart, S. 2004. *Ewenny Priory, Glamorganshire: Treatment of the original decoration on the east wall of the presbytery*. London.
Perks, J.C. 1946-1948. 'The Architectural History of Chepstow Castle during the Middle Ages' *TBGAS*, 67, 307-46.
Perks, J.C. 1967. *Chepstow Castle*, 2nd edn. London.
Picton Turberville, E. 1928. 'Ewenny Church', *Arch. Camb.*, ser. 7, 8, 371-74.
Plant, R. 2003. 'Architectural developments in the Empire North of the Alps: The patronage of the Imperial Court', in Hiscock 2003, 29-56.
Platt, C.P.S. 1982. *The Castle in Medieval England and Wales*. London.
Pritchard, E.M. 1907. *History of St Dogmael's Abbey: together with her cells, Pill, Caldey, and Glascareg, and her mother abbey of Tiron*. London.
Pryce, H. 2001. 'British or Welsh? National Identity in Twelfth-century Wales', *English Historical Review*, 116, 775-801.
Pugh, T.B. (ed). 1971. *Glamorgan County History, III, The Middle Ages*. Cardiff.
Radford, C.A.R. 1948-1949. 'Bangor Cathedral in the Twelfth and Thirteenth Centuries: Recent Discoveries', *Arch. Camb.*, 100, 256-61.
Radford, C.A.R. 1949. *Strata Florida Abbey*. London.
Radford, C.A.R. 1960. 'Tretower: The Castle and the Court', *Brycheiniog*, 6, 1-50.
Radford, C.A.R. 1961. 'Presidential Address', *Arch. Camb.*, 111, 1-24.
Radford, C.A.R. 1962. *St Dogmael's Abbey*. London.
Radford, C.A.R. 1963. 'The Native Ecclesiastical Architecture of Wales (c. 1100-1285): The Study of a Regional Style', in *Culture and Environment: Essays in Honour of Sir Cyril Fox*, ed. I. LL. Foster and L. Alcock (London), 355-72.
Radford, C.A.R. 1976. *Ewenny Priory*, 6th edn. London.
Radford, C.A.R. 1986. *Tretower Court and Castle*, 3rd edn, ed. & revised by David Robinson. Cardiff.
Radford, C.A.R., and Hemp, W.J. 1959. 'Pennant Melangell: the church and the shrine', *Arch. Camb.*, 108, 90-98.
Randall, H.J. 1928. 'Ogmore Castle', *Arch. Camb.*, ser. 7, 8, 389-90.
Redknap, M. 2000 *Vikings in Wales: an Archaeological Quest*. Cardiff.
Redknap, M. and Lewis, J.M, forthcoming. *A Corpus of Early Medieval Inscribed Stones and Stone Sculpture in Wales, vol. 1, Breconshire, Glamorgan, Monmouthshire, Radnorshire, and geographically contiguous areas of Herefordshire and Shropshire*. Cardiff.
Rees, S. 2001. 'The Priory Buildings', in *A History of the Benedictine Priory of the Blessed Virgin Mary and St Florent at Monmouth*, ed. D.H.W. and K.E.K. (Monmouth), 41-64.
Rees, S. 2004. 'Benedictine Houses in South East Wales: Continuity and Conservation', *Papers in Honour of David Henry Williams: The Monmouthshire Antiquary*, 20, 83-94.
Reeve, M. 1998. 'The Retrospective Effigies of Anglo-Saxon Bishops at Wells Cathedral', *Somerset Archaeology and Natural History*, 142, 235-59.
Remfrey, P.M. 1995. *Oystermouth Castle, 1066 to 1326*. Worcester.
Remfrey, P.M. 1995. *Ogmore Castle, 1066 to 1282*. Worcester.
Remfrey, P.M. 2000. *White Castle*. Worcester.
Remfrey, P.M. 2003. *A Political Chronology of Wales 1066 to 1282: An annual breakdown of events*. Shrewsbury.
Renn, D.F. 1962. 'The Round Keeps of the Brecon Region', *Arch. Camb*. 111, 129-43.
Renn, D. 1973. *Norman Castles*. 2nd edn. London.
Renn, D. 1987. '"Chastel de Dynari": the first phases of Ludlow', in Kenyon & Avent (eds.), 55-73.
Renn, D. 1994. 'Burhgeat and Gonfanon: Two sidelights from the Bayeux Tapestry', *ANS*, 16, 177-98.
Renn, D. 2000. 'The Norman Military Works', in Shoesmith and Johnson 2000, 125-38.
Rhys, J. 1905. 'The Englyn. The origin of the Welsh Englyn and kindred metres. Part I: Inscriptional Data', *Y Cymmrodorion*, 13: 1-102.
Richard, A.J. 1927. 'Kenfig Castle', *Arch. Camb.*, ser. 7, 7, 161-82.
Rickards, R. 1904. *Church and Priory of St Mary, Usk*. London.
Ridgway, M.H. 1994. 'Furnishings and Fittings in Pennant Melangell Church', *Mont. Coll.*, 82, 127-38.
Rigold, S. 1969. *Lilleshall Abbey*. London.
Rigold, S. 1977. ' Romanesque bases, in the South-east of the Limestone Belt' in Apted, Gilyard-Beer and Saunders, 99-137.
Rivoira. G.T. 1933. *Lombardic Architecture: Origin, Development and Derivatives*. Oxford (reprinted New York 1975).
Roberts, G. 1847. *Some Account of Llanthony Priory*. London.
Robinson, D.M. 1996. 'The Twelfth-Century Church at Tintern Abbey', *Mon. Ant.*, 12, 35-39.
Robinson, D.M.1998. *The Cistercian Abbeys of Britain, Far from the Concourse of Men*. London.
Robinson, D.M. forthcoming. *The Cistercians in Wales: Architecture and Archaeology 1130-1540*. London.

Robinson, D. and Platt, C. 1992. *Strata Florida Abbey, Talley Abbey*. Cardiff.
Rodwell, W. 1998. *Wells Cathedral: Excavation and Structural Studies*, 1978-93, 2 vols. London.
RCAHMW, *Caernarvonshire*, 3 vols. London, 1956-1964.
RCAHMW, *County of Montgomery*, London 1911.
RCAHMW, *County of Flint*, London 1912.
RCAHMW, *County of Radnor*, London 1913.
RCAHMW, *County of Carmarthen*, London 1917.
RCAHMW, *County of Merioneth*, London 1921.
RCAHMW, *County of Pembroke*, London 1925.
RCAHMW, *Anglesey*, London 1937.
RCAHMW, *County of Glamorgan, I, Pre-Norman, Part III, The Early Christian Period*. London 1976.
RCAHMW, *County of Glamorgan, III, Pt 1a, Medieval Secular Monuments, The Early Castles from the Norman Conquest to 1217*. London 1991.
Rouquette, J.M. 1980. *Provence romane*, I, 2nd edn. La Pierre-qui-Vire (Yonne).
Round, J.H. 1901. *Studies in Peerage and Family History*. London.
Rowley-Morris, E. 1891. 'History of the Parish of Kerry', *Mont. Coll.* XXV, 363-94.
Ruprich-Robert, V. 1884. *L'architecture normande aux XIe et XIIe siècles en Normandie et en Angleterre*, 2 vols. Paris.
Rydén, T. 1995. *Domkyrkan i Lund*. Malmö.
St Clair Baddeley, W. 1913. 'Ewenny Priory or St Michael of Ogmore', *Arch. Camb.*, 6S, 13 pt 1, 1-50.
Salter, M. 1991a. *The Old Parish Churches of Gwent, Glamorgan and Gower*. Malvern.
Salter, M. 1991b. *The Old Parish Churches of Mid-Wales*. Malvern.
Salter, M. 1993. *The Old Parish Churches of North Wales*. Malvern.
Salter, M. 1994. *The Old Parish Churches of South-West Wales*. Malvern.
Sampson, J. 1998. *Wells Cathedral West Front: Construction, Sculpture and Conservation*. Stroud.
Schiller, G. 1972. *Iconography of Christian Art, II, The Passion of Christ*. London.
Scott, G.G. 1862. *Report Made by the Order of the Dean and Chapter on the State of the Fabric of St. David's Cathedral*. London.
Scott, G.G. 1870. *Second Report...on the Bangor Cathedral Restoration*. London.
Scott, G.G. 1877. 'Hereford Cathedral', *Archaeol. J.*, 34, 323-48.
Serbat, L. 1908a. 'Église de Thaon', *Cong. Arch.*, 75, 222-31.
Serbat, L. 1908b. 'Église de Saint-Contest', *Cong. Arch.*, 75, 232-41.
Sharret, F. and Sharret, P. 1985. *Écosse romane*. La Pierre-qui-Vire (Yonne)
Shoesmith, R. and Johnson, A. (ed.) 2000. *Ludlow Castle: Its History and Buildings*. Logaston.
Smith, J.B. 1971. 'The Kingdom of Morgannwg and the Norman Conquest of Glamorgan', in Pugh 1971, 1-44.
Soden, R.W. 1984. *A Guide to Welsh Churches*. Llandysul.
Spurgeon, C.J. 1991. 'Glamorgan's First Castles', *Fortress*, 8, 3-14.
Stalley, R.A 1971. 'A Twelfth-Century Patron of Architecture: a Study of the Buildings erected by Roger, Bishop of Salisbury, 1102-1139', *JBAA*, 34, 62-83.
Stalley, R.A. 1979. 'The Medieval Sculpture of Christ Church Cathedral, Dublin', *Archaeologia*, 106, 107-122.
Stalley, R.A. 1981. 'Three Irish Buildings with West Country Origins', *Medieval Art and Architecture at Wells and Glastonbury, BAA CT*, IV, ed. Nicola Coldstream and Peter Draper, 62-80.
Stalley, R.A. 1987. *The Cistercian Monasteries of Ireland*. New Haven and London.
Stalley, R. A 2000. 'The construction of the medieval cathedral *c*. 1030-1250', *Christ Church Cathedral, Dublin: A History*, ed. Kenneth Milne. Dublin, 53-74.
Stalley, R.A. 2002. 'The Architecture of St Davids Cathedral: Chronology, Catastrophe and Design', *Antiq. J.*, 82, 13-45.
Stratford, N. 1978. 'Notes on the Norman Chapter House at Worcester', *Medieval Art and Architecture at Worcester Cathedral: BAA CT*, I, ed. G. Popper, 51-70 (Leeds 1978).
Swynnerton, C. 1921. 'The Priory of St Leonard of Stanley, Co. Gloucester, in light of recent discoveries, documentary and structural', *Archaeologia*, 71, 119-226.
Swarzenski, H. 1967. *Monuments of Romanesque Art*, 2nd edn. London.
Tatton-Brown, T. 1989. *Great Cathedrals of Britain*. London.
Tatton-Brown, T. 1994. 'The Medieval Fabric', in Chichester Cathedral: An Historical Survey, ed. Mary Hobbs (Chichester), 25-46.
Tatton-Brown, T. 1996. 'Archaeology and Chichester Cathedral', in *The Archaeology of Cathedrals*, ed. Tim Tatton-Brown and Julian Munby, Oxford, 47-55.
Taylor, A.J. 1946-1947. 'Usk Castle and the Pipe Roll of 1185', *Arch. Camb.*, 99, 249-55.
Taylor, H.M. and Taylor, J. 1965. *Anglo-Saxon Architecture*, 2 vols. Cambridge.
Thacker, A. 2000. 'The Early Medieval City and its Buildings', in *Medieval Archaeology, Art and Architecture at Chester: BAA CT*, ed. Alan Thacker (Leeds), 16-30.

Thacker, A. and Sharpe, R. (ed.) 2002. *Local Saints and Local Churches in the Early Medieval West*. Oxford.
Thompson, A.H. 1912. *Military Architecture in England during the Middle Ages*. Oxford.
Thompson, H.M. 1925. 'Llandaff Cathedral: A Bibliography Raisonne', *Arch. Camb.*, ser. 7, 5, 392-404.
Thompson, M.W. 1986. 'Associated Monasteries and Castles in the Middle Ages: A Tentative List', *Archaeol. J.*, CXLIII, 305-21.
Thurlby, M. 1976. 'Breaking Away From Formality (English Medieval Figure Sculpture)', *Country Life* (June 3, 1976), 1508-09.
Thurlby, M. 1982. 'Fluted and Chalice-Shaped: The Aylesbury Group of Fonts', *Country Life* (January 28), 228-29.
Thurlby, M. 1984a. 'A note on the former barrel vault in the choir of St John the Baptist at Halesowen and its place in English Romanesque Architecture', *TWAS*, 3rd Series, 9, 37-43.
Thurlby, M 1984b. 'A note on the romanesque sculpture at Hereford Cathedral and the Herefordshire School of Sculpture', *Burlington Magazine*, CXXVI, no. 973, 233-34.
Thurlby 1985a. 'The Romanesque Elevations of Tewkesbury and Pershore', *JSAH*, XLIV, 5-17.
Thurlby, M. 1985b. 'The Elevations of the Romanesque Abbey Churches of St Mary at Tewkesbury and St Peter at Gloucester', *Medieval Art and Architecture at Gloucester and Tewkesbury: BAA CT*, VII, ed. T.A. Heslop and V. Sekules (Leeds), 36-51.
Thurlby, M. 1988a. 'The Former Romanesque High Vault in the Presbytery of Hereford Cathedral', *JSAH*, XLVII, 185-89.
Thurlby, M. 1988b. 'The Romanesque Priory Church of St Michael at Ewenny', *JSAH*, XLVII, 281-94.
Thurlby, M. 1991a. 'The Romanesque Cathedral of St Mary and St Peter at Exeter', *Medieval Art and Architecture at Exeter Cathedral: BAA CT*, XI, ed. Francis Kelly, 19-34.
Thurlby, M. 1991b. 'The Romanesque Cathedral [of Exeter] circa 1114-1200', in *Exeter Cathedral: A Celebration*, ed. Michael Swanton (Exeter), 37-44.
Thurlby, M. 1993. 'The Early Gothic Transepts of Lichfield Cathedral', *Medieval Archaeology and Architecture at Lichfield: British Archaeological Conference Transactions*, XIII, ed. John Maddison (Leeds), 50-64.
Thurlby, M. 1994a. 'The Roles of the Patron and the Master Mason in the First Design of Durham Cathedral', in *Anglo-Norman Durham 1093-1193*, ed. David Rollason, Margaret Harvey and Michael Prestwich (Woodbridge), 161-84.
Thurlby, M. 1994b. 'The Romanesque Apse Vault of Peterborough Cathedral', in *Studies in Medieval Art and Architecture presented to Peter Lasko*, ed. David Buckton and T.A. Heslop (Stroud), 171-86.
Thurlby, M. 1994c. 'St Andrews Cathedral-Priory and the Beginnings of Gothic Architecture in Northern Britain', in *Medieval Art and Architecture in the Diocese of St Andrews: BAA CT*, XIV, ed. John Higgitt (Leeds), 47-60.
Thurlby, M. 1995a. 'Hereford Cathedral: The Romanesque Fabric', in *Medieval Art, Architecture and Archaeology in Hereford: BAA CT*, XIV, ed. David Whitehead (Leeds), 15-28.
Thurlby, M. 1995b. 'The Lady Chapel of Glastonbury Abbey', *Antiq. J.*, 65, 107-70.
Thurlby, M. 1995c. 'Observations on Romanesque and Early Gothic Vault Construction', *Arris*, 6, 22-29.
Thurlby, M. 1995d. 'Some Design Aspects of Kirkstall Abbey', in *Yorkshire Monasticism: Archaeology, Art and Architecture: BAA CT*, XVI, ed. Lawrence R. Hoey (1995), 62-72.
Thurlby, M. 1995e. 'Jedburgh Abbey Church: The Romanesque Fabric', *PSAS*, 125, 793-812.
Thurlby, M. 1996. 'The Abbey Church, Pershore: An Architectural History', *TWAS*, 3rd Series, 15, 146-209.
Thurlby, M. 1997a. 'L'abbatiale romane de St. Albans', in *L'architecture normande au Moyen Age*, ed. Maylis Baylé (Caen), 79-90.
Thurlby, M. 1997b. 'Aspects of the architectural history of Kirkwall Cathedral', *PSAS*, 127, 855-88.
Thurlby, M. 1997c. 'The Elder Lady Chapel at St Augustine's, Bristol, and Wells Cathedral', in *'Almost the Richest City': BAA CT*, XIX, ed. Laurence Keen, 31-40.
Thurlby, M. 1999. *The Herefordshire School of Romanesque Sculpture*. Logaston.
Thurlby, M. 2000a. 'Roger of Pont l'Évêque, Archbishop of York (1154-81), and French Sources for the beginnings of Gothic architecture in Northern Britain', *England and the Continent in the Middle Ages: Studies in Memory of Andrew Martindale*, ed. John Mitchell (Stamford: Paul Watkins), 35-47.
Thurlby, M. 2000b. 'Aspects of Romanesque Ecclesiastical Architecture in Dorset: Wimborne Minster, Sherborne Abbey, Forde Abbey chapter house, and St Mary's, Maiden Newton', *PDANHS*, 122 (2000), 1-19.
Thurlby, M. 2001. 'The Place of St Albans in Regional Sculpture and Architecture in the Second Half of the Twelfth Century', in *Alban and St Albans: Roman and Medieval Architecture, Art and Archaeology, BAA CT*, XXIV, ed. Martin Henig and Phillip Lindley (Leeds 2001), 162-75.
Thurlby, M. 2002. 'Minor Cruciform Churches in Norman England', *ANS*, 24, 239-277.
Thurlby, M. 2003a. 'Anglo-Saxon Architecture Beyond the Millennium: Its Continuity in Norman Building', in Hiscock 2003, 119-37.
Thurlby, M. 2003b. 'Did the late 12th-century nave of St David's Cathedral have stone vaults?', *Antiq. J.*, 83, 9-16.
Thurlby, M. 2003c. '[Tewkesbury Abbey] The Norman Church', in Richard K. Morris and Ron Shoesmith (ed.), *Tewkesbury Abbey: History, Art and Architecture* (Logaston), 89-108.

Thurlby, M. 2004a. 'The Use of Tufa Webbing and Wattle Centering in English Vaults down to 1340', *Villard's Legacy: Studies in medieval technology, science and art in memory of Jean Gimpel*, ed. Marie-Therese Zenner (Aldershot), 157-72.
Thurlby, M. 2004b. 'Aspects of Romanesque Architecture in Dorset: Corfe and Sherborne Castles, Milton Abbey, Powerstock, Milborne St Andrew, Loders, Godmanstone, the Stoke Abbott Font, and Worth Matravers', *PDANHS*, in press.
Thurlby, M. 2004c. 'Romanesque Architecture and Sculpture in the Diocese of Carlisle', *Carlisle and Cumbria: Roman and Medieval Architecture, Art and Archaeology: BAA CT*, XXVII, ed. Mike McCarthy (Leeds), 269-90.
Thurlby, M. 2004d. 'Romanesque Churches in the Diocese of Rochester', *Archaeologia Cantiana*, CXXIV, 51-73.
Thurlby, M. 2004e. 'The Architectural Context of the late 12th-century Fabric of Keynsham Abbey', *PS ANHS* (2004), 95-102.
Thurlby, M. 2005. 'The Romanesque Churches of St Mary Magdalen at Tixover and St Mary at Morcott' *Ecclesiology Today*, 35 (September 2005), 23-41.
Thurlby, M. and Baxter, R. 2002. 'The Romanesque Fabric of Reading Abbey Church', *Windsor: Medieval Archaeology, Art and Architecture of the Thames Valley: BAA CT*, XXV, ed. Laurence Keen and Eileen Scarfe, Leeds, 282-301.
Thurlby, M. & Kusaba, Y. 1991.'The Nave of St Andrew at Steyning and Design Variety in Romanesque Architecture in Britain', *Gesta*, XXX/2, 163-75.
Tomaszewski, A. 1974. *Kocecio³ y romañskie z emporami zachodnimi*, (*Romanesque Churches with Western Tribunes*), Wroclaw.
Turberville, J.P. 1901. *Ewenny Priory: Monastery and Fortress*. London.
Turner, R. 2002. *Chepstow Castle*. Cardiff.
Turner, R. 2004. 'The Great Tower, Chepstow Castle, Wales', *Antiq. J.*, 84, 223-318.
Turvey, R, *The Welsh Princes 1063-1283*. London.
Tweddle, D. 1995. *Corpus of Anglo-Saxon Stone Sculpture, IV, South-East England*. Oxford.
Tyrrell Green, E. 1913. 'Cardiganshire Fonts', *TCAS&AR*, 1 no. 3, 11-21.
Tyrrell Green, E. 1914. 'Cardiganshire Fonts', *TCAS&AR*, 1 no. 4, 9-25.
Tyrrell Green, E. 1916-17. 'The Church Architecture of Wales', *THSC*, Session 1916-17, 52-118.
Tyrrell Green, E. 1918-19. 'Types of Baptismal Fonts as Illustrated by Welsh Examples', *THSC*, Session 1918-19, 30-127.
Tyrrell Green, E. 1920-21. 'The Ecclesiology of Pembrokeshire' *THSC*, Session 1920-21, 10-62.
Tyrrell Green, E. 1928. *Baptismal Fonts Classified and Illustrated*. London.
Vergnolle, E. 1994. *L'art roman en France*. Paris.
Victory, S. 1977. *The Celtic Church in Wales*. London.
Wakeman, T. 1855. 'On the Town, Castle, and Priory of Usk'. *JBAA*, X, 257-65.
Walker, D. 1974. 'Brecon Priory in the Middle Ages', in *Links with the Past: Swansea and Brecon Historical Essays*, ed. O.W. Jones & D. Walker. Llandybie, Carmarthenshire, 37-65.
Walker, D. (ed.) 1976. *A History of the Church in Wales*. Cardiff.
Walker, D. 1977. *A New History of Wales: The Norman Conquerors*. Swansea.
Walker, D. 1978. 'The Norman Settlement in Wales', *Proceedings of the Battle Abbey Conference on Anglo-Norman Studies*, I, 131-43.
Wallace, P.F. and and Ó Floinn, R. 2002. *Treasures of the National Museum of Ireland*. Dublin.
Wallace, R. (ed.) 1904. *Eleanor Ormerod, LL.D. Economic Entomologist. Autobiography and Correspondence*. London.
Ward-Perkins, J.B. 1981. *Roman Imperial Architecture*. Harmondsworth.
Webb, G. 1956. *Architecture in Britain: The Middle Ages*. Harmondsworth.
Welander, D. 1991. *The History, Art and Architecture of Gloucester Cathedral*. Stroud.
West, J.K. 1988. 'Architectural Sculpture in Parish Churches of the 11th- and 12th-Century West Midlands: some Problems in Assessing the Evidence', in Blair 1988, 159-67.
Westwood, J.O. 1856. 'Inscribed Font at Patrishow, Brecknockshire', *Arch. Camb.*, ser. 3, 2, 286-90.
Westwood, J.O. 1876. *Lapidarium Walliae: the Early Inscribed and Sculptured Stones of Wales*. Oxford.
Westwood, J.O. 1879. 'Malpas Church, Monmouthshire', *Arch. Camb.*, ser. 4, 10, 193-94.
White, P. 2000. 'Changes to the Keep', in Shoesmith and Johnson 2000, 139-44.
Whittingham, S. 1970. *A Thirteenth-Century Portrait Gallery at Salisbury Cathedral*. Salisbury.
Wightman, W.E. 1966. *The Lacy Family in England and Normandy 1066-1194*. Oxford.
Williams, A. 1992 ' A Bell-house and a Burh-geat: Lordly Residences in England before the Norman Conquest', in *The Ideals and Practice of Medieval Knighthood*, ed. C. Harper-Bill and R. Harvey, iv, 221-40.
Williams, A.G. 'Norman Lordship in south-east Wales during the reign of William I', *Welsh History Review*, Vol. 16, no. 4 (1993), pp. 445-66.
Williams, D. 1986. 'Catalogue of Welsh Eccelsiastical Seals as known down to A.D. 1660, Part III: Capitular Seals', *Arch. Camb.*, 135, 154.

Williams, D.H. 1980. 'Usk Nunnery', *The Monmouthshire Antiquary*, IV, 44-45.
Williams, S.W. 1886. 'Architectural Notes upon Usk Church, Monmouthshire', *Arch. Camb.*, 5S, 3, 90-93.
Williams, S.W. 1889a. *The Cistercian Abbey of Strata Florida*. London.
Williams, S.W. 1889b. 'On Further Excavations at Strata Florida Abbey', *Arch. Camb*, ser. 5, 6, 24-58.
William, S.W. 1891. 'Report on Excavations at Strata Marcella Abbey, near Welshpool', *Mont. Coll.*, 25, 161-96.
Williams, S.W. 1892. 'The Cistercian Abbey of Strata Marcella', *Arch. Camb.*, ser. 5, 9, 1-17.
Willis, R. 1845. *Architectural History of Canterbury Cathedral* (London, 1845), reprinted in *Architectural History of some English Cathedrals*, I (Chicheley, 1972).
Willis, R. 1862-3. 'The Crypt and Chapter House of Worcester Cathedral', *Transactions R.I.B.A.*, 1st Ser., 13, 213-25, reprinted in *Architectural History of some English Cathedrals*, II, Chicheley, 1973.
Willis, R. 1863. 'The Architectural History of Worcester Cathedral', *Archaeol. J.*, 20, 83-113, reprinted in *Architectural History of some English Cathedrals*, II, Chicheley, 1973.
Willmot, E.C.M. 1907. *The Cathedral Church of Llandaff*. London.
Wilson, C. 1978. 'The Sources of the Late Twelfth-Century Work at Worcester Cathedral', *Medieval Art and Architecture at Worcester Cathedral: BAA CT*, ed. G. Popper (Leeds), 80-90.
Wilson, C. 1985. 'Abbot Serlo's Church at Gloucester (1089-1100): Its Place in Romanesque Architecture', *Medieval Art and Architecture at Gloucester and Tewkesbury: BAA CT*, VII, ed. T.A. Heslop and V. Sekules (Leeds), 52-83.
Wilson, C. 1986. 'The Cistercians as "missionaries of Gothic" in Northern England', in Norton and Park 1986, 86-116.
Wilson, D.M. 1984. *Anglo-Saxon Art from the Seventh Century to the Norman Conquest*. Woodstock, New York.
Wood, M 1965. *The English Mediaeval House*. London.
Wood, R. 2001. 'Geometric Patterns in English Romanesque Sculpture', *JBAA*, 154, 1-39.
Wyatt, T.H. 1848. 'Llandaff Cathedral: its History, Condition and Contemplated Restoration'. *The Builder*, 6, 182-83, 211-12.
Wynne-Edwards, R. 1871. 'Norman Column and Arch Discovered in Meifod Church in September 1871', *Mont. Coll.*, IV, xxiii-xxv.
Zarnecki, G. 1951. *English Romanesque Sculpture 1066-1140*. London.
Zarnecki, G. 1953. *Later English Romanesque Sculpture 1140-1210*. London.
Zarnecki, G. 1998. 'The Romanesque Font at Lenton', in *Southwell and Nottinghamshire: Medieval Art, Architecture and Industry, BAA CT*, XXI, ed. Jennifer S. Alexander, 136-42.
Zienkiewicz, J.D. 1986. *The Legionary Fortress Baths at Caerleon*. Cardiff.

References

Preface
1. Walker 1977.
2. Carr 1995; Maund 2000; Turvey 2002.
3. Jones and Owen 2003.
4. Thurlby 1988.
5. Thurlby 1999.
6. Carr 1995, 44.
7. Gerald of Wales, 151.
8. *The Builder*, 7 (1848), 29. My thanks to Peter Coffman for this reference.
9. Tessa Garton, *Transactions of the Ancient Monuments Society*, 45 (2001), 150-51.

Introduction
1. See now, Draper 1999, Stalley 2002, Thurlby 2003b.
2. Barker 1987; Higham and Barker 2000.
3. Thurlby 2000.
4. Stalley 2002, 40.
5. *B/W Pembrokeshire*, 40
6. *B/W Pembrokeshire*, 388.

Chapter 1 Chepstow and Ludlow
1. Thompson 1986; Cunliffe 1977, 105-20; Cunliffe and Munby 1985, 12-19; Impey 1999.
2. Fernie 1986; Fernie 2000, 19-33.
3. Binns 1989, 102.
4. *CDF*, no. 145; Binns 1989, 93.
5. Binns 1989, 103.
6. *DB Gloucestershire*, S1.
7. Lewis 1988, 16.
8. Turner 2003; Turner 2004. I am very grateful to Rick Turner for generously sending me the text of the last article prior to publication.
9. Perks 1967, 31.
10. *B/W Gwent/Monmouthshire*, 180.
11. Turner 2004.
12. Turner 2004.
13. Turner 2004, 226-31.
14. Marshall 2002, 31.
15. Fernie 2000, 68-71; Goodall 2001, 8-12.
16. Turner 2004; Impey 2002, 197-98.
17. Ruprich-Robert 1884-1888, pls XXXVIII and XXXIX.
18. Baylé 1979; Baylé 1997, 50-51.
19. Baylé 1991, pls. 333-35.
20. Baylé 1991, pl. 328.
21. Zarnecki 1951, pls. 6 and 8.
22. Ruprich-Robert 1884-88, pl. XLII.
23. See below, 20-40.
24. *VCH Gloucestershire*, XI (1976), 147. See also, Galbraith and Tait 1950, 115.
25. *DB Herefordshire*, 1.11.
26. Lewis 1988, 15. Thanks to Rick Turner for this reference.
27. Thurlby 2004, 61, pl. IX (Eynsham).
28. Ward-Perkins 1981, ill. 309.
29. Gerald of Wales, 114.
30. Fernie 2000, figs. 132 and 173. On the bishop's chapel, see Bony 1958; Gem 1986, 94; Halsey 1985, 29; Fernie 2000, 233-36; Böker 1998. Professor Böker kindly informs me that he now prefers to date the Hereford Bishop's Chapel to the time of Robert de Losinga rather than to that of Gilbert Foliot (1148.-.63), as he suggested in his article.
31. Perks 1946-48, 327-28.
32. Purser 1998, 135.
33. Fernie 2000, 55 and 61.
34. *Monasticon*, IV, 652; *Calendar of Inquisitions post mortem*, iv, 299; Graham 1929, 103; Binns, 1989, 96.
35. Coxe 1801.
36. For the later architectural history of the priory church, see, *B/W Gwent/Monmouthshire*, 164-66.
37. Coxe 1801, pl. opp. 362; Wallace 1904, pl. VI. Thanks to Ann Rainsbury for this and the following two references.
38. Chepstow in Monmouth Shier, iconographically described. 1686, by Jacob Millerd of Bristol. Charles Heath, *Descriptive Accounts of Persfield and Chepstow....* (Privately Printed 1793), 32.
39. Freeman 1851a, 2.
40. Coxe 1801, 361.
41. Hensley, 1890-92, 332.
42. Lynam 1905; Fernie 2000, 239.
43. Clapham 1934, 56; McAleer 1984, 481.
44. On Romanesque vaulting in the West Country, see Hoey and Thurlby 2004; Thurlby 2004a; Thurlby 2003c; Thurlby 1996; Thurlby 1995a; Thurlby 1988a; Thurlby 1988a; Thurlby 1985a; Thurlby 1985b; Thurlby 1984; Wilson 1985.
45. Scott 1877, 327, ill. opp. 328; Thurlby 1988b, fig. 1.
46. Ormerod 1861, 82. See also, *B/W Gwent/ Monmouthshire*, 165. Ormerod's mention of 'Hoare's elevation' presumably refers to an engraving in William Coxe, *An Historical Tour of Monmouthshire illustrated with views by Sir R.C. Hoare, Bart* (London 1801), opp. 362, although the engraving in question is by Thomas Jennings.
47. Thurlby 1985, Thurlby 1988; Thurlby 1993a and b; Thurlby 1994; Thurlby 1995; Thurlby 2004; Gardner 1982.
48. *The Oxford English Dictionary*, v. 11 (Oxford, 1933), 452. Thurlby 2004a.
49. *The Oxford English Dictionary*, v. 11 (Oxford, 1933), 452.
50. Thurlby 2003c, 98.
51. Willis 1862-3, 222.
52. Zienkiewicz 1986, 103-14.
53. Gerald of Wales, 114.
54. Thurlby 1995b, Thurlby 2004a.

55. Willis 1845, 60.
56. The term 'West Country School of Romanesque architecture', is adapted from Harold Brakspear's article entitled 'A West Country School of Masons', *Archaeologia*, 81 (1931), 1-18. Brakspear discussed early Gothic churches in which he identified sufficient regional traits to identify a 'school'. These traits appear in buildings from Coventry and Lichfield in the midlands, to Chester in the north, Exeter in the south-west, Llandaff and St Davids in Wales, and Christ Church, Dublin, and Waterford in Ireland. A number of the motifs used by these masons are inherited or adapted from Romanesque antecedents. These motifs, along with many others, used by Romanesque masons from Cheshire and Staffordshire, through Worcestershire and Gloucestershire, down to Wiltshire and Dorset, Devon and Cornwall, and in Wales and Ireland, make the 'West Country School' label the most appropriate one.
57. For the Hereford presbytery, see Thurlby 1995a, pl. IA.
58. Thurlby 2001.
59. For the Basilica Julia, see Rivoira 1933, figs. 116 & 117.
60. For Bernay, see Ruprich-Robert 1884 - 88, pl. XI: Musset 1975, II, 45-57; Baylé 1997, II, 27-31.
61. Thurlby 2003c, pl. 7.
62. Thurlby 2003c, figs. 9.9, 9.23 and 9.24.
63. Taylor and Taylor 1965, figs. 426 and 427; Thurlby 2002, fig. 50.
64. Ruprich-Robert 1884, pl. XI.
65. Wilson 1978, 81. For Wells, see Bilson 1928, pl. 4.
66. On St John's Chester, see Gem 2000.
67. Kidson 1962, 44.
68. Baylé 1991, 114-16, pl. 394.
69. Binns 1989, 106.
70. Dimock 1853, 269-70, pl. 32. I am most grateful to Peter Coffman for this reference and for many stimulating discussions on its implications. See now, Coffman 2001.
71. Meyer 1997, I, 250, II, ills, on 716.
72. For the Great Paxton piers, see Taylor and Taylor 1965, fig. 238. For related pier forms in Germany and at Saint-Remi at Reims, see Fernie 1983, 130-33.
73. Fernie 2000, 124-28, esp. 126; Fernie 2003, 97-103.
74. Quatford was founded as a collegiate church by Roger, Earl of Shrewsbury (*VCH Shropshire*, II, 123).
75. Barker 1994, 40.
76. *VCH Gloucestershire*, II (1907), 103.
77. Fernie 2000, 211-13.
78. Fernie 1983, figs. 89 and 97.
79. Fernie 2000, 93.
80. Musset 1975, 105; Vergnolle 1994, 358 n.154.
81. Musset 1975, pl. 34 and colourplate 1.
82. Ruprich-Robert 1884 – 88.
83. Gem 1985.
84. Tatton-Brown 1994, 25-27; Tatton-Brown 1996, 52. See also, Gem 1981, and Fernie 2000, 130-31.
85. Thurlby 2004b.
86. Fernie 2000, fig. 162.
87. Blair 1985, 134; Keynes 1988, 185-222; Gem 1988, 27; Fernie 2000, 214.
88. Fernie 2000, fig. 160 (Hadstock); Fernie 1983, 165-66, fig. 98 (Wareham).
89. For references to Romanesque Gloucester, Tewkesbury, Pershore and Hereford, see above, note 44. On the crossings at Dorchester and Wimborne Minster, see Thurlby 2003a, 123, fig. 46; Thurlby 2002, 241-43; Thurlby 2000b, 1-9.
90. Coffman and Thurlby 2001.
91. Thurlby 2003c, 104, fig. 9.4.
92. Thurlby 1995a, pl. IIC.
93. Thurlby 1995a, pl. IC; Morris 2000, fig. 58.
94. Baylé 1991, ill. 615.
95. For the St John's chapel capitals, see Baylé 1991, pls. 693 and 694; for Blyth, see Coffman and Thurlby 2001.
96. Musset 1974, pl. 65.
97. Thurlby 1995a, 22.
98. Thurlby 1995b.
99. Thurlby 1988a, fig. 2.
100. Gethyn-Jones 1979, pl. 34a & b (Hereford) and pl. 42c (Bridstow).
101. Fernie 2000, 55.
102. Baylé 1997, 52, gives 1023 - 58; Fernie 2000, suggests after 1058.
103. Fernie 2000, 58, 233-36, 239; Hoey and Thurlby 2004, 165, 170.
104. Wilson 1985; Thurlby 1985b, Thurlby 1996; Thurlby 2003c.
105. Hoey and Thurlby 2004, 136, 166, 172.
106. Stalley 1981, 62-65, 80; O'Keeffe 2003, 125-65.
107. Thurlby 1995d; Hoey and Thurlby 2004, 170-71.
108. Kidson 1996, 134.
109. Kidson and Murray 1962, 50.
110. Moore 1912, 19-20; Hoey and Thurlby 2004, fig. 12; Thurlby 2003c, fig. 9.9.
111. Coffman 1994.
112. Coplestone-Crow 2000, 21-22; Renn, 2000, 125; White 2000, 144; Fernie 2000, 50-52.
113. Coplestone-Crow 2000, 21. B/E Shropshire, 181, attributes the start to Roger de Lacy or Roger de Montgomery, Earl of Shrewsbury.
114. On the Lacy family, see Wightman 1966.
115. Shoesmith and Johnson 2000.
116. Goodall 2001, 16.
117. For Sherborne, see *RCHM West Dorset*, 64, pl. 90; for Newark, see Marshall 1998, fig. 6.
118. Renn 2000, 136-37.
119. For a summary of the origins and use of the cushion capital in England, see Fernie 2000, 278-79.
120. Gem 1987.
121. Fernie 2000, 120, 211, 278-79; Cambridge, 'Early Romanesque', 151-52.
122. For Notre-Dame at Huy, see Barral I Altet 1989, pls. 80-82.
123. Tweddle 1995, 127, part of a cross shaft TR 155578,

ills. 20-23, C10-C11.
124. For Beckermet St Bridget and Gosforth, see Bailey and Cramp 1988, 54-56, 100-04, ills. 41-46, ills. 288-308. See also Kendrick 1949, pls. XLIV and XLVII, and pl. XLVI for Clulow (Cheshire) and Stapleford (Notts.).
125. Harvey 1984, 27.
126. *DB Kent*, 3.10.
127. Bony 1981, 83.
128. Fernie 2000, 106.
129. Zarnecki 1951, 14.
130. Barker 1994, 32.
131. Barker 1994, 40-41.
132. Taylor and Taylor 1965, fig. 201.
133. Marschall and Slotta 1984, pls. 9, 10, 129 and 136.
134. The Knook south portal is illustrated in Keyser 1927, fig. 34. The chancel arch at Knook is wooden and probably dates from William Butterfield's restoration of the church in 1874-1876. There is no indication that there was ever one of stone.
135. Clapham 1930, 136-37, fig. 44.
136. Kendrick 1949, 40-41; Taylor and Taylor 1965, 364-65.
137. *B/E Wiltshire*, 282.
138. Harrison 1890.
139. Vitruvius, *The Ten Books on Architecture*, I.D. Rowland and T.N. Howe (eds.) (Cambridge 1999), Book V, chapter 1.
140. Thurlby 2003c, 93.
141. Brakspear 1931.
142. Gethyn-Jones 1979, pl.12a; Thurlby 1999, 21, 105, 133, figs 5, 24 and 171.
143. Renn 2000, 125.
144. Renn 2000, 125.
145. *DB Gloucestershire* 39.1, records that Roger de Lacy held Kempley from the king.
146. On such design variety in arch ornamentation, see Thurlby and Kusaba 1991.
147. Later examples are in the transepts and nave aisles at Malmesbury abbey, in the chancels at St John at Devizes and St Mary at Devizes (Wilts.), and in the central axial tower at Englishcombe (Somerset).
148. Gethyn-Jones 1979.
149. Gethyn-Jones 1979.
150. Gethyn-Jones 1979, pl. 42c.

Chapter 2 Norman Church Architecture in the March and Glamorgan down to 1120

1. RCAHMW *Radnorshire*, 136, cat. 561, states that 'about midway' in the north wall 'is a round-headed doorway now blocked up'. This is incorrect.
2. Taylor and Taylor 1965, 497-99.
3. Taylor and Taylor 1965, 497-98.
4. Taylor and Taylor 1965, 498.
5. Taylor and Taylor 1965, 499.
6. Parsons 1995, 67. For the use of tufa in Romanesque churches in west Kent, see Thurlby 2004d, 51-54.
7. Gethyn-Jones 1979, pl. 9c.
8. Eric Fernie has made pioneer studies of proportion in the planning of Anglo-Norman architecture, see Fernie 2000, 288-90, with further references.
9. *Hist. et Cart. S. Petri Glos.*, I, 93.
10. Victory 1977, 116-17.
11. Fox 1933.
12. *Arch. Camb.*, 85, 1933, 400.
13. Butler 1971, 387, suggested that the Llyswyrny stone 'is probably part of a twelfth-century memorial slab'.
14. RCAHMW *Glamorgan*, I, 1976, 62.
15. Marshall 1918-1920, 56-59; Keyser 1927; Gethyn-Jones 1979; Zarnecki 1951; George Zarnecki and Ron Baxter, 'St Andrew, Bredwardine, Herefordshire', *The Corpus of Romanesque Sculpture in Britain and Ireland*, http://www.crsbi.ac.uk/crsbi/frhesites.html. There is also a related lintel reused as a sill in the east window of the south nave aisle at Eardisley (Herefs.), George Zarnecki and Ron Baxter, 'St Mary Magdalene, Eardisley, Herefordshire', *The Corpus of Romanesque Sculpture in Britain and Ireland*, http://www.crsbi.ac.uk/crsbi/frhesites.html.
16. Gethyn-Jones 1979; Thurlby 1999.
17. RCHM *Herefordshire, I, South-West* (London 1931), 26; Zarnecki 1951, 29, and Gethyn-Jones 1979, 9, stated that the lintel of the north doorway at Bredwardine is inserted. RCHM *Herefordshire*, I, 26, and Gethyn-Jones 1979, 9-10 considered that the lintel and capitals of the south doorway at Bredwardine, and the lintel of the south doorway at Letton were all inserted into earlier doorways. George Zarnecki and Ron Baxter, 'St Andrew, Bredwardine, Herefordshire', *The Corpus of Romanesque Sculpture in Britain and Ireland*, http://www.crsbi.ac.uk/crsbi/grhesites.html also suggest that the capitals of the south doorway and the lintels of both doorways at Bredwardine are inserted.
18. Gem 1986; Böker 1998; Fernie 2000, 233-36.
19. Gethyn-Jones 1979, fig. 12a.
20. Renn 2000, fig. 11.
21. Gethyn-Jones 1979, figs 48a and 56b.
22. Gethyn-Jones 179, fig. 23a.
23. Glass 1991, fig. 28.
24. Decaëns 1979, pl. 29.
25. A number of examples are discussed by Wood 2001.
26. Sunley, H. 1995 ,'Holy Cross, Morton Morrel, Warwickshire', *The Corpus of Romanesque Sculpture in Britain and Ireland*, http://www.crsbi.ac.uk/crsbi/frame23.html
27. Gethyn-Jones 1979, pl. 11c.
28. Baxter, R. 2004, 'St Mary, Bowdon, Cheshire', *The Corpus of Romanesque Sculpture in Britain and Ireland*, http://www.crsbi.ac.uk/crsbi/frchsites.html
29. Stone 1955, pl. 31A.
30. Keyser 1927, fig. 13.
31. Keyser 1927, fig. 37.
32. Keyser 1927, fig. 70.
33. Keyser 1927, fig. 54.
34. Keyser 1927, fig. 93.

35. Keyser 1927, figs 22 and 23.
36. Keyser 1927, fig. 137.
37. Stone 1955, pls 30A and 31A.
38. Wood 2001, 5-6, 8-9.
39. Clapham 1934, 128.
40. George Zarnecki, 'Romanesque Sculpture in Normandy and England in the Eleventh Century', *Anglo-Norman Studies*, I (1978), 168-89 at 181; reprinted in idem, *Further Studies in Romanesque Sculpture* (London 1992); Thurlby 1996.
41. Wilson 1984, fig. 34.
42. Chester 1890, 140; *Country Life*, 31 May 1919, cited by Marshall, 1918-20, 57 n.1.
43. Marshall, 1918-20, 57.
44. Keyser 1927, 8.
45. Zarnecki 1951, 29, cat. 23.
46. Thurlby 1999, fig. 134.
47. Gethyn-Jones 1979, pls. 18c and 59b and c.
48. Marshall 1918-20, 58.
49. Marshall 1918-20, 58.
50. Redknap and Lewis, forthcoming.
51. RCAHMW *Glamorgan*, I, 1976, 62.
52. B/W *Glamorgan*, 394.
53. Nash-Williams 1950, 138, cat. 218.
54. On Sutton Hoo, see Evans 1989.
55. *Arch. Camb*, 6th ser., 20 (1920), 310-313 at 312.
56. Thurlby 1999, fig. 7.
57. Cramp 1992, fig. 50.
58. For the Cava dei Tirreni pulpit, see Glass 1991, fig. 65.
59. Allen 1888, 174; Alexander 1978, cat. 72, ills. 329 and 331.
60. Nordenfalk 1977, 39, pl. 4 (Durrow), 48-49, pl. 10 (Echternach).
61. De Paor 1977, 182-83, cat. 57.
62. Baylé 1991, pl. 340.
63. Keyser 1927, fig. 135.
64. Cramp 1992, fig. 59; Thurlby 1999, fig. 169.
65. Redknap and Lewis, forthcoming.
66. Redknap and Lewis, forthcoming.
67. Hohler 1999, vol. 2, 171, cat. 98, pl. 214; Hoftun and Franceschi 2002, pl. 112.
68. Hohler 1999, vol. 2, 17.
69. Redknap and Lewis, forthcoming.
70. Nash-Williams 1950, cat. 224; RCAHMW, *Glamorgan*, I, 63; Redknap and Lewis, forthcoming.
71. Thurlby 1999, 145, fig. 228.

Chapter 3 Cathedral, Castle and Monastery post 1120

1. Birch 1912; Butler 1971; Conybeare 1850; Freeman 1850; James 1929; King 1873; Lovegrove 1929; Lovegrove 1933; North 1957; Ollivant 1860; Thompson 1925; Willmot 1907; Wyatt 1848.
2. Ollivant 1860, 14-22, with illustration of the proposed west front and south elevation (pl. 5), and presbytery interior (pl. 8); King 1873, 8-11, with an illustration of the proposed west front on 10; Davies 1956.
3. Buttress 1965; Thompson 1925.
4. Walker 1976, 29-30.
5. On St John's, Chester, see Gem 2002; Baxter 2004; for Hereford cathedral, see Thurlby 1995; Thurlby 1999, fig. 1.
6. Welander, ill. on 82.
7. Zarnecki 1953, ill. 8.
8. For capitals without abaci at Ludlow castle, see above, 44-45.
9. Gethyn-Jones 1979, pl. 43a.
10. Thurlby 1995, pl. 1C.
11. Thurlby 1999, 116, fig. 182.
12. Stalley 1971; Kealey 1972; King 1990; 1995 and 1996; Thurlby 2000b.
13. Stalley 1981, 61-65; O'Keeffe 2003, 161-65.
14. Kenyon 2002, 4.
15. Kealey 1972, 231-233.
16. Thurlby 2000b, fig. 14.
17. RCAHMW *Glamorgan, Early Castles*, 43.
18. RCHME *Herefordshire, II, East*, pl.
19. King 1873, 36.
20. Freeman 1850a. James 1929, pl. between 22 & 23, follows Freeman's reconstruction. Butler 1971, 383, fig. 1, erroneously shows aisles to the Romanesque presbytery.
21. King 1873, 36.
22. See below, 242-245.
23. See below, 193-196 and 242-245.
24. Lovegrove 1929.
25. James 1929, 11.
26. James 1929, 11.
27. RCHME *Herefordshire*, SW, 92-93; Thurlby 1991; Thurlby 1995a, 16; Stalley 1981, 62-65; O'Keeffe 2003,
28. Lovegrove 1933, 366. See also, Williams 1986, cat. 197, pl. XIII, where the Llandaff seal is illustrated alongside the very similar seal of Hereford cathedral
29. Crouch 1988, xiv.
30. Lord 2003, 57, ill. 69, dates the apex head of the bishop ca 1120, which is to ignore both the architectural setting and the naturalism of the head that belong in Saltmarsh's time.
31. Bond 1912, 454-55, compared the chevron of the Llandaff doorways with St Davids nave arcades, Glastonbury Abbey Lady Chapel, Wells Cathedral north porch, the arch from the north transept of the north choir aisle at Lichfield Cathedral, and the doorway of the west slype at Worcester Cathedral.
32. Fernie 1986; Gem 1983; Thurlby 1997a.
33. Thurlby 1994a.
34. Davies 2002; Davies 2003.
35. *DB Herefordshire*, 1.48.
36. *CDF* #1133, #1138; Binns 1989, 106.
37. Cowley 1977, 15.
38. *CDF* #1142.
39. *CDF*, 406-14.
40. B/W *Gwent/Monmouthshire*, 396.
41. Rees 2001, 45-48.

42. Hoey 1989; Gem 1978, 28-31.
43. Rees 2001, 47.
44. Rees 2001, 49.
45. For the Ledbury arcades, see RCHME *Herefordshire, II, East*, pls 136 and 137.
46. Rees 2001, 49.
47. Thurlby 1999, 130-131, figs 4, 6 and 204.
48. Thurlby 1999, 131; Gethyn-Jones 1979, pl. 39b.
49. Thurlby 1995, 15.
50. Morris 1983, 201; Thurlby 1999, 129-131, fig. 202.
51. Thurlby 1999, fig. 203.
52. *CDF*, #1142.
53. Pugh 1971, 286. For the Normans in Glamorgan, see Smith 1971, especially 'Robert Fitzhamon (d.1107) and the Norman Conquest of Glamorgan', 9-27; Cowey 1971; Bazeley 1908; Nicholl 1936; Walker 1978.
54. Morey and Brooke, 80, 82, letter 45; *Archaeol. J.*, 68 (1911), 391-396; *Arch. Camb.*, 111 (1962), 21 n. 53; Radford 1976, 7.
55. Haddan and Stubbs 1964, 1, 306.
56. Dugdale IV 1823, 523. Leland 1964, III, 50-51.
57. Nicholas 1874, 65-66.
58. *ByT*, 89-90.
59. *Hist. et Cart. Glouc.*, I, 224-25.
60. *Hist. et Cart. Glouc.*, I, 75-76, trans. Radford, Ewenny, 7.
61. Radford 1976, 7.
62. Picton Turberville 1928, 371.
63. Butler 1971, 381-82; Hague 1984, 183.
64. Thurlby 1988b.
65. O'Keeffe 2003, 161; *B/W Glamorgan*, 343.
66. Cowley 1977, 13.
67. Orrin 1988, 152.
68. Paine and Stewart 2004. I am most grateful to Sophie Stewart for sending me a copy of her report on the painting at Ewenny.
69. Grose 1786, ill. opp. 59, also illustrated in Orrin 1988, 152.
70. Cadw file 664//35.
71. The drawing is reproduced by Orrin 1988, 152. Carter's drawing is in Cadw file 664//33.
72. Thurlby 2002.
73. Thurlby 2002.
74. Lozendio and Rodriguez 1966, pls. 72 and 74.
75. For Ventemiglia, see Chierici and Citi 1979, pl. 117; for Saint-Paul-Trois-Chateaux and Saint-Gabriel, see Rouquette 1980, pls. 12 & 18.
76. While there is no doubt that the Gloucester presbytery had a Romanesque high vault, opinion is still divided on its form. Wilson 1985, reconstructed a groin vault while Thurlby 1985, opted, and still opts, for a barrel.
77. On Christchurch (Twyneham) transept crypt vaults, see Moore 1912, 19-20; Hoey and Thurlby 2004, 165, fig 12.
78. On Boscherville, see Wilson 1985, pl.XIF.
79. For Heddon-on-the-Wall, see Thurlby 1988, fig. 22; for Warkworth, see *B/E Northumberland*, pl. 18b.
80. Thurlby 1985b, 47-48.
81. Thurlby 1988, 291n 40; Hoey and Thurlby 2004.
82. Thurlby 2003c, 98.
83. For York Minster, see Fernie 2000, colourplate I; for Blyth, Coffman and Thurlby, 2001.
84. *DB Gloucestershire*, 3.7; *DB Worcestershire*, 2.31.
85. RCAHMW *Glamorgan, Early Castles*, 162-211; D'Elboux, 1923, 114-116.
86. RCAHMW *Glamorgan, Early Castles*, 274-288; Kenyon and Spurgeon 2001, 5-9, 42-45.
87. Randall 1928, 390.
88. *B/W Glamorganshire*, 477.
89. Binns 1989, 100-101.
90. Thurlby 1991.
91. Thurlby 2004d, 57-58, pl. VI.
92. Elliston-Erwood 1931, 247-254, plans on 251.
93. Stephen Heywood, 'The so-called tower-nave churches of Kent', in Malcolm Thurlby (ed.), *Romanesque Architecture in Great Britain and Ireland*, forthcoming.
94. Thurlby 2004d, pl. VII.
95. Ruprich-Robert 1884, 162.
96. Binns 1989, 103.
97. Binns 1989, 104.
98. Radford 1962, 7.
99. *AC*, 41; Pritchard 1907, 49; Redknap 2000, 101.
100. Radford 1962. See also, Pritchard 1907 and Clapham 1921.
101. Radford 1962, 8.
102. *B/W Pembrokeshire*, 433.
103. Radford 1962, 16.
104. The numbers are taken from Stuart Harrison's report for Cadw on the loose stonework at St Dogmael's abbey. I am grateful to Stuart Harrison for details of this report and images of the stones discussed here.
105. Radford 1962, 24.
106. Rigold 1977, 127.
107. Thurlby 1991b, ill on 43.
108. Thurlby 1995b, figs. 1 and 2.
109. Brakspear 1931.
110. Binns 1989, 64.
111. Thurlby 1999.
112. Thurlby 1999, 148-50.
113. Thurlby 1999, figs. 140 and 141.
114. Muthesius 1997, 97-98, pl. 50B.
115. The Morville font is illustrated by Bond 1908, 180.
116. Thurlby 1999, fig. 156.
117. Macalister 1922, 207.
118. Binns 1989, 113.
119. It is reproduced in *B/W Gwent/Monmouthshire*, 376.
120. Westwood 1879.
121. Westwood 1879.
122. Westwood 1879, 194.
123. Welander 1991, ills. on 54 and 55.
124. Binns 1989, 98.
125. Robinson 1996.

126. Robinson 1996, 39.
127. Richard 1927; RCAHMW *Glamorgan, Early Castles*, 314-26.
128. RCAHMW *Glamorgan, Early Castles*, 322-323, figs. 235 and 237; Richard 1927, fig. 7.
129. RCAHMW *Glamorgan, Early Castles*, 314.
130. RCAHMW *Glamorgan, Early Castles*, 316.
131. Colvin 1963, 578; VCH *Gloucestershire*, II, 74; Renn 1973, 117-18.
132. Binns 1989, 64-65; Birch 1897, 14-15.
133. Birch 1897, 14-15.
134. Butler 1984.
135. Collier 1925-1926; Robinson 1998, 204-05.
136. For a plan, see *B/W Glamorgan*, 424. Butler 1971, 393, fig. 4a, erroneously shows seven bays in the present nave.
137. Robinson 1998, 140.
138. Grose 1786, VII, ill. opp. 61. Carter's drawing is reproduced in Birch 1897, 89. See also, David 1929, 319.
139. Wilson 1978.
140. For examples in the Soissonais, see Lefevre-Pontalis 1894; and northern France, see Enlart 1895.
141. Wilson 1986; Thurlby 2000a, Thurlby, 2004e.
142. There is also a heavily restored example on the west doorway at Storgursey prory (Somerset).
143. *B/W Glamorgan*, 551.
144. Stalley 1979, 114, fig. 3
145. Stalley 1979, 115-16; Stalley 2000.
146. Newman 1995, 160.
147. RCAHMW, *Glamorgan, Early Castles*, 331. See also, Kenyon and Spurgeon 2001, 9.
148. Stalley 1971, 65-68; RCHME, *Dorset, West*, 64-66.
149. West 1988, 161-3. Stoneleigh chancel arch is illustrated in *VCH Warwickshire*, VI (1951), opp. 238.
150. Stalley 1971, 76-80.
151. *Hist. et Cart. Glouc.*, I, 109.
152. *VCH Wiltshire*, X (1975), 69-70.
153. John Goodall kindly supplied these examples and information on Dover castle. For Egremont, see Thurlby 2004b.
154. Thanks to Stephen Heywood for the examples at Bury St Edmunds and Wissington. For Bury St Edmunds, see Drewett and Stewart 1975/6, pl. XX; for High Ongar, see *B/E Essex*, ill. 6.
155. For Newcastle and Durham, see Halsey 1980, 68; for Dover and Canterbury, see Thurlby 2004, 157-58.
156. Colvin 1963, 650-51.
157. King and Perks 1970, 84.
158. Gerald of Wales, 151.
159. Gerald of Wales, 150. See map in King and Perks 1970, fig. 1.
160. King and Perks 1970, 95.
161. Wood 1965, 17-20.
162. Thompson 1912, 207-209; Wood 1965, 68.
163. Heslop 1991, 48, 57 n.27.
164. Binns 1989, 116.
165. Clark 1876; Clark 1884, II, 499-503; Radford 1960; Radford and Robinson 1986.
166. Renn 1961, 138-39.
167. Clark 1884, II, 500.
168. Radford and Robinson 1986, 24; Clark 1884, II, 501.
169. On the borough foundation, see Courtney 1994, 97-110; a marginally earlier date is preferred in Mein 1986.
170. The precise nature of the borough 'defenses' remains open. For a discussion of the evidence, and an analysis of the town plan, see Courtney 1994, 103-7.
171. The priory was said to be 'a flight shot' from the Castle by the Tudor antiquary, John Leland; see Smith (ed.) (1906), 50. The square keep at Usk is clearly a twelfth-century structure, and could possibly be pre-1174. The castle was greatly expanded by the Marshals in the early thirteenth century. For a fuller discussion, see Knight 1977.
172. Davies 1987, 181.
173. Wales was poorly served with Women religious. Apart from Usk, the only foundations of significance were the Cistercian nunneries at Llanllyr and Llanllugan. For the Cistercian houses, see Williams 1975.
174. Williams 1980.
175. The confirmation charter is British Library, Additional Charter 5342; it appears in *Monasticon*, IV, 591.
176. Confusion over the chronology of the de Clare family, and of Strongbow's identity, led Williams 1886 to suggest a date of about 1135 for the foundation. His interpretation must be dismissed, as must the analysis by Rickards 1904, 6-7, who was also confused over the descent of the de Clare family. Cowley 1977 chose to be cautious, concluding that the relevant member of the de Clare family could not be identified. He followed Dugdale in accepting a date of before 1236. Williams (1980), who at the time suggested a date of before 1135 for the foundation of the priory, seems to have followed Rickards in part.
177. Mein 1986, 35-45.
178. Crouch's note appears as an appendix in Courtney 1994, 110.
179. The arrangement is not unlike that at the somewhat earlier great tower at Chepstow castle (Knight 1991).
180. Mein 1992, 45.
181. Williams 1886.
182. Mein 1993.
183. Alas, there are no records of the 1964 'excavation'. The 'story' of the work was recounted to Mein by one of the excavators some twenty years later.
184. Maylan 1992, 32.
185. Gilchrist 1994, 97.
186. Clapham 1913; Baker 1969.
187. Gilchrist 1994, 118.
188. Gilchrist 1994, 52.
189. Interestingly, at Usk, the introduction of the brick

vault with ribs under the crossing after the dissolution demonstrates a continuation of the iconography of the rib set over the sanctuary area. On the construction of this later vault see Rickards 1904, 32, in which he corrects Williams 1886, 91, who believed it to be part of the original Romanesque fabric.
190. Swynnerton 1921.
191. Wilson 1978, 82.
192. The scene in question is the Confessor's funeral procession. On Romanesque Westminster see Gem 1980, where Terry Ball's reconstruction provides a striking illustration of the possible form of the crossing tower.
193. Taylor 1946-1947; Knight 1977; *B/W Gwent/Monmouthshire*, 589-91. I am grateful to Rosie Humphries and Jeremy Knight for much fruitful discussion on the fabric of Usk castle.
194. Knight 1977, 145-46.
195. Knight 1977, 149-50, fig. 3.
196. Knight 1977, 140-41.
197. Evans *et al*, 1982-1984, 50; *Monasticon*, VI, 128-34 at 129; Roberts 1847, 47-63 at 51-52.
198. *Giraldi Cambrensis Opera*, VI, ed. J.F. Dimock (Rolls Series, 1877), 37.
199. *Monasticon*, VI, 128-34; Roberts (1847), 47-63; *Opera*, VI, 37-41; Lovegrove (1942-43), 219.
200. Brakspear 1931.
201. Wilson 1978.
202. Binns 1989, 138; Lowe et al 1987; Thurlby 2004e.
203. Binns 1989, 157.
204. Rigold 1969.
205. Thurlby 2004a.
206. Hearn and Thurlby 1997.
207. Hearn and Thurlby 1997; Thurlby 1993; Thurlby 1996; Thurlby 1997.
208. Harrison and Thurlby 1997, 58-59.
209. Harrison and Thurlby 1997, 46.

Chapter 4 Church Architecture and Sculpture for Norman Patrons

1. *VCH Gloucester*, II, 53-54.
2. Caröe 1933, 389, reported that the 'archway had originally an inner order, but this is lost'.
3. Morgan 1885, 285-86.
4. Morgan 1885, 286.
5. Morgan 1885, 286.
6. Swarzenski 1967, fig. 121.
7. Deshman 1995, 45-54, pl. 19.
8. Caröe 1933, 389.
9. Newman 2000, 20.
10. Zarnecki 1953, 61, ill. 100; Thurlby 1982; Thurlby 2001
11. Edwards 2002, 237.
12. Edwards 2002, 234.
13. Gerald of Wales, 115, 223.
14. *B/W Gwent/Monmouthshire*, 114.
15. *B/W Gwent/Monmouthshire*, 382-83.
16. Lundgren and Thurlby 1999.
17. Lord 2003, pl. 169.
18. *B/W Gwent/Monmouthshire*, 398.
19. http://www.churchplansonline.org/show full image. asp?resource id=01224.tif
20. Stalley 1971; O'Keefe 2003, figs 91-93, 115, 119, 146 and 168.
21. Lord 2003, 70.
22. Lord 2003, 70 n.45.
23. Davies 2003, 193.
24. Davis-Weyer 1971, 21.
25. Henry 1965, pls 22 (Clonamery) and 23 (Fore).
26. Knight 1991.
27. *B/E Gloucestershire: The Vale and the Forest of Dean*, 19.
28. The church is illustrated in: http://www.churchcrawler.pwp.blueyonder.co.uk/churchcrawler/gwent.htm
29. Gardner 1917, 266.
30. Newman 2000, 21.
31. Gardner 1917, 258, 264-65. Kilpeck font is illustrated in Bond 1908, 150.
32. *B/E Gwent/Monmouthshire*, 329.
33. *B/W Glamorgan*, 549.
34. *Hist. et Cart. Glouc.*, I, 75.
35. Illustrated in Orrin 1988, 88.
36. Crook 2002, ill. 5.6.
37. For Harpole, see Bond 1908, ill. on 184; for Lichtenhagen, see Drake 2002, 93, pl. 190.
38. Krautheimer 1942.
39. Butler 1971, 385, related the Marcross capitals with the presbytery arch at Llandaff.
40. The Gloucester corbel is illustrated in Welander 1991, ill. on 87.
41. Thurlby 1999, figs 83, 85 and 89.
42. Newman 1995, 39, 420.
43. The font is illustrated in ill. Orrin 1988 opp. 325.
44. Orrin 1988, 287.
45. For illustrations, see Orrin 1988, 120, Colwiston, ext. S and int. to E; 197, Llandow, ext SE; 198, Llandow, int. to E; 418, Wick, ext. S and int. to E.
46. Orrin 1988, ill. on 38.
47. The St Lythans font is illustrated in Orrin 1988, 88.
48. RCAHMW *Glamorgan, Early Castles*.
49. Lewis 1845, 530.
50. *B/W Glamorgan*, 378.
51. Butler 1971, 384.
52. Lewis 1845, 71.
53. Knight 1976, 33, 40.
54. Knight 1976-78, 58-59.
55. Knight 1976-78, 43-46.
56. Knight 1976-78, 60-61; RCAHMW *Glamorgan, Early Castles*, 346.
57. Illustrated in Freeman 1850b, pl. opp. 41.
58. Maurice de Londres gave Oystermouth church to St Peter, Gloucester (*Hist et Cart. Glouc.*, 75-76).
59. Freeman 1850b, 55.
60. Orrin 1988, 358 gives a plan of St Fagans.

61. *B/W Glamorgan*, 401.
62. A sketch of the interior of the nave before rebuilding is reproduced by Lewis 1975, between 32 and 33.
63. *B/W Glamorgan*, 44, 401, 535. Lewis 1975 believed the font to be Norman.
64. Allen 1896.
65. Bond 1908, ill. on 40.
66. Westwood 1856, 287-288; Westwood 1876, 71.
67. Westwood 1856, 287n.
68. Rhys 1905, 62-63; Bond 1908, 127.
69. Tyrrell-Green 1918-19, 64-66.
70. Nash-Williams 1950, 79.
71. *B/W Powys*, 363-364; Lord 2003, 48-49.
72. *B/W Powys*, 317; Lord 2003, 48-49.
73. RCAHMW *Denbighshire*, 36.
74. Salter 1993, 47.
75. *B/W Clwyd*, 128.
76. http://www.cpat.demon.co.uk/projects/longer/churches/wrexham/16745.htm
77. Bond 1988, 145-147, figs 36-40.
78. Fenton 1811, 371.
79. RCAHMW, *Pembrokeshire*, fig. 60.
80. RCAHMW, *Pembrokeshire*, fig. 121.
81. Tyrrell-Green 1918-19, fig. 23; Tyrrell-Green 1928, 34, fig. 12.
82. Coffman and Thurlby 2001.
83. Lord 2003, 80.
84. Boak's unpublished research is reported by Lord 2003, 79-80.
85. Tyrrell Green 1928, 81, fig. 51; RCAHMW, *Pembrokeshire*, fig. 48ix.
86. Bond 1908, 151.
87. Bond 1908, ill. on 49.
88. RCAHMW, *Pembrokeshire*, fig. 154.
89. RCAHMW, *Pembrokeshire*, fig. 48ii.
90. RCAHMW, *Pembrokeshire*, fig. 48x.
91. RCAHMW, *Pembrokeshire*, fig. 48vi.
92. RCAHMW, *Pembrokeshire*, fig. 125.
93. RCAHMW, *Pembrokeshire*, fig. 48iv.
94. RCAHMW, *Pembrokeshire*, fig. 239A.
95. *Arch. Camb.*, ser. 5, 5 (1888), ill. opp. 132.
96. RCAHMW, *Pembrokeshire*, fig. 48ii.
97. RCAHMW, *Pembrokeshire*, fig. 48v.

Chapter 5 The Patronage of Gruffudd ap Cynan, Prince of Gwynedd

1. On Gruffudd ap Cynan, see most recently the entry by Huw Pryce in *Oxford DNB*, 24 (2004), 133-35 with full bibliography.
2. *ByT*, 117.
3. Jones 1910; Evans 1977; Evans 1990; Maund 1996.
4. Jones 1910, 155.
5. Jones 1910, 155-157.
6. *ByT*, 81.
7. *ByT*, 105.
8. Lewis 1996, 75 citing Jones 1910, 151-55.
9. Lewis 1996, 75.
10. *DNB*, V, 566; *Oxford DNB*, 15, 282-84 at 283.
11. Lewis 1996, 76.
12. Lewis 1996, 75; *DNB*, V, 565-67; *Oxford DNB*, 15, 282-84.
13. Lloyd 1912, 454-455; Barlow 1979, 84; Lewis 1996, 75.
14. *Oxford DNB*, 15, 283.
15. William of Malmesbury, *Gesta regum Anglorum*, II, (Oxford 1998), 498-99, 502.
16. Ó Riain-Raedel 2000, 326.
17. Jones 1910, 105; Pryce 2001, 789n.5.
18. Evans 1990, 81.
19. Lloyd 1912, 448.
20. Jones 1910, 82.
21. Hughes 1901, 185, claimed that the lower portion of the stair turret at the north-east angle of the north transept was Norman. This is not supported by the evidence in the fabric.
22. Scott 1870; Hughes 1901a; RCAHMW *Caernarvonshire, II, Central*, 1-9; Radford 1948-1949, 257-59.
23. Fernie 2000, 239-242; Gem 1989.
24. Fernie 1983, 97-101, 121-24.
25. Thurlby 1995a, 23-24.
26. Thurlby 2002, 255, figs. 16 and 17.
27. Gem 2000.
28. McKenna 1996, 135.
29. Hughes 1901a, 188-189.
30. Nash-Williams 1950, 86, cat. 79, fig. 64. Hughes 1901a, 182. I am indebted to Aimee Pritchard for bringing this and the related stone in Bangor cathedral to my attention.
31. Hughes 1901, 183, suggested that the slab 'may have formed part of the stem of an upright cross'. This would be most unusual.
32. O'Keeffe 2000, 315; O'Keeffe 2003.
33. Stalley 1981, 62-65; O'Keeffe 2003, 123-65.
34. Fernie 1993b.
35. Thurlby 1997b.
36. RCAHMW *Anglesey*, xci.
37. Thurlby 2002, 251-52.
38. Holme 1926, 26; RCAHMW *Anglesey*, 120. *The Builder*, November 3, 1855, 524, gives an account of the reopening of the church, and the work done 'in accordance with plans prepared by Messrs. Weightman, Hadfield, and Goldie, of Sheffield'. I owe *The Builder* reference to Peter Coffman. See also, Ellis 1855.
39. Holme 1926, 26-27.
40. Holme 1926, 26.
41. Hughes 1930b, 446; Jones 1849.
42. RCAHMW *Anglesey*, 120.
43. Radford 1961, 23.
44. Radford 1963, 367.
45. Lord 2003, 75.
46. Redknap 2000, 101.
47. Leask 1955, 36.

48. Nordenfalk 1977, pl. 28.
49. Nordenfalk 1977, pl. 4.
50. Henry 1970, pls 35 and 36.
51. Baxter, 'Barthomley'.
52. The restoration was by Messrs. Weightman, Hadfield and Goldie, of Sheffield, at a cost of about £1180: see *The Builder*, November 3, 1855, 524. I owe this reference to Peter Coffman.
53. Knight 1976-1978.
54. Lundgren and Thurlby 1999.
55. Holme 1930, 58, citing Bloxham 1859, 122.
56. Serbat 1908, 240.
57. Lefèvre-Pontalis 1908, 662 and pl. opp. 660 for Ver-sur-Mer and Basly.
58. Ruprich-Robert 1884 pls. XXXI and XXXIII.
59. Nash-Williams 1950, 123-25, cat. 182, pl. XXXVI.
60. Nash-Williams 1950, 167, cat. 276, pl. LX.
61. Baxter, 'St John's, Chester'.
62. Thurlby 1996, 155.
63. Stalley 1981, 62-65; O'Keeffe 2003, 161-65.
64. Baxter, 'Chester Cathedral'.http://www.crsbi.ac.uk/crsbi/frchsites.html
65. Baxter, 'Shotwick'.
66. *DB Cheshire*, A12.
67. Thacker 2000.
68. http://www.crsbi.ac.uk/crsbi/frchsites.html
69. Willis 1863, 93-94.
70. Kidson 1996, 131.
71. Bartrum 1966, 99. I owe this reference to Richard Gem.
72. Leask 1955, 36.
73. Lloyd 1912, 468.
74. Bond 1908, 99.
75. Nash Williams 1950, 51, cat. 1.
76. RCAHMW *Anglesey*, 121.
77. The Rhodo-Geidio font is illustrated in RCAHMW *Anglesey*, pl. 61.
78. The frontispiece of RCAHMW *Anglesey*, gives a general view of the island. RCAHMW Anglesey, 141-44.
79. http://www.anglesey-history.co.uk/places/penmon/
80. http://news.bbc.co.uk/1/hi/wales/1133023.stm
81. Edwards 1986.
82. Jones 1849, 129; RCAHMW *Anglesey*, 141.
83. Hughes 1901.
84. RCAHMW *Anglesey*, 141
85. Hughes 1930b, 248.
86. Hughes 1901, 90, and 1930b, 245.
87. Hughes 1901, 90.
88. Hughes 1901, 91.
89. Hughes 1901, 91-92.
90. Hughes 1901, 93.
91. Hughes 1901, 93.
92. Brown 1903, 162.
93. Cadw file AN 64.
94. Leask 1951, fig. 52.
95. Leask 1955, 38.
96. Leask 1955, 27, fig. 8. On Irish churches with stone roofs above barrel vaults, see O'Keeffe 2003, 87-91.
97. On holy wells, saints and churches, see Edwards 1994; Jones 1992.
98. Lord 2003, 21, fig. 8.
99. *B/W Pembrokeshire*, 491.
100. *B/W Clwyd*, 194. Jones 1992, 27, reports that at Ffynnon Gybi (Caern.) there is a 'building of dry stone walling and corbelled vaulting similar to early Irish cells'. The holy well at Llanllawer is located in a 'roughly vaulted chamber' (*B/E Pembrokeshire*, 25).
101. Lundgren and Thurlby 1999, which includes a list of examples.
102. Hughes 1930b, 245.
103. Hughes 1930b, 249.
104. RCAHMW *Anglesey*, 1, pl. 27.
105. Henry and Zarnecki 1957-1958.
106. Lord 2003, 63-64, cites the Nuns' Church at Clonmacnois in connection with the Aberffraw arch.
107. O'Keefe 2003, 262.
108. On the architecture of Dunfermline abbey, see Fernie 1994; for the west portal, see Cameron 1994.
109. Cameron 1994.
110. Garton 1981; Garton 2001.
111. Bradley and King 1985.
112. Sharret and Sharret 1985, pl. 102.
113. Baxter, 'Prestbury'.
114. RCAHMW *Anglesey*, 1; Lord 2003, 63.
115. The interior of the church is illustrated in RCAHMW *Anglesey*, pl. 34; plan on 1.
116. Lewis 1845, 16.
117. In a report on the visit of the Cambrians' visit to Aberffraw church, Harold Hughes discussed the possibility that the arch occupies its original position [*Arch. Camb.*, 85 (1930), 463].
118. Thurlby 2005.
119. The arch and tower were rebuilt in the seventeenth century but, as Pevsner pointed out, there is no space in the extant Norman fabric for a chancel arch (*B/E Northamptonshire*, 322). It must therefore be concluded that the arch led to the tower in the Norman church. See now, Ron Baxter, 'St Peter, Northampton, Northamptonshire', http://www.crsbi.ac.uk/crsbi/frnhsites.html
120. *B/E Northamptonshire*, 321.
121. Lloyd 1912, 231, 682; Jones 1910, 155; Moore 1996, 47; Caerwyn Williams 1996, 174, 184.
122. Lloyd 1912, 108; citing *Arch. Camb.*, I, I (1846), 62; Radford 1963, 367. Lord 2003, 63, observed that Aberffraw was the site of the court of Gruffudd ap Cynan but did not suggest that Gruffudd was the patron of the church. In the text he stated that the church was rebuilt in the first half of the twelfth century, and in the caption to the illustration of the arch gives a mid-twelfth-century date. RCAHMW *Anglesey*, suggested that the arch is late twelfth century.

123. Henry and Zarnecki 1957-1958; Baxter and Harrison 2002.
124. King 1990; King 1995; King 1996; Thurlby 2000b.
125. Lord 2003, 64, denies any influence from Norman sources in the Aberffraw arch.
126. Hughes 1930. 355.
127. Hughes 1930, 357.
128. Hughes 1930b, 249.
129. Hughes 1930b. 249.
130. Jones and Owen 2003, 59.
131. Hughes 1930b, 249. Skinner's watercolour of the Llanbabo south doorway is reproduced by Lord 2003, ill. 94.
132. Hughes 1930b, 249.
133. Ford 1970.
134. Thurlby 1999, figs 12 and 45.
135. *DNB*, V, 566; *Oxford DNB*, 15, 283..
136. Hughes 1923, 54.
137. Lord 2003, 50.
138. RCAHMW *Anglesey*, 21, 40.
139. Hughes 1923, 54.
140. Cone 1977, cat. 58.
141. Hughes 1924, 39.
142. Hughes 1924, 39.
143. Lasko 1972, 137, pl. 145.
144. Lasko 1972, 127.
145. Wallace and Ó Floinn 2002, 5.27, ills on 206 and 207.
146. Crosby 1972.
147. Thurlby 1982; Thurlby 2001.
148. Bond 1908, ill. on 44.
149. Thurlby 1995, figs 9 and 10.
150. Drake 2002, 86.
151. RCAHMW A*nglesey*, 107, pl. 59.
152. Lord 2003, 49; RCAHMW *Caernarvonshire*, III, 89.
153. Kermode 1907, 40; Lord 2003, 46, pls 48 and 49.
154. Wilson 1984, 143, pls 169 and 186.
155. Drake 2002, 157-158, pls 348 and 349.
156. Drake 2002, 104.
157. Wilson 1984, 209, pl. 271.
158. Radford 1963, 367.
159. Lord 2003, 49.
160. Lord 2003, 49.
161. Nash Williams 1950, 53, cat 4; RCAHMW *Anglesey*, 20.
162. RCAHMW *Anglesey*, 76, pl. 61.
163. Drake 2002, 25-26, pls. 47-49.
164. Hughes 1923, 60-62, figs 68 and 69.
165. RCAHMW *Anglesey*, cxxviii, 99, 114, pl. 62.
166. The Llanfair Caer Einion doorway is illustrated in *Arch. Camb.*, ser. 5, 2 (1885), 43.
167. Drake 2002, xv.
168. Lewis 1845, 481.
169. Lewis 1845, 239, 447.
170. Lewis 1855, 49.
171. Lewis 1855, 107.
172. Lewis 1855, 69.
173. Lewis 1845, 491.
174. Lewis 1855, 24.
175. Lewis 1855, 33.
176. Lewis 1855, 316.
177. Lewis 1855, 19.
178. Lewis 1855, 66.
179. Lewis 1855, 19.
180. Lewis 1855, 175, 237.
181. Lewis 1855, 23.
182. Lewis 1855, 260.
183. RCAHMW *Anglesey*, 97.
184. O'Keeffe 2003, 68.
185. Davis-Weyer 1971, 72.
186. O'Keeffe 2003, 69.
187. Herity 1993; O'Keefe 1998; O'Keeffe 2003, 69.
188. RCAHMW *Anglesey*, 32.
189. RCAHMW *Caernarvonshire*, II, 36-42, plan on 37.
190. Sharret and Sharret 1985, 261 (plan), 263-65.
191. RCAHMW *Anglesey*, 62 with plan.
192. *Arch. Camb.*, 1S, II (1847), 170-71.
193. RCAHMW *Anglesey*, 75 with plan.
194. Heitz 1963, 31, 43, 79-80, 144.

Chapter 6 Church Architecture, Shrines and Fonts for Welsh Patrons

1. *Hist. et Cart. Glouc.*, I, 106, II, 73-76; Lloyd 1912, 432.
2. Gerald of Wales, 180.
3. Gerald of Wales, 180.
4. Gerald of Wales, 180.
5. RCAHMW *Merioneth*, cat. 538, 170 inc. plan.
6. RCAHMW *Merioneth*, 170; Radford 358.
7. RCAHMW *Merioneth*, 170.
8. RCAHMW *Merioneth*, 170.
9. RCAHMW *Merioneth*, 170; Lord 2003, 61.
10. Lord 2003, 61, citing Bradley 1994, 9-32 esp. 17, lines 23-36, plus discussion in the Appendix.
11. McKenna 1996, 124; Jones and Owen 2003, 57.
12. McKenna 1996, 135.
13. McKenna 1996, 130.
14. http://www.cpat.demon.co.uk/projects/longer/churches/montgom/75.htm
15. For an aerial photograph of the churchyard, see http://www.cpat.demon.co.uk/projects/longer/churches/churches.htm
16. Henken 1987, 270; http://www.britannia.com/bios/ebk/tysilpw.html
17. Jones and Owen 2003, 46.
18. Wynne-Edwards 1871, xxiii.
19. Lewis 1855, 201.
20. Jones 1955, 133-135.
21. Lewis 1855, 201.
22. RCAHMW *Montgomeryshire*, 150.
23. Lewis 1855, 201.
24. Wynne-Edwards 1871, xxiv.
25. Kubach and Verbeek 1976, II, 1219-1231, figs 2156-2158 and 2165.

26. Kubach and Verbeek 1976, I, 582-594, figs, 974-976 and 979.
27. Kubach and Verbeek 1976, II, 801-807, figs 1344-1346.
28. Heitz 1963, 25, 79-80, 98.
29. Kubach and Verbeek 1976, I, 582; Plant 2003, 42-44.
30. Kubach and Verbeek 1976, I, 582; Plant 2003, 44.
31. Leo Hugot, *Kornelimünster. Untersuchung über die baugeschichtliche Entwicklung der ehemaligen Benediktinerklosterkirche* (Rheinische Ausgrabungen, II). Köln, Böhlau, 1968. Thanks to Hans Böker for this reference.
32. See above, 207-208.
33. See above, 191-192.
34. Taylor and Taylor 1965, 135, fig. 62; Fernie 1983, 44-45.
35. Fernie 1983, 42.
36. Davis-Weyer 1971, 21; Fernie 1983, 43.
37. Mackie 2003.
38. Sharret and Sharret 1985, 261 (plan), 263-265.
39. Manning 2000; O'Keeffe 2003, 71-72.
40. O'Keeffe 2003, 71-72.
41. Jones and Owen 2003, 49.
42. Cowley 1977, 231.
43. *ByT*, 183.
44. Williams 1889a; Williams 1889b; Williams 1892; Robinson and Platt 1992; Robinson 1998.
45. Williams 1889b, 30-31.
46. Stalley 1987, 84-87. In the late-twelfth-century presbytery of the parish church at Ledbury (Herefs.) the short columns of the main arcades sit on tall square plinths that read like reduced versions of the Strata Florida walls.
47. Stalley 1987, 182.
48. Stalley 1987, 86, fig. 29.
49. Reported in Robinson and Platt 1992, 46.
50. Radford 1949, 2; Robinson and Platt 1992, 30; Robinson 1998, 177.
51. Robinson and Platt 1992, 13, 30; Robinson 1988, 177.
52. Radford 1949, 2.
53. Robinson and Platt 1992, 49, Robinson 1998, 177.
54. See above, 126.
55. Evans 1995, ill on 14.
56. On the starting date of Wells cathedral, see Colchester and Harvey 1974; Draper 1995, 120; Thurlby 1997b, 31-32; Reeve 1998; Sampson 1998, 13; and Rodwell 2001, 130. On the basis of stylistic typology, Malone 2004a, 17-26, and Malone 2004b, 351-353, placed the start of construction around 1186, a view she had earlier expressed in her 1973 Ph.D. dissertation.
57. *B/E Herefordshire*, 68.
58. Stalley 1987, pls. 47 and 191.
59. Williams 1891; Williams 1892; Robinson, 1998, 179-180.
60. Williams 1891, pl. 15.
61. Williams 1891, pls 4, 5, 12 and 13.
62. Tyrrell Green 1913, 19.
63. Bond 1908, ills on 54 (Shobdon), 110 (Stafford), and 177 (Hereford). For Sutton, see RCHME, *Herefordshire, II, East*, pl. 54.
64. Drake 2002, 59-60, fig. 123.
65. Bond 1908, 110.
66. Barber 1993, 24-25.
67. Krautheimer 1942; Thurlby 1982a.
68. Tyrrell Green 1913, 15. The comparison was earlier made by Meyrick 1808, 223. Green 1913, 17, and Green 1928, 81, stated that the Henfynyw font is in the porch of Holy Trinity church Aberaron, and this is repeated by Lord 2003, 79 note 66, but the font is now returned to Henfynyw.
69. Tyrrell Green 1914, 19; Tyrrell-Green 1918-19, 67-70; Tyrrell-Green 1928, 81-82.
70. Tyrrell Green 1913, 21, ill. 6.
71. Tyrrell Green 1928, 66; Lord 2003, 85, pl. 111, illustrates all four symbols.
72. Lord 2003, 85.
73. Lord 2003, 83.
74. Tyrrell Green 1914, 21, ill. 13.
75. Drake 2002, 39, 41 n.19, ill 76.
76. RCAHMW, *Radnorshire*, xx.
77. Lloyd 1937, 66.
78. Thurlby 1997c; Whittingham 1970.
79. RCAHMW *Merioneth*, 148 cat 483, fig. 24, dates the Llanmawddy font C14; Til-Châtel (Côte d'Or) is illustrated in Drake 2002, fig. 144.
80. Reported by V. Cotterill Scholefield, clerk of works, in Rowley-Morris 1891, 384.
81. Scholefield in Rowley-Morris 1891, 384.
82. Scholefield in Rowley-Morris 1891, 383.
83. *B/W Powys*, 113; http://www.cpat.demon.co.uk/projects/longer/churches/montgom/16413.htm
84. Gethyn-Jones 1979.
85. Jordan 1911.
86. Thurlby 1999, figs. 24 and 25.
87. Keyser 1911.
88. Thurlby 1999, fig. 54.
89. Tyrrell Green 1928, 19.
90. Lord 2003. 48.
91. RCAHMW *Caernarvonshire, III, West*, 1-2, plan, fig. 40; Ellis 1951, 7.
92. O'Keeffe 2003, 68-71.
93. RCAHMW *Caernarvonshire, III, West*, 1.
94. Nash-Williams 1950, 168-170, cat. 281.
95. Nash-Williams 1950, 167, cat. 276.
96. Gem 1987.
97. Nash-Williams 1950, 123-125, cat. 182.
98. For Beckermet St Bridget and Gosforth, see Bailey and Cramp 1988, 54-60, 100-104, ills. 41-46, ills. 288-308. See also Kendrick 1949, pls. XLIV and XLVII, and pl. XLVI for Clulow and Stapleford.
99. RCAHMW *Flint*, 23, cat. 77; Nash-Williams 1950, 126-127, cat. 185 and 186.
100. Harrison and Barker 1999.
101. Lord 2003, fig. 174.
102. Lord 2003, figs. 90 and 169.

103. Drake 2002, 46-59; King 2002.
104. RCAHMW, *Denbighshire*, 50.
105. Tyrrell-Green, 1918-19, 52-53; Tyrrell Green 1928, 139-140. Tangmere font is illustrated in Drake 2002, pl. 10.
106. Thurlby 1982; for Eydon, see Drake 2002, pl. 53, for Flitwick, see Hazel Gardiner, 'St Peter and St Paul, Flitwick, Bedfordshire', http://www.crsbi.ac.uk/crsbi/frbdsites.html
107. Drake 2002, 28; pl. 56 for Abbotsham.
108. Heaton and Britnell 1994, 106, 109-110; Britnell and Watson 1994, 165; Crook 2000, 279-281.
109. Crook 2000, 276-77, fig. 107.
110. Radford and Hemp 1959.
111. Radford and Hemp 1959.
112. Heaton and Britnell 1994, 109.
113. Britnell and Watson 1994, 158.
114. Stalley 1971.
115. Hope 1913-14, 115, fig. 11.
116. Tyrrell Green 1914, 11, ill. 8.
117. Tyrrell Green 1918-19, 75.
118. Tyrrell Green 1918-19, 75.
119. Tyrrell Green 1928, 34, fig. 12.
120. Tyrrell Green 1914, 19, ill. 12.

Chapter 7 St. Davids Cathedral
1. Thurlby 2000a.
2. Stalley 2002, 40.
3. *B/W Pembrokeshire*, 40
4. *B/W Pembrokeshire*, 388.
5. Brakspear 1931.
6. See above, 292-294.
7. *AC*, 55.
8. Brewer 1861, VI, 110; Gerald 1978, 169.
9. Brewer 1861, I, 84-85, III, 71, 285.
10. *AC*, 61.
11. *AC*, 75.
12. *AC*, 87.
13. Jones and Freeman 1856,
14. Jones and Freeman 1856.
15. Scott 1862, 6.
16. *The Builder*, 53 (Dec. 3, 1892), 440-42.
17. Lovegrove 1926, 257, 261.
18. Lovegrove 1926, 261.
19. Lovegrove 1926, 261.
20. Lovegrove 1926, 271.
21. Lovegrove 1926, 262-263.
22. Lovegrove 1926, 271.
23. Boase 1953, 222.
24. Webb 1956, 87.
25. Webb 1956, 92.
26. Webb 1956, 93.
27. Tatton-Brown 1989, 73.
28. Stalley in *B/W Pembrokeshire*, 392-400.
29. Jones and Freeman 1856, 142.
30. Scott 1863, 78.
31. King 1873, 114; Robson 1901, 23; Lovegrove 1926, 264-265.
32. Bond 1912, 468; Bond 1913, 321, n1.
33. Lovegrove 1922, 370.
34. Lovegrove 1922, 370.
35. Evans and Worsley 1981, 63.
36. Webb 1956, 92-3.
37. Tatton-Brown 1989, 73.
38. Hearn and Thurlby 1997, 52; Draper 1999, 111-12.
39. Bony 1949, 12.
40. Thurlby 2003b.
41. Scott 1862, 4.
42. Lovegrove 1922.
43. Brakspear 1931, 16.
44. Boase 1953, 222.
45. Draper 1999; Stalley 2002.
46. Brakspear 1931,
47. Evans and Worsley 1981, 39-43, figs. 17-24.
48. Thurlby 1985, 47-8; Thurlby 1993, 49-50.
49. The uninterrupted coursing of the rubble masonry above the high-vault capitals at Llanthony does not support Stalley's contention that stone vault springers have been removed.
50. Stalley 2002, fig. 19.
51. Stalley 2002; see above,
52. Thurlby 1985, 40, pl. VIIIA.
53. Thurlby 2003b, fig. 7.
54. Lovegrove 1926, 260.
55. Brakspear 1931, pls IA and XI.
56. Stalley 2000, 62.
57. Wilson 1978, 85-86.
58. Thurlby and Kusaba 1991.
59. Gardner 1956; Lowe 1987, 120, fig. 37.
60. Thurlby 1976; Thurlby 1995b.
61. Stalley 1971; Stalley 1981; Stalley 1987.
62. Colchester and Harvey 1974; Thurlby 1997c.
63. Stalley 2002, 32.
64. The inner north porch at St Mary Redcliffe, Bristol, probably dates from around 1200, but it has nothing in common with the work at St Davids.
65. Stalley in *B/W Pembrokeshire*, 399.
66. Thurlby 1995e; Thurlby and Baxter 2002.
67. Crossley 1987, 69; Crossley 1988
68. Carley 1988, 111.
69. Pre- and post-restoration photographs are conveniently juxtaposed in Robson 1901, 56-57.
70. Brakspear 1931, 16.
71. Thurlby 1991a.
72. Thurlby 2000b.
73. Thurlby 1995a, pl. IIC.
74. Evans 2003.
75. Stalley in *B/W Pembrokeshire*, 397.
76. Draper 1999, 106-109.
77. Thurlby 1994c.
78. Draper 1995; Draper, 1999, 107.
79. Willis 1845.
80. Draper 1999, 106-109.

Epilogue
1. See above, Chapter 5.

Index

Aachen, palace chapel 43-43
Abbey Cwmhir (Radnor) 118, 343
Abbotsbury (Dorset) 308
Aberdaron, St Hywyn (Gwynedd) 270-271
Aberffraw, St Beuno (Anglesey) 213-218, 222
Abergavenny, St Mary (Gwent) 4, 172
Aberporth (Cardigan) 280
Ahun, St-Sylvain (Creuse) shrine 276
Aiziers (Eure) 206
Alexander, Bishop 275
Allen, J. Romilly 182
Ambleston (Pemb.) 188
Amroth (Pemb.) 188
Angle (Pemb.) 188
Anglo-Saxon influences 16, 31, 34, 35, 43-44, 45, 65, 162, 175, 183, 194
Anguerny, St-Martn (Calvados) 206
Anselm, Abbot 129
Ardfert cathedral (Kerry) 19
Astley (Worcs.) 63
Attleborough (Norfolk) 31
Avington (Berks.) 128
Aylesbury group 164, 275
Aymestrey (Herefs.) 255

Baltinglass (Wicklow) 252
Bangor cathedral 193-196, 243, 244, 245
Bampton (Oxon) 226
Bapchild, St Lawrence (Kent) 105
Barfreston (Kent) 69
Barker, Philip 34, 44
Barking nunnery (Essex) 144
Barnack (Northants.) 217
Barrow (Salop) 63
Bartholmley, St Botoline (Cheshire) 201
Basly, St-Georges (Calvados) 206
Bassaleg (Gwent) 165
Baxter, Ron 208
Bayeux 32
Bayvil (Pemb.) 188
Beaumais (Calvados) 16, 17, 67, 224
Beckermet, St Margaret (Cumbria) 272
Beckford (Worcs.) 140
Beckington (Somerset) 309
Begelly (Pemb.) 188
Belstone (Herefs.) 221
Bernard, Bishop of St Davids 107, 118, 191, 284, 336
Bernay abbey (Eure) 30, 31, 34
Bettws Bledrws, St Bledrws (Cardigan) 257
Bettws Newydd (Gwent) 172
Bewcastle (Cumbria) cross 224
Bindon abbey (Dorset) 336
Binham priory (Norfolk) 31
Bishop's Cleeve (Glos.) 42, 103, 335
Blithere 43
Blois, Bishop Henry of 103, 275, 310, 343
Blyth priory (Notts.) 37, 38, 57, 67, 102, 187

Boase, T.S.B. 287
Bond, Francis 183, 210, 287
Bony, Jean 388
Boothby Pagnell (Lincs.) 132
Bosham, Holy Trinity (Sussex) 34-35, 36
Bowdon, St Mary (Cheshire) 64
Boyle abbey (Roscommon) 256
Bradford-on-Avon, St Laurence (Wilts.) 59
Brakspear, Harold 46, 111, 288, 333
Bramber (Sussex) 100
Brawdy (Pemb.) 188
Brecon priory (now cathedral) 111-113, 164
    St Mary 182-183, 269
Bredon (Worcs.) 308, 335
Bredon-on-the-Hill (Leics.) 69
Bredwardine, St Andrew (Herefs.) 61-63, 64, 65, 66, 67, 116-117, 172
Breteuil castle 16
Brewood priory (Staffs.) 145
Bridstow (Herefs.) 38, 48
Brinkburn (Northumberland) 100
Brinsop (Herefs.) 47
Bristol cathedral (St Augustine's) 83, 84, 310, 314, 315, 260
    St Mary Redcliffe 313, 314, 315
    St James' priory 309, 255
    St Philip & St Jacob 188
Brough castle (Cumbria) 133
Brown, Gerald Baldwin 211
Bruera, St Mary (Cheshire) 217
Buildwas abbey (Salop) 145, 156, 255
Burton (Pemb.) 188
Burton Agnes (Yorks.) 132
Burry Holms (Glamorgan) 180
Bury St Edmunds abbey 31, 129
Butler, Lawrence 93
Buttington (Salop) 256

Cadwaladr 107
Caen (Calvados), Exchequer 27, 65, 128
    La Trinité / Abbaye-aux-Dames 17, 31, 38, 39
    Saint-Etienne 34, 37, 38, 39, 70, 87, 146, 156
    Saint-Nicholas 17, 34, 35
Caerleon (Gwent) 19, 29, 121, 164-165
Caerwent (Gwent) 19
Caldicot, St Mary (Gwent) 165-166
Cambridge, St Benet's 16, 217
    St Radegard's 145
Cambridge, Eric 43
Camden Society 75
Campania, S. Agata dei Goti 63
Camrose (Pemb.) 188
Canterbury, St Augustine's 43, 335
    St Peter and St Paul 248
    cathedral 34, 9, 106, 129, 156, 321, 337, 341, 343
Capel Lligwy (Anglesey) 211, 234

377

Cardiff castle 129
Carlisle cathedral 208
Caröe, W.D. 162
Carter, John 98, 99
Cashel, Cormac's chapel (Tipperary) 38, 39, 80, 81, 82,
    108, 109, 196, 205, 207, 208, 209, 211, 216,
    221, 225, 342
Castle Frome (Herefs.) 62, 66, 91, 171
Castle Hedingham (Essex) 15, 140, 156
Castle Rising (Norfolk) 91, 140, 166, 206, 212
Castlemartin (Pemb.) 187, 188
Castlemorton (Worcs.) 62
Cava dei Tirreni abbey, nr. Salerno 70
Cenarth (Cardigan) 258, 259
Centual, St Riquier 248
Cerisy-la-Fôret (Calvados) 65, 187
Cerrigceinwen, St Ceinwen (Anglesey) 228, 229, 231,
    232
Chaddesley Corbett (Worcs.) 72
Charlemagne 41
Chartres cathedral 296
Chatillon-sur-Seine (Côte d'Or), St Vorles 194
Chelwood (Somerset) 188
Chepstow 3-4
    castle 3, 129, 343-344
        great tower 4-20, 64, 65, 67, 103, 132
        priory 3, 20-40, 87, 88, 121, 162
Chesney, Bishop Robert of London 275
Chester cathedral (St Werburgh's) 103, 195, 202, 207,
    209
    St John's 31, 48, 79, 145, 206, 208, 216, 217,
    222
Chichester cathedral 35
Chirk, St Mary (Denbigh) 185-187
Christchurch (nr. Newport, Gwent) 166
Christchurch priory (Dorset) 40, 101, 132
Christon (Somerset) 206, 212
Churton (Wilts.) 128
Cistercian architecture in Wales 120-121, 249, 256
Clapham, Sir Alfred 22, 44-45
Clark, G.T. 136, 137
Clayton (Sussex) 31
Clermont abbey (Mayenne) 121
Clocaenog (Denbigh) 280
Clonfert cathedral 279
Clonmacnois cathedral (Offaly) 235, 271
    nuns' church 215-216
    Teampill Chiarmin 235
Clovelly (Devon) 187
Clulow (Cheshire) 272
Clun (Salop) 270
Clwyd-Powys Archaeological Trust 185
Clynnog Fawr (Gwynedd) 236
Cogan, St Peter (Glamorgan) 51, 56
Colchester castle 15
    priory 38
Cologne, St Pantaleon 42, 248
Colvington (Glamorgan) 56
Colwinston (Glamorgan) 178

Compton (Surrey) 70
Copford, St Mary the Virgin (Essex) 22
Corfe castle (Dorset) 35
Cork cathedral 216
Cormeilles abbey (Eure) 20
Corrington (Lincs.) 217
Corvey abbey 19
Corwen cross 206, 271-272
Coxe, William 20, 23, 113, 115
Crick (Northants.) 225
Croxdale (Co. Durham) 65
Crouch, David 142
Cullompton, St Andrews (Devon) 102
cushion capitals, Anglo-Saxon or not? 43-44
Cwmyoy, St Martin (Gwent) 171
Cyfeliog, Owain 256
Cynddelw 245, 248

Dalmeny, St Cuthbert (Lothian) 216
damliac (stone church) tradition 234-235
Davington priory (Kent) 30
de Ballon, Hamelin 4
    Berthune, Bishop Robert of Hereford 85
    Breteuil, Roger 20
    Chandos, Robert 117
    Clare, Richard fitz Gilbert (Strongbow) 140, 142
    Glanville, Richard 177
    Lacy, Hugh 40
        Roger 40
        Walter 40, 47
    Leia, Bishop Peter 285, 337
    Londres, Maurice 92, 93, 104, 105
        William 92, 93, 104, 105
    Losinga, Bishop Robert 29
    Luffa, Bishop Ralph 35
    Montgomery, Arnulph 106
    Neufmarché, Bernard 111, 135
Deerhurst priory (Glos.) 34, 69, 79, 233
Defynnog, St Cynog (Brecon) 184
Devizes, St John's (Wilts.) 80
Dimock, James 32-33
Dinas (Pemb.) 188
Diocletian's Palace, Split 14, 18
Diserth, St Fraid (Flint) 224, 272, 273, 274
Dixton, St Peter (Gwent) 56
Domfront, Notre-dame-sur-L'Eau (Orne) 39, 100, 128,
    194
Dorchester abbey (Oxon) 37, 128
Dore abbey (Herefs.) 145, 156, 256, 307
Dover castle (Kent) 129
    St Mary-in-Castro 31, 100, 156
Drake, C.S. 228
Draper, Peter 288, 337
Dublin, Christ Church cathedral 126, 308, 310
Dugdale, William 92
Dunblane cathedral 105
Dunfermline abbey 216
Durham castle 17
    cathedral 28, 34, 39, 101, 102, 129, 196, 304,

378

335, 337
Dymock, St Mary's (Glos.) 47, 48, 62, 66, 103, 139, 140
Dymock School of Sculpture 48, 61, 227

Eardisley (Herefs.) 89
Earls Barton (Northants.) 35, 43, 236
East Dean, St Simon & St Jude (Sussex) 105
Edvin Loach (Herefs.) 54
Edward the Confessor 31
Efenechidyn, St Michael (Denbigh) 275
Egremont castle (Cumbria) 128
Eliseg Pillar (Denbigh) 206, 272
Elkstone (Glos.) 221, 308
Elstow nunnery (Beds.) 29, 144
Ely cathedral 34, 128, 274, 335
Ernisius, chaplain to Queen Matilda 148
Esley, Saint-André (Lorraine) 44
Evans, Wyn 336
Ewenny priory 39, 92-104, 122, 145, 156, 174, 207, 243, 245, 308, 309
Exeter castle 43
    cathedral 82, 105, 109
        tomb of William Marshal 274
Eynsford (Kent) 18

Fardd, Llewelyn 244
Fernie, Eric 43
Ferrey, Benjamin 247
fitz Baderon, William(s) 84, 85, 92
    Hamon, Robert 57, 92, 127
    Martin, Robert 107
    Osbern, William 4, 5, 16, 17, 18, 20, 39, 40
    Richard, Walter 117
    Stephen, Robert 247
Findern (Derbs.) 65
Flaxley abbey 308
Fleece Hotel, Gloucester 46
Fontenay (Côte d'Or) 119, 120, 124, 125
Forde abbey (Dorset) 336
Fordwich (Kent) 175
Forthampton (Glos.) 221
Fountains abbey (Yorks.) 120, 145
Fownhope (Herefs.) 89
Freeman, Edward A. 22
Freystrop (Pemb.) 188
Froville (Lorraine) 44
Fulchard, Abbot 107
Furneaux 257

Gardner, Illtyd 172
Gem, Richard 43, 208
Gerald of Wales 130, 165, 180, 285
Gervase 337
giant or colossal order, the 45
Gilchrist, Roberta 144
Glastonbury abbey 29, 38, 39, 110, 133, 140, 156, 166, 288, 304, 305, 310, 311, 313, 321, 327, 336, 337, 343
    Lady Chapel 225

Glendalough, St Kevin (Wicklow) 212
    St Saviour and Trinity 69
Gloucester abbey/cathedral, St Peter's 28, 31, 32, 37, 38, 40, 42, 46, 47-48, 57, 79, 85-86, 87, 89, 100, 101, 103, 108, 115, 134, 140, 145, 159, 162, 163, 166, 170, 174, 176, 177, 195, 220, 241, 243, 263, 267, 304, 307, 309, 335
    St Nicholas 103
    St Oswald's priory 79
Gloucester, Miles of 48
Gnosall (Staffs.) 103
Godmersham (Kent) 18, 105
Goetre, St Peter (Gwent) 172
Goldcliffe (Gwent) 117
Goodrich castle (Herefs.) 47, 62, 89, 91, 140
Gosforth (Cumbria) 221, 222, 227, 272
Gothic, arrival of 343-344
grave church tradition 275-276
Graville-Ste-Honorine (Seine-Maritime) 17, 38
Great Clacton (Essex) 39
Great Durnford (Wilts.) 221
Great Kimble (Bucks.) 164
Great Malvern priory (Worcs.) 243
Great Paxton (Hunts.) 16, 31, 33
Great Salkold, St Cuthbert (Cumbria) 213, 216
Great Tey (Essex) 146
Great Washbourn (Glos.) 64
Grose, Francis 98
Gruffudd ap Cynan 191-193, 196, 207-208, 209, 218, 220, 221, 222, 233, 234, 237-238, 245, 247, 248, 274
Gumfreston (Pemb.) 187
Gwaunysgor, St Mary (Flints) 274-275
Gwynedd, Owain 107, 197, 234

Haddon, Arthur West 92
Hadstock, St Botolphs (Essex) 35
Hague, D.B. 93
Hampton Bishop (Herefs.) 64, 67
Haroldston West (Pemb.) 188
Harpole (Northants.) 175
Harrison, J. Park 45
    Stuart 253
Haslam, Richard 184
Hatfield, St Leonard's (Herefs.) 17, 18, 269
Haughmond abbey (Salop) 126, 145
Haycastle (Pemb.) 188
Heath, Charles 21
Heath chapel (Salop) 186
Heddon-on-the-Wall (Northumberland) 101
Heneglwys (Anglesey) 220-222, 224, 225, 227, 228, 308
Henfynyw, St David (Cardigan) 257
Hemel Hempstead, St Mary's (Herts.) 146
Hemp 276, 278
Henry I, King 191, 194
    II, King 129
Henry IV, Holy Roman Emperor 208
    V 192

Henry (of Abergavenny), Bishop 84
Henry (of Warwick), Lord of Gower 105
Henry's Moat (Pemb.) 187
Hensley, Rev. E.J. 22, 27
Herbrandston (Pemb.) 188
Hereford, bishop's chapel 19, 29, 37, 38, 39, 42, 44, 62,
    80, 103, 105, 119, 134
   cathedral 27, 28, 37, 38, 48, 65, 79, 80, 82,
    88, 898, 109, 194, 208,
    222, 335, 336
Herefordshire School of Sculpture 61, 72, 89-90, 111-
   113, 163, 168, 269, 310
Hervé, Bishop of Bangor 85, 193
Heywood, Stephen 105
High Ongar (Essex) 128, 129
Hinton Blewett (Somerset) 188
Hoare, Sir Richard Colt 113
Hodgeston (Pemb.) 188
Holme, G.G. 196, 206
Holy Roman Empire 44, 191, 192, 194, 242
Holyhead, St Cybi (Anglesey) 218, 235
Hough-on-the-Hill (Lincs.) 17
Hubbard, Edward 212
Hubberston (Pemb.) 188
Hughes, Harold 195, 196-197, 210, 211, 213, 224
Huy, Notre-dame 43

Idwal, Prior of Penmon 197, 207, 208
Iffley (Oxon.) 35
Instow (Devon) 187
Inwardleigh (Devon) 187
Iona, St Oram 216, 236, 248

James, J.H. 81-82
Jedburgh abbey 321
Jeffreyston (Pemb.) 188
Jerpoint (Kilkenny) 252, 255
Jervaulx abbey 335
John, King 254
Johnston (Pemb.) 188
Jones & Freeman 285, 287
Jordanston (Pemb.) 188
Jumièges abbey 31, 41, 42

Kells, St Columba's House 211
Kempley (Glos.) 48, 103, 145, 177
Kempsford (Glos.) 221
Kencott (Oxon.) 65
Kendrick, Sir Thomas 45
Kenfig castle (Glamorgan) 118, 129, 156
   St Mary Magdaleine 175, 178
Kenilworth, St Nicholas (Warwks.) 117
Kermode 227
Kerry, St Michael's (Montgomery) 145, 261-263
Keynsham abbey 29, 125, 126, 156, 308, 310, 312, 313
Keyser, Charles E. 65, 269
Kidson, Peter 40
Kidwelly (Carmarthen) 80
Kilkhampton, St James (Cornwall) 216

Killaloe, St Flannan's Oratory (Clare) 197, 208
Kilmalkedar cathedral (Kerry) 216
   81, 205, 211
Kilpeck (Herefs.) 38, 47, 69, 72, 89, 91, 112, 163, 172,
   176, 177, 269
King, Richard 81
Kingston Seymour (Somerset) 187
Kinlet (Salop) 47, 62
Kirk Michael, Giants Cross (Isle of Man) 227
Kirkburn (Yorks.) 129
Kirkstall abbey (Yorks.) 39, 120, 145, 156
Knight, Jeremy 146, 147, 206
Knook, St Margarets (Wilts.) 44, 45
Kornelimunster, nr Aachen 248

Lambston (Pemb.) 188
Lampeter (Cardigan) 259
Lampeter Velfrey (Pemb.) 188
Lamphey (Pemb.) 188
Lanfranc, Archbishop 34
Langeais castle (Indre-et-Loire) 133
Langford (Oxon.) 166, 206, 212
L'Asne, Hugh 18, 20
Lastingham priory (Yorks.) 100, 187
Lawrenny (Pemb.) 187
Leask, Harold 197, 211
Leckhampstead (Bucks.) 64, 65
Ledbury (Herefs.) 88, 335
Leland, John 92, 180
Leominster priory (Herefs.) 30, 103, 194, 277
Leonard Stanley (Glos.) 100, 145, 336
Lessay abbey (Manche) 39
Letton, St John the Baptist (Herefs.) 61, 63, 64, 65, 66
Lewis, Samuel 179, 217, 247
Lichfield cathedral 156
Lichtenhagen (Germany) 175
Lilleshall priory (Salop) 129, 145, 156
Limburg-an-der-Hardt 43
Lincoln cathedral 39, 40
Lindisfarne priory 28, 39, 304
Linley (Salop) 113
Lion-sur-mer (Calvados) 106
Little Newcastle (Pemb.) 188
Little Trefgarn (Pemb.) 118
Llanaber (Gwynedd) 343
Llanarth (Cardigan) 256, 257
Llanbabo (Anglesey) 218, 219-220, 221, 231, 233, 234
Llanbadarn Fawr (Cardigan) 241, 245
Llanbadarn Fawr, St Padarn (Radnor) 267-269
Llanbadrig, St Padrig (Anglesey) 225, 233
Llanbeulan (Anglesey) 222-224, 227, 231, 233
Llancarfan, St Cadoc (Glamorgan) 51, 57
Llandaff cathedral 51, 75-84, 105, 114, 115, 117, 129,
   175, 176, 177, 182, 259, 308, 341
   dedication of 84
Llandenny, St John (Gwent) 170
Llandeussant (Anglesey) 224-225
Llandew, St David (Brecon) 51, 58, 59, 60, 61, 66
Llandew, Holy Trinity & St David (Gwent) 172-173

Llandewi Skirrid, St David (Gwent) 173, 174
Llandewi Velfrey (Pemb.) 188
Llandewi Ystradenni, St David (Radnor) 269-270
Llandough, St Dochdwy (Glamorgan) 179-180
Llandow (Glamorgan) 56, 178
Llandrillo-yn-Rhos, Capel Trillo (Denbigh) 212
Llandrinio, St Trinio, St Peter & St Paul (Montgomery) 264-265
Llandyssiliog, St Tyssilio (Cardigan) 258, 259
Llanegryn, St Egryn (Merioneth) 260, 261
Llaneillian (Anglesey) 225-226
Llanelly (Gwent) 174
Llaneugrad (Anglesey) 234, 236
Llanfair Caer Einion (Montgomery) 232
Llanfair Cilgedin (Gwent) 174
Llanfair Clydogan, St Mary (Cardigan) 259
Llanfairgynghornwy (Anglesey) 236
Llanfair-yn-Neubyll, St Mary (Anglesey) 229-230
Llanfair ym Cwmws (Anglesey) 231
Llanfechain, St Garmon (Montgomery) 265-267
Llanfilo, St Bilo (Brecon) 51, 58, 59, 61, 66
Llanfihangel Abercywyn (Carmarthen) 167, 274
Llanfihangel Pontymoile (Gwent) 174
Llanfihangel-y-Pennant, St Michael (Merioneth) 260, 261
Llanfihangel-y-Traithau, St Michael (Merioneth) 271
Llanfihangell Ystrad (Cardigan) 280
Llanfinnian, St Finnian (Anglesey) 230, 234
Llangadwaladwr (Anglesey) 234
Llangaffo, St Caffo (Anglesey) 228-229, 232, 233
Llangefni, St Cyngar (Anglesey) 231
Llangeinwen, St Ceinwen (Anglesey) 232, 233
Llangennith, St Cennydd (Glamorgan) 105-106, 181
Llangoedmore (Cardigan) 280
Llangollen, shrine 278
Llangristiolus (Anglesey) 228, 229, 233, 274
Llangwm (Gwent) 174
Llangwm (Pemb.) 188
Llangwyfan (Anglesey) 234, 235
Llangwyllog, St Cweyllog (Anglesey) 231, 232
Llanhowell (Pemb.) 188
Llanidan, St Idan (Anglesey) 232, 233, 234
Llaniestyn, St Jestyn (Anglesey) 226-227, 233
Llanllwchaiarn (Cardigan) 259
Llanlowell, St Lywell (Gwent) 51, 58, 66, 67
Llanmadoc (Glamorgan) 180-181
Llanreithan (Pemb.) 188
Llanrhaeadr-ym-Mochant, St Dogfan 278
Llanrhidian, St Rhidian and St Illtyd (Glamorgan) 51, 58, 67-71
Llanrwst, St Grwst (Denbigh) tomb of Llewelyn ab Iorwerth 274
Llansantffraed (Cardigan) 257
Llansantffraed, St Bridget (Gwent) 172
Llanstinian (Pemb.) 188
Llanthony priory (Gwent) 111, 145, 148-156, 305, 306, 307, 309
Llantilio Crosseny, St Teilo (Gwent) 172
Llantrisant (Anglesey) 232, 233
Llantrisant (Glamorgan) 181, 182

Llantwit Major (Glamorgan) 51, 71-72, 175, 274
Llantysilio yn Ial (Denbigh) 279
Llanvapley, St Mable (Gwent) 173
Llanwenarth (Gwent) 174
Llanwenog, St Gwenog (Cardigan) 258, 259
Llanwrthwl (Brecon) 259, 260
Llanymawddwy, St Tydecho 260, 261
Llechcynfarwg, St Andrew (Anglesey) 228-229, 232, 234
Lloyd, Thomas 218, 284
Llyswynny, St Tydfil (Glamorgan) 51, 58, 60, 66, 67, 71
Loches (Indre-et-Loire) 39
London cathedral 335
Londres, Sir John 92
Longtown castle (Herefs.) 80
Longueville Jones, H. 197, 210
Lord, Peter 368, 227, 232, 244, 259, 269, 274
Lorsch gatehouse 19, 33
Lovegrove, E.W. 81, 82, 287, 288, 307
Ludlow castle 62, 147
    chapel 47-48, 103, 206
    great tower 40-47, 80
Lullington (Somerset) 168
Lynam, Charles 22

Maestir, St Mary (Cardigan) 259
Magor, St Mary (Gwent) 171
Malmesbury abbey 42, 83, 108, 117, 140, 145, 221, 304, 308, 322, 327, 335, 336
Malpas, St Mary (Gwent) 113-117
Malvern priory 65, 80, 103, 145
Manorbier castle (Pemb.) 41, 130-133
    church 187, 188
Marcross, Holy Trinity (Glamorgan) 108, 129, 133, 175-177
Margam abbey (Glamorgan) 118-126, 129
Markbury (Somerset) 187
Marloes (Pemb.) 188
Marshal, William 343
Marshall, G. 65, 66
    Pamela 15
Martletwy (Pemb.) 187, 188
Mathern, St Tewdric (Gwent) 165
Mathon (Herefs.) 47, 62
Maylen, C.N. 143
McAleer, J.P. 22
Mears Ashby (Northants.) 182
Meifod, St Tysilio & St Mary (Montgomery) 145, 219, 245-249
Mein, Geoffrey 142
Melbourne, palace chapel (Derbys.) 194, 218
metalworker, art of 225
Meuvaines (Calvados) 38, 64
Mew F. 167
Middleton-on-the-Hill (Herefs.) 48, 57, 103
Milan, San Nazaro Maggiore 40
    Sant Ambrogio 100, 101
Milborne Port (Somerset) 35, 44, 115, 134, 146
Millerd, Joseph 21
Mitchel Troy (Gwent) 174

Moccas (Herefs.) 54, 66
Modena cathedral 70
Molland (Devon) 188
Monknash, St Mary (Glamorgan) 56, 177
Monkton Farleigh (Wilts.) 308
Monkton priory (Pemb.) 4, 106-107
Monmouth castle 84, 90-92, 103, 138
         priory 84-90, 168
Mont St Michel 34, 39
Montacute 113
Montgaroult (Orne) 71
Montivillers (Seine-Maritime) 146
Morcott (Rutland) 217
Moreton Valence (Glos.) 65
Morfan, Abbot of Tywyn 241, 244
Morgan, C.O.S. 162
Morton Morrel, Holy Cross (Warwickshire) 64
Morville (Salop) 113
Mosan font (Belgium) 256-257, 259
Moylgrove (Pemb.) 188
Much Wenlock priory (Salop) 29, 101, 102, 156
Munstereifel 248
Mynt (Cardigan) 280

Nash (Pemb.) 188
Nash-Williams, V.E. 67, 72, 195, 210, 224, 229, 272, 273
Neath abbey 118
Nevern (Pemb.) 188
New Moat (Pemb.) 188
New Shoreham (Sussex) 335
Newborough, St Peter (Anglesey) 232, 234
Newcastle, Bridgend 41, 127-130
Newcastle-upon-Tyne castle (Northumberland) 128, 129
Newman, John 5, 67, 93
Newnham-on-Severn (Glos.) 80
Newport castle (Gwent) 129
         St Woolos 103, 145, 159-164, 243, 343
Newport (Pemb.) 188
Newton Purcell (Oxon.) 65
Nice-Cimiez (Alpes-Maritimes) 19, 63
Nicholas, Thomas 92
Nolton (Pemb.) 188
Northampton, St Peter 217
Norwich castle 140
         cathedral 31, 34, 156, 335
Noyon cathedral 274

Oakham castle (Rutland) 133, 337
Ogmore castle (Glamorgan) 104-105, 129
O'Keefe, Tadhg 93
Old Radnor, St Stephen (Radnor) 269
Old Sarum — see Sarum
Oratory of Gallerus (Kerry) 70
Orcop, St Mary (Herefs.) 186, 187
Orford castle (Suffolk) 128
Ormerod, George 27-28
         Mrs. 24, 32
Orpington, All Saints (Kent) 106
Over Monnow (Gwent) 167-168

Ougy (Burgundy) 64
Owain, King 271
Oxford, St Frideswide's 156, 321, 336
Oxwich, St Illtyd (Glamorgan) 180, 181
Oystermouth (Glamorgan) 181

Pamber (Hants.) 100
Parsons, David 54
Patrishow (Brecon) 183-184
Pauntley, St John's (Glos.) 47, 48
Pembroke, St Mary (Pemb.) 188
Penally (Pemb.) 188
Penbryn (Cardigan) 280
Pencareg (Carmarthen) 259, 260
Penmark (Glamorgan) 178-179
Penmon priory (Anglesey) 48, 195, 196-210, 217, 218,
         220, 221, 222, 224, 231, 232, 234, 237
Penmynydd (Anglesey) 218-219, 220, 228
Pennant Melangell, St Melangell (Montgomery) 69, 70,
         275-280
Pennington (Lancs.) 65
Penrise (Glamorgan) 181
Penterry, St Mary (Gwent) 171
Pen-y-Clawdd (Gwent) 174
Perks, John Clifford 5
Pershore abbey 28, 31, 37, 39, 48, 103, 108, 156, 206
Peterborough cathedral 335
Petersfield (Hants.) 194
Pevsner, Sir Nikolaus 45
Picard 135
         Roger 140
Pistyll, St Beuno (Gwynedd) 227, 228, 230, 234
Poitiers, St Radegarde (Vienne) shrine 276
Pont Audemer, Saint-Germain (Eure) 29, 30
Pontigny (Yonne) 120
Porchester castle (Hants.) 133
Portskewett, St Mary (Gwent) 165
Prendergast (Pemb.) 188
Prestbury (Cheshire) 217
Presteigne, St Andrew (Radnor) 51-55
Preston-by-Dymock (Glos.) 62
Pritchard, Aimee 280
         John 75, 113, 114, 115, 181
Provence 100
Pugin, A.W. 75, 247

Quatford (Salop) 34
Quenington (Glos.) 128
Quillebeuf (Eure) 146

Radford, R.A. Raleigh 93, 108, 136, 107, 218, 254, 276,
         278
Randall, H.J. 104
Raunds (Northants.) 206
Ravenna, S Croce 248
Reading abbey (Berks.) 166, 218, 277, 321
Reculver (Kent) 206
Rees, Sian 87, 88
Regenbald, Alan 15

Renn, Derek 41, 47
Rhayader (Radnor) 259
Rhodgeidio (Anglesey) 234
Rhoscrowther (Pemb.) 188
Rhossili, St Mary the Virgin (Glamorgan) 182
Rhys, Lord of Deheubarth 242, 259, 256, 259, 260, 285
Richmond castle (Yorks.) 20, 40
    Scolland's Hall 15, 91
Rigold, Stuart 109
Ripple (Worcs.) 103
Robert, earl of Gloucester 118
Robertson West (Pemb.) 188
Robinson, David 117, 136
Rochester cathedral 38, 255
Rock (Worcs.) 113
Roger (of Pont L'Evéque), Archbishop of York 125, 255, 274
Roger, Bishop of Salisbury 218, 221, 237, 259, 279, 342
Roger, Bishop of Worcester 125
Rogiet (Gwent) 174
Roman derivation 16, 18, 19, 20, 29, 63, 112, 133, 160
Rome, Basilica Julia 29
    Old St Peter's 100
Romsey abbey (Hants.) 145, 321
Roscrea cathedral (Tipperary) 168
Rosemarket (Pemb.) 187
Rudbaxton (Pemb.) 188
Rudford (Glos.) 103
Rufus, Alan 15
Runston, St Keyna (Gwent) 170
Ruprich-Robert, W. 34, 106, 206

St Albans abbey 29, 87, 156, 335
St André-de-Sorrede (Rousillon) 64
St André-d'Hébertot (Calvados) 106
St Andrews (Scotland) 336, 337
St Athan, St Tathan (Glamorgan) 178
St Arvans, St Arvan (Gwent) 170, 171
St Augustine 248
St Baruch's chapel, Barry Island 180, 206
St Bees (Cumbria) 216
St Brides (Pemb.) 188
St Brides Major, St Bridget (Glamorgan) 174
St Brides-super-Ely (Glamorgan) 126
St Cadfan 244
St Caradog 324
St Clears (Carmarthen) 108, 117, 129, 133-134, 176, 177
St Collen 278
St Cuthbert 276
St David 148, 164, 324
St Davids cathedral 81, 83, 107, 125, 126, 156, 166, 244, 255, 256, 283-338, 343
St Dogmaels priory (Pemb.) 100, 107-111, 133
St Dogwells (Pemb.) 188
St Donats, St Donat (Glamorgan) 117, 174-175
St Dubricius/Dyfrig 75, 84, 164
St Fagans, St Mary (Glamorgan) 178
St Florence (Pemb.) 188

St Génis-des-Fontaines (Pyrénées-Orientales) 64
St Georges-de-Boscherville, Saint Martin
    (Seine-Maritime) 101
St Germer de Fly (Oise) 274
St Gwynllyw 164
St Harmon (Radnor) 259
St Ishmaels (Pemb.) 188
St Justinian 324
St Leger-de-Rôtes (Eure) 17
St-Loup-Hors (Calvados) 106
St-Loyer, St Lotharius (Orne) 175
St Lythans (Glamorgan) 178
St-Martin-de-Boscherville, St Georges (Seine-Maritime) 38
St Mary Hill (Glamorgan) 178
St Maughans (Gwent) 174
St Pierre, St Peter (Gwent) 51, 54, 55, 66
St-Savin-sur-Gartempe (Vienne) 64
St Teilo 84
St Twynnels (Pemb.) 187
St Tysilio 219, 245
Salisbury cathedral 160
Salter, Mike 185
Saltmarsh, Bishop William 82, 83, 84
San Miguel de Escalada, nr. Leon 72
Santa Cristina de Lena, nr, Oviedo 72
Sarnau (Cardigan) 280
Sarum cathedral, Salisbury 80, 103, 117, 168, 180, 218, 220, 221, 222, 225, 279, 310, 322, 335, 337
Scholefield, V. Cotterill 261-262
Scolland's hall — see Richmond castle
Scott, George Gilbert 286, 287, 288, 298, 325, 332, 337
    Taylor 286
Sherborne abbey (Dorset) 42, 80, 127, 128, 335
    castle 41, 140, 147, 218
Shobdon (Herefs.) 112
Shrewsbury abbey 86, 103, 162, 194, 195, 196, 208
    St Chad's 111
    Old St Chad's 111
    St Mary's 111, 126, 129, 156, 308, 309
Siddington (Glos.) 221, 308
Silian, St Sulian (Cardigan) 258, 259
Silvington (Salop) 63
Skinner, Rev. John 219
Slimbridge, St John (Glos.) 288, 332, 333, 334
Smith, Telfer 142
Solva (Pemb.) 188
Soria, San Juan de Duero (Castille) 100
South, Francis 85
South Cerney (Glos.) 128, 308
Southwell Minster 32-33, 40, 42, 44
Speyer cathedral 196, 206, 248
Spittal (Pemb.) 188
Stafford, St Mary 257
Stalley, Roger 352, 256, 279, 284, 287, 288, 306, 308, 314, 315, 336
Stapleford (Notts.) 272
Stewart, Sophie 94, 95
Stewkley (Bucks.) 38

Steyning (Sussex) 336
Stogursey priory (Somerset) 32, 100, 126
Stoke-sub-Hamden (Somerset) 105, 106
Stoneleigh abbey (Warks.) 109, 128
Stottesden (Salop) 112
Stowe Missal 223
Strata Florida abbey 126, , 249-256, 258, 318, 342-343
Strata Marcella 118, 232, 256
Stratton (Glos.) 64
Street, G.E. 85
Stubbs, William 92
Studland (Dorset) 165, 206, 212
Sully (Glamorgan) 180
Sutton (Northants.) 70

Tangmere (Sussex) 275
Tardouet (Calvados) 106
Tarrington (Herefs.) 80
Tatton-Brown, Tim 35, 287, 288
Taylor, H.M. & Joan 45, 52
Tedstone Delamere (Herefs.) 54, 69
Tewkesbury abbey 28, 29, 30, 31, 36, 37, 38, 39, 45, 48, 101, 103, 108, 156, 195, 243, 263, 307, 321, 335
Thacker, Alan 207
Thaon (Calvados) 206
Til-Châtel (Côte d'Or) 261
Tintern abbey (Gwent) 117
Tissington (Derbs.) 65
Tixover (Rutland) 217
Tower of London 20
    St Johns Chapel 17, 28, 32, 38, 39
Tredunnock, St Andrews (Gwent) 170
Trefdraeth (Anglesey) 232
Tregaian (Anglesey) 227
Tremain (Cardigan) 280
Tretower castle (Brecon) 135-140
tufa, use of 28-29, 51, 53, 54, 156, 211
Turbeville, Miss E. Picton 93
Turner, Rick 6, 14
Twyning, St Mary Magdalene (Glos.) 69
Tywyn, St Cadfan (Merioneth) 81, 145, 242-245, 343
Tyrrell-Green, E. 183, 275

Upleadon (Glos.) 62
Upton (Pemb.) 188
Upton Hellions (Devon) 187
Urban, Bishop 51
Usk castle 140, 146-147
    priory 140-146
Uzmaston (Pemb.) 188
    Higgons Well 212

Valle Crucis abbey 232, 233, 255, 275, 277
Ventemiglia cathedral (Liguria) 100
Ver (Calvados) 206
Verdun, Saint-Vanne (Lorraine) 44
Vitruvius 45
Voel, Genillin 183

Walton East (Pemb.) 188
Walton West (Pemb.) 188
Wareham, St Martin (Dorset) 35
Warkworth (Northumberland) 101, 171
Warmington (Northants.) 156
Weaverthorpe (Yorks.) 171
Webb, Geoffrey 287
Wells cathedral 31, 140, 156, 164, 288, 311, 312, 313, 314, 332, 333, 336, 337
Welsh sculptural tradition 51, 72
Werden, St Lucius 33
    St Saviour 247-248
West Country School of Romanesque 28, 31, 32, 34, 37, 38, 40, 48, 108, 109, 133, 139, 145, 195, 206, 230, 243, 307, 308, 309, 313, 322, 335
    of masons 46, 148, 166, 284, 314
West Kingsdown, St Edmund (Kent) 105, 106
West Malling (Kent) 145
Weston-in-Gordano (Somerset) 187
Westwood, J.O. 114-115, 183
Wheathill (Salop) 46
Whitchurch Canonicorum (Dorset) 336
Whitland 107, 118-119, 249, 256
Whitson (Gwent) 166
Wick, St James (Glamorgan) 178
Wigmore abbey (Herefs.) 156, 255, 311
Wihenoc of Monmouth 4
Wilcrick (Gwent) 174
Wilkinson, Nathaniel 85
Willersley, St Mary Magdalene (Herefs.) 61, 67
William I 5, 16, 17, 20, 35, 39
William of Tiron, Abbot 107
William, Earl of Gloucester 118, 127, 129, 130
Williams, David 141
    Stephen 142, 250, 256
Wilson, Christopher 308
Wimbourne Minster (Dorset) 37
Winchester cathedral 34, 70, 335
    St Cross 103, 310, 335, 337
Winstone, St Bartholomews (Glos.) 17, 64
Winson (Glos.) 56
Wissington (Suffolk) 128, 129
Wiston (Pemb.) 188
Wittering, All Saints (Northants.) 34, 59
Wootton, St Mary Magdalene (Glos.) 79-80
Wooton Wawen (Warks.) 204
Worcester cathedral 29, 31, 34, 42, 44, 48, 80, 87, 103, 125, 156, 166, 167, 255, 272, 307, 310, 335
Wyatt, A.M. 167
    T.H. 75

Yarnscombe (Devon) 105
York, St Mary's abbey 17, 67
    minster 102, 125, 255, 310, 335
Ynys Seriol (Anglesey) 206, 210-213

Zarnecki, George 44, 65